THE GOOD
SHOPPING GUIDE

THE GOOD SHOPPING GUIDE

Published by the Ethical Marketing Group

7th edition published 2008 by The Ethical Marketing Group for The Ethical Company Organisation

The Ethical Company Organisation
105 Westbourne Grove, London W2 4UW
www.ethical-company-organisation.org

© Ethical Company Organisation, 2008

0845 257 6818 (Switchboard)

Research and Editorial Director - William Sankey
Publishing & Company Liaison Director - Kat Alexander
Editor – Sarah Edwardes
Research Manager – Gabriella Icardi
Designed by Deborah Barrow & Gary White & Lindsey Johns
Media consultancy and public relations by 86 Ltd (*www.86.co.uk*)

ISBN 978-0-9552907-4-9

Printed and bound in Great Britain on paper certified from sustainable forests using vegetable dyes.

Distributed by Central Books (*orders@centralbooks.com*; 0845 458 9911)
Sales enquiries to Signature Books (*sales@signaturebooks.co.uk*; 01904 633 633)

Thanks to everybody at The Ethical Company Organisation, the pioneers at the ECRA and all the NGOs we work with.

Legal Disclaimer
The Good Shopping Guide aims to provide an independent and authoritative list of mainstream brands and companies according to research executed by The Ethical Company Organisation between March 2005 and August 2008. While every reasonable care is taken to ensure the accuracy of the information in *The Good Shopping Guide* , neither the publisher, the printers nor any distributor is responsible for errors or omissions. Pictures and advertisements are vetted to ensure there is no conflict with this editorial policy.

Contents

Contents (continued)

Foreword

by the Ethical Company Organisation

Welcome to this 7th annual edition of *The Good Shopping Guide*, revealing the good, the bad and the ugly of the UK's companies and brands.

As businesses get bigger and corporate influence increases, the importance of individuals' brand choices has never been so clear: by choosing to buy from ethical and avoid irresponsible companies we can minimise the damage that we do to the world around us.

Most of us are now aware of our carbon footprint, but we should also know that we leave an ethical footprint every time we shop. Each purchase supports activities throughout the supply chain and beyond; activities that may include animal testing, unfair trade in developing countries or investment in weapons and nuclear power.

The Good Shopping Guide exposes many of these connections, listing the level of corporate social responsibility of the companies behind hundreds of everyday products. It reveals which brands are implicated in abuses such as child labour, human rights violations, green-washing and environmental destruction in the UK and worldwide – and also shows which companies are deserving of your support.

We believe that the key to a progressive 21st century lies in the persuasive power of intelligent consumer action. *The Good Shopping Guide* shows you how to channel your spending power towards only the most responsible companies.

Thank you to Friends of the Earth, Cafédirect, Christian Aid, the World Development Movement, the Ethical Investment Research Service, Good Energy, AECB, Tourism Concern, the Environmental Transport Association, Survival International and a host of other NGOs for all their help with this edition.

'your till receipt is as important as your vote'

WELCOME TO THE GOOD SHOPPING GUIDE

Now, more than ever before, the world's consumers are choosing to use their spending power pro-actively. The information in this book can empower us all to really make a difference to the world around us.

The Good Shopping Guide aims to help consumers make informed decisions about which brands are best for the planet, best for animals and best for people world-wide. With your help, we hope to make a positive difference to the environment, to animal welfare and to communities who are living in poverty across the globe.

We can all make a contribution to a better world though the simple choices we make while out shopping. Most of us are aware that by choosing to buy one kind of coffee over another we can help the farmers of Africa or Asia, and that buying an eco-friendly washing-up liquid helps to reduce pollution in the UK. But how many of us know which television manufacturer has the best human rights record, which consumer goods companies are involved in the arms trade and which health and beauty products are kindest to animals? *The Good Shopping Guide* tells all – in detail.

We don't have to feel powerless about the world's problems. Our till receipts are like voting slips – they can easily be used constructively. This is something that the big corporations will have to notice tomorrow, even if they seem to be unaware

of it today. If you care about global warming, pollution, animal testing, factory farming, the arms trade and the exploitation of people, you are certainly not alone. More shoppers are taking an interest in the origins of their purchases. Consumers are realising that they don't have to join a campaign or become a political activist to make their voices heard: speaking out is as easy as making good choices about where you shop and what you buy.

SMALL DECISIONS, BIG EFFECTS

These choices can support progressive companies who want to improve the way their business is done. Our shopping habits can force changes in the day-to-day workings of even the largest corporations. It's already happening in supermarkets, where fair trade, GM-free and organic foods are appearing in larger numbers because the companies know that these products will be sought out by more and more of their customers.

The big companies have noticed this too, and have begun to pursue the 'halo' effect

"Your shopping can make a real difference. *The Good Shopping Guide* shows you how."

Anne MacCaig – Chief Executive – *Cafédirect Plc*

that comes with an association with these types of product. In recent months, one of the most widely criticised brands, Nestlé, has launched its own fair trade Partners Blend coffee. L'Oreal's controversial acquisition of The Body Shop, and Green & Black's take-over by Cadbury, might provide an opportunity for their ethical business principles to filter up through the company groups.

As an individual, you can make a difference in lots of ways. Begin by looking for products carrying *The Good Shopping Guide*'s ethical certification logo. Also look for fair trade, organic and GM-free foods. You could also choose to buy sustainably-produced or recycled products. Buying eco-friendly cleaning fluids or washing-up liquids gives progressive manufacturers more funds to invest in clean technology, and helps to persuade other manufacturers to consider changing their policies.

Each of these decisions has an impact: small in itself but huge overall when millions of others are doing the same. This book shows that you can be part of the solution, rather than part of the problem. It provides all the information you need to make your shopping decisions the first step towards a cleaner, fairer and kinder world.

WHAT IS ETHICAL SHOPPING?

'Good' shopping is ethical shopping. This means buying products that are made in an ethical manner by companies who do not cause harm to or exploit humans, animals or the environment.

Ethical shopping encourages innovative products and companies, and discourages others that prefer to ignore the social and environmental consequences of their practices. It also empowers you, the consumer, by giving you a say in how the products you buy are made and how the manufacturers conduct their business.

Our choices can be both positive, by buying products that we know to be ethical, and negative, by refusing to buy the ones of which we disapprove. For example, one aspect of ethical shopping might be supporting actions such as the Nestlé boycott, which targeted all the brands and company subsidiaries to try and force the company to change its marketing of formula baby milk in the Third World.

With this book you will also be able to follow a fully screened approach. This means looking at all the companies and products together and deciding which brand is the most ethical. It is this information that *The Good Shopping Guide* brings together in the following pages.

The Ethical Company Organisation is part of an ever-growing network of organisations committed to making the world a better place: groups such as Oxfam, Fairtrade Foundation, Traidcraft, Friends of the Earth, Naturewatch, the Soil Association, the Vegetarian Society and the Forest Stewardship Council. Their work helps to put pressure on governments, whether directly or indirectly, to use legislation to make ethical trade not just a choice, but a fundamental part of the way we do business.

By using this book you will discover more than you ever knew about what goes into the goods you buy. You will have the information you need to make clear and informed decisions, either to choose the products of green and progressive companies or to boycott those of unethical companies. From here on, it's up to you.

How to use this book

The Good Shopping Guide takes you through all the ethical factors you may want to consider when making decisions about which products to buy. It is the essential reference guide for ethical shopping, and includes up-to-date information on all the major manufacturers and their brands.

This guide gives you the essential environmental, animal welfare and human rights background to a wide range of products, summarising the most important ethical attributes of the different brands that are available in the UK. It also details the changes that are being made by manufacturers to improve their ethical records, and gives the names of the most progressive companies.

To make it easy to find the product you are interested in, the book is divided into seven sections: Home & Office, Energy, Travel, Money, Food & Drink, Health & Beauty and Fashion. Within each section you will find chapters on a wide range of different products.

For each type of product there is a long table showing a clear ethical rating (the Ethical Company Index) for each brand. This is based upon the company's record for environmental reporting, pollution, animal testing, factory farming, workers' rights, involvement in armaments or genetic engineering and other ethical factors.

The table includes a separate rating for each of these areas, so you can check how the company scores on the issues that concern you most.

Alongside the long table is a short table, which gives an at-a-glance overview of which brands come from the most ethical companies. You will also find background information about the environmental and social impact of each product.

At the back of the book is a reference guide called the Good Network, which includes information on all the organisations mentioned in the book. It also has details of the companies who, having scored well in *The Good Shopping Guide*'s ethicality test, can display the Ethical Company logo as an independent mark of endorsement. Look out for this badge of authority on the labels of several leading and progressive brands.

After consulting *The Good Shopping Guide*, you will have all the information you need to make some really switched-on decisions – so don't forget to take it with you next time you visit the shops.

How to read the tables

THE LONG TABLES: READING THE SYMBOLS

The long tables that run in each product section are designed to give readers an in-depth view of the ethical performance of different companies and brands.

All the tables in this book are based on extensive research carried out by *The Good Shopping Guide*. The methodology behind their easy-to-read format is outlined below.

● **Top rating:** a green circle indicates that we have found no criticisms or negative records

○ **Middle rating:** an empty red circle shows that there are some criticisms or negative records in this category

● **Bottom rating:** a full red circle indicates the highest level of criticism and negative records in this category

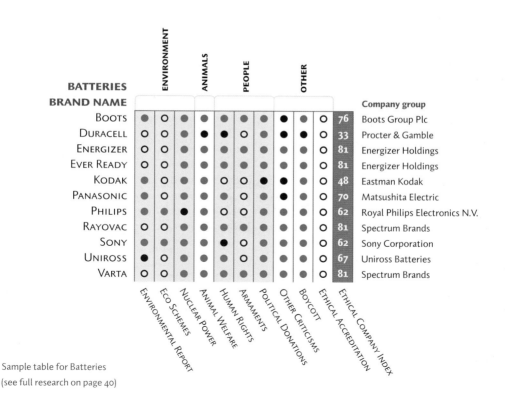

BATTERIES BRAND NAME	ENVIRONMENT			ANIMALS	PEOPLE			OTHER			Ethical Company Index	Company group
	Environmental Report	Eco-Schemes	Nuclear Power	Animal Welfare	Human Rights	Armaments	Political Donations	Other Criticisms	Boycott	Ethical Accreditation		
Boots	●	○	●	●	●	●	●	●	●	○	76	Boots Group Plc
Duracell	○	○	●	●	●	○	●	●	●	○	33	Procter & Gamble
Energizer	○	○	●	●	●	●	●	●	●	○	81	Energizer Holdings
Ever Ready	○	○	●	●	●	●	●	●	●	○	81	Energizer Holdings
Kodak	●	○	●	●	○	○	●	●	●	○	48	Eastman Kodak
Panasonic	●	○	●	●	●	○	●	●	●	○	70	Matsushita Electric
Philips	●	●	●	●	○	○	●	●	●	○	62	Royal Philips Electronics N.V.
Rayovac	○	○	●	●	●	●	●	●	●	○	81	Spectrum Brands
Sony	●	●	●	●	●	○	●	●	●	○	62	Sony Corporation
Uniross	●	○	●	●	●	○	●	●	●	○	67	Uniross Batteries
Varta	○	○	●	●	●	●	●	●	●	○	81	Spectrum Brands

Sample table for Batteries
(see full research on page 40)

The table on the previous page is organised with the brand name, under which the product is sold, on the left. On the right is the name of the company group which is ultimately responsible for the brand. At the bottom of the table are the categories, which are explained in detail over the following pages.

The marks on these tables represent criticism from environmental and human rights organisations across the world. Information from a wide variety of sources – from government agencies as well as NGOs – has been compiled by the Ethical Company Organisation's team of researchers between May 2005 and August 2007.

THE CATEGORY DEFINITIONS

Each table is divided into the broad areas of Environment, Animals and People and then sub-divided into more specific categories. Most are self-explanatory but it is useful to understand the practical issues and dilemmas behind some of the categories.

The tables have been tailored to each particular industry so that we can now reveal more detailed information about all of the companies. For instance, in Good Food & Drink we reward companies that are involved in fair trade, and in Good Money we penalise banks which have invested in projects that have caused outrage among environmental and human rights campaigners.

The following categories are included in each section of the book:

THE ENVIRONMENT

ENVIRONMENTAL REPORT

The quality of a company's environmental reporting can say a lot about its ethical standards. As such reports become more commonplace it is getting easier to rate companies on their efforts: a good report will contain fixed targets as opposed to vague statements of intent.

Companies which fail to publish a report get a bottom rating (●); companies with inadequate reports get a middle rating (○). To earn the top rating (◉) the report must be dated within the last two years and must set concrete and company-wide performance targets; it also has to demonstrate an understanding of the company's main impacts. Many of the corporations that have attracted most criticism have actually produced exemplary environmental reports.

Exception is made for small companies without the resources to publish an elaborate annual report (i.e. companies whose turnover is less than £2 million a year). Companies which were launched with the aim of helping people, animals or the environment are rewarded with the top rating. These include businesses that provide fair trade, organic, vegetarian, cruelty-free or environmentally-friendly alternatives.

NUCLEAR POWER

Nuclear power is a target for social and environmental campaigners for two main reasons: its link to the production of nuclear weapons and the pollutant properties of radioactive waste. Nuclear waste remains dangerous for 250,000 years, and this greatly increases the security problem attached to its potential for use in nuclear weapons.

The nuclear industry argues that, as an electricity generator which does not produce greenhouse gases, it should have a role in combating climate change. However, environmental campaigners would prefer to support a sustainable future through energy conservation and the development of 'cleaner' power sources such as sun, wind and wave power.

Some nuclear industry specialists are also involved in the production of consumer goods and these are reflected in the tables. A full red circle (●) indicates the company is involved in the design, construction or operation of nuclear power stations, radioactive waste handling and/or the mining, processing or reprocessing of uranium. It also may indicate the production of other nuclear-related equipment, such as monitoring facilities.

GENETIC MODIFICATION (GM)

No one really knows the possible effects of GM food on our health and the environment and the public and certain NGOs are therefore anxious about their use. Releasing genetically altered organisms into the environment could disrupt ecosystems, and genetically modified crops have been proved to be more harmful to many groups of wildlife than their conventional equivalent.

New 2004 EU regulations for the labelling of genetically modified foods and feed require that all food products that make direct use of GMOs at any point in their production are subjected to labeling requirements, regardless of whether or not GMO content is detectable in the end product. GMO content that is below the prescribed threshold remains unlabelled, as long as it is due to an unintentional and technically unavoidable mixture. The threshold only applies to GMO content that has been authorized in the EU, and therefore is considered safe. (Source: GM Compass).

A bottom rating indicates that the company uses GM ingredients in any of their products. A middle rating is given to companies which do not have a stated policy on their website regarding the use of food or ingredients which contain GMO in their products but where no negative records were found. The top rating is awarded to companies which clearly state that they do not use GM ingredients in their products.

This category only applies to the Food & Drink and Health & Beauty sections of the book.

In our chapter on cafés, the top rating is awarded if no criticisms relating to genetic modification have been found. In our chapter on supermarkets, the top rating is given if no own-brand products contain GM ingredients or ingredients derived from animals fed on GM crops; the middle rating indicates that no own-brand product contains GM ingredients.

In the Health & Beauty sector, the bottom rating is given to companies involved in the non-medical genetic modification of plants or animals or to companies that use GM in their products.

ORGANIC

Non-organic farming reduces biodiversity, encourages irreversible soil erosion and generates run-off that is awash with harmful chemicals. Organic produce is grown or made without the use of synthetic fertilisers, pesticides, herbicides, fungicides and other man-made 'inputs'.

The green circle (●) indicates that one or more of the company's products is approved by the Soil Association (*www.soilassociation.org*) or another organic certification body.

In our chapter on cafés, the top rating indicates that only organic coffee is served; the middle rating indicates that some organic products are available; the bottom rating indicates that no organic products are sold at all. In our chapter on supermarkets, the top rating is given to those companies that have the widest range of own-brand organic products (i.e. over 100 product ranges). The bottom rating indicates that no own-brand organic products are sold.

This category only applies to the Food & Drink and Health & Beauty sections of the book. In High Street Fashion a company only gets the top rating if they sell one or more product lines made of organic materials.

HOME & OFFICE ECO SCHEMES

Energy Saving Recommended
The Energy Saving Recommended logo was established by the Energy Saving Trust (*www.est.org.uk*) and guarantees a high standard of energy efficiency. The logo appears on a wide range of household appliances, including fridges, freezers, dishwashers, washing machines, tumble dryers, light bulbs, light fittings, gas boilers and heating controls.

A green circle (●) indicates that one or more of the company's products is recommended by the Energy Saving Trust.

European Eco-label
Products that bear the EU Eco-label flower have passed a number of criteria relating to the environment and performance. The scheme covers everything from paints to tissues to computers, but remains very much in a nascent state in the UK.

A green circle (●) indicates that one or more of the company's products bears the Eco-label.

TCO
This category only applies to office products.

TCO Development sets the world's toughest standard for environmental and employee-friendly office equipment. To earn the TCO badge each product has to pass at least 50 tests relating to emission levels, energy consumption, ergonomic design and ecological soundness.

A green circle (●) indicates that one or more of the company's products is approved by TCO Development.

RAINFOREST TIMBER

This category only applies to our chapter on furniture.

The logging of rainforest timber results in the destruction of biodiversity and the oppression of the indigenous people who live there. The Forest Stewardship Council (FSC) operates the only system of forest certification recognised by NGOs. The top rating (●) is given to companies that only sell garden furniture derived from FSC forests or from forests working towards FSC certification; the bottom rating (●) is given to companies who source less than 50 per cent of their garden furniture from FSC sources or from forests working towards FSC certification.

We rely on the information gathered by Greenpeace in their *Garden Furniture Guide* (2005).

ENVIRONMENTAL DESTRUCTION

This category only applies to the Good Money section, and to our chapter on cars.

The bottom rating (●) represents involvement in a project in the last five years that has drawn widespread criticism from environmental NGOs and campaigners.

RENEWABLES

This category only applies to our chapter on petrol stations.

The top rating (●) indicates that the company is investing a significant proportion of its net income (about 5 per cent) into renewable energy. The middle rating (○) shows that the company has put some investment into renewables; companies who have not invested at all receive the bottom rating (●).

NB. BP does not quite invest 5 per cent of its net income into renewable energy but, since it invests considerably more than the other oil giants (Shell is the closest competitor), it has been awarded the top rating.

ANIMALS

ANIMAL WELFARE

At the end of the 20th century, nearly three million animals per year were used in UK experiments alone. Worldwide, over 100 million animals are subjected to tests. Most tests are carried out on mice, rats, guinea pigs, birds, fish and rabbits, but other animals including dogs, cats and primates will be used. The testing of consumer products such as lipstick and washing-up liquid accounts for a tiny fraction of animal tests. The vast majority is done in the name of medical research, to test new drugs. But animals are also used in the testing of weapons, pesticides, food additives, and in psychology experiments.

All new chemical ingredients are required by law to be tested on animals. Regulatory bodies list a number of tests that must be carried out before an ingredient can be registered.

Alternative, non-animal tests such as tissue and cell cultures, computer production, clinical studies and the use of skin fragments do exist for all the standard toxicity and irritancy tests. But the process of 'validating' these alternative methods has been obstructed, according to BUAV, by industry and regulatory bodies' reluctance to accept these new methods.

Companies need to do two things in order to behave responsibly:

• Invest heavily in developing alternative, non-animal tests and lobby to get them validated

• Postpone the search for new ingredients and use the 8,000 established ingredients until non-animal alternatives to all animal tests have been validated.

Companies are penalised in the Animal Welfare column if they conduct or commission animal testing, whether for medical or cosmetic purposes. They are also penalised if they have been the subject of continuing criticism from animal rights organisations such as the British Union for the Abolition of Vivisection (BUAV) and

People for the Ethical Treatment of Animals (PETA).

In the Health & Beauty section of the book, the green circle (●) is only given to those companies which have been approved by the BUAV's Humane Cosmetics Standard. These companies operate a fixed cut-off date (FCOD), and avoid ingredients which were tested on animals after a specified year. Companies that do not conduct or commission animal testing get the middle rating (○).

VEGETARIAN

This column rewards companies' support for a meat-free lifestyle. Apart from the moral questions that surround killing animals for food, going vegan is better from an ecological standpoint too, since animal products are extremely inefficient to produce.

The green circle (●) indicates that one or more of the company's products is approved either by the Vegetarian Society (*www.vegsoc.org*) or the Vegan Society (*www.vegansociety.com*).

Products approved by the Vegetarian Society are awarded with the seedling showcase logo and must meet the following criteria:
- Free from animal flesh (meat, fowl, fish or shellfish), meat or bone stock, animal or carcass fats, gelatine, aspic or any other ingredients resulting from slaughter
- Contain only free range eggs, where eggs are used
- Free from GMOs
- Cruelty free – no animal testing
- No cross contamination during the production process. If the production line is shared with non-vegetarian products,

thorough cleaning must be carried out before vegetarian production commences. Strict procedures must be in place to ensure packaging mix-ups and other errors do not occur

For a product to be approved by the Vegan Society, there must be no animal ingredients, animal-derived additives, animal fibres, milks, or milk derivatives; there must be no bee products, dairy products or by-products, eggs, human-derived substances, and slaughter by-products.

This category only applies to the Food & Drink and Health & Beauty sections of the book.

PEOPLE

HUMAN RIGHTS

In the 1990s NGOs and labour organisations began to look more closely at the global supply chains of big companies, and discovered that people working for these companies in the developing world were regularly subjected to 80-hour weeks, enforced overtime, unsafe factories and humiliating physical tests. These problems have not gone away, and multinational companies are only beginning to take responsibility for the unacceptable working conditions of their suppliers.

Companies are penalised in this column if, in the last 5 years, they have been implicated in human rights abuses (either through their supply chain, or through their involvement in a project that has proven links with human rights abuses, or through their economic presence in Burma). A full red circle (●) indicates more than one serious criticism.

This category is used in the Good Home & Office and Good Fashion sections. In the rest of the book, it is subsumed in the more widely defined Public Record Criticisms category.

ARMAMENTS

In the table, the middle rating (◐) represents involvement in the manufacture or supply of nuclear or conventional weapons, including ships, tanks, armoured vehicles and aircraft; components of weapons systems; fuel, computing and communications services; systems aiding the launch, guidance, delivery or deployment of missiles. Non-strategic parts of the military, such as catering services, are not included in this list.

The bottom rating (●) indicates that the business was listed as one of the world's 100 biggest arms-producing companies in 2003 by the Stockholm International Peace Research Institute (SIPRI).

POLITICAL DONATIONS

We include this column because we do not believe that corporations should fund political parties. There is considerable evidence that the huge wealth of corporations can distort the political process. Elections in the USA in particular can appear to be 'bought' by the candidate with the biggest budget, and parties that are critical of business are quickly marginalised. In some countries, such as Germany, corporate funding is quite sensibly prohibited by law. Until that occurs in the

UK, consumers who agree with this position can use our tables to withdraw their custom from political donors.

The middle rating (◐) indicates that the company has donated more than £10,000 (or more than $18,900) in the last 5 years to a party-political organisation in the UK or the US, as listed by the Center for Responsive Politics in the US (*www. opensecrets.org*) and the Electoral Commission in the UK (*www. electoralcommission.gov.uk*). The bottom rating shows that the company has donated more than £50,000 (or more than $94,500) since 2000 to a party-political organisation in the UK or the US.

FAIR TRADE

Fair trade ensures that producers are paid regularly and guaranteed a minimum price. This price covers the cost of production, the payment of workers, and the development of farms and small-holdings. Fair trade protects small farmers from the fluctuating prices that have previously pushed many below the poverty line.

The green circle (●) indicates that one or more of the company's products is certified by the Fairtrade Mark (*www. fairtrade.org.uk*).

In our chapter on cafés, the top rating is awarded to those companies that serve exclusively fair trade coffee; the middle rating indicates that some fair trade coffee is served; the bottom rating shows that fair trade coffee is not served at all. In our chapter on supermarkets, the top rating is awarded to those supermarkets that have a range of own-brand fair trade products; the bottom rating (●) is given to supermarkets which do not sell own-brand fair trade products at all.

This category only applies to the Food & Drink section of the book, with the exception of the Fashion section where a top rating is given to those companies selling Fair Trade clothing.

IRRESPONSIBLE MARKETING

All consumers in free-market economies learn to accept that the language of marketing accentuates the positive and plays down the negative. The point at which this becomes 'irresponsible' is difficult to define, but we focus mainly on those practices that have direct health implications. The bottom rating (●) indicates the marketing of products in a way that has been criticised for its effect on public health.

This category only applies to the Health & Beauty section of the book.

OTHER CATEGORIES

BOYCOTT CALL

This column can be problematic since a boycott may be called by groups across the political spectrum. It is important, therefore, to be clear about the reasons why a particular boycott has been called.

Some campaign groups have problems with boycotts. For example, development charities CAFOD and Oxfam contend that boycotts of companies involved in workers'

rights abuses could put workers' livelihoods at risk. However, boycotts can be a useful means of exerting economic pressure and can encourage companies to change their policies.

A full red circle (●) indicates that a boycott of either the brand or the company group has been called (and has not been dropped). For more information on specific ongoing UK boycotts, visit *www.ethicalconsumer.org*.

PUBLIC RECORD CRITICISM

A full red circle (●) indicates more than one serious criticism in the last five years from NGOs such as Human Rights Watch and Friends of the Earth. The huge range of criticism covered in this column mainly relates to the environment and human rights. Undue political influence, exercised through lobby groups and industry associations, and involvement in political corruption, are also represented in this column.

Companies have been penalised if they are part-owned by a separate company which has been the subject of severe criticism from campaign groups or is heavily involved in the armaments and nuclear industries. For instance, Pret a Manger has received the full red circle because it is a third-owned by McDonalds. If a company owns more than half of another company's shares, it is listed as the company group.

In the Good Home & Office and Good Fashion sections of the book, this category is split into the Human Rights and Other Criticism columns.

ETHICAL COMPANY ACCREDITATION

While there are many single-issue certification bodies which ensure standards for organic produce, fair trade or energy-efficiency, the Ethical Company badge covers the whole spectrum of ethical concerns and grants approval at a corporate rather than product level. The badge certifies the company rather than the product, so that, while Nestlé's Partner's Blend may be approved by the Fairtrade Foundation, Nestlé itself would not qualify for Ethical Company status.

The companies who have joined the Ethical Company Accreditation Scheme have been thoroughly screened by our team of researchers.

ETHICAL COMPANY INDEX

The Ethical Company Index provides one overall score for each company.

The top, middle and bottom ratings on the rest of the tables count as ten, five and zero points respectively. Some categories, however, are weighted slightly differently according to the level of NGO and consumer concern. For instance, due to the number of reported human rights violations in the supply chains of electronics manufacturers and clothes companies, a clean record scores 20 points in these product sectors.

Each company's total score is then converted into a percentage, which becomes the Ethical Company Index.

GOOD MONEY

LEGAL STATUS

In this column, mutual building societies and organisations which are not for the profit of shareholders are identified with a full green circle (●). Mutuals only invest in mortgages, and so never get involved in business projects condemned by many of the world's NGOs. They make important policy decisions democratically, with each saver entitled to one vote.

THIRD WORLD DEBT

All UK banks have sold or written off the bulk of 'Third World' debts, but some still have lending relationships with developing country governments. A full red circle (●) indicates that Third World debts are still held.

We have relied on the *Guide to Responsible Banking* (2003) drawn up by the Ethical Investment Research Service (EIRIS).

ETHICAL INVESTMENT POLICY

It is promising to see our financial institutions starting to introduce ethical criteria into their lending policies. While for now these are often no more than token gestures, we hope that the trend will continue to grow.

The middle rating (○) is given for any kind of ethical policy; the full green circle (●) represents a policy that goes beyond negative screening, and gives priority to projects that are socially or environmentally beneficial.

ENVIRONMENTAL DESTRUCTION

The bottom rating (●) represents involvement in a project in the last six years that has drawn widespread criticism from environmental NGOs and campaigners.

OTHER IRRESPONSIBLE LENDING

A full red circle (●) indicates involvement in a project in the last five years that has drawn widespread criticism from human rights groups.

POLITICAL ACTIVITY

A full red circle (●) indicates either that donations over £50,000 (or $94,500) have been made to a political party in the UK or the US in the last five years, or that the bank/financial institution has been criticised by NGOs such as the World Development Movement (WDM) for its involvement in lobby groups.

GOOD FASHION

CODE OF CONDUCT

The top rating (●) is awarded to those companies which have drawn up a comprehensive code of conduct that formally acknowledges the right to form a union. The code must be publicly available, and it must regulate against excessive working hours and forced or child labour.

ETHICAL TRADING SCHEMES

The top rating (●) is awarded to those companies which are members of the Ethical Trading Initiative (ETI) or are affiliated to the Fair Labor Association (FLA). This guarantees that the company's supply chain is subject to independent scrutiny.

GOOD ENERGY

ENERGY MIX

Since 2002 under the Renewables Obligation schemes for England, Scotland and Northern Ireland, energy companies have been required to source an increasing proportion of their energy from renewable sources. The minimum requirement for 2006/07 was 6.7% (2.65% for Northern Ireland whose order came into effect in April 2005). These schemes were introduced by the Department of Trade and Industry, the Scottish Executive and the Department of Enterprise, Trade and Investment respectively and are administered by the Gas and Electricity Markets Authority (whose day to day functions are performed by Ofgem). The top rating indicates that over 50% of the company's energy is generated only from renewable sources. The middle rating indicates that the company generates more than 6.7% of its energy from renewable sources. Companies that do not reach the minimum target are given a bottom rating.

THE SHORT TABLES: READING THE SYMBOLS

The summary tables that appear in each product section are designed to give readers a quick, at-a-glance view of the overall ethicality scores awarded to different companies and brands.

The Good Shopping Guide methodology for these tables involved mathematically amalgamating the results of the long tables, based on the Ethical Company Index, to produce three broad groups.

Sample table for Batteries (see full research on page 38)

- Energizer
- Ever Ready
- Rayovac
- Varta

- Boots
- Uniross

- Duracell
- Kodak
- Panasonic
- Philips
- Sony

The Good Shopping Guide Ethical Company group contains brands and companies which, taking every category into account, score well in that particular product sector. These companies may apply to use the logo on packaging and marketing materials.

We apply the question mark symbol to brands and companies which score in the middle section of their individual product sector. This will mean that they have scored highly in some areas of the ethicality audit but have done less well in others.

The cross symbol is applied to brands and companies which score in the lowest section of their product sector. This will mean that they have not scored as highly as other companies in a number of categories included in the ethicality audit.

History of ethical shopping

In the last twenty years, ethical shopping has grown from a niche concern to a genuine phenomenon, practised by everyone from parents to politicians. The timeline below charts some of the key events in its history.

1986
- General Electric boycotted for its involvement in nuclear weapons

1989
- Avon stops animal testing in response to consumer pressure
- Iceland forced to stop whaling in response to Greenpeace campaign

1990
- Dolphin-friendly logos launched following campaign against Heinz's use of purse-seine nets

1991
- Protests lead to huge drop in number of animals used in cosmetics testing
- Consumers stage general boycott of companies involved in Gulf War

1993
- Boycott of goods from Taiwan leads to ban on sale of endangered rhino products

- General Motors stops using live animals in crash tests after three year boycott
- Nestlé reports falling sales following Baby Milk Action boycott over its marketing of breast milk substitutes

1994
- L'Oreal changes animal testing policy following extended boycott
- Friends of the Earth persuades 'big six' DIY chains to stop selling tropical timber
- Consumer power used to convince companies to remove CFCs from their products

1995
- Campaign against dumping of Brent Spar oil platform decimates Shell's petrol sales
- France forced to cancel some of its nuclear testing programme following trade boycott

1997
- Organic food market is reported to be worth £200 million

2002
- First annual edition of *The Good Shopping Guide* is published

2003
- Companies begin to pull out of Burma following continued protests from consumers and NGOs

2004
- *GOOSHING.CO.UK* becomes world's leading ethical shopping portal reaching over 1 million users

2005
- Sales of Fairtrade food and drink reach over £100 million per year

2006
- Report reveals sales of organic products have soared by 30 per cent to £1.6bn

Ethical shopping success

Over the years, and especially since the 1980s, consumers have been making an ever-increasing impact on the way governments and companies behave in all parts of the world. These are just a few examples:

- The campaign against testing cosmetics on animals changed the behaviour of nearly all the main cosmetics companies.

- A boycott in the US against Heinz forced the company to stop catching tuna with purse-seine fishing nets, which used to kill tens of thousands of dolphins each year. It also led to the introduction of the 'dolphin friendly' logo.

- In 1991, Friends of the Earth launched a campaign against the stocking of tropical timber from unsustainable sources by the six largest DIY chains – the campaign eventually became a consumer boycott, and by 1994 all six had agreed to stop selling mahogany.

- Probably the most dramatic single environmental boycott was Greenpeace's campaign in 1995 against the dumping of Shell's oil platform Brent Spar – sales of Shell petrol went down by 70 per cent in some German outlets and the company gave in after only a few days.

- Increasing numbers of clothing companies and sports shoe manufacturers have adopted codes of conduct to protect the conditions of the workers making their goods.

- The success of socially responsible companies Green & Blacks and The Body Shop has led to their high profile take-overs, by Cadbury's and L'Oreal respectively. Although controversial, these take-overs suggest that big businesses are beginning to see ethical commitments as an asset.

- Ethical consumerism encouraged the phasing out of the worst ozone-depleting and greenhouse gases used in fridges and freezers. In 1994, Electrolux followed manufacturers Bosch, Siemens, Liebherr and AEG in replacing ozone-damaging HCFCs and HFCs with hydrocarbons.

- The UK campaign against genetically modified (GM) foods was so successful that the leading companies changed their policies. Eight supermarket chains in the UK now sell their own GM-free own-brands.

- The consumer boycott of fruit, wine and other products from apartheid South Africa helped to free Nelson Mandela and bring about democratic change.

- The first edition of *The Good Shopping Guide* sold out in just three months, showing there is a real consumer demand for reliable information.

www.gooshing.co.uk is set to take ethical shopping global (see page 370).

The Ethical Accreditation Scheme

The Ethical Company Organisation runs the UK's Ethical Accreditation Scheme. Companies that pass our full ethicality audit can show independent certification by displaying the Ethical Company logo.

Accreditation is designed to support ethical companies' reputations and sales by clearly showing that the company is independently endorsed by the Ethical Company Organisation. The logo can be displayed on product packaging, websites, advertising, press releases and stationery, so that consumers can easily identify the most ethical companies.

A number of companies have already joined the scheme and are using the logo as an independent mark of endorsement. The research process takes between four and eight weeks and scans over 40,000 public record documents, including court reports, criticisms from NGOs, boycott calls and environmental reports.

Listed below are some of the companies who have already joined the Ethical Company Organisation's Accreditation Scheme. We can wholeheartedly recommend the following list of E.C.O. accredited companies, as our research team is contracted to re-test their Ethical Company status every 12 months.

- Animal Tails
- Annirac
- Arena Flowers
- Aromatherapy Direct
- Atmos
- Brother UK
- Brother Norway
- Brother Sweden
- Bulldog
- Burns Pet Nutrition
- Caurnie
- Charity Bank
- Chelsea Building Society
- Chococo – The Purbeck Chocolate Company
- The Clean Space

- CO2 Balance
- Designs by Taran
- Ecosoapia
- Essential Care
- ETA
- Europa Pet Foods
- Everything Environmental
- Fair*
- Fushi
- Good Energy
- Green Energy
- Green Garden Group
- Green People
- The Green Shopping Guide
- Green Stationery
- Hemp Garden

- Highland Spring
- Holz Toys
- Honesty
- Innocent
- IT Ambulance
- Kanzi Home
- Mooncup
- Nash Partnership
- Natural by Nature Oils
- Natural Curtain Company
- Natural Organic Soap
- Natura Organics
- New Look
- OrganiPets
- Organico
- OSMO

- Plain Lazy
- Po-Zu
- Redwood Wholefoods
- Sainsbury's
- Satellite
- Seasalt
- Shared Interest
- Terramar Organics
- The Little Pet Food Company
- The Luberation Laboratory
- The Tide Has Turned
- Trophy Pet Food
- Tropical Wholefoods
- Zed PR

Good shopping principles

- **TRY TO ONLY BUY BRANDS FROM THE 'GOOD SHOPPING' LISTS FEATURED IN THIS BOOK**
  Don't worry if you have some questionable brands around you today – just gradually try to replace them with brands approved by *The Good Shopping Guide* over the next few years.

- **LOCAL SHOPS**
  Look out for local, independent stores. Using them means you use your car less. They also offer a more personal service and they help to support the local community.

- **HEALTH FOOD SHOPS**
  These are the best places to support. They tend to stock fair trade, vegetarian and organic products as well as vitamins and herbal remedies.

- **FAIR TRADE**
  Look out for Fairtrade Foundation marked products, which guarantee that workers have been fairly rewarded for their labour. Organisations such as Oxfam (0870 333 2700) and Traidcraft (0191 491 0591) also sell fair trade goods on the high street or via mail order catalogues.

- **PRODUCTS NOT TESTED ON ANIMALS**
  Look for 'not tested on animals' labels or contact the British Union for the Abolition of Vivisection (0207 700 4888) or Naturewatch (0124 225 2871) for an approved products guide.

- **VEGETARIAN AND VEGAN PRODUCTS**
  Look out for the Vegetarian Society symbol. It is hard to completely avoid animal products, but the Vegan Society publishes a useful guide called *Animal Free Shopper*.

- **ORGANIC PRODUCE**
  Organic food is free from chemical fertilisers and pesticides. Look out for the Soil Association symbol or contact the association on 0117 314 5000 to find your nearest outlet.

- **NON-GM FOOD**
  Although 70 per cent of the public oppose the use of genetically modified food, it is increasingly finding its way into our diet. Look out for GM-free labels, the Vegetarian Society symbol or the Soil Association symbol. These all guarantee GM-free.

- **ETHICAL MONEY**
  Choose an ethical investment fund as well as one of the more ethical banks and mortgages. These decisions are key as they involve such large amounts of money.

- **RECYCLING**
  Recycled products save resources and reduce pressure on landfill sites. Many everyday things, especially paper, printer cartridges and TVs, can be recycled. For advice on recycling points in your area contact Wasteline (0870 243 0136).

- **WOOD PRODUCTS**
  Many timber products originate from virgin rainforests or unsuitably managed forests. The Forest Stewardship Council (0168 641 3916) operates independent verification of sustainable timber and paper products. Look out for the FSC logo.

- **GETTING AROUND**
  Walk as much as you can and use public transport (where it's any good!). When you use a car, try to journey share as often as possible – too many of us drive solo in our cars.

- **ENERGY**
  Choose energy efficient brands where you can. There are several different rating and labelling systems, including one from the Energy Saving Trust, a non-profit organisation partly run by the government. Also make sure you switch to one of the greener electricity suppliers.

- **SECOND-HAND GOODS**
  Like recycled products, these help to save resources. Unwanted items that are in good condition can be donated to charity rather than thrown away.

- **PLASTIC BAGS**
  Good shopping is not just about what you buy, but how you carry it home. Avoid using non-biodegradable plastic bags – invest in a re-useable shopping bag from an ethically sound company.

- **GREEN EVENTS**
  Supporting the green events listed at the back of this book helps to send a positive message to the organisations and local communities involved (see page 354 for more information).

- **SUPPORT THE ADVERTISERS IN THIS BOOK**
  All our advertisers are ethical brands and have been vetted. We would never accept low scoring brands. So please, support these brands (see The Ethical Marketplace, page 360).

- **DON'T BUY BAD BRANDS**
  Avoid the brands that do not score well in *The Good Shopping Guide*. Together we have the power to make companies change.

- **GOOSHING**
  If you shop online, make sure you do it at *www.gooshing.co.uk*. It compares the ethics of 250,000 products and searches 350 shops to deliver you the cheapest prices on the internet.

- **LOOK OUT FOR *THE GOOD SHOPPING GUIDE* ETHICAL COMPANY LOGO**
  If you see this logo you know that the brand has scored well on our ethical audit.

GOOD
HOME & OFFICE

Introduction

It is often said that change starts at home, and with ethical shopping this can certainly be the case. Most modern houses are filled with consumer goods, many of which will see a lot of wear and tear – particularly if you have young children or unruly teenagers! Offices, too, are now populated as much by computers as by people, and in almost all cases it is the machines that give up working long before the humans. For these reasons, and to avoid the environmental and financial damage of unnecessary replacements, it is crucial that we choose the most long-lasting goods for our homes and offices.

While an unacceptable number of 'white' goods, such as kitchen appliances, still end up in landfill sites each year, steps are finally being taken to address the amount of waste we produce. Many progressive companies are setting up their own facilities to re-use and recycle their products, and websites such as *www. wasteonline.org.uk* have helped to create an online community where even your outdated VCR might be found a new home.

On the domestic front, the government has considered introducing a 'rubbish bag tax' as an incentive for people to reduce their non-recyclable waste. A controversial idea, undoubtedly, but perhaps a necessary one when you consider that Britain manages to recycle barely 20 per cent of its municipal waste: many countries in Europe, such as the Netherlands, have increased this figure to over 50 per cent.

Although the prospect of government legislation suggests that the eco-friendly message has made it to the top, many of the larger manufacturers still don't seem to have got the idea. It is up to us to make a stand. With the arrival of sustainable building it is now possible to build environmental considerations into the very foundations of your home or office; failing that, take a look at the tables on the following pages and make the right decision.

All-in-ones

When it comes to equipping your office there's no doubt that an all-in-one machine is the superior choice both financially and ecologically. Instead of running a printer, copier, fax and scanner with all their subsequent maintenance costs, an all-in-one consumes far less energy, costs less to buy at the outset and is cheaper to run in the long term. With less raw materials and energy being employed to produce one machine instead of four, the environment is also better off.

A SMART CHOICE

Perhaps a little slower and not quite as precise as separate units, the all-in-one machine more than makes up for this by occupying less storage space, costing less plus and not being such a burden on the environment. For these reasons, it is an ideal choice for smaller businesses and home offices, especially where there are limited queues for the photocopier.

LASER OR INKJET?

As with regular printers, all-in-ones can use either inkjet or laser technology. Laser printers work in a similar way to a photocopier and run at a lower overall cost per sheet. They require a drum and toner cartridge, both of which need intermittent replacing or refilling. When choosing a laser printer, ensure these two parts are housed separately as they run out at different times. If the drum is located inside the cartridge you won't be able to replace or refill it individually, which will produce extra waste. Beware of consumable parts in colour laser printers –

some can have up to nine in total.

Inkjets produce superior colour and photo quality prints to laser printers. They are far cheaper to buy too, but are much more expensive to maintain. The cartridges run out quickly and the glossy paper they need is far pricier. Whichever you choose, try to refill your empty toners and cartridges, rather than taking the more wasteful (and also more expensive) option of replacing them.

Out of the 44 million laser jet printer cartridges sold in Europe each year, 73% are only used once. It takes two litres of oil to make a typical laser printer cartridge plus aluminium and steel which release toxins and gas into the atmosphere when thrown into landfill. A cartridge can take several decades to decompose. With all this in mind the refilling option suddenly seems increasingly appealing. You can either do it yourself or send the cartridges away to be filled professionally. The other choice is to buy remanufactured cartridges which have been used, then cleaned and refilled. Remanufactured cartridges are available for most machines today.

brother. supports ethical shopping
at your side

THOUGHTFUL USE

In spite of the recent barrage of campaigns alerting us to the vast amount of energy consumed by electronic goods left on stand-by when not in use, people are still not switching off. Just as you wouldn't leave the light on, make it a reflex to turn all machines off when you leave the office at the end of the day. This small gesture will have major consequences in the long run. Avoid printing unnecessarily and always use both sides of the paper. Thankfully email has rendered the fax machine almost archaic – so if you can live without faxes get an all-in-one without this facility, saving even more money and materials!

RECYCLING

Electronic goods become obsolete, or appear to become obsolete, long before they really are. This is because technology is moving so fast in this sector. The importance of extending the life-span of IT equipment has been repeatedly highlighted by Greenpeace, which remains concerned about the amount of electronic waste that is dumped in countries such as China. Much of this waste comes from overseas, because it is cheaper for companies to send their waste abroad than deal with reusing and recycling at home.

The truth is that, for a normal user, an existing all-in-one with a printer, scanner, copier and fax should suffice for a number of years. When it is no longer good enough for your needs there's certain to be someone else for whom it would be ideal. It's possible to find these people through second-hand outlets or some of the schemes available for passing on electronic equipment, such as *www.wasteonline.org.uk*. You can also try your local freecycle group (*www.uk.freecycle.org*).

- Amstrad
- Brother
- BT
- Konica Minolta
- Lexmark
- Olivetti
- Ricoh
- Xerox

- Canon
- Epson
- Kyocera Mita
- NEC
- Panasonic

- Hewlett-Packard
- Sagem
- Samsung

brother at your side   supports ethical shopping

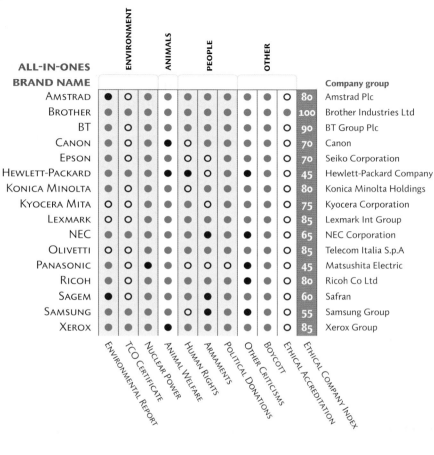

Key
- ● Top rating
- ○ Middle rating
- ● Bottom rating

Source: The Ethical Company Organisation (2008)

Batteries

Batteries are so small that it's easy to believe they're harmless, so who can blame us when we throw them in the bin? Unfortunately, the little devices that power so much of the technology we now consider indispensable (such as watches and mobile phones) are anything but. Read on to find out more about their potential effect on the environment, and what you can do to avoid adding to the problem.

TOXIC INGREDIENTS

Batteries inevitably contain a number of either toxic or corrosive chemicals, but so far manufacturers and environmental groups have failed to find much common ground in their debate about how these chemicals should be produced and disposed of. Until these issues are fully resolved, it is up to the consumer to look for products that have the least impact on the environment.

Nickel cadmium batteries, or NiCads, are the ones most often sold as 'rechargeable', a fact that rightly attracts many environmentally-concerned buyers. Nevertheless, cadmium is still a highly toxic heavy metal. To get around this problem, the five main manufacturers (Ever Ready, Panasonic, Rayovac, Uniross and Varta) have facilities to collect their own-brand NiCads and send them away for recycling. Just return the batteries to the relevant company when their four to five year life-span is up.

OTHER BATTERY TYPES

Nickel metal hydride (NiMH) batteries avoid the cadmium problem, and are generally longer-lasting than NiCads. Unfortunately, at the moment they tend to be available only as battery packs for camcorders, computers and mobile phones. As these batteries become more widespread, it must be hoped that the manufacturers will put in place a clear and accessible recycling system that their customers will want to adhere to.

Zinc and alkaline batteries are also rechargeable, although they are far less effective than NiCads. The main problem with these battery types is that there are virtually no facilities for recycling them in the UK. While the industry maintains that their impact on landfills is negligible, environmentalists are convinced that they will leave problem chemicals in the ground for future generations.

BUTTON CELLS

Button cells are the small flat batteries used in watches, hearing aids and some cameras. Their formulations include lithium, zinc air, silver oxide and alkaline. From this list, silver oxide is the best option; lithium batteries should be avoided if possible. Mercuric oxide cells used to be available but these have been phased out in recent years following concerns about the toxic effects of mercury on the environment.

WHAT NEXT?

The elimination of mercury is a significant step forward in the fight against battery waste, and there have also been considerable improvements in the collection of NiCads from larger commercial users of power tools, mobile phones and emergency lighting. However, with the average household using over 20 batteries a year, and only 2 per cent

of these being recycled, there is much left to be done.

So far, the number of reprocessing facilities has begun to increase, and some local authorities, including Bristol, have started to collect batteries as part of their recycling schemes. In the ideal future, though, all battery waste would be collected and recycled. For the industry this would mean proper labelling and the establishment of recycling schemes for all batteries. For consumers, the message should be to buy rechargeable batteries from retailers that promise to accept them back for recycling, either as single batteries or as packs.

Check *www.gooshing.co.uk* for price searches and ethical information on batteries – or why not eliminate them entirely by choosing an appliance that uses renewable energy such as wind or solar power? See the section on Good Energy for more information.

- Energizer
- Ever Ready
- Rayovac
- Varta

- Boots
- Uniross

- Duracell
- Kodak
- Panasonic
- Philips
- Sony

BATTERIES

BRAND NAME	ENVIRONMENT			ANIMALS	PEOPLE			OTHER				Company group
	Environmental Report	Eco Schemes	Nuclear Power	Animal Welfare	Human Rights	Armaments	Political Donations	Other Criticisms	Boycott	Ethical Accreditation	Ethical Company Index	
Boots	●	○	●	●	●	●	●	●	●	○	76	Boots Group Plc
Duracell	○	○	●	●	●	○	●	●	●	○	33	Procter & Gamble
Energizer	○	○	●	●	●	●	●	●	●	○	81	Energizer Holdings
Ever Ready	○	○	●	●	●	●	●	●	●	○	81	Energizer Holdings
Kodak	●	○	●	●	○	○	●	●	●	○	48	Eastman Kodak
Panasonic	●	○	●	●	●	○	●	●	●	○	70	Matsushita Electric
Philips	●	●	●	●	○	○	●	●	●	○	62	Royal Philips Electronics N.V.
Rayovac	○	○	●	●	●	●	●	●	●	○	81	Spectrum Brands
Sony	●	●	●	●	●	○	●	●	●	○	62	Sony Corporation
Uniross	●	○	●	●	●	○	●	●	●	○	67	Uniross Batteries
Varta	○	○	●	●	●	●	●	●	●	○	81	Spectrum Brands

Key

● Top rating
○ Middle rating
● Bottom rating

Source: The Ethical Company Organisation

Boilers

Utility bills have a habit of arriving when least expected, and usually seem unreasonably high, especially after a long winter. Often the main reason for the expense is an inefficient boiler. Replacing an old boiler with a gas condensing model, or even a solar-powered system, may cost a bit more initially, but once installed they can be much cheaper to run. It's an ideal opportunity to both help the environment and save money.

WHAT IS CONDENSING?

Of the central heating boilers available, the most popular usually provide a combination of central heating and hot water for household use. Most systems are gas-fired, although there is also the option of using LPG or fuel oil. The most important question to ask when thinking of buying a new boiler is whether it works on a condensing or a non-condensing system.

Environmental campaigners are all agreed that gas condensing boilers (GCBs) are the best technological choice for most people. This is because they operate at about 90 per cent efficiency, compared to only 70 per cent efficiency for the more common, and cheaper, non-condensing boilers.

GCBs include heat exchangers, which mean that they retrieve heat that would otherwise disappear in water vapour emissions, and then return it to the system. This process helps to reduce emissions, not only of carbon dioxide, but also of nitrous oxide – a positive step for all of us.

Of course this advantage comes at a price, and GCBs tend to cost between £700 and £1,400 – about twice as much as non-condensing boilers. However, GCBs are more efficient and their annual running costs usually turn out to be around 20 per cent lower than most other boilers. So, calculating how much is spent every year on gas or other fuels, these apparently rather expensive machines can pay for themselves in little more than five years. If the initial outlay still seems like a lot of money, the Big Green Boiler Scheme at *www.green-boilers.co.uk* has enabled some local authorities to make subsidies available to boost sales of GCBs.

EFFICIENCY LABELS

Just like fridges and several other domestic appliances, all new boilers are now required by European law to display energy efficiency labels. These run on an A to G scale, with A being the best. The most extensive details of boiler models and their efficiencies are available on a British government-sponsored website at *www.sedbuk.com*. There were, at the time of writing, over 400 different models labelled with an A rating.

SUPPLIERS

The table opposite features some of the main companies supplying the UK market. They all produce A-rated gas condensing boilers and were taken from the Sedbuk and Energy Saving Trust (*www.est.org.uk*) websites. Half are relatively small, privately-owned British companies which specialise in heating systems. Several others belong to European-based heating specialists. Such companies may also make air conditioning and other heating systems, such as showers, for household or corporate customers.

The Ethical Company Organisation's recommended company is Atmos (*www. atmos.uk.com*), which is a member of the accreditation scheme and sells a range of boilers including standard and solar-powered systems.

THE PRICE FACTOR

- After installing a gas condensing boiler, the average user in a small house should recoup the extra cost in well under ten years and then make substantial savings over the 20-year life of the product.
- In some local authority areas there is a £70 grant available through the Big Green Boiler Scheme, *www.green-boilers.co.uk.* Tel: 0800 028 2855 / 0193 486 3650.
- British Gas also operates a scheme whereby it sells low-cost GCBs from a limited range of manufacturers.
- *www.gooshing.co.uk* has a cost comparison function, getting you the best boiler prices from across the web.

- Ariston
- Atmos
- EcoMax
- GLOW Worm

- Arena
- Barcelona
- Baxi
- British Gas
- Eclipse ESS
- Gas 210 ECO
- Keston Boilers
- Potterton
- Quinta

- Bosch
- Carfield/ Geminox
- Ideal Boilers
- Worcester Greenstar

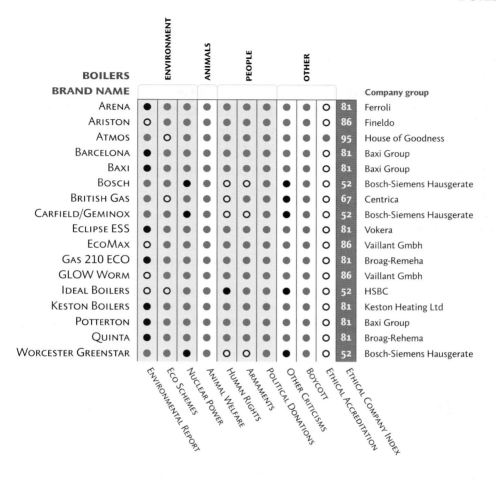

Ratings by brand. Categories: ENVIRONMENT (Environmental Report, Eco Schemes, Nuclear Power), ANIMALS (Animal Welfare), PEOPLE (Human Rights, Armaments, Political Donations), OTHER (Other Criticisms, Boycott, Ethical Accreditation), and Ethical Company Index.

Ratings key: T = Top rating, M = Middle rating, B = Bottom rating.

BOILERS BRAND NAME	Environmental Report	Eco Schemes	Nuclear Power	Animal Welfare	Human Rights	Armaments	Political Donations	Other Criticisms	Boycott	Ethical Accreditation	Ethical Company Index	Company group
Arena	B	T	T	T	T	T	T	T	T	M	81	Ferroli
Ariston	M	T	T	T	T	T	T	T	T	M	86	Fineldo
Atmos	T	M	T	T	T	T	T	T	T	B	95	House of Goodness
Barcelona	B	T	T	T	T	T	T	T	T	M	81	Baxi Group
Baxi	B	T	T	T	T	T	T	T	T	M	81	Baxi Group
Bosch	T	T	B	T	M	M	T	B	T	M	52	Bosch-Siemens Hausgerate
British Gas	T	M	T	T	M	T	T	B	T	M	67	Centrica
Carfield/Geminox	T	T	B	T	M	M	T	B	T	M	52	Bosch-Siemens Hausgerate
Eclipse ESS	B	T	T	T	T	T	T	T	T	M	81	Vokera
EcoMax	M	T	T	T	T	T	T	T	T	M	86	Vaillant Gmbh
Gas 210 ECO	B	T	T	T	T	T	T	T	T	M	81	Broag-Remeha
GLOW Worm	M	T	T	T	T	T	T	T	T	M	86	Vaillant Gmbh
Ideal Boilers	M	M	T	T	B	T	T	B	T	M	52	HSBC
Keston Boilers	B	T	T	T	T	T	T	T	T	M	81	Keston Heating Ltd
Potterton	B	T	T	T	T	T	T	T	T	M	81	Baxi Group
Quinta	B	T	T	T	T	T	T	T	T	M	81	Broag-Rehema
Worcester Greenstar	T	T	B	T	M	M	T	B	T	M	52	Bosch-Siemens Hausgerate

Key

● Top rating
○ Middle rating
● Bottom rating

Source: The Ethical Company Organisation

Cleaners

Every year, the big detergent manufacturers come up with dozens of new ideas for keeping homes sparkling clean and free from bacteria, from germ-busting sprays to disposable mops. Ignore the hype and keep things simple: one multi-surface cleaner will suffice for nearly all household tasks, including kitchens and bathrooms alike. Cutting down the use of chemicals in the home is the first step towards reducing their impact on the environment.

PETROLEUM DERIVATIVES

Household cleaners are formulated from a wide range of ingredients, and almost always contain surfactants (detergents) which help to remove dirt and grease and allow them to disperse in water. Natural surfactants can be derived from vegetable substances, but many big brands continue to use petroleum derivatives such as the much-criticised sodium lauryl sulphate.

Petroleum-based surfactants are derived from a non-renewable resource and often biodegrade more slowly and less completely than those produced from vegetables. During the degradation process, they can form compounds that are even more dangerous than the original chemicals themselves.

European countries, including the UK, have been discussing a strategy that would enforce the consumer's right to know about all the chemicals present in cleaning products. At the moment, manufacturers of household detergents can continue to use toxic and potentially toxic chemicals in their products.

BIODEGRADABILITY

A general claim of 'biodegradable' on the labels of many products is misleading, because all such products are biodegradable; the question is how readily the elements biodegrade. There is a big difference between products breaking down entirely in hours or days, rather than partially over months or years. Read the label carefully: terms such as 'surface active agents', 'cleaning agents', 'soil suspending agents', 'grease cutters' and 'grease removers' are often just clever names for petroleum-based surfactants.

A regrettable side-effect of companies' quest to find different products to do what is essentially the same job (cleaning a surface) has been an increase in animal testing.

More and more cleaners are now being marketed as being 'especially formulated' for the bathroom or kitchen sink, when in reality there is very little difference between the cleaning requirements of the two areas.

CUTTING DOWN ON BLEACH

Greater quantities of bleach and detergent are discharged directly into sewers from domestic premises than from the factories making them. Several types of bleach exist, all of which act by oxidising, and thus sterilising, organic matter. This powerful antibacterial effect has been seen to persist beyond the u-bend, undermining the bacterial action that helps break down sewage. For this reason bleach should be used in diluted form, if at all, and should never be poured neat down drains. Neither Ecover nor Bio-D produce household bleach, because they believe the action is unnecessarily powerful. Their toilet cleaners rely on acids which dislodge waste rather than sterilise it.

Another reason for not using bleach is the danger it poses to humans. When chlorine-based bleaches are mixed with ammonia they release dangerous chlorine gas. An estimated 6,000 infant and toddler accidents are attributed to household cleaners each year.

WATER AND PACKAGING

The most common ingredient (up to 90 per cent) of general-purpose cleaners is water. When this excess water is transported, energy and packaging is wasted and more solid waste is created for our landfills. Concentrated products in smaller bottles are a better option.

Cleaning product bottles are usually made from plastic. Greenpeace urges consumers to make a conscious effort not to buy things in polyvinylchloride (PVC) containers. There is usually a symbol on the bottom of the bottle indicating the type of plastic: PVC is indicated by a '3' in a recycling symbol. High and low density polyethylene (HDPE and LDPE), polypropylene (PP), polyethylene (PE) and polyethylene tetraphthalate (PET) all have fewer environmental problems associated with their manufacture and disposal than PVC.

Why not avoid synthetic chemicals altogether with some old-fashioned remedies? Try white vinegar, baking soda, salt, lemon juice and olive oil as handy DIY cleaners.

- Astonish
- Bio D
- Ecover
- Orange Plus

- 1001
- Dettol
- Jeyes Fluid
- Mr Muscle

- Ajax
- Cif
- Flash
- Stardrops

CLEANERS BRAND NAME	Ethical Company Index	Company group
1001	81	WD-40 Company
Ajax	62	Colgate-Palmolive Companies
Astonish	86	The London Oil Refining Company Ltd
Bio-D	90	Bio-D Company
Cif	43	Unilever
Dettol	67	Reckitt Benckiser
Ecover	90	Ecover Belgium EV
Flash	33	Procter & Gamble
Jeyes Fluid	71	Jeyes Group Ltd
Mr Muscle	67	SC Johnson and Sons, Inc
Orange Plus	86	Earth Friendly Products
Stardrops	57	Thornton and Ross

Rating categories: ENVIRONMENT (Environmental Report, Eco Schemes, Nuclear Power), ANIMALS (Animal Welfare), PEOPLE (Human Rights, Armaments, Political Donations), OTHER (Other Criticisms, Boycott), Ethical Accreditation, Ethical Company Index

Key

● Top rating
○ Middle rating
● Bottom rating

Source: The Ethical Company Organisation

Computers

Advances in the computer industry have revolutionised our work and leisure time, but the never-ending drive for the latest technology has had some alarming consequences. The escalating problem of electrical waste has been exacerbated by the seemingly built-in obsolescence of many machines, and the enormous demand for replacements has led to unsatisfactory working conditions in factories world-wide. One potential answer is reconditioning old machines; another, as ever, lies in informed consumer choice.

WHO MAKES YOUR COMPUTER?

More than one-third of electronic goods are made in poor countries, notably China, Thailand and Mexico. Some of the larger manufacturers have been accused of ignoring labour regulations by preventing workers from forming associations and enforcing compulsory overtime in their factories.

The Catholic Agency for Overseas Development (*www.cafod.org.uk*) runs a campaign highlighting abuses in this sector, and has been a catalyst in the introduction of codes of conduct in the industry. Despite this progress, the current guidelines still contain significant omissions, and do not insist on a working week of less than sixty hours or cover the right of all workers to associate.

Before buying a new computer, be sure to investigate working conditions at the company. Check the table overleaf and use *www.gooshing.co.uk* to find out about the most ethically-produced machines.

ENVIRONMENTAL PRESSURES

Electrical waste is the most rapidly growing waste problem in the world. Every year, an estimated 1 million tonnes of electronic equipment is discarded in the UK alone, and information technology products account for 39 per cent of this figure. Landfill disposal or incineration is entirely inappropriate for computers, which contain dangerous chemicals including mercury and hexavalent chromium.

An EU directive on Waste Electrical and Electronic Equipment came into European law in August 2005, based on the principle of 'extended producer responsibility'. This requires manufacturers to pay for the safe disposal of their own goods. However, the British government was slow to follow this directive, and has only recently begun to provide local authorities with the recycling equipment necessary for its implementation.

Despite this sluggishness, many companies and local authorities already operate take-back or collection schemes.

If your computer is ageing it is worth contacting the manufacturer to try and arrange for an environmentally sound disposal, but be sure to find out where the machine will end up. Greenpeace has found that some manufacturers are dumping their used products in countries such as China which have less stringent laws.

UPGRADING AND RECONDITIONING

As an alternative to disposal, an attractive possibility is to arrange for the computer's re-use. Ageing machines can be reconditioned and then re-sold to another user. This process has the advantage of conserving the raw materials and energy used in manufacturing. The refurbishment of computers can also provide a social benefit, enabling less wealthy institutions and individuals to purchase the equipment at a lower price. Several charities arrange for unwanted computers to be sent to schools or developing countries after reconditioning.

Even if the computer as a whole is too old to be passed on, the individual parts may nevertheless be suitable for re-use. The Waste Online website (*www.wasteonline.org.uk*) has a comprehensive list of contact details for refurbishment schemes across the UK.

Another possibility to consider is upgrading an existing machine rather than buying a new model. Upgrading the computer memory, for example, can often prove a simple and cost-effective way to reduce waiting times and increase the file handling capacity of a PC.

Upgrades and re-use can help to alleviate the environmental pressures created by the increasingly rapid manufacture of new machines. At the moment only 26 per cent of waste IT equipment is recycled, so any diversion of waste from landfill can really make a difference.

- AMD
- Evesham
- Intel
- Sun
- Thinkpad
- Tranquil PC
- VIA Eden-N
- Viglen

- Acer
- Apple
- Dell
- Fujitsu Siemens
- NEC
- Packard-Bell

- Compaq
- Hewlett-Packard
- Sony
- Toshiba

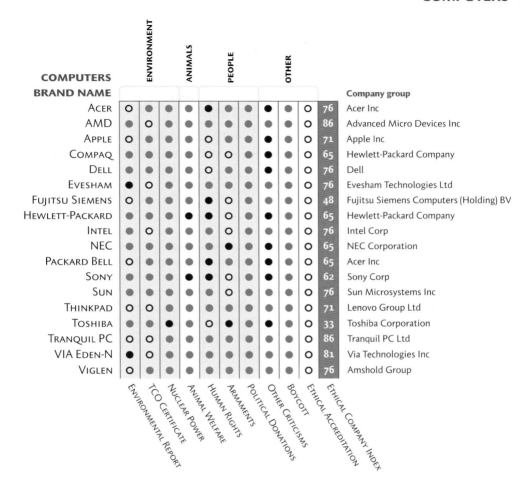

COMPUTERS BRAND NAME

Brand Name	Ethical Company Index	Company group
ACER	76	Acer Inc
AMD	86	Advanced Micro Devices Inc
APPLE	71	Apple Inc
COMPAQ	65	Hewlett-Packard Company
DELL	76	Dell
EVESHAM	76	Evesham Technologies Ltd
FUJITSU SIEMENS	48	Fujitsu Siemens Computers (Holding) BV
HEWLETT-PACKARD	65	Hewlett-Packard Company
INTEL	76	Intel Corp
NEC	65	NEC Corporation
PACKARD BELL	65	Acer Inc
SONY	62	Sony Corp
SUN	76	Sun Microsystems Inc
THINKPAD	71	Lenovo Group Ltd
TOSHIBA	33	Toshiba Corporation
TRANQUIL PC	86	Tranquil PC Ltd
VIA EDEN-N	81	Via Technologies Inc
VIGLEN	76	Amshold Group

Column categories:
- **ENVIRONMENT**: Environmental Report, TCO Certificate, Nuclear Power
- **ANIMALS**: Animal Welfare
- **PEOPLE**: Human Rights, Armaments, Political Donations
- **OTHER**: Other Criticisms, Boycott, Ethical Accreditation
- Ethical Company Index

Key

● Top rating

○ Middle rating

● Bottom rating

Source: The Ethical Company Organisation (2008)

Cookers

Most of us won't buy more than one or two cookers in our lifetime, so getting the right one is crucial. The ideal appliance will strike a perfect balance between convenience and efficiency, making light work of everything from a family meal to a dinner party, without impacting on the environment in the long term. The key question here is whether to choose gas or electric, and the relative merits of both are considered below.

CONVENIENCE AND EFFICIENCY

Ease of use is an important consideration when choosing a cooker, which is probably why British consumers seem to prefer electric ovens to gas ones, while gas hobs (whose temperature tends to be more controllable) are marginally more popular than electric. Most manufacturers acknowledge these preferences and offer dual fuel products.

Unfortunately, popularity is no guide to energy efficiency, and government research shows that there is room to improve the efficiency of ovens and hobs alike. Self-cleaning oven features – which can be found in both gas and electric ovens – contribute to energy efficiency because they provide extra insulation. However, as the process itself requires an extra 1.4kW of energy each time it is used, in order to save energy overall the self-cleaning function should not be operated more than once a month.

Fan ovens also have lower energy needs because they cut the heating-up time and the amount of heat lost, which reduces the overall time used for cooking. The fan also creates an even temperature throughout, although models are available that allow the fan to be turned off in order to increase the temperature at the top of the oven.

Even if there is little to choose from in terms of functionality between gas and electric, the issue of carbon emissions may tip the balance. Gas is commonly accepted to be the preferable option, with lower emissions than electricity. A UK study calculated that the 'carbon intensity' of cooking with electricity was 0.12kgC/kWh, compared to 0.05kgC/kWh for gas. However, switching to a 100 per cent renewable electricity company would be a positive step in reducing your carbon emissions – see the Good Energy section on renewable energy suppliers for more information.

INDUCTION HOBS

For electric cookers, the latest 'induction hobs' use less than half the energy expended by standard coils.

The induction system involves a high frequency coil being housed beneath a ceramic glass surface. Electromagnetic energy in the form of heat is transferred to the pan, which must be magnetic, with the cooker surface remaining fairly cool. These are currently an expensive option, particularly as aluminium and glass pans are not suitable for them, but prices look set to come down in future years.

Induction hobs have been assessed by the European Commission to be 82 per cent efficient. Ceramic hobs with halogen elements come next at up to 70 per cent, followed by sealed hobs at 50 per cent. Solid disc elements are the worst in terms of efficiency, using high wattages yet heating up slowly. Regardless of the choice of hob, there must be good contact between pan and element for them to work efficiently, so that battered old saucepan could be wasting more energy than you'd expect.

The best prices on energy efficient cookers and 250,000 other products can be found at *www.gooshing.co.uk*, which searches 350 retailers to bring you the cheapest prices on the most ethical goods available.

- Ariston
- Aga
- Candy
- Baumatic
- Belling
- Cannon
- Creda
- Hotpoint
- Leisure
- Miele
- New World
- Rosieres
- Scholtes
- Stoves

- AEG
- Bauknecht
- Brandt
- De Dietrich
- Electrolux
- Ocean
- Parkinson-Cowan
- Tricity Bendix
- Whirlpool
- Zanussi

- Bosch
- Gaggenau
- GE
- Neff
- Siemens

COOKERS

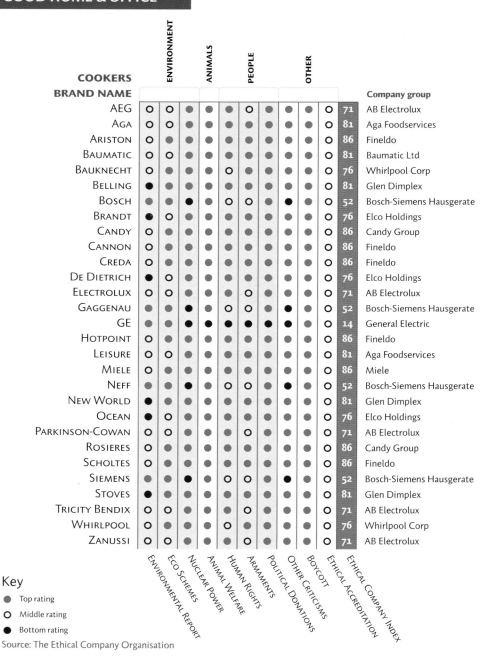

Ratings key: T = Top rating, M = Middle rating, B = Bottom rating

BRAND NAME	Environmental Report	Eco Schemes	Nuclear Power	Animal Welfare	Human Rights	Armaments	Political Donations	Other Criticisms	Boycott	Ethical Accreditation	Ethical Company Index	Company group
AEG	M	M	T	T	T	M	T	T	T	M	71	AB Electrolux
AGA	M	M	T	T	T	T	T	T	T	M	81	Aga Foodservices
ARISTON	M	T	T	T	T	T	T	T	T	M	86	Fineldo
BAUMATIC	M	M	T	T	T	T	T	T	T	M	81	Baumatic Ltd
BAUKNECHT	M	T	T	T	M	T	T	T	T	M	76	Whirlpool Corp
BELLING	B	T	T	T	T	T	T	T	T	M	81	Glen Dimplex
BOSCH	T	T	B	T	M	M	T	B	T	M	52	Bosch-Siemens Hausgerate
BRANDT	B	M	T	T	T	T	T	T	T	M	76	Elco Holdings
CANDY	M	T	T	T	T	T	T	T	T	M	86	Candy Group
CANNON	M	T	T	T	T	T	T	T	T	M	86	Fineldo
CREDA	M	T	T	T	T	T	T	T	T	M	86	Fineldo
DE DIETRICH	B	M	T	T	T	T	T	T	T	M	76	Elco Holdings
ELECTROLUX	M	M	T	T	T	M	T	T	T	M	71	AB Electrolux
GAGGENAU	T	T	B	T	M	M	T	B	T	M	52	Bosch-Siemens Hausgerate
GE	T	T	B	B	B	B	B	B	T	M	14	General Electric
HOTPOINT	M	T	T	T	T	T	T	T	T	M	86	Fineldo
LEISURE	M	M	T	T	T	T	T	T	T	M	81	Aga Foodservices
MIELE	M	T	T	T	T	T	T	T	T	M	86	Miele
NEFF	T	T	B	T	M	M	T	B	T	M	52	Bosch-Siemens Hausgerate
NEW WORLD	B	T	T	T	T	T	T	T	T	M	81	Glen Dimplex
OCEAN	B	M	T	T	T	T	T	T	T	M	76	Elco Holdings
PARKINSON-COWAN	M	M	T	T	T	M	T	T	T	M	71	AB Electrolux
ROSIERES	M	T	T	T	T	T	T	T	T	M	86	Candy Group
SCHOLTES	M	T	T	T	T	T	T	T	T	M	86	Fineldo
SIEMENS	T	T	B	T	M	M	T	B	T	M	52	Bosch-Siemens Hausgerate
STOVES	B	T	T	T	T	T	T	T	T	M	81	Glen Dimplex
TRICITY BENDIX	M	M	T	T	T	M	T	T	T	M	71	AB Electrolux
WHIRLPOOL	M	M	T	T	M	T	T	T	T	M	76	Whirlpool Corp
ZANUSSI	M	M	T	T	T	M	T	T	T	M	71	AB Electrolux

Column groupings: ENVIRONMENT (Environmental Report, Eco Schemes); ANIMALS (Nuclear Power, Animal Welfare); PEOPLE (Human Rights, Armaments, Political Donations); OTHER (Other Criticisms, Boycott, Ethical Accreditation)

Key

- ● Top rating
- ○ Middle rating
- ● Bottom rating

Source: The Ethical Company Organisation

Digital cameras

Digital cameras are the Polaroids of the computer generation, allowing snap happy photographers to see their prints instantly. At first glance, they also seem to offer extra environmental value, removing the need for extensive chemical processing, and meaning that only a select few pictures actually make it onto paper. However, there are inescapable problems associated with the disposal of digital cameras, and they are one of the most battery-hungry devices available.

BATTERIES GALORE

Most digital cameras come with standard non-rechargeable batteries, so it is up to the buyer to make the switch to rechargeable. Although rechargeable batteries are more expensive, they will soon pay for themselves. The most environmentally friendly option are nickel metal hydride (NiMH) batteries. Unlike the more widespread nickel cadmium (NiCad) variety, they do not contain toxic metals and will usually last for longer.

Alkaline batteries (such as ordinary AAs) will run down remarkably quickly if used in digital cameras. This is because they can't supply energy quickly enough to satisfy the vast demands of the camera. Even when an alkaline battery fails in a digital camera the chances are it will still have plenty of energy left – try it in a device that needs less power before disposing of it. The best choice, as ever, is to buy rechargeables.

To reduce the camera's battery use, switch it off between photographs and avoid looking at the LCD display for too long each time, as this will drain the power. Some models will automatically switch off if left unattended.

MANUFACTURE AND DISPOSAL

Digital cameras are included in the Waste Electrical and Electronic Equipment Directive 2003, which requires producers and retailers of electrical equipment to establish a scheme whereby they can be collected after use to be recycled or recovered. Local authorities will have details of such schemes, or the manufacturer can be contacted directly.

Like all electrical goods, digital cameras are made of dozens of different materials, which can make them difficult to recycle. The LCD display, which allows photos to be viewed, contains toxic components and should not be disposed of in landfill.

Wasteonline (*www.wasteonline.org.uk*) lists four ways in which the materials used to make a device such as a digital camera can be recycled. Most obviously, the equipment can be manually dismantled and its recyclable components separated out. This can also be done mechanically, with the item being shredded so that recyclable raw materials can be removed. Raw materials can also be isolated through incineration, which burns off combustible matter and leaves metals behind. Finally, chemical processes can be used to recover precious metals from complicated circuit boards and components.

All of these processes reduce the need for new raw materials to be sourced, which helps to protect the environment from the damage caused by mining and processing.

PRINTING

It is now possible get print-outs of digital pictures at most high-street chemists, but some amateur photographers instead choose to develop their pictures at home. Many manufacturers have realised this and begun marketing specially designed equipment for digital cameras, but for most needs a good quality inkjet printer will suffice.

Pictures from cheaper cameras tend not to print as well as more expensive ones. This is because they store the image using fewer pixels, so the picture appears less crisp on paper. As a general rule, the higher the number of megapixels, the better the camera.

The three main types of paper available for printing photos are gloss, semi-gloss and matt, all of which give a slightly different finish to the picture. Choose acid-free brands and use sparingly, as recycled versions of these high quality papers are difficult to find.

- Benq
- Casio
- Fuji
- Konica Minolta
- Ricoh

- Canon
- Kyocera
- Nikon
- Oregon
- Pentax
- Vivitar
- Yakumo

- Hewlett Packard
- Kodak
- Olympus
- Panasonic
- Samsung
- Sanyo
- Sony

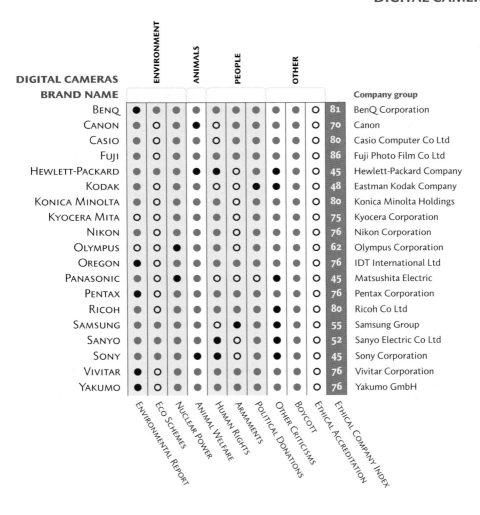

DIGITAL CAMERAS BRAND NAME	ENVIRONMENT			ANIMALS	PEOPLE			OTHER			ETHICAL COMPANY INDEX	Company group
	Environmental Report	Eco Schemes	Nuclear Power	Animal Welfare	Human Rights	Armaments	Political Donations	Other Criticisms	Boycott	Ethical Accreditation		
BENQ	●	●	●	●	●	●	●	●	●	O	81	BenQ Corporation
CANON	●	O	●	●	O	●	●	●	●	O	70	Canon
CASIO	●	O	●	●	O	●	●	●	●	O	80	Casio Computer Co Ltd
FUJI	●	O	●	●	●	●	●	●	●	O	86	Fuji Photo Film Co Ltd
HEWLETT-PACKARD	●	●	●	●	●	O	●	●	●	O	45	Hewlett-Packard Company
KODAK	●	O	●	●	O	O	●	●	●	O	48	Eastman Kodak Company
KONICA MINOLTA	●	O	●	●	●	O	●	●	●	O	80	Konica Minolta Holdings
KYOCERA MITA	O	●	●	●	●	O	●	●	●	O	75	Kyocera Corporation
NIKON	●	O	●	●	●	O	●	●	●	O	76	Nikon Corporation
OLYMPUS	O	O	●	●	●	O	●	●	●	O	62	Olympus Corporation
OREGON	●	O	●	●	●	●	●	●	●	O	76	IDT International Ltd
PANASONIC	●	O	●	●	O	O	O	●	●	O	45	Matsushita Electric
PENTAX	●	O	●	●	●	●	●	●	●	O	76	Pentax Corporation
RICOH	●	O	●	●	●	●	●	●	●	O	80	Ricoh Co Ltd
SAMSUNG	●	●	●	●	O	●	●	●	●	O	55	Samsung Group
SANYO	●	●	●	●	●	O	●	●	●	O	52	Sanyo Electric Co Ltd
SONY	●	●	●	●	●	O	●	●	●	O	45	Sony Corporation
VIVITAR	●	O	●	●	●	●	●	●	●	O	76	Vivitar Corporation
YAKUMO	●	O	●	●	●	●	●	●	●	O	76	Yakumo GmbH

Key

● Top rating

O Middle rating

● Bottom rating

Source: The Ethical Company Organisation (2008)

DVD players

It's hard to believe that ten years ago few of us knew what a DVD player was, let alone owned one. The format now accounts for about 60 per cent of the rental market, and many filmmakers even go to the trouble of filming behind-the-scenes material especially for the DVD. The promise of 'extra features' is only one of the bonuses of DVD players, but the inevitable downside is their contribution to electronic waste.

E-WASTE

The number of electronic products discarded globally has skyrocketed in recent years, with 20 to 50 million tonnes of waste being generated every year. To put this in perspective, if our estimated annual electronic waste was put into containers on a train it would stretch once around the world. E-waste now makes up 5 per cent of all municipal solid waste world-wide – nearly as much as is produced from plastic packaging. Unfortunately though, e-waste is much more hazardous.

Electronic devices are made from a complex mixture of up to several hundred materials, many of which contain toxic heavy metals such as lead, mercury, cadmium and beryllium. They can also include brominated flame retardants, which have been the subject of a Friends of the Earth campaign following concerns about their potential effect on human health. These chemicals are thought to disrupt the thyroid hormone system and have been linked to behavioural changes in mice.

In addition to the well-publicised problems associated with lead and mercury, all of these substances are hazardous to the people who have to work with them, and can cause serious pollution if not properly disposed of. Companies were given until June 2006 to exclude lead from their products, but the metal will still be found in many appliances that were made before this date.

WHAT CAN COMPANIES DO?

Removing toxic chemicals from products such as DVD players reduces pollution and makes re-use and recycling cheaper and less hazardous. Greenpeace (*www.greenpeace.org*) publishes rankings for the major electronics companies showing the level of toxic chemicals in their products.

Some companies, such as Sony, have made pledges to reduce, substitute and where possible eliminate the use of substances that are potentially damaging to the environment. Environmental groups hope that these commitments will be honoured, and that they will provide an incentive for other companies to follow suit.

DISPOSAL

Many old electronic goods gather dust in storage waiting to be reused, recycled or thrown away. Due to the level of harmful chemicals in e-waste, appliances such as DVD players must be disposed of carefully, and should only be recycled in controlled conditions.

The dumping of electronic products in landfill sites not only results in the potential leaching of toxic substances into the environment, but causes a net loss of resources. For example, the six million tonnes of electronic waste dumped each year in the UK contains over 600,000 tonnes of copper. If this copper is not re-used, more of the raw material has to be extracted, meaning that extra resources are expended in mining, transport and refinement.

It's not just the players that need recycling: DVDs and CDs also make a significant contribution to landfill. Unwanted discs can easily be given to charity to be re-sold, or a company called Polymer Reprocessors (*www.polymer-reprocessors.co.uk*) will happily take them off your hands to be made into anything from burglar alarms to bird feeders. Failing that, they also make very good coasters.

DVD WARS

A VHS-style war is shaping up in the DVD world, with new Blu-ray technology set to take on HD-DVD to become the future of home entertainment. With this in mind, anyone thinking of buying one of the next generation of appliances would be advised to wait – just in case their brand new player turns out to be the Betamax of the noughties.

- Alba
- Bush
- Goodmans
- Sharp

- Denon
- Panasonic
- Philips
- Sony

- Hitachi
- Samsung
- Sanyo
- Toshiba

DVD PLAYERS

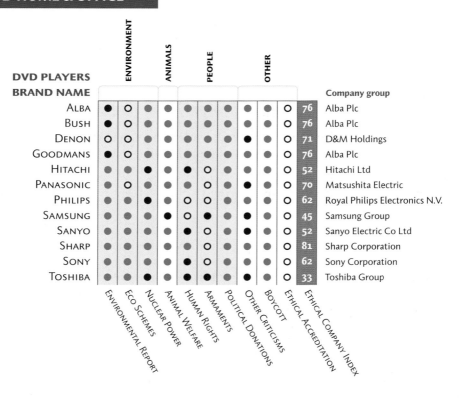

BRAND NAME	ENVIRONMENT	ANIMALS	PEOPLE	OTHER	Ethical Company Index	Company group
ALBA					76	Alba Plc
BUSH					76	Alba Plc
DENON					71	D&M Holdings
GOODMANS					76	Alba Plc
HITACHI					52	Hitachi Ltd
PANASONIC					70	Matsushita Electric
PHILIPS					62	Royal Philips Electronics N.V.
SAMSUNG					45	Samsung Group
SANYO					52	Sanyo Electric Co Ltd
SHARP					81	Sharp Corporation
SONY					62	Sony Corporation
TOSHIBA					33	Toshiba Group

Column categories: Environmental Report, Eco Schemes, Nuclear Power, Animal Welfare, Human Rights, Armaments, Political Donations, Other Criticisms, Boycott, Ethical Accreditation, Ethical Company Index

Key

- ● Top rating
- ● Middle rating
- ○ Bottom rating

Source: The Ethical Company Organisation

 supports ethical shopping

Fax machines

A veritable communication revolution at the outset, the fax machine is long past its heyday. Competition from email has rendered this eighties throwback almost redundant, but for some offices it is still an essential and trusty component. Those with copying and printing facilities certainly reduce the need for several machines and their environmental credentials can be boosted by using recycled paper and switching off when not in use.

CHOICE OF PAPER

Plain paper fax machines use ordinary sheets of A4 paper, while thermal fax machines use rolls of thermal paper. At first glance, plain paper machines seem the better option, but two factors are worth thinking about: firstly, a plain paper machine also requires a replaceable ink or toner cartridge or drum, and second, a thermal fax machine cuts messages to length and thus saves on paper and energy.

Plain paper made from 100 per cent post-consumer waste is widely available. Look for the Nordic Swan symbol, a Scandinavian labelling scheme which requires the production process to have the minimum possible environmental impact. Contrary to popular opinion, thermal paper is recyclable, although it is considered 'low-grade' waste and there are no known sources of recycled thermal paper.

One way to reduce paper is to send and receive faxes through a computer. The drawbacks of this option are that computers cannot receive faxes when they are switched off or working offline, and only material already stored in the computer can be faxed, meaning that a separate scanner may be required. For offices that already have this capability, however, it may be the ideal solution.

RECYCLING

When you buy a new fax machine, make sure you find out how many parts are consumable and whether or not they can be recycled.

A few years ago, some companies began producing ink and toner cartridges with 'anti-recycling devices'. These usually consisted of an electronic chip which prevented the cartridge from being refilled, forcing the owner to buy a brand new one (and ensuring the company retained the potential recycler's custom). This alarming practice became the subject of much debate, and was widely criticised by the remanufacturing industry. All anti-recycling devices have since been banned in the EU.

Just like printers, using remanufactured cartridges for your fax machine will save

you money and help the environment. To find the best distributors of recycled cartridges simply contact The United Kingdom Cartridge Recyclers Association (UKCRA). This independent body encourages producers of remanufactured cartridges to maintain high standards and offer high quality products. Their website (*www.ukcra.com*) has detailed profiles on the companies that provide remanufactured cartridges plus information on developments in the recycling industry.

MINIMISING PAPER USE

Switching off the automatic header page function is an instant paper saver. Every so often a fax machine gives out a transmission report; try to use scrap paper for these. Big logos may look good and instantly attract attention as they come shuffling out of the machine, but they also consume much more paper than a cleverly designed smaller one. It could make all the difference between getting all your information on one page instead of two.

ETHICAL-MINDED COMPANIES

One fax machine manufacturer, Brother UK, has been awarded international environmental management standard, ISO 14001:2004. To achieve this status, Brother's environmental performance was assessed according to various criteria, including distribution and transport, carbon dioxide emissions, natural resources, packaging, waste and impact on the local environment.

Brother is also a member of the Ethical Company Organisation's accreditation scheme, awarded to companies that meet the highest ethical standards. See *www.ethical-company-organisation.org* for more details on the scheme and its members.

Other manufacturers consistently come up with disappointing results in our league tables. The Samsung Group has yet to remedy their involvement with armaments or improve their track record concerning human rights.

- Amstrad
- Brother
- BT
- Olivetti
- Ricoh

- Canon
- NEC

- Panasonic
- Sagem
- Samsung

Are you interested in saving your business money and reducing waste?

You can start by following Brother's Print Smart Charter.

1. Print on both sides of a sheet of paper wherever possible.

2. Introduce a recycling scheme for all waste paper.

3. Monitor print levels within the office and set targets for reduced paper usage.

4. Always consider manufacturers with an accredited environment standard such as ISO-14001* and who have an established product and consumables recycling scheme.

5. Ensure all staff are trained in the smart printing techniques available on your office printer (e.g. duplex printing, scan to USB).

6. Ensure your printer is switched off every night and the energy save mode is activated when not in use.

7. To make sure all your workers are aware of (and adhere to) these guidelines.

*ISO 14001 – a universal standard specifying requirements for an environmental management system. See www.iso-14001.org.uk for more details

Visit **www.brother.co.uk/printsmartcharter** to find out more and download Brother's Print Smart guide.

 supports ethical shopping
at your side

FAX MACHINES

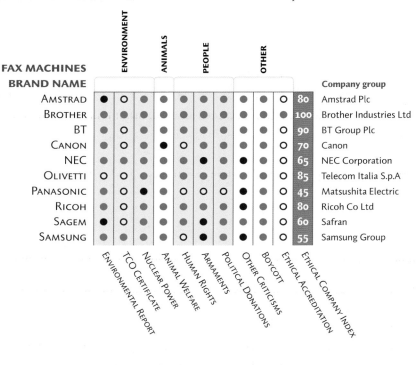

BRAND NAME	Ethical Company Index	Company group
AMSTRAD	80	Amstrad Plc
BROTHER	100	Brother Industries Ltd
BT	90	BT Group Plc
CANON	70	Canon
NEC	65	NEC Corporation
OLIVETTI	85	Telecom Italia S.p.A
PANASONIC	45	Matsushita Electric
RICOH	80	Ricoh Co Ltd
SAGEM	60	Safran
SAMSUNG	55	Samsung Group

Rating categories (columns): ENVIRONMENT (Environmental Report, TCO Certificate, Nuclear Power); ANIMALS (Animal Welfare); PEOPLE (Human Rights, Armaments, Political Donations); OTHER (Other Criticisms, Boycott, Ethical Accreditation)

Key

● Top rating
O Middle rating
● Bottom rating

Source: The Ethical Company Organisation (2008)

Fridges and freezers

Chill with a clean conscience by bearing a few things in mind when buying a fridge or freezer unit. Firstly, and most importantly, look for the most energy-efficient model available. Secondly, be sure that the kind of coolant gas the appliance uses does as little harm to the environment as possible, and finally, take a look at the manufacturing company and their wider policies such as workers' rights, pollution and marketing.

ENERGY USE

A fridge or freezer probably costs about twice as much to run over its lifetime as it did to purchase. This is one reason to look out for the most energy-efficient machines. A less efficient one may be cheaper to buy, but powering it will be more expensive from the moment it is switched on.

Energy labelling is now compulsory for fridges and freezers, and most brands have models available that are classed as 'A' or 'B'. A-rated models use about half as much energy as C-rated ones. 'Energy plus' ratings are awarded to models (so far only fridge-freezers) that are even more efficient, using as little as half the electricity of the average appliance. The EU also awards 'eco-labels' to energy efficient models that are manufactured with minimal environmental impact. Vestfrost of Denmark is one of the companies that has received this label.

RUNNING FRIDGES AND FREEZERS EFFICIENTLY

- Place freezers in a cool place out of the sun and away from heaters, boilers and cookers
- Open doors for as little time as possible
- Keep fridges about three-quarters full for maximum efficiency
- Defrost regularly
- Keep the temperature right – no warmer than 5°C. The colder you keep it the more energy it will use

COOLANTS

When CFC coolant gas was taken out of production because it was harming the ozone layer, manufacturers switched to HCFCs and then to HFCs. There is still widespread use of HFCs in fridges, even though they could contribute to climate change. The methods used to produce HFCs also results in toxic waste.

One of the best options to look for in a new fridge or freezer is the R600a hydrocarbon coolant (labelled 'CFC and HFC-free'). This has a lower global warming potential, is non-toxic and is more efficient than HFCs.

DISPOSAL

Old fridges and freezers contain a number of toxic substances, including CFC and HFC coolants and flame-retardant chemicals, so it is essential that they are disposed of safely and correctly. The gases need to be removed at a specialist facility that deals with hazardous waste. Some manufacturers and retailers take back old models and may offer trade-ins, so they should be the first place to try. Local councils can also offer advice on recycling and safe disposal of units.

At *www.gooshing.co.uk* you can save money on fridges and save the planet. Gooshing finds you the cheapest and most ethical deals available.

60-SECOND GREEN GUIDE

- Buy an A-rated hydrocarbon (R600a) appliance (it will be labelled 'CFC- and HCFC-free')
- When buying a fridge/freezer consider opting for a two-control model so that one of the units (for example the fridge) can be switched off when you go on holiday
- Chest freezers are more energy efficient than upright models
- Make sure your old appliance is professionally de-gassed and preferably recycled, as it will probably contain CFCs or HFCs

- Ariston
- Beko
- Candy
- Creda
- Hoover
- Hotpoint
- Indesit
- LEC
- Merloni
- Miele
- New World
- Proline

- AEG
- Bauknecht
- Brandt
- Electrolux
- Ignis
- Liebherr
- Ocean
- Tricity Bendix
- Whirlpool
- Zanussi

- Bosch
- Iceline
- Kyoto
- Neff
- Siemens

FRIDGES AND FREEZERS

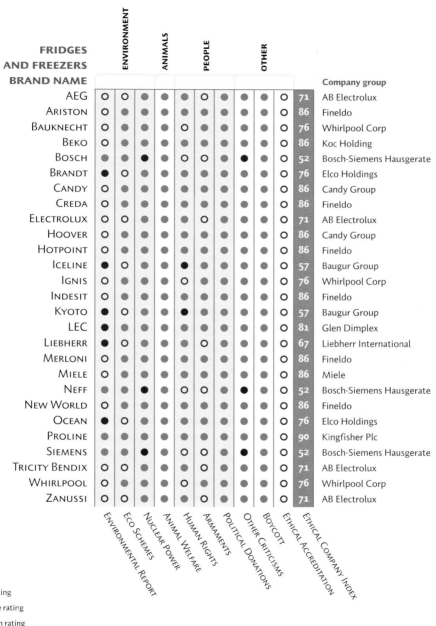

FRIDGES AND FREEZERS BRAND NAME	ENVIRONMENT			ANIMALS	PEOPLE			OTHER				
	Environmental Report	Eco Schemes	Nuclear Power	Animal Welfare	Human Rights	Armaments	Political Donations	Other Criticisms	Boycott	Ethical Accreditation	Ethical Company Index	Company group
AEG	Middle	Middle	Top	Top	Top	Middle	Top	Top	Top	Middle	71	AB Electrolux
Ariston	Middle	Top	Top	Top	Top	Top	Top	Top	Top	Middle	86	Fineldo
Bauknecht	Middle	Top	Top	Top	Middle	Top	Top	Top	Top	Middle	76	Whirlpool Corp
Beko	Middle	Top	Top	Top	Top	Top	Top	Top	Top	Middle	86	Koc Holding
Bosch	Top	Top	Bottom	Top	Middle	Middle	Top	Bottom	Top	Middle	52	Bosch-Siemens Hausgerate
Brandt	Bottom	Middle	Top	Top	Top	Top	Top	Top	Top	Middle	76	Elco Holdings
Candy	Middle	Top	Top	Top	Top	Top	Top	Top	Top	Middle	86	Candy Group
Creda	Middle	Top	Top	Top	Top	Top	Top	Top	Top	Middle	86	Fineldo
Electrolux	Middle	Middle	Top	Top	Top	Middle	Top	Top	Top	Middle	71	AB Electrolux
Hoover	Middle	Top	Top	Top	Top	Top	Top	Top	Top	Middle	86	Candy Group
Hotpoint	Middle	Top	Top	Top	Top	Top	Top	Top	Top	Middle	86	Fineldo
Iceline	Bottom	Middle	Top	Top	Bottom	Top	Top	Top	Top	Middle	57	Baugur Group
Ignis	Middle	Top	Top	Top	Middle	Top	Top	Top	Top	Middle	76	Whirlpool Corp
Indesit	Middle	Top	Top	Top	Top	Top	Top	Top	Top	Middle	86	Fineldo
Kyoto	Bottom	Middle	Top	Top	Bottom	Top	Top	Top	Top	Middle	57	Baugur Group
LEC	Bottom	Top	Top	Top	Top	Top	Top	Top	Top	Middle	81	Glen Dimplex
Liebherr	Bottom	Middle	Top	Top	Top	Middle	Top	Top	Top	Middle	67	Liebherr International
Merloni	Middle	Top	Top	Top	Top	Top	Top	Top	Top	Middle	86	Fineldo
Miele	Middle	Top	Top	Top	Top	Top	Top	Top	Top	Middle	86	Miele
Neff	Top	Top	Bottom	Top	Middle	Middle	Top	Bottom	Top	Middle	52	Bosch-Siemens Hausgerate
New World	Middle	Top	Top	Top	Top	Top	Top	Top	Top	Middle	86	Fineldo
Ocean	Bottom	Middle	Top	Top	Top	Top	Top	Top	Top	Middle	76	Elco Holdings
Proline	Top	Top	Top	Top	Top	Top	Top	Top	Top	Middle	90	Kingfisher Plc
Siemens	Top	Top	Bottom	Top	Middle	Middle	Top	Bottom	Top	Middle	52	Bosch-Siemens Hausgerate
Tricity Bendix	Middle	Middle	Top	Top	Top	Middle	Top	Top	Top	Middle	71	AB Electrolux
Whirlpool	Middle	Top	Top	Top	Middle	Top	Top	Top	Top	Middle	76	Whirlpool Corp
Zanussi	Middle	Middle	Top	Top	Top	Middle	Top	Top	Top	Middle	71	AB Electrolux

Key

- ● (grey) Top rating
- ○ Middle rating
- ● (black) Bottom rating

Source: The Ethical Company Organisation

Furniture

According to Friends of the Earth, as much as 60 per cent of the timber coming into the UK is likely to have been sourced illegally. Alarmingly, this means that much of the furniture in our own homes could be made from illegally logged tropical timber. The easy way to avoid buying furniture with such origins is to look out for products that are certified by the Forest Stewardship Council (FSC).

RAINFOREST TIMBER

In recent years a number of well-known chains and supermarkets have been exposed for selling furniture made from wood sourced illegally. In 2003, Friends of the Earth accused Tesco of selling garden furniture made out of illegal Indonesian timber. The logging in Indonesia endangers species including the tiger, the elephant and the orang-utan, and results not only in widespread rainforest destruction but also in the brutal oppression of indigenous peoples, whose land and livelihood are seized with impunity by criminal gangs and international companies.

The latest report, released by Greenpeace in October 2005, traced wood from Britain's building sites and building merchants back to the rainforests of Papua New Guinea, where locals complain of police brutality and intimidation from logging company managers. Their horrifying tales of human rights abuse include allegations of rape and torture. Companies that buy illegally logged wood are effectively supporting these abuses.

FSC WOOD

Buying furniture certified by the Forest Stewardship Council (FSC) provides peace of mind about the origins of the wood. It's the only standard of sustainable forestry recognized by NGOs, and it ensures that forests are managed in a way that benefits both the environment and the people who live and work there. Indigenous peoples, forest workers, and all who are affected by what happens in the forest are able to agree on how it is managed. Nick Cliffe, the Director of FSC UK, said: "Buying paper or furniture that comes from FSC sources allows consumers to have an impact on the other side of the world and support the rights of workers and indigenous peoples."

Each year Greenpeace publishes a table to see how retailers compare in the sourcing of their garden furniture. In 2005, B&Q, Asda, Tesco and Woolworths sold the greatest proportion of FSC-certified furniture, whereas Argos, Wyevale and Habitat were seen as the least responsible in their sourcing. Harrods and House of Fraser failed to report.

Of the major retailers, B&Q is the best place to find FSC-certified furniture, but it's also worth checking out Arbor Vetum (*www.arborvetum.co.uk*) and Pendlewood (*www.pendlewood.com*), both of whom sell furniture made exclusively from FSC wood. If you can't find the FSC-certified item you are looking for, consider contacting the organisation via their website (*www.fsc-uk.org*) to see if they can help – the more demand there is for certified furniture, the more likely it is to go into production.

RECYCLED OR REFURBISHED

There is also the option of buying second-hand or recycled furniture. You can buy refurbished furniture from Emmaus (*www.emmaus.co.uk*) and support a good cause at the same time. Emmaus, which has shops in England and Scotland, is a charity that offers homeless men and women a place to live and an opportunity to work full-time, refurbishing donated furniture. Similar projects that help the homeless and the unemployed exist across the country, such as Morph in east London (*www.morph.org.uk*) and Revive in Liverpool (*www.frcgroup.co.uk*).

There are plenty of options for buying recycled furniture too. Reel Furniture (*www.reelfurniture.co.uk*), Living Concepts (*www.livingconcepts.co.uk*), Reclaimed Pine Online (*www.reclaimed-pine-online.co.uk*) and Re-Form Furniture (*www.re-formfurniture.co.uk*) all offer recycled or reclaimed furniture available to order online.

- B&Q
- Marks & Spencer

- Argos
- Benson's For Beds
- DFS
- Furniture Village
- Harveys
- Homebase
- House of Fraser
- Ikea
- John Lewis
- Laura Ashley
- MFI

- Bhs
- Habitat
- Heal's

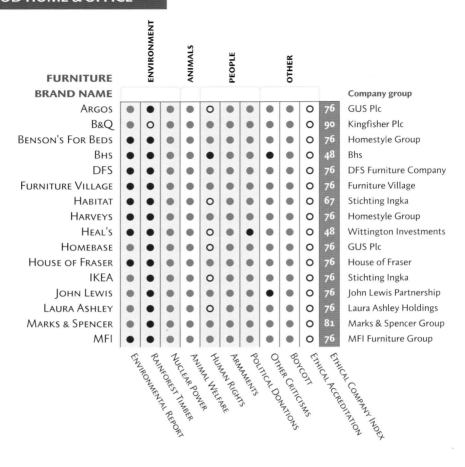

FURNITURE BRAND NAME	ENVIRONMENT			ANIMALS	PEOPLE			OTHER			Ethical Company Index	Company group
	Environmental Report	Rainforest Timber	Nuclear Power	Animal Welfare	Human Rights	Armaments	Political Donations	Other Criticisms	Boycott	Ethical Accreditation		
ARGOS	●	●	●	●	○	●	●	●	●	○	76	GUS Plc
B&Q	●	○	●	●	●	●	●	●	●	○	90	Kingfisher Plc
BENSON'S FOR BEDS	●	●	●	●	●	●	●	●	●	○	76	Homestyle Group
BHS	●	●	●	●	●	●	●	●	●	○	48	Bhs
DFS	●	●	●	●	●	●	●	●	●	○	76	DFS Furniture Company
FURNITURE VILLAGE	●	●	●	●	●	●	●	●	●	○	76	Furniture Village
HABITAT	●	●	●	●	○	●	●	●	●	○	67	Stichting Ingka
HARVEYS	●	●	●	●	●	●	●	●	●	○	76	Homestyle Group
HEAL'S	●	●	●	●	○	●	●	●	●	○	48	Wittington Investments
HOMEBASE	●	●	●	●	○	●	●	●	●	○	76	GUS Plc
HOUSE OF FRASER	●	●	●	●	●	●	●	●	●	○	76	House of Fraser
IKEA	●	●	●	●	○	●	●	●	●	○	76	Stichting Ingka
JOHN LEWIS	●	●	●	●	●	●	●	●	●	○	76	John Lewis Partnership
LAURA ASHLEY	●	●	●	●	○	●	●	●	●	○	76	Laura Ashley Holdings
MARKS & SPENCER	●	●	●	●	●	●	●	●	●	○	81	Marks & Spencer Group
MFI	●	●	●	●	●	●	●	●	●	○	76	MFI Furniture Group

Key

● Top rating

○ Middle rating

● Bottom rating

Source: The Ethical Company Organisation

Kettles

Boiling and re-boiling more water than necessary for a single cup of tea or coffee wastes a phenomenal amount of energy every day. Fortunately, the efforts of energy-efficiency campaigners have persuaded most manufacturers to come up with new kettle designs to tackle the problem. These modern kettles are much less wasteful than the traditional varieties: of the ones currently available, jug kettles are good, but those with concealed elements are even better.

SAVE WATER, SAVE POWER

In the UK we each drink an average of 27 cups of tea and coffee each week. It has been calculated that by boiling 1.5 cups of water each time rather than the average 3.5 we could save enough electricity each week to run a TV for 26 hours.

The designers of an award-winning eco-kettle in Australia identified consumer behaviour as the key to improving energy efficiency. Behavioural studies of the product found that the main problem was not the efficiency of the kettle but the way in which it was used. The study found that only 26 per cent of people used the water gauge even when they had one, and that the majority re-boiled the kettle when there was no need. By putting a large gauge on the top of the kettle, the designers found that consumers were more likely to use it. In addition, a feature where the top of the kettle turned red at temperatures over 80°C made people less tempted to re-boil so often. The Axis eco-kettle is produced in Australia by MEC Kambrook, but is not currently distributed in the UK.

Re-boiling is not only a waste of energy but often makes a worse drink. Coffee, for example, should be brewed with water at between 85-90°C, so as not to damage the delicate oils in the bean. Water straight out of the kettle will be over 100°C.

Stove-top kettles for gas cookers have long been an environmental favourite because, although they use slightly more energy than a jug kettle to boil the water, the inherent inefficiency of conventional electricity production makes them a better choice in terms of carbon emissions. However, with the evolution of '100 per cent green' electricity it is possible to run an electric kettle with practically zero carbon impact. Electric kettles can, therefore, represent the best environmental option.

COUNTRIES OF ORIGIN

The production of most household appliances is now 'out-sourced', meaning that the company which owns the brand name is only directly involved in the design and sourcing of the item, but not in the actual production. Some companies' goods

Growers...
are the heart
of Cafédirect

Cafédirect partner with over 260,000 farmers from 39 grower organisations, across 13 developing countries, to bring you the highest quality, best tasting coffees and teas.

As well as paying our growers above market prices, over the last 3 years we have reinvested an average of 60% of our profits into their businesses and communities.

CAFÉDIRECT ®
BRINGING QUALITY
TO LIFE

Join our network at
www.cafedirect.co.uk

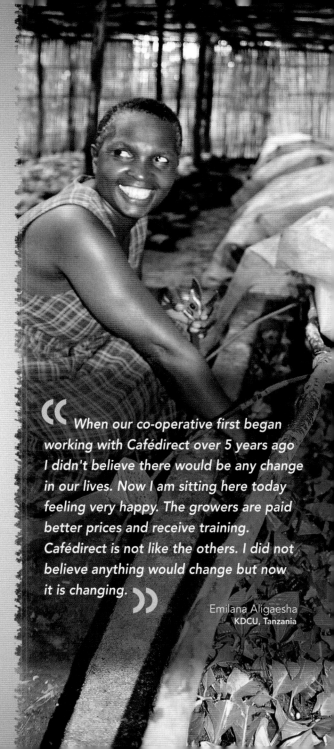

" When our co-operative first began working with Cafédirect over 5 years ago I didn't believe there would be any change in our lives. Now I am sitting here today feeling very happy. The growers are paid better prices and receive training. Cafédirect is not like the others. I did not believe anything would change but now it is changing. "

Emilana Aligaesha
KDCU, Tanzania

are produced by over 25 unaffiliated manufacturers located primarily in Far East locations, such as Hong Kong, China and Taiwan. Such companies do not often maintain long-term purchase contracts with manufacturers, preferring to work on the basis of a single contract that is not reliant on any individual supplier.

Although such practices are standard, they reflect the fundamental problem of globalisation: flexibility for a company in the 'north' means job insecurity and a lack of long-term investment in the 'south'. Such a multitude of suppliers also makes it very difficult for consumers to hold corporations to account for the conditions under which their goods are produced. With labour costs in Taiwan and South Korea rising, China has now become the main producer of kitchen appliances.

GOOD PRACTICE

- When buying a new kettle, look for one with a covered element. These permit the boiling of smaller quantities of water, reducing the amount that is wasted
- Boil only as much water as you need each time – look for a kettle with a gauge so you can tell exactly how much you need
- If you live in a hard water area, leave the kettle empty after each use and descale it every month with a little vinegar
- Gas kettles' efficiency can be improved by the addition of a 'heat-ring' around the base
- Go to *www.gooshing.co.uk* for information on a wide selection of kettles. It's a free service where you can buy online, find the cheapest deals and compare ethical ratings on over 250,000 products.

- Morphy Richards
- Moulinex
- Rowenta
- Swan
- Tefal

- Breville
- Bush
- De'Longhi
- Haden
- Hinari
- Kenwood
- Pifco
- Russell Hobbs
- Salton

- Bosch
- Braun
- Philips

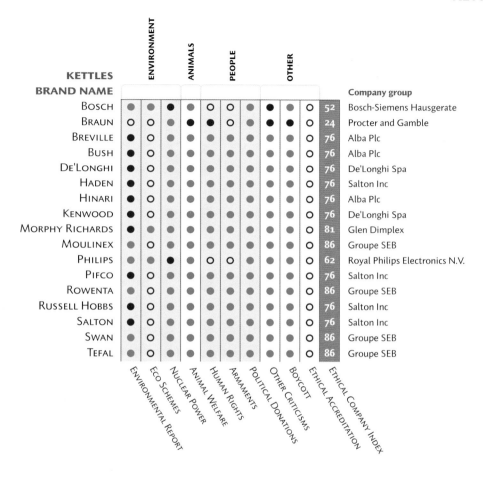

KETTLES BRAND NAME	ENVIRONMENT			ANIMALS	PEOPLE			OTHER			Ethical Company Index	Company group
	Environmental Report	Eco Schemes	Nuclear Power	Animal Welfare	Human Rights	Armaments	Political Donations	Other Criticisms	Boycott	Ethical Accreditation		
BOSCH	●	●	⬤	●	○	○	●	⬤	●	○	52	Bosch-Siemens Hausgerate
BRAUN	○	○	●	⬤	⬤	○	●	⬤	⬤	○	24	Procter and Gamble
BREVILLE	⬤	○	●	●	●	●	●	●	●	○	76	Alba Plc
BUSH	⬤	○	●	●	●	●	●	●	●	○	76	Alba Plc
DE'LONGHI	⬤	○	●	●	●	●	●	●	●	○	76	De'Longhi Spa
HADEN	⬤	○	●	●	●	●	●	●	●	○	76	Salton Inc
HINARI	⬤	○	●	●	●	●	●	●	●	○	76	Alba Plc
KENWOOD	⬤	○	●	●	●	●	●	●	●	○	76	De'Longhi Spa
MORPHY RICHARDS	⬤	●	●	●	●	●	●	●	●	○	81	Glen Dimplex
MOULINEX	●	○	●	●	●	●	●	●	●	○	86	Groupe SEB
PHILIPS	●	●	⬤	●	○	○	●	●	●	○	62	Royal Philips Electronics N.V.
PIFCO	⬤	○	●	●	●	●	●	●	●	○	76	Salton Inc
ROWENTA	●	○	●	●	●	●	●	●	●	○	86	Groupe SEB
RUSSELL HOBBS	⬤	○	●	●	●	●	●	●	●	○	76	Salton Inc
SALTON	⬤	○	●	●	●	●	●	●	●	○	76	Salton Inc
SWAN	●	○	●	●	●	●	●	●	●	○	86	Groupe SEB
TEFAL	●	○	●	●	●	●	●	●	●	○	86	Groupe SEB

Key

● Top rating

○ Middle rating

⬤ Bottom rating

Source: The Ethical Company Organisation

Good buy

 Energy saving lightbulbs use up to 80% less electricity

 The ECO kettle uses 31% less energy than conventional kettles

 Wind-up radios that give you hours of carbon free listening

 Solar rechargeable LED torch gives 15 hours use from 1 hour of sunlight

Goodbye

 Global warming globes

 Carbon clunky kettles

 Carbon reckless radios

 Battery bingeing torches

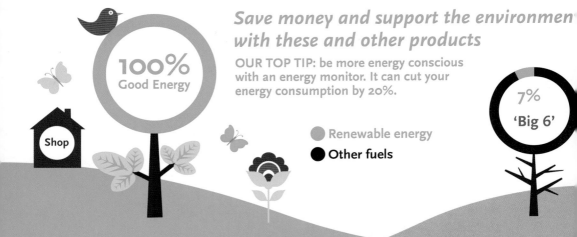

Save money and support the environmen with these and other products

OUR TOP TIP: be more energy conscious with an energy monitor. It can cut your energy consumption by 20%.

100% Good Energy

Shop

● Renewable energy
● Other fuels

7% 'Big 6'

Visit Good Energy Shop before you buy. And switch your electricity supply to Good Energy who only buy power from wind, water and sunlight.

www.goodenergyshop.co.uk

Good Energy
THE NATURAL CHOICE

Source: BERR Fuel Mix Disclosure Table based on 2008 disclosed figures. 'Big 6' figures are straight averages of 2007/8 disclosed fuel mix for npower/RWE; E.ON; British Gas; EDF; Scottish Power; Scottish & Southern.

Kitchen appliances

Kitchen appliances that wear out so fast they often have to be replaced are a good example of the built-in obsolescence at the heart of our consumer culture. Here, the environmentalist's motto 'reduce, re-use, recycle' is particularly important. Many of the gadgets in the average kitchen (such as juicers, blenders and deep fat fryers) go unused, but for those that are truly necessary it is crucial they are disposed of carefully.

OUR THROWAWAY CULTURE

At least six million kitchen appliances are discarded each year. As most of them are thrown into dustbins, very few are recycled as they could be. Friends of the Earth would like to see much higher recycling or re-use targets for waste electrical and electronic equipment. The organisation argues in favour of making products last longer, designing them for easy repair or for easy replacement of worn-out components, as well as for easy recycling for parts that cannot be re-used. FoE says that this should be the responsibility of the manufacturers, so that they carry the cost of recycling or disposal of their products.

Even if a piece of equipment seems to have reached the end of its life, that doesn't mean it's no longer usable. Second-hand shops often take old equipment and there are schemes around the UK to recover discarded electrical equipment. Wastewatch recommends that old appliances are not dumped in the bin but taken to a civic amenity site where they can be added to other scrap for recycling. Information is available from the local authority, which will have a recycling officer, or from Wastewatch (*www. wastewatch.org.uk*).

MATERIALS USED

Various materials, such as stainless steel, iron and plastics, are used in most kitchen appliances. All the associated ills of mining and manufacturing come in to play – toxic waste, pollution, energy wastage and greenhouse gas emissions. Of course these things will continue to exist anyway, but a good way to minimise their impact on a personal level is to avoid buying new products, by choosing second-hand or reconditioned items instead.

TRIMMING DOWN

Weighing up how often an item will be used can be useful in deciding how necessary it is. If it is unlikely to be used on a weekly, or even monthly, basis, is it really needed? It also helps to think about ease of use, as there may be another way to do a job without resorting to over-complicated gadgets that are often difficult to clean.

For example, a blender does many of the same jobs as a food processor but uses a smaller quantity of energy. A standard grill can easily be used instead of a toaster, and electric can openers have mostly been made redundant by the addition of ring-pulls to cans.

ENERGY USE

The energy efficiency of electrical appliances varies from model to model. As there is no eco-labelling scheme for small kitchen appliances, consumers have to rely on the energy usage being displayed on the product's packaging. A kettle draws up to 3KW, and when millions are turned on at about the same time (such as during television ad-breaks) the increase in demand is massive. Compared to electricity, gas is 30 per cent more energy efficient. This is why kettles used on gas cookers can be a better option than electric ones.

Hand-operated kitchen appliances, naturally enough, are the most energy-efficient kinds you can buy, not least the whisks, forks and knives that are absolutely essential for cooking!

You can save money on kitchen appliances by using *www.gooshing.co.uk*. This service searches over 300 shops to find the cheapest price on your chosen brand – and gives ethical ratings on the manufacturers.

- Morphy Richards
- Moulinex
- Prima
- Rowenta
- Swan
- Tefal

- Breville
- Bush
- De'Longhi
- Dualit
- Goodmans
- Hinari
- Kenwood
- Pifco
- Russell Hobbs
- Salton

- Braun
- Philips

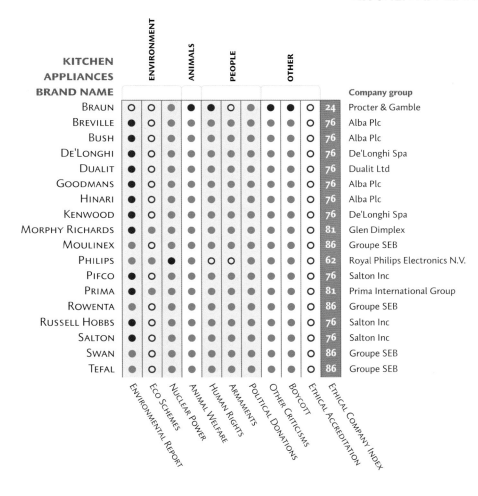

Rating key: T = Top rating, M = Middle rating, B = Bottom rating

KITCHEN APPLIANCES BRAND NAME	Environmental Report	Eco Schemes	Nuclear Power	Animal Welfare	Human Rights	Armaments	Political Donations	Other Criticisms	Boycott	Ethical Accreditation	Ethical Company Index	Company group
BRAUN	M	M	T	B	B	M	T	B	B	M	24	Procter & Gamble
BREVILLE	T	M	T	T	T	T	T	T	T	M	76	Alba Plc
BUSH	T	M	T	T	T	T	T	T	T	M	76	Alba Plc
DE'LONGHI	T	M	T	T	T	T	T	T	T	M	76	De'Longhi Spa
DUALIT	T	M	T	T	T	T	T	T	T	M	76	Dualit Ltd
GOODMANS	T	M	T	T	T	T	T	T	T	M	76	Alba Plc
HINARI	T	M	T	T	T	T	T	T	T	M	76	Alba Plc
KENWOOD	T	M	T	T	T	T	T	T	T	M	76	De'Longhi Spa
MORPHY RICHARDS	T	T	T	T	T	T	T	T	T	M	81	Glen Dimplex
MOULINEX	T	M	T	T	T	T	T	T	T	M	86	Groupe SEB
PHILIPS	T	T	B	T	M	M	T	T	T	M	62	Royal Philips Electronics N.V.
PIFCO	T	M	T	T	T	T	T	T	T	M	76	Salton Inc
PRIMA	T	T	T	T	T	T	T	T	T	M	81	Prima International Group
ROWENTA	T	M	T	T	T	T	T	T	T	M	86	Groupe SEB
RUSSELL HOBBS	T	M	T	T	T	T	T	T	T	M	76	Salton Inc
SALTON	T	M	T	T	T	T	T	T	T	M	76	Salton Inc
SWAN	T	M	T	T	T	T	T	T	T	M	86	Groupe SEB
TEFAL	T	M	T	T	T	T	T	T	T	M	86	Groupe SEB

Column groupings: ENVIRONMENT (Environmental Report, Eco Schemes, Nuclear Power); ANIMALS (Animal Welfare); PEOPLE (Human Rights, Armaments, Political Donations); OTHER (Other Criticisms, Boycott, Ethical Accreditation)

Key

● Top rating
○ Middle rating
● Bottom rating

Source: The Ethical Company Organisation

Laundry detergents

The fact that every day is washing day for many families means that, collectively, we are expending far more energy, water and detergent on our laundry than ever before in history. None of these are good for the environment – particularly the detergents, which are often derived from rather unappealing petroleum by-products. Nevertheless, many companies produce eco-friendly alternatives, which can be just as effective and rarely cost much more than your usual brand.

OVER-PERFORMANCE

The mega-wash companies Procter & Gamble and Lever Brothers churn over 84 per cent of the British clothes that are washed every day. Their research and development divisions are masters at devising new and impressive-sounding formulations for their products, dazzling consumers with promises of whiter and whiter whites. While performance and value for money are undoubtedly important, most of the things put in the average British wash simply don't need the highest level of performance. As small, environment-conscious companies often point out, most of our clothes just require gentle freshening up – not full-scale decontamination.

INGREDIENTS TO WATCH

Detergents from the mega-wash companies are more likely to contain petroleum-based surfactants, which can take many years to biodegrade. Look for vegetable-based alternatives, and avoid detergents that contain other chemical ingredients such as phosphates, phosphonates and carboxylates. Phosphates are a known cause of eutrophication, a process that disrupts the natural balance of rivers and streams and can cause problems for fish and other wildlife.

Enzymes used in detergents are not directly bad for the environment, but have in the past been reported to cause problems for workers in the factories making them. The good news is that these problems have been almost entirely eradicated in recent years.

Ecological brands including Ecover and Bio-D dispense with the most environmentally damaging ingredients found in the mega-wash products, particularly the petrochemical-based surfactants. Many of their products are certified by BUAV and the Vegan Society, so look out for the logos on their packaging. Some users find eco-friendly brands less efficient at removing the most stubborn stains, but their eco-credentials balance out the occasional use of something stronger!

OTHER INNOVATIONS

Some companies such as Ecover have begun to offer a refilling facility, so that detergent bottles do not have to be thrown away when empty. The sellers (such as a specialist shops and health food stores) are provided with a supply of the product so that customers can return their bottles to the nearest available outlet and fill them back up. As most detergent packaging is not suitable for recycling, this is a significant step in reducing the amount of household waste produced.

Also available are products that claim to reduce the amount of laundry detergent required, or to remove the need for it altogether. Some work using enzymes, while others help to soften the water in the washing machine. Reception to these innovations has been mixed, with some saying that the products have lower stain-removing power, but they are nevertheless worth researching.

For most clothes, *The Good Shopping Guide* recommends a combination of Ecover/Bio-D or an equivalent eco-friendly detergent, plus a quarterly wash in biological powder for the dirtiest items. This will provide the best possible trade-off between efficiency and environmental impact.

60-SECOND GREEN GUIDE

- If using a mainstream brand, choose a washing powder over a liquid. Concentrated powder is better than standard powder
- Use soap-based detergents, or ones with a high soap content
- Vegetable-based surfactants are better than petrochemical-based ones
- Use a product without phosphates, phosphonates or carboxylates
- Make eco-products work better in hard water areas by using a water softener
- Choose a low wash temperature, or select the 'economy' cycle

- Bio-D
- Clear Spring
- Ecover

- ACDO
- Advance
- Co-Op
- Cyclon
- Logic
- Novon
- Surcare

- Ariel
- Bold
- Daz
- Dreft
- Fairy
- Persil
- Surf

LAUNDRY DETERGENTS

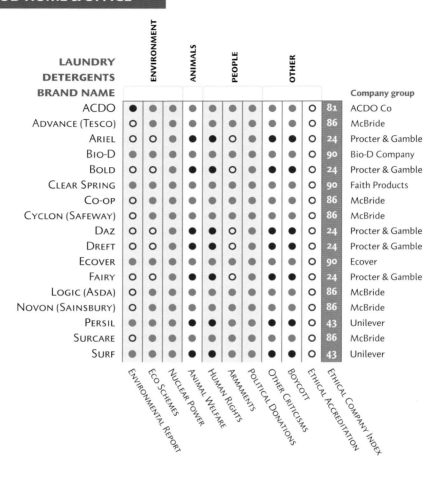

BRAND NAME	ENVIRONMENT			ANIMALS	PEOPLE			OTHER			Ethical Company Index	Company group
	Environmental Report	Eco Schemes	Nuclear Power	Animal Welfare	Human Rights	Armaments	Political Donations	Other Criticisms	Boycott	Ethical Accreditation		
ACDO	●	●	●	●	●	●	●	●	●	○	81	ACDO Co
ADVANCE (TESCO)	○	●	●	●	●	●	●	●	●	○	86	McBride
ARIEL	○	○	●	●	●	○	●	●	●	○	24	Procter & Gamble
BIO-D	●	●	●	●	●	●	●	●	●	○	90	Bio-D Company
BOLD	○	○	●	●	●	○	●	●	●	○	24	Procter & Gamble
CLEAR SPRING	●	●	●	●	●	●	●	●	●	○	90	Faith Products
CO-OP	○	●	●	●	●	●	●	●	●	○	86	McBride
CYCLON (SAFEWAY)	○	●	●	●	●	●	●	●	●	○	86	McBride
DAZ	○	○	●	●	●	○	●	●	●	○	24	Procter & Gamble
DREFT	○	○	●	●	●	○	●	●	●	○	24	Procter & Gamble
ECOVER	●	●	●	●	●	●	●	●	●	○	90	Ecover
FAIRY	○	○	●	●	●	●	●	●	●	○	24	Procter & Gamble
LOGIC (ASDA)	○	●	●	●	●	●	●	●	●	○	86	McBride
NOVON (SAINSBURY)	○	●	●	●	●	●	●	●	●	○	86	McBride
PERSIL	●	●	●	●	●	●	●	●	●	○	43	Unilever
SURCARE	○	●	●	●	●	●	●	●	●	○	86	McBride
SURF	●	●	●	●	●	●	●	●	●	○	43	Unilever

Key

● Top rating
○ Middle rating
● Bottom rating

Source: The Ethical Company Organisation

Mobile phones

Although 50 million people own a mobile phone in the UK, we don't yet know enough about the potential health implications of this new technology. Whilst there is no firm evidence for a direct link between mobile phone use and health risks, experts tend to suggest we should remain cautious. This section will explore some of these health issues, and suggest the networks and handsets that are the most environmentally friendly.

ERRING ON THE SIDE OF CAUTION

The independent Stewart Report, published in 2000, analysed the links between mobile phones and ill-health, and concluded that there was no proof that using mobile phones led to health problems. However, it maintained that 'gaps in our knowledge are significant enough to justify a precautionary approach'.

The major potential health danger is that radiation emitted from the handset could lead to cancer. A recent Swedish report, which found that incidents of ear tumours increased fourfold among people who used mobile phones just once a day for ten years, suggested that this theoretical risk may be a reality.

More worryingly still, it has been proven that the radiation from mobile phones can alter DNA and proteins. While these DNA changes have not been linked to any specific health problems, many scientists believe more research needs to be carried out, and this development strengthens the argument for caution.

WHAT TO DO

Simple steps can reduce the potential risks. Try to avoid making calls when your phone has low signal, don't touch the aerial when the phone is turned on, and switch off the phone when it is not in use. It is also possible to choose a safer phone. Following the Stewart Report's recommendations, all mobile phones should display a SAR (specific absorption rate) value, showing the amount of radiation emitted by the phone. The maximum legal rate in the UK is 2.0 w/kg, but in the US phones must have a SAR value of 1.6 or less. Find the lowest SAR value at *www.mobile-phones-uk.org.uk/sar*.

The most important advice is directed towards children, who are more susceptible to the possible effects of radiation because their skulls are not fully thickened, their nervous systems are still developing, and they will use a mobile phone for longer during their lifetime. The Stewart Report advises that young people only use mobiles for essential calls and discourages companies from marketing their phones directly to children.

MAST DEBATE

Mobile phone masts have been the focus of much anxiety and campaigning, but in reality the health concerns associated with handsets are more serious than those linked to masts. In the UK, masts have been shown to emit radiation between seven hundred and ten million times below internationally agreed limits. Nevertheless, the Stewart Report recommends that they should be surrounded by an exclusion zone and located away from schools.

RECYCLING

Many toxic chemicals go into mobile phones, making their disposal a potential health hazard. This often takes place in the developing world, where labour costs and environmental standards are lower.

Greenpeace highlights the danger that some workers are exposed to when processing old mobile phones without proper equipment, and has persuaded some companies, including Sony Ericsson and Nokia, to eliminate harmful chemicals including flame retardants and PVC plastic from their products. Other companies, such as Motorola, have so far made no such commitment.

If you are one of the 15 million people in the UK who are disposing of a mobile phone this year, you can help to alleviate the environmental strain by recycling your handset. Many supermarkets, charity shops and mobile phone retailers offer recycling services, often for a good cause. Have a look at *www.futureforests.com/recyclephone* or *www.childadvocacyinternational.co.uk* for two charities who would be glad to receive your old phone.

Networks
- O2
- Orange
- T-Mobile
- Vodafone

Phones
- NEC
- Nokia
- Motorola

Networks
- Virgin Mobile

Phones
- Panasonic

Networks
- Three

Phones
- Samsung
- Siemens
- Sony Ericsson

MOBILE PHONES

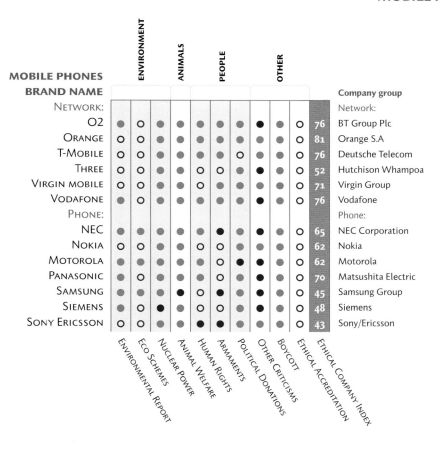

BRAND NAME	Environmental Report	Eco Schemes	Nuclear Power	Animal Welfare	Human Rights	Armaments	Political Donations	Other Criticisms	Boycott	Ethical Accreditation	Ethical Company Index	Company group
NETWORK:												Network:
O2	T	M	T	T	T	T	B	T	T	M	76	BT Group Plc
ORANGE	M	M	T	T	T	T	T	T	T	M	81	Orange S.A
T-MOBILE	M	M	T	T	T	M	T	T	T	M	76	Deutsche Telecom
THREE	M	M	T	M	M	T	B	T	T	M	52	Hutchison Whampoa
VIRGIN MOBILE	M	M	T	T	M	T	T	T	T	M	71	Virgin Group
VODAFONE	T	M	T	T	T	T	B	T	T	M	76	Vodafone
PHONE:												Phone:
NEC	T	T	T	T	B	T	B	T	T	M	65	NEC Corporation
NOKIA	M	M	T	T	M	M	T	T	T	M	62	Nokia
MOTOROLA	T	T	T	T	M	B	B	T	T	M	62	Motorola
PANASONIC	T	M	T	T	M	T	T	T	T	M	70	Matsushita Electric
SAMSUNG	T	T	T	B	M	B	T	T	T	M	45	Samsung Group
SIEMENS	T	M	B	T	M	M	B	T	T	M	48	Siemens
SONY ERICSSON	M	M	T	T	B	B	T	T	T	M	43	Sony/Ericsson

Key

● Top rating
○ Middle rating
● Bottom rating

Source: The Ethical Company Organisation

Paint

It goes without saying that paint is a concoction of chemicals, but what is never really disclosed about those chemicals is how much damage they can cause to the environment and to human health. This chapter looks at some of the environmental claims behind conventional and 'natural' paints that are used to decorate interior walls (emulsions) and woodwork (glosses), and how safe they are in manufacture, application and disposal.

CHEMICALS

Modern paints are complex chemical concoctions, but most contain petroleum-based by-products from the oil industry, a sector not renowned for its commitment to environmental protection. Indeed, two of the largest paint companies on the table, Azko Nobel and ICI, are thought to be amongst the most environmentally damaging in the world.

Paint production is hazardous and uses a lot of energy. Making just one tonne of paint can produce up to ten tonnes of waste, much of which is toxic. However, the main issue with household paint is that of volatile organic compounds (VOCs). These occur in gloss paint more than emulsion. They evaporate during use, and can contribute to the formation of ground-level ozone. Several major paint brands now have a voluntary labelling scheme, which states the level of VOCs in their products using five categories from 'minimal' to 'very high'. Consumers in high-street stores looking to avoid high-level VOCs are usually offered new generations of water-based gloss paints. These contain extra chemicals, so the eco-paint producers argue that it may be better to buy a solvent-based gloss paint from an environmentally aware company.

Conventional paints can emit an alarming array of noxious gases, including known carcinogens such as toluene and xylene. But the fumes given off by natural paints can also be noxious, so both types of paint may get a similar VOC rating. Other concerns are the use of synthetic alkyl phenols, alkyds and acrylics, and whether the product is biodegradable.

Titanium dioxide is used to improve the coverage or 'opacity' of the paint, and is also an important ingredient of many 'brilliant white' paints. Despite being in plentiful supply, titanium has a significant environmental impact because of the amount of energy used in its manufacture, which has led some companies to offer a choice of paints either with or without titanium.

15 to 25 per cent of paint sold in the UK is never used, so if you have waste paint at home contact your Environmental Health

Department for safe disposal or recycling. Remove paint from brushes before rinsing and don't pour it down the drain.

NATURAL PAINT?

The 'natural' paints on the market claim to be both safer to use and kinder to the environment than conventional products. Not all 'natural' paints are the same; some contain only organic ingredients, and several are based on traditional formulations that have been in use for centuries, whilst others, although free from VOCs, may contain synthetic alkyds, usually in order to improve their performance. Some also contain a small percentage of white spirit, sometimes labelled as 'aliphatic hydrocarbons'. The most common ingredients found in 'natural'

paints are linseed oil, lime, turpentine, d-limonene, natural earth and mineral pigments, chalk, casein and borax.

OSMO's products have been certified for ethicality by the Ethical Company Organisation's accreditation scheme.

PITY THE POOR PAINTER

Many consumers are turning to eco-paints, not only for the environmental benefits but also out of concern for their own health. In 1989, the World Health Organisation's cancer research agency found that professional painters and decorators faced a 40 per cent increased chance of contracting cancer, and went so far as to deem painting and decorating to be a carcinogenic activity by definition.

- Auro
- B&Q
- Biofa
- Casa
- Ecos
- Green Paints
- Keim
- Livos
- Nutshell
- Osmo

- Craig & Rose
- Farrow & Ball
- Fired Earth
- Focus
- Johnstone's
- Leyland
- Mangers
- Wickes

- Benetton
- Crown
- Dulux
- Homebase

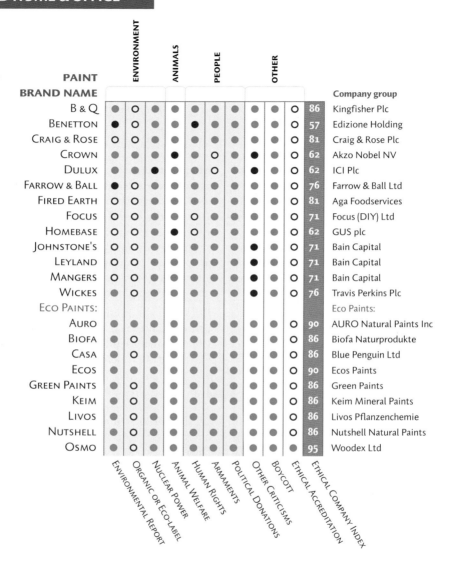

PAINT
BRAND NAME

Ratings: T = Top rating, M = Middle rating, B = Bottom rating

Brand Name	Environmental Report	Organic or Eco-Label	Nuclear Power	Animal Welfare	Human Rights	Armaments	Political Donations	Other Criticisms	Boycott	Ethical Accreditation	Ethical Company Index	Company group
B & Q	T	M	T	T	T	T	T	T	T	M	86	Kingfisher Plc
BENETTON	B	M	T	T	B	T	T	T	T	M	57	Edizione Holding
CRAIG & ROSE	M	M	T	T	T	T	T	T	T	M	81	Craig & Rose Plc
CROWN	T	T	T	B	T	M	T	B	T	M	62	Akzo Nobel NV
DULUX	T	T	B	T	T	M	T	B	T	M	62	ICI Plc
FARROW & BALL	B	M	T	T	T	T	T	T	T	M	76	Farrow & Ball Ltd
FIRED EARTH	M	M	T	T	T	T	T	T	T	M	81	Aga Foodservices
FOCUS	M	M	T	T	M	T	T	T	T	M	71	Focus (DIY) Ltd
HOMEBASE	M	M	T	B	M	T	T	T	T	M	62	GUS plc
JOHNSTONE'S	M	M	T	T	T	T	T	B	T	M	71	Bain Capital
LEYLAND	M	M	T	T	T	T	T	B	T	M	71	Bain Capital
MANGERS	M	M	T	T	T	T	T	B	T	M	71	Bain Capital
WICKES	T	M	T	T	T	T	T	B	T	M	76	Travis Perkins Plc
ECO PAINTS:												Eco Paints:
AURO	T	T	T	T	T	T	T	T	T	M	90	AURO Natural Paints Inc
BIOFA	T	M	T	T	T	T	T	T	T	M	86	Biofa Naturprodukte
CASA	T	M	T	T	T	T	T	T	T	M	86	Blue Penguin Ltd
ECOS	T	T	T	T	T	T	T	T	T	M	90	Ecos Paints
GREEN PAINTS	T	M	T	T	T	T	T	T	T	M	86	Green Paints
KEIM	T	T	T	T	T	T	T	T	T	M	86	Keim Mineral Paints
LIVOS	T	M	T	T	T	T	T	T	T	M	86	Livos Pflanzenchemie
NUTSHELL	T	M	T	T	T	T	T	T	T	M	86	Nutshell Natural Paints
OSMO	T	M	T	T	T	T	T	T	T	T	95	Woodex Ltd

Key
- ● Top rating
- ○ Middle rating
- ● Bottom rating

Source: The Ethical Company Organisation

 supports ethical shopping

Printers

While we are increasingly aware of the colossal (and avoidable) paper wastage that goes on in offices, it is almost impossible to create a paper-free environment. A few strict rules can help keep paper use to a minimum while a careful choice of brand and model ensures that we support those manufacturers who do most to promote good labour practices. Purchasing printers with the smallest number of consumable parts and recycling cartridges can also make a big difference.

THE GREEN OFFICE

With a little common sense and a lot of encouragement, every office can become a more environmentally friendly place to work in. From the smallest gestures, such as using both sides of the paper to print on, to the more financially weighty ones, e.g. investing in an ecologically conscious printer, it all makes a difference. When it comes to choosing a printer, look for one with a recognised eco-label, in particular the TCO Development label. TCO labelling was launched by a Swedish initiative in 1993 and has since become the recognised benchmark for environmentally friendly office goods. It requires that the companies meet certain standards concerning the emissions, ergonomics, ecology and energy.

ENVIRONMENTAL MATTERS

The companies in this section are subject to many manufacturing regulations, which mean that their production processes demonstrate admirable environmental concern. However, the impact of printers comes mostly from their use and disposal. To save energy, support those machines that meet the TCO and other energy efficient standards. Products from Brother have set the standard for environmentally friendly printers, and the company scores highly when evaluated under the Ethical Company Organisation's accreditation scheme.

DISGARDING PRINTERS

Of the million tonnes of waste electronic and electrical equipment (WEEE) that is thrown away on the UK every year, 39% is IT equipment. With these products made from a wide range of materials waste management is particularly difficult... in other words discarded computer hardware is an environmental health hazard just waiting explode.

While it's possible to upgrade certain appliances, which saves purchasing replacements, there comes a time when this option is no longer viable and it is vital that machines are correctly and safely disposed of. To find the companies who can collect and dispose of electrical waste nearest you,

brother supports ethical shopping
at your side

visit *www.wasteonline.org.uk*. There is also the possibility of donating your unwanted equipment to local charities and schools or even having them exported to developing countries(try www.donateapc.org.uk).

CARTRIDGES AND CONSUMABLES

Printers use either inkjet or laser technology, and both have their advantages and disadvantages (see the section on All-in-ones for more information). Of particular concern is the number of consumable parts contained in many colour laser printers, which can almost reach double figures in some cases. All require a drum and toner cartridge that will almost certainly need to be replaced or refilled at some point, but using printers with a separate cartridge for each allows the parts to be replaced independently, saving on unnecessary waste.

In 2003, only 30 to 40 per cent of the 40 million inkjet and toner cartridges sold in the UK were remanufactured or recycled. 12,000 to 14,000 tonnes ended up in landfills. Recycling and refilling old cartridges reduces the amount of waste

created, and there are several companies and charities that can do this for you. Check out *www.cartridgeworld.org*, which supplies refills and buys used cartridges. For a generally more environmentally-friendly printer, look for long-life drums, refill the ink and toner cartridges, and change ozone filters where applicable. For a more environmentally friendly consumption of ink, print in 'draft' mode as often as possible. Print in black and white instead of colour, this uses less ink and is cheaper. If you have a lot to print, try printing two sheets to a side in landscape format.

LABOUR LAWS

With cheap labour being exploited for mass computer hardware production, there are few sound labour practices in the industry. CAFOD the Catholic Agency for Overseas Development runs a campaign for pressuring multinational computer manufacturers to adhere to recognised standards. Choose brands with high scores in 'People' section of the table opposite. See www.gooshing.co.uk for the best ethical office equipment at the best price.

- Brother
- Konica Minolta
- Lexmark
- Xerox

- Epson
- Kyocera Mita

- Hewlett-Packard
- Samsung

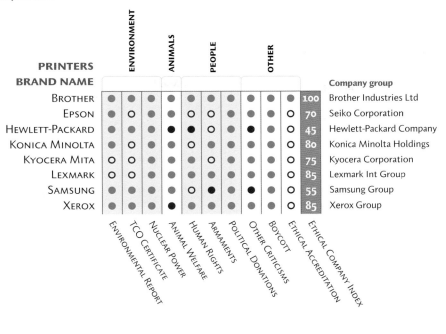

PRINTERS BRAND NAME	ENVIRONMENT			ANIMALS	PEOPLE			OTHER			Ethical Company Index	Company group
	Environmental Report	TCO Certificate	Nuclear Power	Animal Welfare	Human Rights	Armaments	Political Donations	Other Criticisms	Boycott	Ethical Accreditation		
BROTHER	●	●	●	●	●	●	●	●	●	●	100	Brother Industries Ltd
EPSON	●	○	●	●	○	○	●	●	●	○	70	Seiko Corporation
HEWLETT-PACKARD	●	●	●	●	●	○	●	●	●	○	45	Hewlett-Packard Company
KONICA MINOLTA	●	○	●	●	○	●	●	●	●	○	80	Konica Minolta Holdings
KYOCERA MITA	○	○	●	●	●	○	●	●	●	○	75	Kyocera Corporation
LEXMARK	○	○	●	●	●	●	●	●	●	○	85	Lexmark Int Group
SAMSUNG	●	●	●	●	○	●	●	●	●	○	55	Samsung Group
XEROX	●	●	●	●	●	●	●	●	●	○	85	Xerox Group

Key

● Top rating

○ Middle rating

● Bottom rating

Source: The Ethical Company Organisation (2008)

brother at your side   supports ethical shopping

Sewing Machines

A sewing machine may seem an unlikely "green" accessory, but there are good environmental arguments for repairing everyday belongings such as clothes and soft furnishings, rather than throwing them away. If you can make these items at home you might save money too. While many of the products in this area are made by specialist companies, others involve much bigger names. Did you know, for example, that car manufacturer Toyota also makes sewing machines?

BUYING A MACHINE

When choosing a sewing machine, look for a model that is easily maintained. Buy from an established company that will be able to provide you with spare parts or a repairs service should the machine break down. Spending a bit more to start off with could be worth it in the long run, and will ensure that your machine doesn't end up in landfill within a few years. If you are upgrading to a new model the company may be required, under the EU's Waste Electrical and Electronic Equipment directive, to take back your old machine for recycling.

Look for an economical machine: the more efficient the motor, the less energy will be wasted when it is in use. Read *The Green Claims Code* (*www.defra.gov.uk/environment*) for guidance on the validity of companies' environmental claims, and check whether the machine carries the ISO 14021 mark. This is a voluntary international standard which guarantees that self-proclaimed "green" products have been fully and accurately labelled. Try Defra's *Shopper's Guide to Green Labels* for more information.

DONATING AND RECYCLING

Many charity shops are unable to accept electrical goods, but with a bit of resourcefulness you should be able to find a good home for your old sewing machine. Local councils will have details of any recycling programmes in your area, and may also be able to recommend options for reuse or refurbishment. Another alternative to disposal is the UK-based charity Tools For Self Reliance (*www.tfsr.org*), which collects goods for donation to communities in Africa.

TFSR works with artisans and small businesses to match unwanted tools to the people that need them. As well as carpentry, plumbing and building tools, they also accept sewing machines. If your old machine is a Singer hand or treadle, or an electric model that can do zigzag stitches and embroidery, and is in good working order, it could be spruced up by the volunteers at TFSR and sent to the developing world. There it will help workers improve their incomes – and become more self-reliant.

 supports ethical shopping

HAND-MADE FASHION

You've bought fair trade t-shirts, recycled trainers and second hand accessories, but why not go one step further and try making your own clothes? Most department stores and haberdashers stock a wide range of fabrics, and will happily offer advice on the best ways to approach a project. Sewing patterns are no longer the preserve of the unfashionable – established names such as Simplicity have updated their designs in recent years, and the internet is the place to go for truly original styles. Try online communities such as Wardrobe Refashion (*http://nikkishell.typepad.com/wardroberefashion*) for useful tips and eco-friendly inspiration. As well as new clothes, don't forget to look after the ones you already own. Washing at lower temperatures not only saves energy but also helps to protect colours and fabrics

from the effects of wear and tear. Most small rips can be sewn up or patched by machine, or your nearest clothing alteration company may offer a mending service. If the problem is too big to fix, be creative: re-use the material elsewhere or send unwearable garments to reclamation services such as *www.traid.org.uk*, who will be able to give them a new lease of life.

ETHICAL FASHION EVENTS

There is a new wave of ethicality entering the fashion industry at every level. From London Fashion Week to the Ethic Fashion Award (which features up-and-coming designers with the winners getting a Brother sewing machine) there is lots to look out for.

- Bernina
- Brother
- Janome

- Husqvarna

- Toyota

SEWING MACHINES

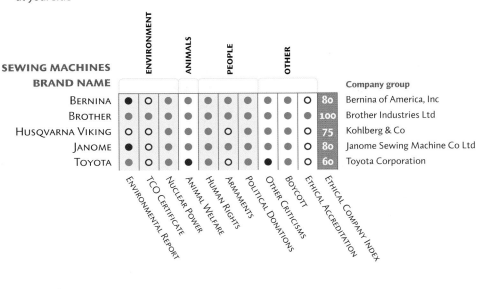

BRAND NAME	ENVIRONMENT			ANIMALS	PEOPLE			OTHER			Ethical Company Index	Company group
	Environmental Report	TCO Certificate	Nuclear Power	Animal Welfare	Human Rights	Armaments	Political Donations	Other Criticisms	Boycott	Ethical Accreditation		
BERNINA	●	○	●	●	●	●	●	●	●	○	80	Bernina of America, Inc
BROTHER	●	●	●	●	●	●	●	●	●	●	100	Brother Industries Ltd
HUSQVARNA VIKING	○	○	●	●	●	○	●	●	●	○	75	Kohlberg & Co
JANOME	●	○	●	●	●	●	●	●	●	○	80	Janome Sewing Machine Co Ltd
TOYOTA	●	○	●	●	●	○	●	●	●	○	60	Toyota Corporation

Key
- ● Top rating
- ○ Middle rating
- ● Bottom rating

Source: The Ethical Company Organisation (2008)

Sustainable building

The aim of sustainable construction is to lessen the environmental impact of a building throughout its life cycle. It gives consideration to the choice of materials used, the building process, how the property affects the occupier and what might happen to the building when it is demolished. By using traditional skills, good management and renewable resources, sustainable building makes the foundations of modern living both ethically and environmentally sound.

UNHEALTHY APPETITE

Building and construction has an unhealthy appetite for energy and resources. 7 per cent of UK primary energy demand and 9 per cent of CO_2 production is used for construction materials. Domestic heating, lighting and cooking is responsible for around 30 per cent of UK energy demand and 30 per cent of CO_2 emissions. Around 115,000kWh of embodied energy are used in the materials, transportation and building of a typical three bedroom masonry house, but this is just 5 per cent of the energy needed to power the house during its life. By getting the design right, the potential for energy and resource savings is massive: a low energy timber frame house can halve both figures easily.

The 7.5 tonnes of CO_2 per year created by an average house could be cut by 50 per cent if simple and established energy conservation techniques were adopted. Government forecasts of climate change (higher winds, higher temperatures and increased flooding) are already evident in our weather, so CO_2 reduction must be a priority.

A sustainable balance between the reasonable requirements of people and nature lies at the heart of environment-conscious building. We must take care of the natural world and use its resources wisely because we are totally dependent on it for our survival. Quality of life for people comes from a sustainable, fair and healthy society, working in harmony with nature.

Sustainable building is as much a philosophy as it is an art, although the wealth of ideas and opportunities that spring from the concept can stimulate artistic talents that most of us never knew we possessed. It requires us to consider what buildings we use, how we build, how the building affects the environment and what happens when the building is taken down.

Design and construction to sustainable criteria will directly benefit local economies and will reduce transport and environmental costs. Since we live in a changing world, it is sensible to design buildings that can be recycled, so that materials and foundations can be easily reused and land is not degraded or polluted.

ENERGY

The facts about CO_2 emissions and the greenhouse effect are well known. Vast amounts of energy are consumed in the production of building materials and during the lifetime of any building. Select materials and products that use the least energy in manufacture (natural or near natural) and can be re-used, or are already recycled. Ensure buildings are insulated to the highest possible standards, as this will reduce fuel bills. When designing a new building take advantage of the sun's free energy. Site orientation and the scrupulous use of glazing can make the best of passive solar energy. Where possible investigate and consider using alternative, renewable forms of energy such as solar, bio-fuels and power from wind and water.

RESOURCES

Many materials used in buildings are from finite sources, so it is important to use those that are sustainable. Timber and bio-crops (such as straw) are generally considered to be the most renewable resource, provided they are grown and harvested in a sustainable way. Timber can also be recycled and reused. Always ask for timber and wood products that bear the Forest Stewardship Council (FSC) logo. The FSC is an independent, international and credible labelling scheme for timber and timber products. For more information visit their website at *www.fsc-uk.org*.

ATMOSPHERE

The effect of CFCs (chlorofluorocarbons) and HCFCs (hydrochlorofluorocarbons) on the ozone layer has been recognised for many years, and the damage associated with CFC emissions has been addressed by international governmental agreements. However, some insulations still use HCFCs. Although these have a lower ozone depletion potential, they carry a very high global warming potential. Alternatives such as cellulose, wool, cork and foamed glass are available and should be considered (see table on page 96).

More details on the use of CFCs and HCFCs in the home and their effects on the environment can be found in the section on fridges and freezers, page 63.

HEALTH

It is well known that exposure to chemicals can cause damage to the environment and human health. Hazardous chemicals are found in many products such as timber preservatives, paint and wood stains, although there are an increasing number of natural alternatives available. In particular, there is still excessive emphasis on treating timbers. For example, many banks, building societies and local authorities insist on extensive chemical treatment of existing woodworm when providing grants or loans. Many of the chemicals approved for use in this country have been banned or restricted overseas.

Within the fabric of a new building there is generally no need to treat sound timber against infestation and rot. Insect infestation and dry or wet rot in older properties can often be dealt with by changing the environmental conditions in the building, through adjusting humidity levels and temperature. There are companies that offer surveys in this respect, including necessary guarantees to satisfy third parties. If action is considered necessary then a boron treatment should be used. Boron is considered to be the least toxic of treatments.

Other issues related to health include the over-use of plastics in buildings, particularly PVC. Hazardous fumes result when PVC is burnt, but more recently it has been suggested that phthalates migrate from the plastic into the atmosphere. There is increasing scientific evidence to suggest that exposure to some of these chemicals may cause widespread problems including immune system damage and cancer, which has prompted Greenpeace to run a campaign highlighting the problems of PVC. Evidence also indicates that some phthalates can disrupt the hormone system. Alternative materials to replace PVC include copper, stainless steel, iron and HDPE (for water pipes and drainage), timber (for cladding and sheeting), timber and aluminium (for windows and doors), clay (for drainage), timber and linoleum (for flooring) and rubber (for electrical cable).

WATER AND WASTE

There is a greater emphasis today on avoiding pollution of water supplies and conserving water. Reed bed sewage systems are an innovative and effective way of disposing of waste in a manner that is ecologically sound. WCs are available which use less water, but the ultimate green loo is the composting toilet, which uses no water, evaporates the urine and turns sewage into a valuable source of nutrients for the garden. There are also urine-separating toilets which isolate urine from faeces. The urine can then be piped onto hay or straw bales to produce nitrogen-rich compost.

Rainwater harvesting systems are available, which save and store rainwater from roofs for flushing toilets, washing and other household chores.

BIODIVERSITY

As more and more land is developed it is important to conserve and encourage wildlife. Trees, hedgerows and ponds can be carefully protected and retained during building operations. Consider setting aside small areas of land as wild nature areas, or establishing a new pond to promote biodiversity. It is also possible to plant indigenous trees and hedgerows, and use dry stone walling to provide a habitat for animals and insects.

DESIGN

Good design is an integral part of sustainable building. Make the structure easily adaptable, for example by using de-mountable partitions so that the internal layout can be altered when necessary. Design also for health and comfort, to provide optimum levels of daylight, sunlight, temperature and fresh air.

COSTS

The cost of any building depends on the design. However, costs for sustainable building can be comparable. In the future they may even be cheaper as the concept of sustainability moves into the mainstream and the economics of scale come into play. Sustainable buildings give added value and avoid the hidden costs, in terms of health and pollution, associated with conventional buildings. Many eco-products are currently manufactured on a smaller scale and can therefore be more expensive or involve higher transport costs.

Comparing the energy costs of various materials (see page 95 for explanation)

PRIMARY EMBODIED ENERGY

MATERIAL	KWH/M3	MATERIAL	KWH/M3
Lead	157,414	Concrete tiles	630
Copper	133,000	Concrete 1 : 3 : 6	600
Steel iron ore (blast furnace)	63,000 - 80,000	Lightweight clinker blocks	600
Aluminium	55,868	Local slate	540
Plastics	47,000	Local stone tiles	450
Steel recycled (electric arc furnace)	29,669	Sand cement render	400
Glass	23,000	Bricks (fletton)	300
Cement	2,860	Mineral fibre insulation	230
Clay Tiles	1,520	Home grown green oak	220
Bricks (non flettons)	1,462	Crushed granite	150
Plastic insulation	1,125	Cellulose (recycled paper) insulation	133
Gypsum plaster / plasterboard	900	Home grown softwood (air dried)	110
Autoclaved bricks	800	Sand and gravel	45
Concrete 1 : 2 : 4	800	Sheep's wool insulation	30
Imported softwood	754		
Foamed glass insulation	751		

SELECTION OF ECOLOGICAL BUILDING MATERIALS

Approximate figures for embodied energy (the energy used in a material's manufacture or mining) allow us to compare the energy costs of various materials, and reveal the advantages of recycling and of using easily won, natural materials. For example, the production of fibreglass requires 15 times more energy than Warmcell recycled cellulose insulation.

The tables showing values for Primary Embodied Energy (page 93) and Thermal Conductivity (page 96) clearly reveal that nature has provided us with a good selection of materials for high performance construction. Most of the ones required for sustainable building can be found near the bottom of each table, while a few such as glass, gypsum, plastic and steel should be used, when unavoidable, in small quantities.

THE WAY FORWARD

Sustainable building needs to be more widely promoted. Ideally, it should be economical, supported by the government and widely accepted as the norm. Building regulations should ensure that the relevant minimum standards are met, such as increased insulation, as we currently fall way behind our European counterparts in this area. The skills shortage problem must also be addressed, and traditional skills (which tend to be more sustainable) must be re-taught.

Some non-renewable fuels are becoming cheaper (in monetary terms) despite their hidden environmental costs, so much more support needs to be given to the renewable energy sector and VAT reduced or removed from this area. It would be helpful if a standard design could be developed for sustainable building, which would encourage the volume builders to embrace this form of construction. This would also make it easier to formulate suitable training programmes to deal with the skills shortage.

The consumer can help by being demanding, and refusing to accept the standard products on offer. We can demand higher levels of energy conservation, knowing that the building will be better for the environment and at the same time benefit the consumer with lower fuel bills and higher living standards. We can also be more demanding over what type of materials are used in the building. All of us should bear in mind the high levels of environmental degradation that are involved in many standard building products, and also take into account the ethicality of their production.

- *The Association for Environment Conscious Building (AECB) can supply more information on green architecture and sustainable building. It has a database of builders who are registered members of the Association, and began the CarbonLite programme for promoting 'carbon liberate' design. It also runs a training scheme, SussEd (Sustainable Skills and Education), which teaches sustainable building skills for the construction industry. For more information about this organisation send an A4 SAE (73p) to AECB, PO Box 32, Llandysul, Carmarthenshire SA44 5ZA, email* info@aecb. net, *visit their website at www.aecb.net or phone 0845 456 9773*

- The Good Shopping Guide *would like to thank John Shore (AA Dipl) for his help in compiling this chapter*

THERMAL CONDUCTIVITY OF MATERIALS

MATERIAL	W/mK	MATERIAL	W/mK
Copper	380.000	Clay board (alternative to plasterboard)	0.140
Aluminium	198.000		
Steel	48.300	Softwood / Plywood	0.138
Granite	3.810	Oil tempered hardboard	0.120
Limestone	1.530	Chipboard	0.108
Dense brickwork	1.470	Strawboard	0.098
Dense concrete	1.440	Snow (average density)	0.090
Sand / Cement render	1.410	Woodwool slab (light)	0.082
Very packed damp soil	1.400	Stony soil (normal)	0.052
Sandstone	1.295	Bitvent 15 sheathing board	0.050
Bricks (engineering)	1.150	Cork	0.043
Dry soil	1.140	Fibreglass insulation	0.040
Clay bricks (compressed, unfired)	0.950	Flax insulation	0.037
Brickwork	0.840	Sheep's wool insulation	0.037
Tile hanging	0.840	Hair	0.036
Damp loose soil	0.700		
Water	0.580	Warmcell (recycled paper)	0.036
Adobe	0.520	Wall insulation	0.036
Glass	0.500	Roof insulation	0.035
Earth blocks	0.340	Expanded polystyrene insulation	0.033
Thermalite blocks	0.140 - 0.190	Polyurethane foam	0.023
Plaster board	0.180	Still air	0.020
Recycled wood fibre / Gypsum plasterboard	0.176		
Hardwood	0.160		

Sources: Centre for Alternative Technology; Environmental Science Handbook; Pittsburgh Corning; Timber Trade Fed; CIRIA; AECB.

Continued from page 95: Ecological building materials have good insulating properties

Reduce your bills and your carbon footprint

Easy steps for a low carbon future

Home is where the heart is, but it's also where most of our CO$_2$ emissions come from. Good Energy Shop provides an extensive range of products to help you reduce your carbon emissions, carefully selected and reviewed by our panel of independent experts. Everything for a low carbon future, from energy monitors to solar thermal panels, and of course 100% renewable electricity from Good Energy.

Good Energy Shop

www.goodenergyshop.co.uk

TVs and videos

If too much television rots the brain, then the advent of digital TV may mean the end of intelligent conversation. Never mind, though, as there will be plenty of makeover and reality shows to fill the silence. Some new televisions contain integrated digital facilities to remove the need for a separate set-top box, which will save energy in the long term – just don't leave it on standby when there's finally nothing left to watch.

DON'T DUMP THAT SET

Around 2.5 million TV sets are dumped every year in the UK. Landfilled or incinerated sets mean a loss of resources and are a potential pollution hazard, as plastics and cathode ray tubes can contain toxic substances. Old sets can be given to second-hand or charity shops or, if they are broken and of no use to a new owner, can be taken to a civic amenity site where they will be used for scrap or recycled. When looking for a new set, aim for a higher quality and more durable model, and preferably one that will be suitable for upgrading in future.

ENERGY EFFICIENCY

Producing the energy necessary to power our televisions creates approximately 7 million tonnes of carbon dioxide and 10,000 tonnes of sulphur dioxide per year. Manufacturers seem to have picked up on this and, as a rule, newer TVs and video recorders are more energy-efficient than earlier ones.

Friends of the Earth has estimated that by leaving our televisions in standby mode we waste around £12 million worth of electricity each year. Studies by *Which?* magazine have shown that some sets use more energy when left on standby than others. Sony, Ferguson, Matsui, Samsung and Sharp came out best, using under five watts in standby mode, compared with more than ten watts used by Mitsubishi, Hitachi, Toshiba and Sanyo models. Either way, the message is to get up from the sofa and switch it off!

MATERIALS

The average television set is 50 per cent glass, and a surprising quantity of raw materials goes into its manufacture. Making the glass screen needs sand and electricity, while the glass for the cathode ray tube contains lead oxide and is coated in graphite to absorb X-rays. These impurities make the tube the hardest component to recycle, and is partly why liquid crystal displays (LCDs) are a less environmentally damaging alternative to conventional screens.

The production of circuit boards uses chemicals, water and energy and generates more hazardous waste than any other part of the TV, including airbourne particulate pollution and chemical waste. TVs and video casings often use brominated flame retardants (BFRs), the making of which can have an effect on human and animal health. Friends of the Earth has been campaigning for BFRs to be outlawed – see their website, *www.foe.co.uk*, for more information.

DAMAGE TO VIEWERS

TVs and videos emit non-ionising radiation over a range of frequencies. Although no proven health risks have been associated with non-ionising radiation, the issue continues to stimulate contentious debate. It is best to be cautious, so sit at least six feet away from the screen and switch off devices, particularly those in bedrooms, after use.

60-SECOND GREEN GUIDE

- Always try to buy second-hand televisions and videos where possible
- Switch off the TV when you're not watching instead of leaving it on standby
- Don't sit too near the television
- Favour smaller sets and/or check out LCD screens
- If the TV or video breaks, see if it can be repaired, and if not make sure it is recycled
- If you are buying new then do it at *www.gooshing.co.uk*. This website compares the ethics and prices of over 250,000 products

- Akai
- Bang & Olufsen
- Beko
- Matsui
- Sharp

- Bush
- Casio
- Ferguson
- Goodmans
- Grundig
- Hinari
- LG
- Thomson

- Aiwa
- Hitachi
- JVC
- Mitsubishi
- Panasonic
- Philips
- Samsung
- Sanyo
- Sony
- Toshiba

TVS AND VIDEOS

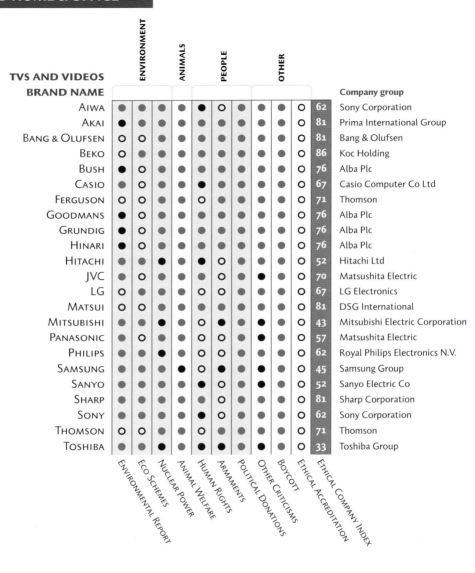

BRAND NAME	ENVIRONMENT			ANIMALS	PEOPLE			OTHER			ETHICAL COMPANY INDEX	Company group
	Environmental Report	Eco Schemes	Nuclear Power	Animal Welfare	Human Rights	Armaments	Political Donations	Other Criticisms	Boycott	Ethical Accreditation		
AIWA	●	●	●	●	●	○	●	●	●	○	62	Sony Corporation
AKAI	●	●	●	●	●	●	●	●	●	○	81	Prima International Group
BANG & OLUFSEN	○	○	●	●	●	●	●	●	●	○	81	Bang & Olufsen
BEKO	○	●	●	●	●	●	●	●	●	○	86	Koc Holding
BUSH	●	○	●	●	●	●	●	●	●	○	76	Alba Plc
CASIO	●	○	●	●	●	●	●	●	●	○	67	Casio Computer Co Ltd
FERGUSON	○	○	●	●	○	●	●	●	●	○	71	Thomson
GOODMANS	●	○	●	●	●	●	●	●	●	○	76	Alba Plc
GRUNDIG	●	○	●	●	●	●	●	●	●	○	76	Alba Plc
HINARI	●	○	●	●	●	●	●	●	●	○	76	Alba Plc
HITACHI	●	●	●	●	●	○	●	●	●	○	52	Hitachi Ltd
JVC	●	○	●	●	●	○	●	●	●	○	70	Matsushita Electric
LG	○	●	●	●	○	○	●	●	●	○	67	LG Electronics
MATSUI	○	○	●	●	●	●	●	●	●	○	81	DSG International
MITSUBISHI	●	○	●	●	○	●	●	●	●	○	43	Mitsubishi Electric Corporation
PANASONIC	●	○	●	●	○	○	●	●	●	○	57	Matsushita Electric
PHILIPS	●	●	●	●	○	○	●	●	●	○	62	Royal Philips Electronics N.V.
SAMSUNG	●	●	●	●	○	●	●	●	●	○	45	Samsung Group
SANYO	●	●	●	●	●	○	●	●	●	○	52	Sanyo Electric Co
SHARP	●	●	●	●	●	○	●	●	●	○	81	Sharp Corporation
SONY	●	●	●	●	●	○	●	●	●	○	62	Sony Corporation
THOMSON	○	○	●	●	○	●	●	●	●	○	71	Thomson
TOSHIBA	●	●	●	●	●	●	●	●	●	○	33	Toshiba Group

Key

● Top rating

○ Middle rating

● Bottom rating

Source: The Ethical Company Organisation

Vacuum cleaners

Beating the dust problem is not just a matter of having a powerful vacuum cleaner, but of having one that is both adaptable and easy to handle around the home. Although a manual carpet sweeper may be a suitable alternative for removing surface dust, most homes will also need a larger, electric machine. To maximise efficiency and reduce energy use, choose a model with good suction power and an effective filter.

POWER AND NOISE

Vacuum cleaners are rated by manufacturers in terms of their wattage, a measure that only reveals the size of the motor. As the average vacuum cleaner wastes most of the electricity it uses in heat and noise, the power rating is not necessarily a helpful indication of its effectiveness.

Only about a quarter of the power output of a vacuum cleaner is actual suction. Electrolux makes a Smart Vac range with 450W of suction from 1,500W input, and this is high compared to most. Miele makes a model called Naturell with an energy-saving 800W motor. Manufacturers might be willing to disclose the suction power data upon request, but this information is not usually found on the label.

There are plans to encourage producers to make more efficient machines by introducing voluntary labelling schemes. One organisation working on this is the Group for Efficient Appliances, a forum of representatives from national energy agencies and European governments. Most EU member states are involved, but in previous years the UK has not put forward a representative.

BAGS AND DUST

Dyson's bag-free machines arguably have less impact on the environment because they do not require paper and other resources for this consumable part, but there is disagreement about whether or not a collection bag interferes with the efficiency of the suction. Dyson asserts that because its machines have no bag their efficiency is constant.

Machines with bags do tend to drop in efficiency as the bag fills, reducing the amount of dust that is picked up. However, manufacturers such as Miele claim that this deficiency is outweighed by the advantages of a bag, which acts as an extra filter for dust particles and also prolongs the life of the motor.

Some companies make vacuum cleaners with 'high efficiency filters' to minimise the re-emission of dust. These include Medivac (*www.medivac.co.uk*), a high scorer in the Ethical Company Organisation's research, whose products are specially designed to offer health benefits to people with dust allergies and asthma. Many high efficiency cleaners have been approved by the British Allergy Foundation (BAF), who operate a system of inspection that includes double-blind testing, ensuring the testers have no idea which product belongs to which manufacturer.

ALTERNATIVES

It is often possible to buy a reconditioned machine second-hand, or to repair a broken one, rather than investing in a brand new cleaner. Hand-held brushes are more efficient than they might appear, and simply require a little elbow grease, although they may not be suitable for households whose occupants suffer from dust allergies. Finally,

there are always old-style carpet sweepers, which are manual, non-electric and work a treat.

Check the ratings on the opposite page for the most ethical types of vacuum cleaner available, then search *www.gooshing.co.uk* for the best prices. It monitors 350 shops to find the cheapest place to buy your chosen brand.

60-SECOND GREEN GUIDE

- When buying a machine, look for the one with the most efficient suction
- Choose a machine that has replaceable dust filters
- Do not allow dust bags to overfill as this can reduce efficiency
- Manual carpet sweepers or hand-held brushes are fine for a quick sweep-up

---

- Medivac
- Miele
- Morphy Richards
- Rowenta

- AEG
- Dyson
- Electrolux
- Hoover
- Nilfisk
- Vax

- Hitachi
- Panasonic
- Philips

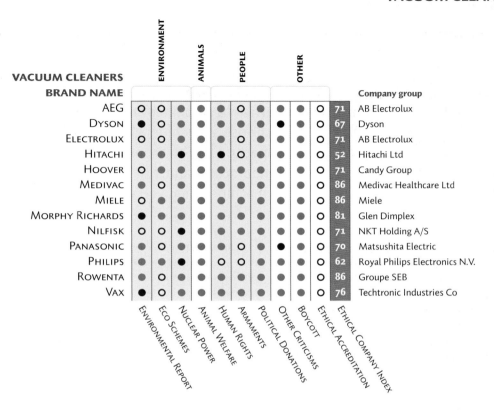

VACUUM CLEANERS BRAND NAME	ENVIRONMENT			ANIMALS	PEOPLE			OTHER			ETHICAL COMPANY INDEX	Company group
	Environmental Report	Eco-Schemes	Nuclear Power	Animal Welfare	Human Rights	Armaments	Political Donations	Other Criticisms	Boycott	Ethical Accreditation		
AEG	O	O	●	●	●	O	●	●	●	O	71	AB Electrolux
DYSON	●	O	●	●	●	●	●	●	●	O	67	Dyson
ELECTROLUX	O	O	●	●	●	O	●	●	●	O	71	AB Electrolux
HITACHI	●	●	●	●	●	O	●	●	●	O	52	Hitachi Ltd
HOOVER	O	●	●	●	●	●	●	●	●	O	71	Candy Group
MEDIVAC	●	O	●	●	●	●	●	●	●	O	86	Medivac Healthcare Ltd
MIELE	O	●	●	●	●	●	●	●	●	O	86	Miele
MORPHY RICHARDS	●	●	●	●	●	●	●	●	●	O	81	Glen Dimplex
NILFISK	O	O	●	●	●	●	●	●	●	O	71	NKT Holding A/S
PANASONIC	●	O	●	●	●	O	●	●	●	O	70	Matsushita Electric
PHILIPS	●	●	●	●	O	O	●	●	●	O	62	Royal Philips Electronics N.V.
ROWENTA	●	O	●	●	●	●	●	●	●	O	86	Groupe SEB
VAX	●	O	●	●	●	●	●	●	●	O	76	Techtronic Industries Co

Key

● Top rating

O Middle rating

● Bottom rating

Source: The Ethical Company Organisation

Washing machines

Washing machines consume a large amount of water and electricity. Fortunately, a wide range of energy-efficient machines are now on the market. Look for the right label, and choose a machine which uses less electricity and will have a reduced impact on the environment. Select the economical modes, wash at lower temperatures and, finally, think carefully about the best way to dispose of the machine when you've finished with it.

ENERGY LABELS

The European Energy Label is required by law to be displayed on many domestic appliances, including all new washing machines. Each product receives an energy efficiency rating, from A (the top rating) down to G (the lowest rating). Also rated on an A to G scale are 'washing performance' (with A giving the cleanest wash) and 'spin drying performance' (with A producing the driest clothes). A figure is also given for energy consumption per cycle (kWh) and water consumption (litres). The main rating here is the one for efficiency. Many 'AA' rated machines are now available, demonstrating that good performance and eco-efficiency can go together.

Sample water consumption for 62 different washing machines ranged from 35 to 78 litres, but averaged at around 53.5. The washing machines in the table all consume less than 50 litres of water and have A-class energy efficiency.

More information about the European Energy label is available at *www.defra.gov.uk/environment*, or call the Energy Advice Centre on 0800 512012.

60-SECOND GREEN GUIDE

BUYING
- Choose the smallest washing machine for your needs
- Look for energy efficient 'A'-rated machines
- Choose one with a fast spin
- Look for an 'eco' button that reduces temperatures
- Choose one with a hot-fill option

USING
- Use a full load if possible
- Avoid the pre-wash cycle, and pre-soak dirty clothes instead
- Try to wash at 40ºC or below
- Don't forget to switch to a 100 per cent renewable energy company. This will mean you are really making a difference.

INTERNET INFORMATION

It's worth checking the details of machines before going shopping for one. The main internet retailers provide the label ranges of their different models. Currys provides particularly detailed information on the technical specifications of each model, including energy and water consumption.

RELIABILITY

A reliable machine not only saves money on repairs, but is also a better environmental choice. The Consumers' Association measured the reliability of each brand and gave good marks to Miele, Candy, Bosch, AEG, Tricity Bendix, Siemens and Zanussi.

DISPOSAL

Every year, nearly one million tonnes of used electrical and electronic goods are discarded in Britain. This includes about eight million large pieces of equipment such as washing machines, cookers and fridges.

EU legislation requires local authorities to put in place 'convenient facilities' for the free take-back of waste goods by final owners, including public collection points where private households should be able to return waste 'at least free of charge'. All equipment designated for collection under this scheme should be marked by a crossed-out wheeled bin symbol.

Next time you buy a washing machine find an ethical brand at *www.gooshing.co.uk*.

- Ariston
- Asko
- Beko
- Candy
- Hoover
- Hotpoint
- Indesit
- Miele
- Servis

- Admiral
- AEG
- Bauknecht
- Brandt
- Dyson
- Hinari
- LG
- Maytag
- Tricity Bendix
- Whirlpool
- Zanussi

- Bosch
- Neff
- Samsung
- Siemens

WASHING MACHINES

BRAND NAME	Environmental Report	Eco Schemes	Nuclear Power	Animal Welfare	Human Rights	Armaments	Political Donations	Other Criticisms	Boycott	Ethical Accreditation	Ethical Company Index	Company group
ADMIRAL	○	○	●	●	●	●	●	⬤	●	○	71	Maytag
AEG	○	○	●	●	●	○	●	●	●	○	71	AB Electrolux
ARISTON	○	●	●	●	●	●	●	●	●	○	86	Fineldo
ASKO	○	●	●	●	●	●	●	●	●	○	86	Antonio Merloni
BAUKNECHT	○	●	●	●	○	●	●	●	●	○	76	Whirlpool Corp
BEKO	○	●	●	●	●	●	●	●	●	○	86	Koc Holding
BOSCH	●	●	⬤	●	○	○	●	⬤	●	○	52	Bosch-Siemens Hausgerate
BRANDT	⬤	○	●	●	●	●	●	●	●	○	76	Elco Holdings
CANDY	○	●	●	●	●	●	●	●	●	○	86	Candy Group
DYSON	⬤	○	●	●	●	●	●	⬤	●	○	67	Dyson
HINARI	⬤	○	●	●	●	●	●	●	●	○	76	Alba Plc
HOOVER	○	●	●	●	●	●	●	●	●	○	86	Candy Group
HOTPOINT	○	●	●	●	●	●	●	●	●	○	86	Fineldo
INDESIT	○	●	●	●	●	●	●	●	●	○	86	Fineldo
LG	○	●	●	●	○	○	●	●	●	○	67	LG Electronics
MAYTAG	○	○	●	●	●	●	●	⬤	●	○	71	Maytag
MIELE	○	●	●	●	●	●	●	●	●	○	86	Miele
NEFF	●	●	⬤	●	○	○	●	⬤	●	○	52	Bosch-Siemens Hausgerate
SAMSUNG	●	●	●	⬤	○	⬤	●	⬤	●	○	45	Samsung Group
SERVIS	○	●	●	●	●	●	●	●	●	○	86	Antonio Merloni
SIEMENS	●	●	⬤	●	○	○	●	⬤	●	○	52	Bosch-Siemens Hausgerate
TRICITY BENDIX	○	○	●	●	●	●	○	●	●	○	71	AB Electrolux
WHIRLPOOL	○	●	●	●	○	●	●	●	●	○	76	Whirlpool Corp
ZANUSSI	○	○	●	●	●	●	○	●	●	○	71	AB Electrolux

Column groupings: ENVIRONMENT (Environmental Report, Eco Schemes, Nuclear Power); ANIMALS (Animal Welfare); PEOPLE (Human Rights, Armaments, Political Donations); OTHER (Other Criticisms, Boycott, Ethical Accreditation)

Key

- ● Top rating
- ○ Middle rating
- ⬤ Bottom rating

Source: The Ethical Company Organisation

Washing-up liquid

For as long as petroleum-based surfactants continue to appear in the most popular washing-up liquid brands, clean dishes will equal a dirty planet. Fortunately, many smaller retailers are beginning to offer a range of environmentally-friendly alternatives, which substitute vegetable oil for petroleum and natural perfumes for chemicals. Some of these companies also use recycled materials in their packaging, and even offer facilities to refill old bottles once they are empty.

INGREDIENTS

The active ingredient in washing-up liquid is a surfactant. This helps to remove grease from an item by emulsifying oils and then dispersing and suspending them so they don't settle back onto its surface. The most commonly found surfactants in hand-washing detergents are anionic, which usually means that they create a lot of suds. Some products also list ionic or non-ionic surfactants.

Surfactants may either be produced from petrochemical sources or from vegetable oils such as coconut. In a life cycle inventory study by a German research body, the vegetable-based or 'oleo' surfactants were shown to be better than their petrochemical equivalents in nine of the 13 categories studied. Not only this, but petrochemical surfactants were found to be slower to biodegrade and were significantly more damaging in terms of aquatic and air eco-toxicity, global warming, depletion of water, acidification, petrochemical oxidant formation and consumption of renewable energy sources.

Synthetic perfumes and colourings in washing-up liquids, also based on petrochemicals, can be slow to degrade and may cause problems for those with sensitive skin. The 'green' brands tend to be colourless and use natural fragrances such as volatile plant oils. Eco-friendly companies favouring these and oleo surfactants include Faith Products, Bio-D, Little Green Shop, Down to Earth, Caurnie and Ecover.

ANTIBACTERIAL ADDITIVES

Since Procter & Gamble launched Fairy Antibacterial in 1997 (which it claims helps kill E-coli, salmonella and campylobacter), many others, including supermarket own brands, have followed with their own disinfectant formulas.

Some scientists believe that our obsession with hygiene could be making us more susceptible to allergies and problems such as asthma. While we obviously need to be very careful around uncooked meats and protein products, and be sure to wash our hands thoroughly before cooking, some argue that a little less cleanliness could actually do us good.

In the case of washing-up liquids, a good kitchen hygiene routine (cleaning items carefully and rinsing the dishcloth thoroughly after use) should offer adequate protection against germs – without the need for extra antibacterial products.

PACKAGING

Most washing-up liquid bottles are made from high density polyethylene (labelled PE or HDPE). This is one of the few plastics that can be recycled in the UK, although provision of local collection schemes is patchy. Look out for the numbers 1 and 2 inside a triangular recycling symbol on the bottom of plastic bottles, as these indicate that they are suitable for recycling.

Bio-D's bottles contain 55 per cent recycled material which, according to a company spokesperson, is the maximum amount possible without the plastic becoming too brittle. Ecover and Bio-D are the only companies providing natural products suppliers with large drums that allow customers to refill their bottles rather than throwing them away.

ALTERNATIVES

In a hard water area it is a good idea to use a water softener to reduce the number of suds generated. Ordinary household soap can be recycled to produce a perfectly good washing-up liquid. Save the scraps from old bars then mix them up in a jar with some boiling water to produce a jelly-like substance.

Make an effort to buy *The Good Shopping Guide*'s ethical brands when you can, and look out for Caurnie, who are one of the Ethical Company Organisation's accredited companies.

- Bio-D
- Caurnie
- Clear Spring
- Ecover

- Morning Fresh
- Surcare

- Fairy
- Persil

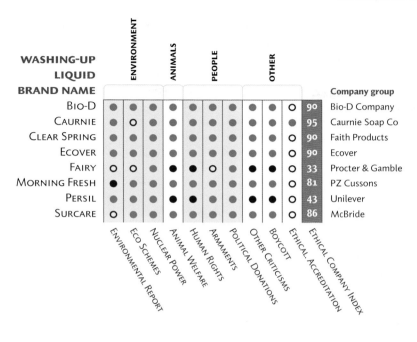

WASHING-UP LIQUID BRAND NAME	ENVIRONMENT	ANIMALS	PEOPLE	OTHER	Ethical Company Index	Company group
BIO-D					90	Bio-D Company
CAURNIE					95	Caurnie Soap Co
CLEAR SPRING					90	Faith Products
ECOVER					90	Ecover
FAIRY					33	Procter & Gamble
MORNING FRESH					81	PZ Cussons
PERSIL					43	Unilever
SURCARE					86	McBride

Column headings: Environmental Report, Eco Schemes, Nuclear Power, Animal Welfare, Human Rights, Armaments, Political Donations, Other Criticisms, Boycott, Ethical Accreditation, Ethical Company Index

Key

● Top rating

O Middle rating

● Bottom rating

Source: The Ethical Company Organisation

GOOD
ENERGY

RENEWABLE ENERGY SUPPLIERS •
ENERGY EFFICIENCY IN THE HOME •
ENERGY SAVING DEVICES •

Introduction

There can't be many people left who aren't aware of the devastating effect that excessive carbon dioxide emissions are having on our environment. The prospect of climate change should be a real concern for all of us. Stories of melting ice caps may seem remote today, but they will not be so irrelevant when the resultant rise in sea levels leaves the waves lapping around our ankles.

It has been said numerous times before that only a few small changes to our lifestyles could have a big impact on the future of the planet. The difference now is that not only is the pressure to make these changes mounting, but governments are beginning to listen to the environmental campaigners and enshrine their objectives in legislation.

One of these changes is a decision to apply Energy Performance Certificates (such as those found on fridges and freezers) to all houses bought and sold in England and Wales. These give every house an A to G rating for its energy efficiency and carbon emissions, as well as offering information on how these ratings can be improved.

Even before these measures come in to place, there is plenty of room for most households to make substantial savings on their CO_2 emissions (and therefore their energy bills) by improving their insulation, installing energy-efficient lightbulbs and buying the most environmentally-friendly appliances for their home.

The most important decision to make is the switch to renewable energy. This is now easier than ever before, particularly as most of the major companies offer their own 'green' energy packages. The best option, however, is to switch to a 100 per cent renewable company – or even to set up a micro-generation site of your own.

This section of *The Good Shopping Guide* includes an in-depth look at renewable energy, as well as tips on home efficiency and a few novel gadgets that could help cut your energy use even further.

Renewable energy suppliers

Switching to a green electricity supplier is a great way to reduce your CO_2 emissions. Green power is a growing area, and the more demand there is for renewable energy, the more pressure there will be on governments and power companies to provide it. Many potential customers are put off from making the switch by the challenge of finding the right tariff, which is why this guide is here to help.

GOOD ENERGY IS GREEN...

The biggest sources of carbon dioxide emissions are power stations, which account for around one third of the total produced. Coal power stations are the least efficient, and although the increased popularity of natural gas burning has reduced our potential CO_2 emissions slightly, the benefits are offset by an increase in energy usage overall. Our rising electricity consumption requires more and more power to be generated, and although consumers' energy efficiency can help reduce this, the only real alternative is to source electricity from renewable resources.

CONFUSING MARKET

The domestic energy market is confusing. A few years ago customers knew that one gas company supplied their gas and nothing else, and another did the same with their electricity. In recent years all customers have been able to change their gas or electricity supplier and over 19 million have swapped in search of a better deal. Now homeowners have a dazzling array of tariffs and service providers, before they even attempt to take the environment into account.

Most of the main energy companies provide some kind of green tariff for electricity. The price and coverage depends on the area in which you live, but it is generally accepted that green electricity tariffs cost the consumer either about the same or just a few pounds per bill more than conventional tariffs.

Green energy supply has been available to some customers in this country from as far back as 1997. However, it did not truly become an option for the average consumer until the energy market was completely opened up to competition in May 1999. Since then the offerings that are available have come a long way.

The green energy revolution has gained significant support at a commercial level. Large energy users and corporations have taken to green energy in a big way. It is not only the large 'green'-centric companies such as The Body Shop that have a green power supply, but also institutions including Oxford University, who have 100 per cent of their energy needs provided for by a green supplier.

Any company, small or large, that claims 'corporate social responsibility' but has not yet switched to a renewable energy supply should think again!

With 14 green energy tariffs now available in the UK, there is a lot of choice around for the consumer. However, it is not the case that these tariffs all offer the same product.

The most important issue for those on a budget may be that of cost. For an average household, as you might expect due to economies of scale, the price of receiving a green energy supply is fractionally higher: the supplement over and above a 'regular' tariff is normally in the order of £20 or £30 a year. However, changing your methods of payment to either direct debit or one annual fee can, in most cases, offset the entire extra cost, so there is no reason not to change your supply today.

WHY SWITCH TO RENEWABLE ENERGY?

When we read the newspapers and watch the news on TV every day, and see the environmental disasters and freak weather conditions that are attributed to global warming, we can see for ourselves the effects of the by-products of traditional energy generation. Electricity production is the single biggest contributor to the emissions that cause climate change.

The prime gas responsible for global warming or the 'greenhouse effect' is carbon dioxide or CO_2. The burning of oil, coal and gas (otherwise known as fossil fuels) in traditional power stations produces a considerable amount of carbon dioxide. The UK, which has 1 per cent of the world's population, emits 2.3 per cent of the world's total emissions of CO_2.

Not only do fossil fuels contribute to the degradation of the environment, they are also finite in nature and increasingly have to be imported into the UK, sometimes from politically unstable areas of the world. It is only a matter of time before the planet's supply of these fuels runs out.

One alternative to traditional fuel burning stations is nuclear power. This, however, is far from being a solution to global pollution. Although British Nuclear Fuels Limited (BNFL) has been pushing nuclear power as the non-polluting solution to climate change, this is certainly not the case. During its lifetime (around 30-40 years) a nuclear reactor can produce radioactive waste that has a 'lifespan' of thousands of years. This waste needs to be disposed of safely, as it is highly dangerous. Although no CO_2 is produced there are other by-products to the nuclear process that could potentially do serious harm to the environment.

In contrast to these more traditional forms of energy supply is renewable or 'green' energy. Not only does green energy not directly result in any by-products that may be harmful to our environment, it also comes from renewable and everlasting sources such as wind and water. In fact, most forms of renewable energy produce very little or no waste, and therefore have a minimal impact on the world around us.

When you switch to a renewable energy supply, you are also supporting the future of the renewable energy industry. By showing the government and mainstream energy suppliers that you wholeheartedly support renewable energy, you can help convince them to increase the support they offer to the industry as a whole.

Wind, water, sunlight...

...and none of the bad stuff

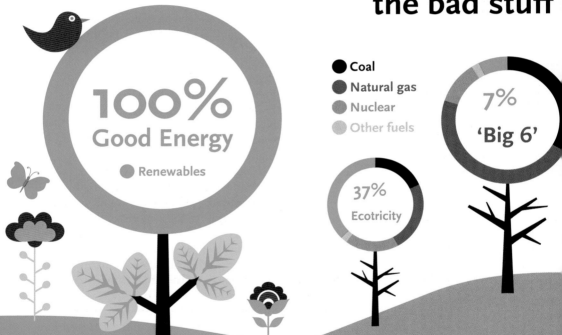

100%
Good Energy

● Renewables

● Coal
● Natural gas
● Nuclear
● Other fuels

37%
Ecotricity

7%
'Big 6'

If you are fighting for the environment, why would you support nuclear and fossil generation? Exactly. That's why at Good Energy we only buy electricity generated from wind, water and sunlight. A little more expensive, sure, but it leaves a lot less mess. We think it's worth it and 25,000 customers agree with us.

Good Energy
THE NATURAL CHOICE

Source: BERR Fuel Mix Disclosure Table based on 2008 disclosed figures. 'Big 6' figures are straight averages of 2007/8 disclosed fuel mix for npower/RWE; E.ON; British Gas; EDF; Scottish Power; Scottish & Sout

'The biggest source of carbon dioxide emissions is power stations, accounting for around one third of the total.'

HOW DO YOU SWITCH?

The great thing about switching to a green energy tariff is that it's incredibly easy to do. There is no need to get the electricians in, or have anything changed physically with your electricity supply. This is down to the nature of the green energy tariffs available to the consumer. These include the energy-based tariff, the fund-based tariff and tariffs that offer a combination of the two.

Of the choices available, the energy-based tariff is the one that actually offers you renewable energy in return for your money. Whilst there is no change in the actual electricity coming down the wires into your home when you subscribe to an energy-based tariff, a proportion of what you pay will be matched by the equivalent amount of energy being fed into the national grid from renewable sources. Tariffs such as the one from Good Energy Ltd (switch at *www.good-energy.co.uk*) promise over the course of the year to match 100 per cent of the units of electricity you buy from them with an equal amount from renewable sources.

With fund-based energy tariffs a proportion of the money you pay the supplier is donated into a fund that supports new renewable capacity, green causes or other related initiatives. An independent body, established either by the supplier or a registered charity, normally administers these funds. In some cases the donation made from the consumer is matched in equal amounts by a donation made by the tariff supplier. A combination tariff is usually some mixture of both fund-based and energy-based supply.

It is extremely easy to switch to a green energy tariff. All you need to do is register your interest with a supplier and they can sign you up over the phone or send you forms to fill out by post. It is also possible to switch your supplier with very little hassle online at *www.gooshing.co.uk*. Here you can arrange to pay by direct debit, which will also save you money.

Over the following pages you will find information about the most widely available tariffs and how they operate, plus *The Good Shopping Guide*'s ratings for each company.

CHOOSING THE BEST SUPPLIER

Since April 1st 2004, energy suppliers have had to make sure that at least 4.9 per cent of all the energy they provide comes from renewable energy sources. For each unit of renewable energy bought they receive a certificate. If companies fail to match their required 4.9 per cent they may buy certificates from those companies that have exceeded their minimum.

In order to reach their minimum requirement, large energy suppliers offer a green tariff to customers. In many cases this does not exceed or match the minimum 4.9 per cent renewable energy that the supplier is required to provide, as demand for traditional tariffs is still considerably greater. These suppliers then have to buy in certificates from smaller niche companies who only offer a green tariff, or whose green tariff makes up more than 4.9 per cent of their total energy supply. If, however, the niche company sells all its certificates other than the 4.9 per cent it retains to meet its own government targets, it results in a net status quo for the energy market. No extra demand for renewable energy supply is generated, as total demand for renewable energy is matched across the board. Trading of certificates at this level will mean that the net average of renewable energy supply will remain at 4.9 per cent nationwide. However, if those suppliers that produce more than the minimum requirement set aside a further percentage of their certificates, above and beyond the required minimum, and refuse to sell them on, additional demand for renewable energy sources is generated. At the moment only Good Energy does this.

When trying to evaluate which tariff is 'better', it's best to look at what green tariffs are trying to achieve. Ultimately the aim is to increase the amount of renewable energy supply there is in the country. By increasing the influence of renewable energy sources, it is possible to lessen the influence of the environmentally degrading sources, fossil fuels and nuclear power. It's for this reason that energy-based tariffs are the most positive choice.

'Any company, small or large, that claims 'corporate social responsibility' but has not yet switched to a renewable energy supplier should think again!'

ENERGY COMPANIES WE RECOMMEND

GOOD ENERGY

Good Energy supplies only 100 per cent renewable electricity to homes and businesses in England, Scotland and Wales. For every unit of electricity used by a Good Energy customer, Good Energy promises to supply the national grid with a unit of electricity generated from renewable power sources including wind, running water and the sun. Therefore every new consumer means Good Energy sources more renewable power. This is verified by an annual green audit carried out by an independent firm of chartered accountants.

In addition, Good Energy supports micro-generators with its Home Generation Scheme, which pays people for all the electricity they generate from small renewable generators. The 100 per cent renewable supply is additional, meaning that it goes over and above the government obligation by setting aside extra renewable obligation certificates. By doing this, Good Energy helps to generate extra demand for renewable energy sources and creates greater environmental benefit.

Good Energy owns the UK's first-ever wind farm at Delabole in Cornwall and has over 1,000 investors, most of whom are Good Energy customers. They recently opened *goodenergyshop.co.uk* for those looking for the complete low carbon lifestyle.

Good Energy is also commended by the Ethical Company Organisation, as a founder member of its company accreditation scheme.
0845 456 1640

GREEN ENERGY UK

Green Energy offer two tariffs: 'Deep Green' which is sourced from water, wind, biomass, solar and tides, and 'Pale Green' which is competitively priced and comes from OFGEM approved low impact combined heat and power. Subscribers also become shareholders. Their electricity comes from small-scall hydro-electric operators, wind turbines, biomass and solar power.

Green Energy has also joined the Ethical Company Organisation's accreditation scheme, which provides full ethical certification every 12 months.
0845 456 9550

ECOTRICITY

Ecotricity is an independent energy supplier that invests in large wind turbines. At Swaffham in Norfolk it built the country's first multi-megawatt wind turbine, which alone provides enough energy for 3,000 people. The renewable energy certificates earned by Ecotricity are sold on to help other energy suppliers meet their government targets. The profits earned from the tariff and the sale of certificates are then used to build further wind farms and turbines. Ecotricity have been particularly pro-active in building new power sources of renewable energy – this helps increase the amount of renewable energy available to the UK market. Ecotricity offers two tariffs: 'New Energy' which comes from a mix of their own wind farms and brown energy sources, and 'New Energy Plus' which is a 100% green tariff and costs a little extra.
0800 032 6100

FINAL THOUGHTS: THE FUTURE

Despite the differences in the available green tariffs, and the ranking of one above another, switching to any green supply is a positive step to take. It is a win-win situation both for the environment and your peace of mind. Whether or not you choose a fund-based tariff or an energy-based tariff, what you are doing when you switch is registering your support for more environmental awareness from the energy suppliers. This will help encourage those suppliers who currently do not offer a green tariff to start one, which is clearly a good thing.

Your vote for a cleaner energy supply also has an impact on the future of government policy. For example, in 2005 all energy suppliers had to disclose the exact sources of their electricity and how much came from renewables. Green energy supplier Good Energy decided to spearhead this disclosure and showed the market the way forward by making their sources available to the public in advance. So by supporting green energy suppliers you can also show your support for government reform.

It has never been easier to switch your energy supplier than it is now. All it takes is a simple phone call or compare further and switch through *The Good Shopping Guide*'s recommended website, *www.gooshing.co.uk/energy.html*. You can start helping to create a cleaner planet. So why wait?

- New Energy Plus
  (Ecotricity)
- Good Energy
- Green Energy 100

- Eco Energy
  (NIE)
  (Viridian)
- RSPB Energy

- Go Green
  (EON)
- Green Energy
  H2O
  (ScottishPower)
- Green tariff
  (EDF Energy)
- Juice
  (N power)

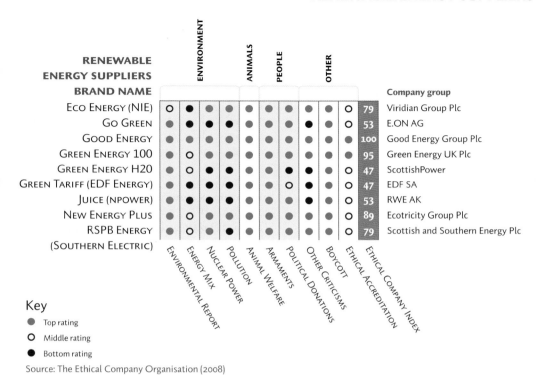

RENEWABLE ENERGY SUPPLIERS BRAND NAME	Ethical Company Index	Company group
Eco Energy (NIE)	79	Viridian Group Plc
Go Green	53	E.ON AG
Good Energy	100	Good Energy Group Plc
Green Energy 100	95	Green Energy UK Plc
Green Energy H20	47	ScottishPower
Green Tariff (EDF Energy)	47	EDF SA
Juice (npower)	53	RWE AK
New Energy Plus	89	Ecotricity Group Plc
RSPB Energy (Southern Electric)	79	Scottish and Southern Energy Plc

Chart column headings: ENVIRONMENT (Environmental Report, Energy Mix, Nuclear Power, Pollution), ANIMALS (Animal Welfare), PEOPLE (Armaments, Political Donations), OTHER (Other Criticisms, Boycott, Ethical Accreditation)

Key

- ● Top rating
- ○ Middle rating
- ⬤ Bottom rating

Source: The Ethical Company Organisation (2008)

ENERGY MIX

Since 2002 under the Renewables Obligation schemes for England, Scotland and Northern wenergy from renewable sources. The minimum requirement for 2006/07 was 6.7% (2.65% for Northern Ireland whose order came into effect in April 2005). These schemes were introduced by the Department of Trade and Industry, the Scottish Executive and the Department of Enterprise, Trade and Investment respectively and are administered by the Gas and Electricity Markets Authority (whose day to day functions are performed by Ofgem).

The top rating indicates that over 50% of the company's energy is generated only from renewable sources. The middle rating indicates that the company generates more than 6.7% of its energy from renewable sources. Companies that do not reach the minimum target are given a bottom rating.

To switch now: Contact

Good Energy

Monkton Park Offices,
Chippenham,
Wiltshire
SN15 1ER
Tel: 0845 456 1640
www.good-energy.co.uk

Green Energy UK: Green Energy 100

9 Church Street,
Ware,
Herts
WG12 9EG
Tel: 0800 783 8851
www.greenenergy.uk.com

Ecotricity

Axiom House,
Station Road,
Gloucester
GL5 3AP
Tel: 0800 032 6100
www.ecotricity.co.uk

Viridian (NIE): Eco Energy

120 Malone Road,
Belfast
BT9 5HT
Tel: 0845 745 5455
www.nie.co.uk

NPower: Juice

Npower Centre,
Oak House,
Bridgewater Road,
Warnden,
Worcester
WR4 9FP
Tel: 0800 316 3370
www.npower.com

ScottishPower: Green Energy H2O

1 Atlantic Quay,
Glasgow
G2 8SP
Tel: 0845 270 6543
www.scottishpower.co.uk

Scottish and Southern Energy plc: RSPB Energy

Southern Electric,
PO Box 6009,
Basingstoke
RG21 8ZD
Tel: 0845 7444 555
www.southern-electric.co.uk

Energy efficiency in the home

With rising energy costs a standard three bedroom detached house can cost £1000 a year to heat. If proper energy efficiency measures are taken it is entirely possible to halve the cost. Heating is not the only area in which energy efficiency in the home can be improved: simple changes to lighting, household appliances and glazing can also help reduce the amount of energy we consume every day.

HEATING

During the cold winter months we all rely on our heating to keep us warm and cosy. However, having an energy inefficient heating system can mean you are spending more than you need to on your heating costs. Here are some tips on how to improve your heating efficiency.

Make sure you have an effective method of heating control, as boilers are unable to tell when you want heat or hot water without one. If some form of heating control is installed then you can regulate when and where you need heat. Controlling heat efficiently around the house can save up to 17 per cent on your heating costs.

If your boiler is more than 15 years old you should think about replacing it. New energy efficient condensing boilers could save you up to 32 per cent on your fuel bills. Even without upgrading to a condensing boiler, modern, more efficient boilers can still save you up to 20 per cent. In addition to this your local council may be able to provide a grant to help you out. If you live in a small property, you could also consider using energy efficient convection heaters or gas heaters to heat your property, rather than relying on central heating.

Turn to the chapter on Boilers (page 41) for more information.

LIGHTING

In the average home you can expect your lighting costs to account for 10-15 per cent of your electricity bill. With lighting accountable for such a sizeable percentage of the costs, it seems only sensible to invest in ways in which you can improve efficiency around the house. With energy saving light bulbs now readily available, they are an ideal option.

Energy saving light bulbs only use a quarter of the energy of standard bulbs. For this reason they are available in much lower wattages (see table overleaf). However, the light from an energy saving bulb is often radiated differently to a conventional one, so you may need to choose a higher wattage bulb than usual to achieve the same lighting effect. At the moment energy saving light bulbs tend to

ORDINARY BULBS	ENERGY SAVING
25W	6W
40W	8-11W
60W	13-18W
100W	20-25W

be more expensive to buy than conventional ones, at around £5 for a 20W bulb. However, the cost benefit makes up for this extra initial outlay. For every conventional bulb you replace with an energy saving one it could save you up to £10 a year on your electricity bill, making back the extra £5 spent on the bulb and leaving you with an extra £5 in your pocket.

To complement energy saving bulbs, consider installing energy saving fittings in which to place them. These are little transformers that fit into the base of the bulb, which regulate the amount of energy that is fed into it. For the few milliseconds it takes for a bulb to light, the transformer provides a surge of energy. Once a bulb is lit it requires far less power to stay alight, so the fitting maintains the electricity flow into the bulb at a very low level.

HOUSEHOLD APPLIANCES

No matter how well you feel your household appliances are running and how few problems they have given you, they could still be extremely energy hungry and inefficient. As a general rule, the older your appliance the more it is going to cost to run. For this reason, it is best where possible to buy your fridges, cookers, dishwashers and washing machines brand new as these will be the most energy efficient. The saving you

make on a second hand purchase will soon be outweighed by the extra cost it takes to run the appliance.

When buying new appliances look out for the Energy Efficiency Recommended logo. To find out more about which currently available appliances are listed as energy efficient, go to *www.saveenergy.co.uk* and browse the extensive database of energy efficient household appliances.

INSULATION

Bad insulation in the home can result in considerable heat loss. Most heat is lost through the walls and the loft space. Fully insulating these spaces can help reduce the amount of heat lost in the home by more than 50 per cent. The walls alone can be responsible for up to 35 per cent of the total heat wastage in the home.

Badly insulated walls can be one of the major sources of heat loss in the home. They could be costing you anywhere up to £200 extra per year. For this reason insulating the walls of your home is one of the most energy efficient ways to make a saving on your heating bills.

If you want to find out what you can do about adding insulation to your walls, the first step is to identify what kind of walls you have in your home. Most houses built after 1930 have cavity walls. To identify whether you have cavity walls you can check by measuring their thickness at a door or window. They are normally around 30cm thick. This is comprised of an inner and an outer layer, and a small air gap in-between. To fill your wall with insulation, small holes are drilled into the outer or inner layer and insulation material is injected into the air gap. This work has to be carried out by a professional, and will be guaranteed for 25 years by the Cavity Insulation Guarantee Agency (CIGA). The cost of the work should be recovered within five years in the savings you make on your heating costs. There are also grants and offers available to help cover the cost of the work.

As air gets hotter it becomes less dense, and as a result rises above cold air, which is denser. This is the reason why it is important to ensure any heat lost through the roof is minimised. Most houses have some space under the roof, normally the loft. Insulating the loft properly can save around 25 per cent on your heating costs. You can insulate your loft easily yourself, and it requires no professional work to be done. By simply adding a 250mm (10 inch) thick layer of insulation the job is done. The material that you need to insulate the roof can easily be picked up at a local DIY store or builder's merchants.

Draughts coming through the edge of the skirting board or up through the cracks in the floor can make a room feel cold and unwelcoming. Sealing up these cracks with a regular tube sealant can save you up to £10 on your heating bills. To make your floors warmer and to stop the chilly draughts coming up through them you could invest in some under floor insulation, which can help save a further £25. Remember, if you fit the insulation yourself, not to block any air bricks on the outside wall. These help maintain adequate ventilation under the floor, and without them it's likely that the floorboards will start to rot.

Heat that escapes through the space under your doors or windows also accounts for a considerable amount of heat lost in the home; as much as 20 per cent. Draught excluders come in many different materials, from brushes to rubber strips. Without double-glazing these can be a cheap and easy way to prevent heat escaping from your home. Do remember that in some rooms ventilation is very important, especially if they have solid fuel burners, gas fires or boilers within.

Badly insulated hot water pipes and water tanks can result in 75 per cent more energy use than those that are fully insulated. British Standard water tank 'jackets' can be found at all good DIY stores and are easy to fit. The saving you make on your water heating bills means the cost can be recouped within a year. If you already have insulation on your water tank check that it's at least 75mm (3 inches) thick. If it isn't it could be a good idea to replace it with a new one to make yours as energy efficient as it can be.

For further information on improving insulation you can get in touch with your local Energy Efficiency Advice Centre. If you don't know where this is you can phone 0845 727 7200 or search on the Energy Savings Trust website at *www.saveenergy.co.uk* or visit *www.gooshing.co.uk/energy*.

GLAZING

Double-glazing your windows is an ideal way to reduce heat loss in the home by up to 20 per cent. Whilst it is an expensive option, it should definitely be considered if you are thinking of replacing your window frames. Not only does double (or even triple-) glazing help prevent heat loss but it can also stop condensation and reduce noise levels and sound from outside. If you are on a tight budget you can always fit secondary glazing, which is less expensive than fitting brand new double-glazing and can still result in annual savings of around £30.

QUICK TIPS TO IMPROVE YOUR ENERGY EFFICIENCY TODAY!

- If you are too warm at home, turn down your thermostat by 1°C. This could save you up to 10 per cent on your heating bill. If you are planning to go away over the winter for any extended period of time, turn the thermostat down to a low level. You can turn it down as far as you want, but be sure to leave it high enough that the house doesn't freeze. Your total saving could be as much as £30 a year.
- There is no need to have the hot water come out of your taps at scalding temperatures. For most people a setting of 60°C/140°F on their cylinder thermostat will be more than enough for taking baths and the washing-up. Doing this can save you as much as £10 a year.
- Never leave the taps running and the plughole unblocked. If you are washing up using hot water, try not to do it with the plughole open. The cost for hot water can soon mount up and leaving the plughole open can flush money away with the waste water.
- Always close your curtains in the evening. Your curtains are a valuable form of insulation. If you close the curtains you can stop extra heat escaping out through the window into the cold night air.
- Try not to use electric lights when there is a good source of natural light available. Open your curtains or blinds fully rather than switching on an electric light. If you do use an electric light make sure you remember to switch it off when you leave the room.

- Electrical devices such as televisions and computers consume almost as much electricity in their standby mode as when switched on. Try to switch off all devices of this nature if you can. Obviously if this will have an effect on the appliance's memory settings then leaving it on standby can be unavoidable, so check the manual before you switch it off.
- Defrosting your fridge or freezer can help it run more efficiently; try to do this as often as possible. Also try not to leave the fridge or freezer door open for more than a few seconds as the cold air will escape, meaning the appliance will have to work harder to cool the air inside down again when you close the door.
- It's important to try to make sure you run a full load in your washing machine and tumble dryer. If this is impossible, use the economy wash settings or run at a low heat. Modern washing powders will work just as effectively at 40°C as at 60°C. These rules can apply to dishwashers too; try to run a full load every time and use the lowest temperature setting available.
- When cooking try to use the best pot or pan available for the job, and match this with the right cooking ring. Ideally the base of the pot should just cover the edges of the ring. If you are using a gas hob the flames should only heat the bottom of the pot, as any flames that rise up the sides of the pot will be wasting heat.
- When boiling water in a kettle, there is no need to fill it all the way to the top if you are not going to use all the water. Fill the kettle with enough water to cover the element, but not more than you plan to use.

- A tap left dripping for a day can waste as much water as it would take to run a good sized bath. This is needless waste, especially if the water is hot. Make sure you firmly close all taps when you have finished with them.
- If you are used to taking baths, consider switching to a shower. An ordinary shower uses less than half of the water that a bath does. You can easily buy devices that convert your bath taps into a shower.

NEW DEVELOPMENTS – HOME GENERATION

The ultimate way to cut your contribution to climate change may be to start your own small-scale renewable energy generation. This could be via solar panels, or you could even buy a small wind generator. Since Good Energy Limited set up its Home Generation tariff you can even sell the energy you generate – customers receive four pence per KWH (unit) for all the renewable electricity produced, including the energy you use yourself!

If you are interested in home generation you can contact Good Energy on 0845 456 1640 or e-mail them at *enquiries@good-energy.co.uk*.

SOLAR PANELS

Solar energy has long been heralded as the obvious answer to our renewable energy production needs. Usage is growing steadily, especially amongst opinion-forming consumers who can quickly see the win-win benefits of the small additional initial investment.

SOLAR ENERGY IN THE UK

The conversion of sunlight to electrical energy is known as photovoltaic (PV) conversion and has several advantages, primarily that the process is emission-free, renewable and noiseless.

Solar energy is an excellent alternative to conventional electricity. The sunshine per square metre available on average on earth is about 1,000 watts of energy. Approximately 4 to 22 per cent of the solar light is converted into electrical energy, the other 78 to 96 per cent is either reflected or turned into heat.

A solar roof is easy to maintain and simply has to be cleaned fairly regularly (otherwise dirt and dust can reduce the energy efficiency). In general the solar panel lasts for about 20 to 25 years, which ensures that significant financial and emissions savings are made. Our government's aim was to reach just 6,000 solar panelled roofs in 2005 – while Germany had 140,000 solar roofs and Japan about 400,000.

DIFFERENT KINDS OF SOLAR PANELS

There are three types of solar panels, and all are made of silicon. The most effective (and also the most expensive) are monocrystalline panels. These are manufactured from silicon slices, which are cut from a single crystal. Polycrystalline panels are made from silicon, which is cast in blocks. These are cheaper but also less efficient than the monocrystalline panels.

However, the lowest cost option is the amorphous panel, manufactured from amorphous silicon. Although less efficient, this method is less expensive and allows the complete replacement of the roof.

ADVANTAGES AND COSTS

The main advantage of solar energy is the fact that sunlight is a renewable and zero carbon emission energy source and there can be real space savings as the panels sit on the roof! The installation of solar panels is not cheap, but in the long term the savings on electricity bills and carbon emissions are considerable. Within the last 30 years the technology has become 90 per cent cheaper than in the 1970s, and the government has established grants for homeowners which mean a 40 to 50 per cent discount to the consumer. See more about installing solar panels at Energy Saving Trust *www.est.org.uk/solar/about* or visit *www.goodenergyshop.co.uk*

HERE IS A LIST OF SUPPLIERS AND INSTALLERS WITH THEIR CONTACT DETAILS. WHY NOT PICK UP THE PHONE AND MAKE IT HAPPEN?

EAGLE POWER
0142 282 3360
www.eaglepower.co.uk
(wind, solar, hydro)

PROVEN ENERGY
0156 048 5570
www.provenenergy.com
(wind)

PV SYSTEMS
0845 458 0250
www.pvsystems.com
(solar)

SOLAR CENTURY
0800 9700 733
www.solarcentury.co.uk
(solar)

SUNDOG ENERGY
0176 848 2282
www.sundog-energy.co.uk
(solar)

WIND AND SUN LTD
0156 876 0671
www.windandsun.co.uk
(wind and solar)

Energy saving devices

Saving energy at home doesn't always require a grand gesture such as solar panels on the roof – the small changes are every bit as worthwhile. Something as simple as gradually replacing conventional light bulbs with the low-energy alternative will make a difference, and the more of us who do it, the greater the effect. The devices suggested here are just the tip of the iceberg, so get on the internet and see what you can find!

WIND-UP TORCHES

The Sherpa wind-up torch by Freeplay is an ideal gadget for camping trips, or to keep around the home in case of a power-cut. The wind-up system offers maximum dependability when dead batteries could leave you vulnerable. The handle folds out from the underside of this compact torch and can be wound clockwise and anti-clockwise: a 30-second wind gives about eight minutes of light on normal beam and you can re-wind at any time.

There are two brightness settings, ultra-bright and energy saving, allowing you to save battery power as necessary. The torch has an LED charge level indicator to tell you the optimum winding speed. With a fully charged battery (about 40 minutes winding), the torch will shine for five hours on normal beam and 30 minutes on high beam. The Sherpa is supplied with a charger and comes in four different colours.

www.freeplayenergy.com

LOW-ENERGY LIGHT BULBS

A huge amount of energy is wasted every day on lighting, but much of this could be saved with the right light bulbs. Low-energy bulbs will fit into standard light fittings and are highly efficient, long-lasting alternatives to conventional bulbs. They consume 75 per cent less energy and can last up to 15 times longer than ordinary light bulbs. A single low-energy bulb can save up to £75 over its lifetime.

Energy saving bulbs come in many different shapes and wattages, and will replace a bulb of up to 175 watts. As they use less energy, a lower wattage bulb will produce the same amount of light. For example, a 25 W low-energy bulb is the equivalent of a standard 100 W bulb. Although they are more expensive to buy, their financial and environmental advantages make low-energy bulbs good value for money.

www.est.org.uk
www.goodenergyshop.co.uk

GOOD ENERGY

SMALL WIND TURBINES

Whitewave, on the Isle of Skye, has become the first property to utilise natural wind resources by employing renewable micro-generation through a 6kW domestic wind turbine. This greatly reduces personal CO_2 emissions without interfering with the natural beauty of the island.

There are two different schemes which offer grants for communities and householders who wish to get involved in micro-generation. Customers installing a turbine at a new house can reclaim the VAT (17.5 per cent) in line with other building costs if they install before the completion date/certificate for the property, so the effective VAT on the wind turbine and associated equipment is zero. Also, customers installing a domestic turbine at an existing house qualify for a special lower rate of VAT at 5 per cent.

Moreover, Good Energy devised the Home Generation scheme, paying small domestic generators a price for every unit they generate. The scheme extends to solar, small-scale wind and small-scale hydro electric generators that are less than 10kW in size.

The electricity produced by the generator is either used on site or contributes to the national grid. The company estimates how much power the home generator is likely to produce and pays the owner accordingly. The Good Energy website also offers advice on setting up a home generator and whether grants might be available to help with the cost.

www.good-energy.co.uk
www.provenenergy.com

WIND-UP PHONES

Have you ever been caught short, needing to make an important call with no battery on your phone? The solution to this familiar problem could come from an unlikely source: the green movement.

Weighing only 90g, the Freecharge wind-up charger allows the talkative phone user to make and receive calls at any time, even when their handset has a flat battery. Since the charger is smaller than most phones, it can easily be kept on hand when you're days from the nearest power-point. The only thing is doesn't guarantee is enough network to make the call.

The Freecharge comes with adapters to fit many models of mobile phone, including Nokia, Ericsson, Motorola, Samsung and Siemens. Versions for other models on the market are currently in development.

The charger produces either 30 to 60 minutes of standby or 2 to 8 minutes of talk time from a three minute wind-up, and can be wound in either direction. It has a built-in LED light to show when the optimum winding speed has been reached and the battery is charging. On average, the Freecharge will charge 60 per cent of the phone's battery, and the phone can be used while it is being recharged.

As if that's not enough, there is also an accessory available that allows you to convert the phone into a wind-up flashlight – and all of the materials in the charger are recyclable. The charger is available via internet stockists, and comes with a standard two year warranty.

www.freeplayenergy.com

BATTERY CHARGERS

Add up the number of torches, personal stereos, digital cameras and other gadgets we keep around the home, and most of us would be surprised at how many of them require batteries.

Buying rechargeables instead of standard disposable batteries is a really easy way to reduce the amount of electrical waste we contribute to landfill sites, and saves a lot of energy in the long term. Nearly 700 million batteries are bought every year in the UK, and almost 90 per cent of these are general purpose ones that could probably be replaced with a recyclable alternative.

Most battery chargers will accept nickel cadmium (NiCad) and nickel metal hydride (NiMh) rechargeable batteries, reaching full charge in three to five hours on any AA, AAA or PP3 battery – less time than it takes to remember to go to the shops and buy some more! These batteries can on average be recharged up to 1,000 times, which means that they have a good life-span and will save the owner a significant amount of money compared to disposables.

It is also possible to find a battery charger that relies on solar power, which would save even more energy. Or switch your electricity supply to a renewable energy company and you may find your batteries are being charged by the wind!

Check out *The Good Shopping Guide*'s chapter on Batteries (page 38) to find out why nickel metal hydride is the best option for rechargeable batteries.

www.battery-chargers.com
www.global-batteries.co.uk

SOLAR GARDEN LIGHTS

Solar lights enhance a garden in an easy-to-use, environmentally-friendly way. They produce a visually pleasing solar light that will last all night long. The units can be mounted around a driveway, decking or patio, and each one is completely self-contained, including a solar panel and LED light.

Solar garden lights require no wiring as they charge during the daytime from the sun's rays, which makes them easy to install. However, they do require a sunny position, although some models will still gain some charge on an overcast day. Solar lights generally come on automatically at dusk, but some have a manual over-ride switch. They do not provide bright surrounding light, but are ideal for marking pathways and garden features with a gentle glowing light.

www.naturalresourcegroup.co.uk

SOLAR DOOR CHIMES

If proof were needed that technology has infiltrated every area of our lives, just look at the doorbell: whatever happened to knocking on the door? Nevertheless, for noisy neighbourhoods and big houses, one company has come up with an innovative, environmentally friendly alternative to the battery-powered doorbell. The solar door chime uses a bell push unit and a solar panel, which keeps a small battery charged so the chime works in all light levels and at night. The unit comes with an electronic two-tone chime, five metres of connecting wire and full installation instructions.

www.greenshop.co.uk

GOOD
TRAVEL

- Cars
- Holidays
- Petrol stations

"Of course I'm worried about climate change, but what can I do?"

If you're worried about climate change, you're certainly not alone.

There are millions of us around the world, and together we can make a powerful difference.

○ We can make the world's governments turn their promises into action.

○ We can campaign for serious investments in wind, wave and solar power.

○ We can persuade the UK Government to reject the dangerous alternative of expanding nuclear power.

Join us today, and be part of the solution.

To join, call us now on 0800 581 051

To find out more or to join online, visit our website www.foe.co.uk

Friends of the Earth

Friends of the Earth inspires solutions to environmental problems, which make life better for people

Introduction

For most people a holiday is time out from the hassles and worries of everyday life, but unfortunately a break for us does not mean time off for the environment. As more holidaymakers choose to travel abroad, and the destinations they travel to become more remote, the impact of tourism on local residents, wildlife and the environment will continue to increase.

Air travel is thought to be one of the biggest causes of climate change, and with the rise of low-cost flights it is only set to get bigger. A return trip from London Heathrow to New York dumps over one and a half tonnes of carbon dioxide into the atmosphere – that's a lot of trees to replant in compensation. Many campaigners believe that although carbon offsetting (planting trees or aiding renewable energy projects to offset the damage caused by your flight) is a positive step for the environment, it is no comparison to not flying at all.

As an alternative to the traditional fortnight in the sun, many smaller companies are now offering eco-tourism packages, which enable holidaymakers to visit areas that are carefully managed to reduce the impact of their visit. Some ask visitors to help with conservation work in the area they stay in. It is possible, with careful planning, to have a relaxing *and* ethical holiday, and the Good Travel section has been designed to help you make the best choices.

Back at home, a car continues to be a necessity for many of us, at least until the day when public transport becomes universally available, affordable and on time. Nevertheless, it is possible to make the best of a bad situation: ignore the continuing trend for 4x4 'Chelsea tractors' and investigate eco-friendly hybrid cars – such as the one driven by Conservative leader David Cameron. In this section are details of the greenest cars on the market today – and, in the chapter on petrol stations, the greenest fuel to go with them.

Cars

The motor industry is a land of real contrasts. Yes, there are still far too many people driving eco-trashing gas guzzlers, but in recent years we have become far more aware of the negative influence cars have on the environment. High profile figures such as David Cameron and Gordon Brown have recognised the political capital of making the switch to green transport, which could turn out to be the first step toward its popularisation.

NASTY EMISSIONS

Road traffic caused 125.3 million tonnes of greenhouse gas emissions in 2002, which accounts for more than 18 per cent of all greenhouse emissions. Experts have been developing new ways to make cars environmentally friendly and ensure the greater safety of passengers. These include finding ways to reduce the level of toxic and greenhouse gases emitted by new cars and improving their efficiency through better maintenance.

The European Union is the biggest car manufacturer in the world with 14,815 million units being made each year, followed by Northern America, which produces half of this number. In Europe, Germany is the biggest manufacturer, producing more than one third of the European total; it is often described as the 'car nation'. The UK is the second largest market with over 2 million new car registrations.

THE BIRTH OF THE CAR

The first car was created in 1876 when Nicolaus August Otto, in co-operation with Eugen Langen, Gottfied Daimler and Wilhelm Maybach, developed the Otto-Motor. The Otto-Motor was the machine that ended the extensive search for a competent main engine. Gottfiend Daimler was the first to use the motor in a vehicle and to further develop the gas motor into a petrol engine. This meant that a gas pipe was no longer necessary, making the engine moveable. In 1886 the first four-wheel vehicle was developed, which travelled at 16 kilometres per hour.

By 1914 55,000 private cars and about 9,000 lorries were on Germany's streets. Four years later the first cars reached the UK market, built mainly from steel. King Edward VII had a strong interest in motoring, so cars soon became accepted for the rich as a convenient method of travel.

CARBON MONOXIDE

In recent years we have recognised that the car is one of the major sources of modern day pollution. In particular they emit high levels of harmful carbon monoxide. Carbon monoxide in low levels is mainly harmless and only a threat to people with cardiovascular disease. But in larger amounts, as in cities, it is a threat to everyone. It is a colourless and odourless poison that affects the oxygen transport in the human body.

CARBON DIOXIDE

Carbon dioxide, which is also emitted by cars, is the most important greenhouse gas and therefore plays a major part in causing climate change. Although there are many more cars on the roads, and cars have become heavier due to higher safety requirements, engines have become much more efficient.

The good news, then, is that in the last few years CO_2 emissions from cars have actually decreased, thanks to agreements between car manufacturers and governments.

NITROGEN OXIDES

The nitrogen oxides released by car exhausts are a major contributor to the production of smog. Sunlight reacts with air pollutants to form a photochemical smog made up of ground-level ozone. Smog is a particular problem in urban areas, where it can have a severe effect on health.

EUROPEAN EMISSION STANDARDS

The European Commission introduced the 'Euro standard' at the beginning of the 1990s, a long-term development plan to reduce emissions from new cars. Each new car has to meet the target, currently the Euro IV standard.

EURO I	31 December 1992
EURO II	1 January 1997
EURO III	1 January 2001
EURO IV	1 January 2006

In 1998 the European Car Manufacturer Association agreed to reduce CO_2 emissions by 25 per cent within ten years – the aim was to reduce averages from 186g CO_2/km to 140g/km by the year 2008.

Heavy diesel engines (buses and lorries) will have to be converted significantly to meet the current Euro IV standard.

The introduction of Euro standards has already yielded fruit. Although car numbers have significantly grown over the last 20 years, the real level of emissions has decreased within the last decade.

The Euro V standard will not be brought in until 2011, but incentives may be used to persuade manufacturers to make the switch earlier. Promisingly, some countries outside the EU have begun to adopt their own versions of the standards.

The 'green' label

In the UK, legislation is going to introduce coloured labels to let potential buyers see at a glance how polluting different cars are. The labels are based on the emissions of CO_2. By 2005, all new four-wheel cars featured these coloured buttons. The lower the emissions, the greener the label. The number in the strip indicates the number of grams of CO_2 emitted per kilometre travelled (e.g. 101-120g CO_2 /km).

Below is a sample of fuel consumption from different cars, showing the huge range in figures.

Honda Insight:	**80g/km**
Toyota Prius:	**104g/km**
Smart City Coupe Hatchback:	**121g/km**
Vauxhall New Astra:	**151g/km**
Ford Mondeo 1.8 Sci Ghia:	**179g/km**
BMW 520I SE:	**219g/km**

Britain's greenest car – the G-Wiz

The G-Wiz is an electric car developed by Reva, an Indian company. It has fast become popular in London where it is distributed by GoinGreen. Apart from the fact that the car is 100 per cent emission free, it is exempt from the London congestion charge, and you get free parking in many areas and car parks.

Costs: The list price is £6,999, which may not seem that cheap but there are few additional costs and the daily running-cost savings really make the difference to your pocket as well as the environment.

Charging the battery: This takes 2.5 to 6 hours. Many car parks offer free charging facilities.

Disadvantage: It can be cold inside the car in winter.

Driving power: The top speed is 40mph with a battery cruising rate of about 40 miles (depending on how you drive it!)

For more information about the G-Wiz, visit *www.goingreen.co.uk*.

TIPS FOR GREENER TRAVEL

BEFORE YOU TRAVEL

- Think about the possibility of selling the car if it is not really necessary. Public transport is a great alternative

- Avoid using the car for short journeys – walk or use a bicycle

- Plan your journey carefully. Listen to the traffic news and try to avoid overcrowded routes to avoid sitting in jams

- Remove roof racks to reduce wind resistance

- Do not carry heavy objects in your car boot as a heavy car consumes more fuel

- Check that your tyres have the right pressure

WHEN DRIVING

- Drive smoothly and efficiently. Avoid fast acceleration and sudden breaking as this uses more fuel

- Driving slowly and in higher gears uses less fuel

- Switch your engine off when you know you will be waiting in a jam for more than two minutes

- Inspect your car regularly to keep your engine efficiency at the highest possible level

- Unnecessary electrical devices and air conditioning increase fuel consumption

- Check your fuel consumption regularly. If you recognise any changes there may be something wrong with the engine

BUYING A NEW CAR

- If you cannot live without a car, think about the possibility of car sharing, perhaps within the family. Maybe one car is enough, instead of two or three

- If you really need to buy a car, buy a new one – the newer the better! New cars are more environmentally friendly and less polluting

- Your car should be as small as possible as these are more fuel efficient

GREEN ADVANCES IN THE CAR INDUSTRY

- In the 1930s the average car travelled 25 miles per gallon with a top speed of 60mph. Today the most efficient models can travel 50 or 60 miles per gallon. Other advances are diesel and unleaded fuel, which are kinder to the environment

- Other areas need increased investment to help lessen the environmental impact of the car. These include fuel alternatives, legislation and further improved engines

THE TEN GREENEST MAINSTREAM CARS

Unless you buy an electric car and have signed up to a renewable energy tariff, it is impossible to drive without creating any pollution, but some cars are less harmful to the environment than others. The Environmental Transport Association recently listed the following as its top ten greenest cars:

1) Honda Civic 1.4 IMA Executive
The Honda Civic 1.3 came top of the ETA's list in 2005. The 1.4 has both a petrol engine and an electric motor for greatest efficiency. When it accelerates or goes uphill the electro motor engages, reducing emissions. The car has very low carbon dioxide emissions at 116g/km, an engine capacity of 1339cc and a fuel cost of £758 per 12,000 miles.

2) Toyota Prius 1.5 VVT-i Hybrid
The Prius has a strange design, is relatively expensive and has little boot space. So why has it been voted 'car of the year' by motoring journalists in 22 countries? The clue is the battery, which is stored under the rear seats and recharges itself when the breaks are applied. It can run off the battery alone but not over long distances. A very economical car with low CO_2 emissions of 104g/km.

3) Citroen C1 1.0i
The Citroen C1 hatchback is a good city car, being small and manoeuvrable – so hopefully easier to park in small spaces. It has a petrol engine and very low CO_2 emissions at 109g/km. The fuel cost of £711 per 12,000 miles is more than reasonable, making this an excellent choice for the green-minded driver.

4) Toyota Yaris 1.0 VVT-i
The Toyota Yaris fell into the supermini category of the ETA's survey, and was the winner of its group. Despite slightly higher CO_2 emissions of 134g/km, the Yaris still has a much lower environmental impact than most cars on the market. Its fuel cost is £866 per 12,000 miles, and the engine capacity is 998cc.

5) Daihatsu New Sirion M300 1.0L Efi
The Daihatsu hatchback is a spacious and economical car. At 118g/km, its CO_2 emissions could be better, but it comes out well in the survey overall. The engine capacity is 998cc and fuel costs are an a verage £772 per 12,000 miles. A good city car.

6) Suzuki Swift 1.3 GLZ
Runner-up in the supermini category, the Suzuki Swift is a stylish diesel car. This three-door hatchback has excellent carbon dioxide emissions of 112g/km and fuel costs of £746 per 12,000 miles. Its carbon monoxide emissions are also particularly low, making this mainstream car a good environmental choice.

7) Vauxhall Corsa 1.3CDTi
The Corsa five-door hatchback has a diesel engine with low CO_2 emissions. The engine also means consumption savings, so although this is not the cheapest model, money can be saved by driving the car. Its fuel consumption works out at a very reasonable £714 per 12,000 miles. The Corsa is a popular choice and comfortable to drive.

8) Peugeot 107 1.0
With a very acceptable CO_2 emission level of 109g/kms, the Peugeot is a good performer with a spacious interior. Slightly less chic than some of the other cars in its supermini category, the 107 nevertheless has a low fuel cost, at £712 per 12,000 miles, and is a good all-round car.

9) Toyota Aygo 1.0 VVT-i
The third Toyota in the list, the Aygo hatchback comes in both a three and five door model. It has a petrol engine of 998cc capacity, and the carbon dioxide emissions of this car are excellent at 109g/km. Fuel costs are £711 per 12,000, one of the lowest in the table.

10) Ford Fiesta 1.4 Duratorq TDCi
The diesel Ford Fiesta hatchback has slightly higher CO_2 emissions of 119g/km but is still a good eco-friendly buy amongst mainstream vehicles. It has a higher engine capacity at 1399cc, and reasonable fuel costs of £730 per 12,000 miles. A user-friendly car with low carbon monoxide emissions.

THE TEN LEAST GREEN CARS

The ETA also publishes a list of the least environmentally friendly cars. The worst are the ones which are the least economical and fuel-efficient. Their CO_2 emissions are twice those of the ten greenest cars, or even higher. Interestingly, all ten cars fall into the luxury or off-road segment of the market.

	Fuel Type	CO2 (g/km)	Fuel costs / 12,000 miles (£)	Tax band
Lamborghini Diablo 132	Petrol	520	3357	F
Bentley Arnage RL	Petrol	495	3186	F
Aston Martin Lagonda V12 Vanquish S	Petrol	448	2929	F
Aston Martin Lagonda DB9	Petrol	421	2762	F
Bentley Continental Flying Spur	Petrol	423	2728	F
Rolls-Royce Phantom	Petrol	385	2452	F
Chrysler Jeep New Grand Cherokee 5.71	Petrol	366	2385	F
Porsche Cayenne S 6 Speed	Petrol	317	2039	F
Corvette C6 7.0 V8	Petrol	350	2273	F
Volkswagen Phaeton 6.0 4Motion	Petrol	374	2411	F

CARS IN THE FUTURE

Although cars remain an enormous threat to our world and our health, the first steps have been taken to make our environment cleaner and more pleasant to live in.

Specialists forecast an enormous fall in car emissions, especially between 2010 and 2020. When the new labels are introduced in the UK it can be assumed that people will become more aware of the impact of car pollution. It is hoped that these labels will then be introduced in all European countries.

The introduction of hybrid cars has shown that manufacturers are aware of the need to improve cars and decrease emissions, and their adoption by a number of high-level MPs may help to increase their profile within the general population. Moreover, the introduction of 100 per cent electronic vehicles is a radical step towards reducing emissions in our cities.

SOURCES

More information on the environmental problems associated with cars and the organisations that are trying to prevent them can be found on the following websites.

- The Environmental Transport Association
  www.eta.co.uk

- Friends of the Earth
  Link to July 2006 report, 'Driving Up Carbon Emissions From Road Transport'
  www.foe.co.uk/resource/ briefings/driving-up-co2-emissions.pdf

- The Department for Transport
  Information on current legislation
  www.dft.gov.uk

- The European Commission
  www.ec.europa.eu

- Aixam Mega
- Citroen C21.4 Diesel
- G-Wiz

- Honda Civic IMA
- Lexus RX400h

- LPG Smart
- Toyota Prius
- Vauxhall Corsa Dual Fuel 1.2
- Volvo V70 Bi-fuel

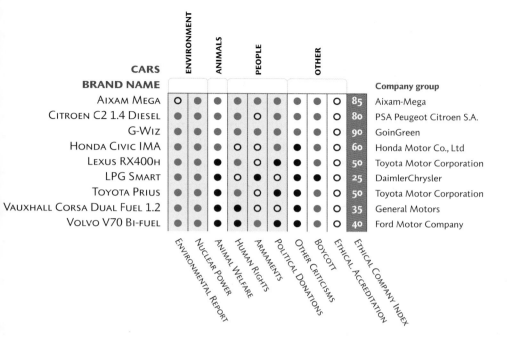

CARS BRAND NAME	ENVIRONMENT		ANIMALS	PEOPLE			OTHER			Ethical Company Index	Company group
	Environmental Report	Nuclear Power	Animal Welfare	Human Rights	Armaments	Political Donations	Other Criticisms	Boycott	Ethical Accreditation		
Aixam Mega	○	●	●	●	●	●	●	●	○	85	Aixam-Mega
Citroen C2 1.4 Diesel	●	●	●	●	○	●	●	●	○	80	PSA Peugeot Citroen S.A.
G-Wiz	●	●	●	●	●	●	●	●	○	90	GoinGreen
Honda Civic IMA	●	●	●	○	○	●	●	●	○	60	Honda Motor Co., Ltd
Lexus RX400h	●	●	●	●	○	●	●	●	○	50	Toyota Motor Corporation
LPG Smart	●	●	●	○	●	○	●	●	○	25	DaimlerChrysler
Toyota Prius	●	●	●	●	●	●	●	●	○	50	Toyota Motor Corporation
Vauxhall Corsa Dual Fuel 1.2	●	●	●	●	○	○	●	●	○	35	General Motors
Volvo V70 Bi-fuel	●	●	●	●	●	●	●	●	○	40	Ford Motor Company

Key

● Top rating

○ Middle rating

● Bottom rating

Source: The Ethical Company Organisation

Holidays

Whether the holiday season takes us to the Caribbean or Croatia, Spain or the Seychelles, tourism can have a potentially devastating effect on the culture, economy and environment of our destination. Air transport, which has been recognised as a significant contributor to climate change, is perhaps the worst culprit. However, by choosing the resort carefully and avoiding developments that impact on the local area, it is possible to plan a guilt-free getaway.

THE COST OF FLYING

As more planes do frequent short-haul flights, staying in the air most of the working day, the cost of flying is coming down. Yet the cost is not just to our own pockets: it's a heavy price for the environment to pay as well. A London-New York return flight releases more carbon dioxide per passenger than the average British motorist produces in 12 months. Crucially, fuel emissions in the upper atmosphere hurt the ozone layer more directly than those on the ground. Scientists predict that by 2015 half the annual destruction of the ozone layer may be caused by aircraft.

Some tourists now 'carbon offset' their flights, by donating money to organisations that work towards reducing the amount of carbon dioxide in the atmosphere. This removes an equivalent amount of CO_2 from the atmosphere through other means, such as planting trees.

Package holidays that include the cost of the flight, hotel and meals may seem to be a great bargain, but there are hidden problems associated with this type of travel.

The money paid for a package holiday benefits the tour operator much more than it does the people who provide the services when we arrive.

More than half the foreign holidays taken by British people every year are sold as packages by the few big companies that dominate the trade. Packages leave less chance for holidaymakers to engage directly with the places they visit.

A WESTERN PASTIME

Tourism is predominantly a Western pastime. It can encourage us to respect different cultures, but it can also add to the difficulties of the faraway communities with which we interact.

Images of local and indigenous people are used in tourist marketing to sell different destinations. Brochures for Kenya nearly always feature Masai warriors, but what they don't tell you is that Masai communities have been evicted from their land to make way for some of Kenya's famous national parks, including Amboseli.

In Goa, developers of a five-star hotel forced farmers to hand over their farms for a golf course by shutting off irrigation for their fields. In Peru, communities of Yagua Indians have been coerced to move nearer the tourist lodges so that they can be photographed more conveniently. In Burma, the government forcibly moved local people so as to develop the site around the temples at Pagan.

In general, the poorer the local people are, the easier it is for the tourism developers to push them aside or employ them in a new way of life, catering for international visitors.

DEGRADATION

It is easy to see how tourism can encourage begging and hustling. It transforms traditions of hospitality into commercial transactions. Tourism can also reduce cultural traditions into meaningless sights and attractions, as when sacred dances are performed as after-dinner shows in luxury hotels.

The expansion of international travel is also a big factor in the growth of international prostitution, contributing to the negative images of great cities like Bangkok, but also occurring in much smaller and more vulnerable societies than Thailand, with distorting cultural and economic effects.

When tourism becomes a big factor in a small economy, it can shift the traditional economic balance away from farming or hunting, and lure away the brightest people in the community, who would otherwise be able to play a productive part in educating the next generation. The hustle of the tourist trade has come to have more importance than the survival of the old traditions and their positive development for the 21st century. If this goes on, there could soon be no 'exotic' people left.

HINTS FOR A GREENER TRAVELLER

- The 'darkest green' travellers may choose to take their holidays in the UK or close to home
- Air travellers with a green conscience can make donations to environmental organisations such as Future Forests (*www.futureforests.com*), Climate Care (*www.climatecare.org*) and Carbon Storage Trust. You pay a levy based on the length of each flight, and they plant trees or find other ways to absorb carbon dioxide. Otherwise you can make back the cost by switching your electricity to a 100 per cent renewable electricity supplier
- Become better informed about the effects of air travel (see *www.chooseclimate.org*)
- When arriving in a strange country, be sure to learn at least some of the language
- Visit local cafés and restaurants and talk to local people away from the main tourist centres
- Choose an eco-friendly holiday company – see the Ethical Network at the back of this book
- Find out more about these and other issues at *www.tourismconcern.org.uk*, who we thank for helping with this section

Petrol stations

Petrol companies are not known for their ethical credentials, but with the right choice it is possible to support the ones that are doing the most to lessen their industry's impact on the environment. There is scope to avoid the most damaging chemicals found in common petrols, but even better would be to invest in a car that runs on one of the many alternative fuels now available, such as bio diesel or ethanol.

CATALYTIC CONVERTERS

Catalytic converters are found on all new cars sold in Britain, and work by converting the gases generated in the combustion of petrol into other substances such as carbon dioxide and water. Carbon monoxide, hydrocarbons and nitrogen oxides in a car's exhaust fumes can cause acid rain, and have been associated with problems for people with lung conditions such as asthma. A catalytic converter can get rid of up to 90 per cent of these gases. They also help reduce the amount of benzene (a known carcinogen) that escapes into the atmosphere during the combustion process.

However, although catalytic converters help to reduce the harmful chemicals found in car exhausts, they don't eliminate them completely – and they have no suppressive effect on the amount of CO_2 the car produces. According to the Environmental Transport Association, 58 per cent of car journeys in Britain are less than the distance it takes for the car's engine to warm up sufficiently for the catalytic converter to work.

ALTERNATIVE FUELS

Petrol is a finite resource, and as the oil it comes from begins to run dry, the car drivers of the world will have to find something else to power their vehicles. But why wait until then when there are many alternatives already available? In the last few years an increasing number of drivers have realised that it is already possible to switch to a 'green' fuel.

The main advantage of running a non-petrol car is that the fuel is much less expensive than normal petrol. Other advantages are that the car is exempt from the London Congestion Charge, and the owner may also qualify for other discounts and concessions.

The Energy Saving Trust (*www.est.org.uk*) publishes a map to help drivers locate refuelling stations for six different types of alternative fuel across the UK. These details are also available from individual retailers.

Alternative fuels can be made out of anything from chip fat to plant matter or even alcohol. The table overleaf includes information about four of the most popular options.

THESE ARE THE MAIN FUEL ALTERNATIVES:

BIO DIESEL

Bio diesel is one of the top alternative fuels. It is similar to normal diesel but is made from mainly renewable resources, such as plants and animal waste. However, it is not a very clean option. It can be used in light or heavy-duty diesel engines, but this needs to be checked with the manufacturer first.

ELECTRICITY

Cars that get their power from a rechargeable battery are completely emission free, although it must not be forgotten that the production of electricity itself is a source of pollution. The capacity of an electric car is restricted as the battery generally only lasts for about 50 miles.

ALCOHOL

Alcohol fuels are generally made from methanol and ethanol. Ethanol is made from agricultural biological waste while methanol is produced from biomasses such as coal. Today it is more often made from natural gas as this is cheaper. Ethanol produces less carbon monoxide and carbon dioxide than conventional cars.

LIQUEFIED NATURAL GAS

This could be one of the best contenders as an alternative to petrol. The energy density of natural gas is better than any other fuel and, with its high octane content, it is extremely efficient. Natural gas cars come either with a single tank dedicated to natural gas, or with two tanks: one for natural gas and a second for another fuel type. Cars which run exclusively on natural gas have the advantage that their engine is entirely optimised for natural gas, plus the fact that they are lighter as they only have one tank.

- Save
- UK

- Jet
- Murco

- BP
- Esso
- Shell
- Texaco
- TOTAL

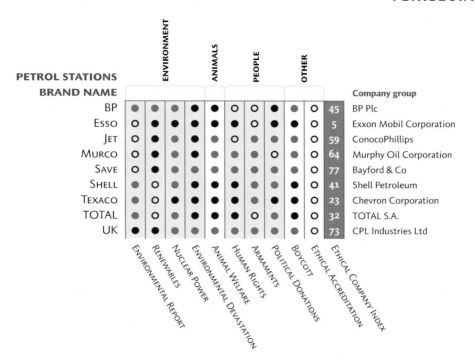

PETROL STATIONS BRAND NAME	ENVIRONMENT				ANIMALS	PEOPLE		OTHER		Ethical Accreditation	Ethical Company Index	Company group
	Environmental Report	Renewables	Nuclear Power	Environmental Devastation	Animal Welfare	Human Rights	Armaments	Political Donations	Boycott			
BP	●	●	●	●	●	○	○	●	●	○	45	BP Plc
Esso	○	●	●	●	●	●	○	●	●	○	5	Exxon Mobil Corporation
Jet	○	●	●	●	●	○	●	●	●	○	59	ConocoPhillips
Murco	○	●	●	●	●	●	●	○	●	○	64	Murphy Oil Corporation
Save	○	●	●	●	●	●	●	●	●	○	77	Bayford & Co
Shell	●	○	●	●	●	●	●	●	●	○	41	Shell Petroleum
Texaco	●	○	●	●	●	●	●	●	●	○	23	Chevron Corporation
TOTAL	●	○	●	●	●	●	○	●	●	○	32	TOTAL S.A.
UK	●	●	●	●	●	●	●	●	●	○	73	CPL Industries Ltd

Key

● Top rating

○ Middle rating

● Bottom rating

Source: The Ethical Company Organisation

GOOD
MONEY

Introduction

So far this book has covered how to spend your money, but what about how to save it? The following pages include all the information you need to make good choices on where and how to invest.

Savers often move their bank accounts to take advantage of the best interest rates, but few of us think of using the same process when it comes to the most ethical banks. With more Britons than ever before living in the red, whether it's through loans, credit cards or student debt, choosing a bank that operates transparently and does not encourage unnecessary spending is crucial. The major credit card companies in particular have been accused of irresponsible marketing, and of making large sums of money available to those who cannot necessarily afford the repayments.

Switching bank accounts no longer needs to be a lengthy and complex ordeal, and with internet banks increasing in popularity most of the research can be done at home. In fact, this section does much of the work for you, looking in depth at the most common criticisms levelled at the high street banks, building societies and mortgage lenders.

One of the most widespread contentions is with the banks' involvement in unethical lending. This can range from investment in questionable corporations to holdings of Third World debt. As well as exposing those brands that still use their money unwisely, this section looks at the companies that are doing the most to promote socially responsible investment.

Amongst these are the funds profiled in the ethical investment section, which finds out how shareholder power can be used to protest against company policies. If the prospect of investing in ethical business seems like a luxury, there are plenty of opportunities to support the charities and associations who campaign on environmental and human rights issues – see the section on charity credit cards, or the non-governmental organisation listings at the back of the book.

Making the switch to a responsible bank is the first, simple step towards ethical spending.

Banks and building societies

Banks and building societies claim to have their customers' best interests at heart, but are they really listening? Most of us choose our banks or building societies for reasons of convenience – simply because there's a branch around the corner or because we had an account with a predecessor of one of today's conglomerates. As customers we should keep tracks on the way our banks behave, particularly in their relationships with the developing world.

DODGY LENDING

The big banks have a notoriously bad history. Even in the last five years, banks have been condemned for funding rainforest destruction, for their involvement in highly controversial dam and gas-pipeline projects, and for lending to governments of the world's poorest countries so they can buy expensive military equipment.

Since some mutual building societies don't take business customers, they can never fund dubious business practices. Of those in the table, the Coventry, Yorkshire, Leeds and Bradford & Bingley do not lend commercially.

Perhaps the most rewarding way to store our money is with banks that have progressive investment policies. Charity Bank, the world's first not-for-profit bank, only invests in the charitable sector, and Triodos Bank lends solely to projects that add cultural value or are of benefit to people and the environment. Of course, the Co-op Bank has a transparent and comprehensive lending policy, available on their website.

THIRD WORLD CONCERNS

Several British banks – most notably Lloyds (now Lloyds TSB) and Midland (now HSBC) – were the focus of campaigns in the 1980s and 90s over their holdings of Third World debt. Much of this has now been written off as the banks realised that they were unlikely to recoup the loans, and that they were acquiring significant bad publicity. Some, such as the Bank of Scotland, 'swapped' their poorest-country debts for commitments by national governments that they would use the money for domestic development programmes. However, the Ethical Investment Research Service (EIRIS) has listed some high street banks as still holding Third World debt – see *www.eiris.org*.

British banks have been the target of other important campaigns about their holding of World Bank bonds, their involvement in the kind of currency speculation that has ruined many developing countries, and their support for the World Trade Organisation's controversial agreement on trade and services. Some of these issues are indicated on the table.

ETHICAL HEALTH CHECK

Information on the environmental and social policies and reporting standards of a range of banks can be found in an EIRIS factsheet, available from 0845 606 0324 or *www.eiris.org*. Charity Bank are the first bank to become members of the Ethical Company Organisation's accreditation scheme.

- Charity Bank
- Chelsea BS
- Co-op Bank
- Ecology BS
- Triodos Bank

- Alliance & Leicester
- Bank of Ireland
- Bank of Scotland
- Bradford & Bingley
- Bristol & West
- Britannia BS
- Chelsea BS
- Cheshire BS
- Coventry BS
- Derbyshire BS
- Leeds
- Nationwide BS
- Norwich & Peterborough BS
- Skipton BS
- Yorkshire BS

- Abbey
- AIB
- Barclays
- Citibank
- Clydesdale
- egg
- Halifax
- HSBC
- Lloyds TSB
- Natwest
- Northern Rock
- Prudential
- Woolwich
- Yorkshire Bank

BANKS AND BUILDING SOCIETIES BRAND NAMES

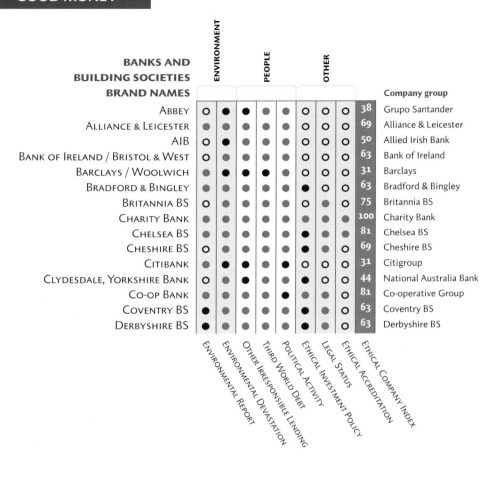

Columns: ENVIRONMENT | PEOPLE | OTHER

Row categories (diagonal labels): Environmental Report, Environmental Devastation, Other Irresponsible Lending, Third World Debt, Political Activity, Ethical Investment Policy, Legal Status, Ethical Accreditation, Ethical Company Index

Brand name	Score	Company group
ABBEY	38	Grupo Santander
ALLIANCE & LEICESTER	69	Alliance & Leicester
AIB	50	Allied Irish Bank
BANK OF IRELAND / BRISTOL & WEST	63	Bank of Ireland
BARCLAYS / WOOLWICH	31	Barclays
BRADFORD & BINGLEY	63	Bradford & Bingley
BRITANNIA BS	75	Britannia BS
CHARITY BANK	100	Charity Bank
CHELSEA BS	81	Chelsea BS
CHESHIRE BS	69	Cheshire BS
CITIBANK	31	Citigroup
CLYDESDALE, YORKSHIRE BANK	44	National Australia Bank
CO-OP BANK	81	Co-operative Group
COVENTRY BS	63	Coventry BS
DERBYSHIRE BS	63	Derbyshire BS

Key

● Top rating
○ Middle rating
● Bottom rating

Source: The Ethical Company Organisation (2008)

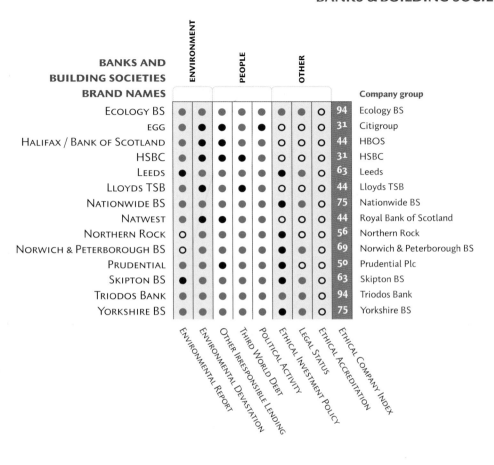

Key

● Top rating

○ Middle rating

● Bottom rating

Source: The Ethical Company Organisation (2008)

Charity credit cards

Credit card loans are a big factor in Britain's soaring consumer debt, and credit card companies have come under attack for irresponsible selling strategies. Sophisticated direct marketing enables companies to target vulnerable people who are more likely to be tempted by credit card loans. A survey by homeless charity Centrepoint revealed that almost a quarter of homeless youngsters had received letters from credit card companies, urging them to apply for loans.

DEBT

There has been much talk of Britain's spiralling debt problem: half a million people have 'crippling debts on their credit cards' according to the National Consumer Council, and advice services such as Debt Free Direct say they received 275 per cent more calls per day in December 2004 than they did a year earlier.

In 2004, after three high-profile suicides by men who had racked up huge credit card debts, HBOS, Lloyds TSB and Capital One were accused by MPs of encouraging young people to get into debt they couldn't handle. Capital One, in particular, was condemned for aggressive marketing and its failure to make clear the cost of repayment.

Many major banks and credit card companies bombard supposedly susceptible households with junk mail and offers of unbeatable deals. The Office of Fair Trading has said that misleading advertising by credit card companies included using introductory rates to lower their overall APR.

CHARITY CREDIT CARDS

Charity credit cards raise money for good causes without serious cost to the customer. Nowadays there are plenty on offer, most of which let the holder choose which charities they wish to support. Single charities issue the cards to raise money and to win publicity. Several banks co-operate closely with them, but not all.

The cards raise money for a charity when the card is first taken out or first used, and from then on a small percentage, for example 25p for every £100 used, goes straight to the charity.

Few affinity cards charge an annual fee, but it is worth checking on this before taking one. Some have low introductory rates of interest in the first few months, but in general the rates are close to the average available at any one time. However, this is irrelevant if the bill is paid off in full, as most affinity cardholders apparently do. As the donations depend on the money spent, not on the size of the outstanding balance, there is no loss to the charity if the card is cleared every month. Many banks have been happy to co-operate not only with conventional charities but also with sports clubs, hobby groups and professional organisations, seeing it as a way to gain market share. In terms of ethics, it makes little difference whether the card is Visa or Mastercard. It is more appropriate to ask which bank the charity has teamed up with to issue its credit card. Some of the banks have resisted becoming involved, considering cards too costly to administer or being reluctant to pay VAT on donations.

THE BANKS

Of the UK high street banks, Royal Bank of Scotland, the Co-op Bank, Halifax and Bank of Scotland (both part of HBOS), all offer charity-linked cards. US bank MBNA jointly issues affinity cards with charities. Co-op Bank cards support, amongst others, Amnesty International, Greenpeace, Help the Aged, Save the Children, Oxfam and the RSPB. Halifax has cards that support Cancer Research UK, Mencap and the NSPCC.

THE PVC ISSUE

The Co-operative Bank's Greenpeace credit card, launched in 1998, was the first non-PVC card to enter the market. Although the bank made a commitment to convert all its cards to non-PVC plastic by 2000, there does not appear to have been any progress on the issue. No other UK card issuers seem to have followed their lead, despite the cumulative toxic effects of some of the chemicals involved in the manufacture and disposal of PVC.

See *www.gooshing.co.uk* for the best deals on a range of ethical financial products.

- Co-op Bank

- Alliance & Leicester
- Bank of Scotland
- Halifax
- MBNA

- Abbey
- Barclaycard
- Capital One
- egg
- HSBC
- Lloyds TSB
- Morgan Stanley
- Natwest
- Royal Bank of Scotland

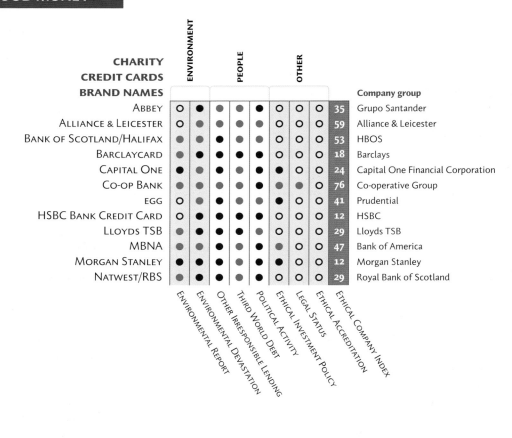

CHARITY
CREDIT CARDS
BRAND NAMES

ENVIRONMENT · PEOPLE · OTHER

Brand Name	Index	Company group
ABBEY	35	Grupo Santander
ALLIANCE & LEICESTER	59	Alliance & Leicester
BANK OF SCOTLAND/HALIFAX	53	HBOS
BARCLAYCARD	18	Barclays
CAPITAL ONE	24	Capital One Financial Corporation
CO-OP BANK	76	Co-operative Group
EGG	41	Prudential
HSBC BANK CREDIT CARD	12	HSBC
LLOYDS TSB	29	Lloyds TSB
MBNA	47	Bank of America
MORGAN STANLEY	12	Morgan Stanley
NATWEST/RBS	29	Royal Bank of Scotland

Column categories:
ENVIRONMENTAL REPORT
ENVIRONMENTAL DEVASTATION
OTHER IRRESPONSIBLE LENDING
THIRD WORLD DEBT
POLITICAL ACTIVITY
ETHICAL INVESTMENT POLICY
LEGAL STATUS
ETHICAL ACCREDITATION
ETHICAL COMPANY INDEX

Key
● Top rating
○ Middle rating
● Bottom rating
Source: The Ethical Company Organisation

Ethical investment

One of the most effective ways to put ethical consumerism into practise is through investment. The idea of using your money wisely has been around for a long time, but only recently has it become a mainstream means of supporting a good cause. With a growth in awareness about ethical investment's benefits on the part of companies as well as investors, it is becoming ever easier to put your money where your mouth is.

A LONG HISTORY

The roots of ethical investment can be traced to the religious movements of the nineteenth century, such as the Quakers and Methodists, whose concerns included issues such as temperance and fair employment conditions. At the beginning of the 1900s, the Methodist Church began investing in the stock market, consciously avoiding companies involved in alcohol and gambling.

During the twentieth century, more churches, charities and individuals began to take ethical criteria into account when making investment choices. An ethical investment ideology began to develop in the US as controversy over American involvement in the Vietnam war led to the founding of the Pax World Fund in 1971, which aimed to avoid investments associated with the war. In the 1980s, the apartheid regime in South Africa was the focal point for ethical investment and, indeed, its success as a tool of protest there accelerated its acceptance and growth around the world.

In 1983 the Ethical Investment Research Service (EIRIS) was established as the UK's first independent research service in ethical investment, providing the underlying research into companies' social, environmental and ethical performance needed by investors to make informed and socially responsible investment decisions. The UK's first ethically screened unit trust – the Stewardship Fund – was launched by Friends Provident a year later. Now there are over 60 ethical retail funds in the UK market, with an estimated value of £3.8 billion. This growth in SRI (socially responsible investment) has been reflected globally. For example, the Asia-Pacific region has seen the launch of several SRI funds in places such as Japan, Australia and Singapore. In Europe there were 170 ethical funds in 1999; by the end of 2001 the number had grown to over 280.

'Ethical' or 'socially responsible' investment describes any area of the financial sector where the principles of the investor inform where they place their money. Companies big and small have an increasingly large impact upon the world around them. How they conduct their business can affect all manner of things beyond the actual product or service they provide. There is a growing awareness that, alongside simply choosing to buy or not to buy their products, those of us who invest our spare money can also influence companies towards better social and environmental behaviour.

With any standard unit trust, investment trust, ISA or pension you may find your money going to companies that you would not wish to support. An ardent anti-smoker, for example, would be dismayed to discover that their savings were invested in a tobacco company. Whether your investments are limited to a pension fund, or if you're more involved in the stock market, knowing as much as you can about the ethics of the financial companies you're investing in can be as important as choosing an environmentally sound washing-up liquid. In fact, as a recent War on Want campaign (encouraging the 10 million people who are occupational pension scheme members to find out where their money is invested) shows, you can use your influence no matter how small your investments might seem.

How do I begin?

The first step towards positive investing is to identify what social, environmental and other ethical issues are most important to you. Areas of concern can be wide ranging, from animal testing to gambling, from human rights to nuclear power, from environmental enhancement to community involvement. Surveys by EIRIS have shown that the most prominent areas of concern are operations in oppressive regimes, breaking environmental regulations and testing products on animals. The companies that respondents preferred their pension funds to be invested in were those with good records on environmental issues and employment conditions. Identifying these areas will reflect the type of companies you want to invest in or to avoid.

Nobody's perfect

It is important, however, to remember that there is no such thing as a perfect company. All are involved in activities that someone somewhere will object to, and none go far enough in terms of positive social and environmental contribution to satisfy all of the people all of the time. Ethical investment is about compromising and prioritising.

Types of funds

Once you've worked out your individual criteria, there are a diverse range of ethical funds available, and different funds suit different investors. Some funds select a set of criteria which they believe will appeal to the widest range of investors. Others take a precisely focused approach, designed to appeal to a particular market. It is therefore very important to look behind the 'green' or 'ethical' label at what the fund is actually investing in before deciding to invest.

Ask:
- How does the fund research the activities of the companies in which it invests?
- Is there an ethical committee or advisory board that is independent of the investment process, to make sure the fund adheres to its published ethical policy?
- How good is the fund's communication with investors, e.g. does it have mechanisms in place to allow investors to voice their concerns?

• How active is the fund in engaging or communicating with companies? Does it encourage companies to improve their social and environmental performance?

ETHICAL STRATEGIES

There are three main strategies that funds can adopt to implement their ethical investment policies:

ENGAGEMENT

• No companies are excluded but areas are identified in which companies can improve their environmental, social and ethical performance. The fund managers then 'engage' with the companies to encourage them to make such improvements

PREFERENCE

• The funds adopt social, environmental or other ethical guidelines which they prefer companies to meet. These guidelines are applied where all other things are equal (e.g. financial performance)

SCREENING

• An acceptable list of companies is created based on chosen positive and/or negative criteria (e.g. avoid companies involved in the arms trade, include companies with good environmental performance and so on). Funds are invested only in those companies on the list

A TWO-PRONGED APPROACH

Ethical investing works in two ways:
• by using the individual's power as a shareholder to influence corporate behaviour
• by their decision to invest only in companies who behave in a socially responsible manner

SHAREHOLDER POWER

One method of shareholder influence, which is particularly useful for the publicity it often receives, is the practice of posting shareholder resolutions which companies then have to consider in public at their annual general meetings. Campaigners say that the rules governing who can put forward a shareholder resolution are more restrictive in the UK than in the US. Nonetheless, a prominent UK example is the resolution placed before BP's spring 2002 AGM, filed by the global environment network WWF, together with an international coalition of ethical investors, on its drilling activities in environmentally and culturally sensitive areas. This is one part of the campaign to prevent BP and others from drilling for oil in places such as the Alaskan Arctic National Wildlife Refuge, which is one of the last pristine areas left in the US and is currently off-limits to oil and gas exploration and development.

The idea of shareholder power is relatively new, but it is becoming more prominent amongst NGOs. It can have some real results, as the case study on the next page shows.

VOTING FOR CHANGE

Shareholder resolutions, one of the more flamboyant ways of investing ethically, have been shown to work. Friends of the Earth used a shareholder resolution as part of its campaign against Balfour Beatty's plans to build a controversial dam in Turkey – the Ilisu dam on the Tiber River, 40 kilometres from the border of Syria and Iraq. Protest groups warned that the dam would make 78,000 local people homeless and drown dozens of towns and villages, including the world historic site of Hasankeyf.

FoE bought £30,000 worth of shares in order to submit a resolution on the dam contract at Balfour Beatty's AGM. Some months later, the company pulled out of the project, announcing that 'after a thorough evaluation of the commercial, environmental and social issues, it is not in the best interests of our stakeholders to pursue the project further'.

ALTERNATIVE INVESTMENT

Ethical investment is not confined to shares traded in stock exchanges. Many investors prefer to back individual projects or causes. Such directed investment is known by a variety of terms including 'alternative' investment, 'mission-based' investment and 'socially directed' investment. Examples of cause-based investment include regeneration projects in Birmingham (through the Aston Reinvestment Trust), and the support of projects in developing countries (through the co-operative lending society, Shared Interest). The cause-based investment sector is currently dominated by financial institutions such as Triodos Bank and the Ecology Building Society, although it also includes ethical companies who raise money directly from stakeholders by selling 'ethical shares'. Such companies include Traidcraft and the Centre for Alternative Technology.

GOOD FOR EVERYBODY

You don't need to worry that concentrating on ethical investments will make your financial performance suffer. Research by EIRIS and others indicates that investing according to ethical criteria may make little difference to overall financial performance, depending on the ethical policy applied. Five ethical indexes created by EIRIS produced financial returns roughly equivalent to the returns from the FTSE All-Share Index. For example, the total return of the Charities' Avoidance Index, which excludes the vast majority of companies involved in tobacco, gambling, alcohol, military sales and pornography, was 0.38 per cent greater than the All-Share.

Companies, too, can benefit. Over £3 billion is already invested in companies screened for good social, environmental and ethical practice by retail investors. Many churches and charities, pension schemes and local authorities are also investing according to socially responsible investment policies. That means money is being consciously diverted from companies that cannot demonstrate this good practice. Many investors are also engaging with companies in which they invest, or are considering investing in, to persuade them to improve their policies and practices.

You can get further information by contacting the organisations listed below:

EIRIS's Guide to Ethical Funds covers the ethical retail funds (such as unit trusts, OEICs and investment trusts) available to the UK investor, giving a summary of each fund's ethical policy, top ten holdings and outlining what products (such as pensions or ISAs) are available with that fund.

EIRIS was established in 1983 by a group of churches and charities, and today it is one of the leading providers of independent corporate research for socially responsible investors. EIRIS has a wealth of information for people who want to apply their principles to their investments and finances. EIRIS can provide a directory of financial advisors who have expertise in advising on ethical investments (available from *www.eiris.org*).
EIRIS, 80-84 Bondway, London SW8 1SD
Tel: 0207 840 5700
Email: *ethics@eiris.org*

The UK Social Investment Forum is a membership network that promotes and encourages socially responsible investment in the UK, including shareholder activism, social banking and community finance (*www.uksif.org*).
Tel: 0207 749 9950

The European Sustainable and Responsible Investment Forum (Eurosif) is a non-profit organisation promoting the concept, practice and development of responsible and sustainable investment (*www.eurosif.info*).

For more information see *www.gooshing.co.uk*. Ethical Investments (*www.ethicalinvestments.co.uk*) and Shared Interest (*http://cust.shared-interest.com*) are members

of the Ethical Company Organisation's accreditation scheme – see the back of the book for more information on these ethically-certified companies.

ETHICAL FUNDS

Below is a list of the ethical funds that *The Good Shopping Guide* was happy to promote and EIRIS was aware of at the time of collating this information and had been given details on by the fund provider. There may be other ethical funds that are on the market that EIRIS was not aware of or had no information on at that time. Note that by providing this list we are not making recommendations. For further information you may want to seek independent financial advice.

EIRIS defines an ethical fund as any fund which decides that shares are acceptable or unacceptable according to positive or negative ethical criteria e.g. environmental criteria, human rights criteria etc. The exception to this rule is that we do not include funds that only exclude companies involved in tobacco products.

AMP NPI GLOBAL CARE FUNDS (GROWTH, INCOME, PENSION AND PENSION MANAGED)

Type of investment: OEIC (Growth and Income),
Pension Fund (Pension and Pension Managed),
Address: NPI House, 55 Calverly Road, Tunbridge Wells, Kent
Phone: 0189 251 5151

AXA WORLD FUNDS II – GLOBAL PORTFOLIO ECOLOGICAL FUND

Type of investment: Off-shore fund
Address: Sun Life Global Management Ltd, Royalty House, Walpole Ave, Douglas, Isle of Man IM1 2SL
Phone: 0162 464 3498
Fax: 0162 464 3541

AXA UK ETHICAL FUND
Type of investment: OEIC
Address: AXA Sun Life Fund Managers Ltd, MFD,
PO Box 1810, Bristol BS99 5SN
Phone: 0117 989 0808
Fax: 0117 989 0604

ABBEY LIFE ETHICAL TRUST
Type of investment: Unit Trust
Address: Abbey Life Investment Services Ltd, Abbey Life
Centre, 100 Holdenhurst Road, Bournemouth BH8 8AL
Phone: 0120 229 2373
Fax: 0120 229 2403

ABERDEEN ETHICAL WORLD OEIC
Type of investment: OEIC
Address: Aberdeen Unit Trust Managers Ltd, One Bow
Churchyard, Cheapside, London EC4M 9HH
Phone: 0845 300 2890
Fax: 0207 463 6507

**AEGON ETHICAL INCOME AND
SOCIALLY RESPONSIBLE FUNDS**
Type of investment: OEIC
Address: Aegon Asset Management plc, Aegon House,
3 Lochside Avenue, Edinburgh Park, Edinburgh EH12 9SE
Phone: 0800 169 5196
Fax: 0131 549 4264

ALLCHURCHES AMITY FUND
Type of investment: OEIC
Address: Allchurches Investment Management Services Ltd,
Beaufort House, Brunswick Road, Gloucester GL1 1JZ
Phone: 0145 230 5958
Fax: 0145 231 1690

**BARCHESTER BEST OF GREEN LIFE,
PENSION AND OFFSHORE FUNDS**
This fund also invests in the Jupiter Ecology Fund
Type of investment: Broker Bond
Address: Barchester Green Investment, Barchester House,
45 – 49 Catherine Street, Salisbury SP1 2DH
Phone: 0172 233 1241
Fax: 0172 241 4191

CIS ENVIRON TRUST
Type of investment: Unit Trust
Address: CIS Unit Trust Managers Ltd, PO Box 105,
Manchester M4 8BB
Phone: 0161 837 5060
Fax: 0161 837 4048

CITY FINANCIAL ETHICAL FUND
Type of investment: OEIC
Address: City Financial Investment Company Ltd, City
Financial Centre, 88 Borough High Street, London SE1 1ST
Phone: 0207 556 8888
Fax: 0207 556 8889

CREDIT SUISSE FELLOWSHIP FUND
Type of investment: OEIC
Address: Credit Suisse Asset Management Funds (UK) Ltd,
Beaufort House, 15 St Botolph Street, London EC3A 7JJ
Phone: 0207 426 2929
Fax: 0207 426 2959

**FRIENDS PROVIDENT STEWARDSHIP FUNDS (INCOME,
INTERNATIONAL, PENSION, LIFE AND UNIT)**
Type of investment: Unit Trusts and Pension Funds
Address: 72-122 Castle Street, Salisbury
Phone: 0870 600 6300
Fax: 0870 600 6366

FAMILY CHARITIES ETHICAL TRUST
Type of investment: Unit Trust
Address: 16 West St, Brighton BN1 2RE
Phone: 0127 372 5272
Fax: 0127 320 6026

HSBC AMANAH FUND
Type of investment: Fund based in Luxembourg
(Islamic Shariah Fund)
Address: 7 Rue du Marche-aux-Herbes, Luxembourg L-1728
Phone: 0035 247 6812 230
Fax: 0035 247 5569
NB: These numbers are for dealing and administration;
marketing materials should be obtained from the local HSBC
Asset Management Representative

HALIFAX ETHICAL TRUST
Type of investment: OEIC
Address: CMIM Retail Funds, 33 Old Broad Street, London EC2N 1HZ
Phone: 0129 639 3100
Fax: 0207 796 4824

HENDERSON ETHICAL FUND
Type of investment: OEIC
Address: Henderson Global Investors, 4 Broadgate, London EC2M 2DA
Phone: 0845 783 2832
Fax: 0207 956 9191

HOMEOWNERS FRIENDLY SOCIETY FTSE4GOOD UK FUND
Type of investment: Single premium bond or savings plans
Address: Homeowners Friendly Society Ltd, Hornbeam Avenue, Harrogate HG2 8XE
Phone: 0500 848 262
Fax: 0142 385 5181

ISIS UK ETHICAL TRUST
Type of investment: Unit trust
Address: 15 Old Bailey, London EC4M 7AP
Phone: 0207 506 1100
Fax: 0207 236 2060

IMPAX ENVIRONMENTAL MARKETS
Type of investment: Investment Company
Address: Crusader House, 145 – 157 St John St, London. EC1V 4RU
Phone: 0207 490 4355
Fax: 0207 336 0865

INSIGHT ETHICAL AND EVERGREEN FUNDS
Type of investment: OEIC sub fund
Address: Clerical Medical Ethical Fund, Narrow Plain, Bristol BS2 0JH
Phone: 0845 777 2233
Fax: 0845 777 2234

JUPITER ECOLOGY AND ENVIRONMENTAL OPPORTUNITIES FUNDS
Type of investment: Unit Trusts
Address: Jupiter Asset Management, 1 Grosvenor Place, London SW1X 7JJ
Phone: 0207 412 0703
Fax: 0207 412 0705

JUPITER GLOBAL GREEN INVESTMENT TRUST PLC
Type of investment: Investment Trust
Address: Jupiter Asset Management Ltd, PO Box 14470, London SW1X 7YM
Phone: 0845 306 0100

LEGAL AND GENERAL ETHICAL TRUST
Type of investment: Unit Trust
Address: Legal and General Investments, Bucklersbury House, 3 Queen Victoria Street, London EC4N 8NH
Phone: 0207 528 6200
Fax: 0207 528 6838

LINCOLN GREEN FUND
Invests in equities and Jupiter Ecology Fund.
Type of investment: Managed Life and Pension Funds
Address: Barnett Way, Barnwood, Gloucester GL4 3RZ
Phone: 0145 237 1371
Fax: 0145 237 4374

MERCHANT INVESTORS ASSURANCE ETHICAL CAUTIOUS MANAGED FUND
Type of investment: Managed Life and Pension Funds
Address: St Bartholomew's House, Lewins Mead, Bristol BS1 2NH
Phone: 0117 926 6366
Fax: 0117 975 2144

MINERVA GREEN PORTFOLIO AND GREEN PROTECTOR PORTFOLIO
Type of investment: Unit Trust
Address: Minerva Fund Managers Ltd, Kelston View, Corston, Bath BA2 9AH
Phone: 0122 587 2300
Fax: 0122 587 2301

MORLEY SUSTAINABLE FUTURE FUNDS
Type of investment: OEIC
Address: Morley Fund Management, 1 Poultry,
London. EC2R 8EJ
Phone: 0207 809 6000

NORWICH UNION UK ETHICAL FUND
Type of investment: Unit Trust
Address: Norwich Union Investment Management,
PO Box 4, Surrey Street, Norwich NR1 3NG
Phone: 0160 362 2200

OLD MUTUAL ETHICAL FUND
Type of investment: Unit Trust
Address: 5th Floor, 80 Cheapside, London, EC2V 6LS
Phone: 0207 332 7500
Fax: 0207 332 7550

QUADRIS ENVIRONMENTAL FUND
Type of investment: OEIC
Address: Regent House, 19 – 20 The Broadway,
Woking, Surrey. GU21 5AP
Phone: 0148 375 6800
Fax: 0148 377 6800

ST. JAMES'S PLACE ETHICAL FUND
Type of investment: Unit Trust
Address: St James's Place House, Dollar Street,
Cirencester. GL7 2AQ
Phone: 0128 564 0302
Fax: 0128 564 0436

SCOTTISH AMICABLE ETHICAL FUND
Type of investment: Unit Trust
Address: Scottish Amicable, Craigforth,
PO Box 25, Stirling FK9 4UE
Phone: 0178 644 8844
Fax: 0178 646 2134

SCOTTISH LIFE UK ETHICAL FUND
Type of investment: Pension Fund
Address: Scottish Life Assurance Company,
19 St Andrew's Square, Edinburgh EH12 1YE
Phone: 0131 456 7777
Fax: 0131 456 7421

**SCOTTISH WIDOWS ENVIRONMENTAL
INVESTOR FUND**
Type of investment: Unit Trust
Address: Scottish Widows Unit Trust Managers Ltd,
Charlton Place, Andover, Hants SP10 1RE
Phone: 0845 300 2244

SKANDIA ETHICAL PORTFOLIO
Type of investment: Managed life and pension fund
Address: Skandia Life, PO Box 37, Skandia House,
Portland Terrace, Southampton SO14 7AY
Phone: 0238 033 4411
Fax: 0238 072 6637

SOVEREIGN ETHICAL FUND
Type of investment: Unit Trust
Address: Sovereign Unit Trust Managers Ltd,
Tringham House, Wessex Fields, Deansleigh Road,
Bournmouth BH7 7DT
Phone: 0800 731 1093
Fax: 0120 243 5027

STANDARD LIFE UK ETHICAL FUND
Type of investment: OEIC
Address: Standard Life Investment Company,
1 George Street, Edinburgh EH2 2LL
Phone: 0800 333 353
Fax: 0131 245 2390

**STANDARD LIFE LIFE ETHICAL AND
PENSION ETHICAL FUNDS**
Type of investment: OEIC
Address: Standard Life Assurance Company,
30 Lothian Road, Edinburgh EH1 2DH
Phone: 0845 60 60 100
Fax: 0131 245 2429

www.gooshing.co.uk will soon feature
a range of 'best deal' and 'best
ethics' information concerning
ethical investment.

Insurance

Choosing insurance companies is a bit of a lottery. They might be offering the best deal today, but who knows what will happen in the future? Increased risk of natural disasters such as flooding could affect the cover these companies offer. Stay ahead of the main players by keeping track of their shares and where they choose to invest, as this is a good indicator as to the ethical standard of their policies.

ETHICAL INSURANCE

A key question for ethical consumers is which shares the money is invested in. According to Friends of the Earth, 'the fate of the global environment is in large part under [institutional investors'] control, and yours too – because it is your money and you are their client'. However, the Ethical Money partnership says that 'no insurer has an "ethical investment" policy where-by they avoid investing in particular types of company'.

Campaigners have become increasingly impatient over unethical corporate activities and they are learning how to put pressure on insurance companies as shareholders. One way to make this pressure work is to keep consumers aware of what their insurers are investing in. Campaigners ask the insurance companies to use their own power as shareholders to vote or create pressure for more ethical or environmentally sound behaviour by the target company. By working together, campaigners and consumers can push these companies to change their policies.

PLUMMETING SHARES

As share prices plummeted in 2001 and 2002, many insurance companies went through a difficult time and saw their assets devalued, as their own investments in stocks, shares and property markets began to mark up losses. Premiums started to rise and companies became much more careful about the risks they were prepared to cover. In the UK, flood cover was withdrawn from a lot of homes that were deemed to be at risk.

So-called natural disasters have required insurers to make huge pay-outs, the rate of which has been doubling every decade. One report in 2002 warned that more frequent natural disasters in future could bring insurers, re-insurers and banks 'to the point of impaired viability or even insolvency'. The insurance companies usually offset their potential liabilities by trading some of the premium (like a bookie 'off-setting' a large bet with another bookie) with a re-insurance company. Many of these companies have now become involved in the UN Environment Programme's Insurance Industry Initiative, which commits them to working together to address issues such as pollution reduction, efficient use of resources and climate change – or in other words to try to work out more sustainable development policies around the world.

ETHICAL INSURANCE

There are some insurers who can be regarded as 'ethical specialists'. Naturesave places 10 per cent of premiums into a fund (The Naturesave Trust) which finances projects that benefit the environment. The company offers a free environmental performance review to businesses and charities to help spread awareness of sustainable development.

The Environmental Transport Association (ETA) aims to bring about positive changes in Britain's travel habits by raising awareness about the impact of excessive car use. It provides travel, house, motor and bicycle insurance (*www.eta.co.uk*).

For those seeking ethical pet insurance, Animal Friends dedicates its profits to the care of animals and their environment (*www. animalfriends.org.uk*).

Choose from the greener companies and source the best insurance deals at *www.gooshing.co.uk*.

- Animal Friends
- Aviva
- CIS
- Ecclesiastical
- ETA
- Naturesave
- Norwich Union
- Royal & Sun Alliance

- Aegon
- Britannic
- Cornhill
- Halifax
- Legal & General
- Liverpool Victoria
- Northern Rock
- Royal London
- Scottish Equitable
- Standard Life

- Allied Dunbar
- Axa
- Churchill
- Direct Line
- Eagle Star
- egg
- First Direct
- Lloyds TSB
- NatWest
- Prudential
- Royal Bank of Scotland
- Zurich

INSURANCE BRAND NAMES	ENVIRONMENT			PEOPLE		OTHER			ETHICAL COMPANY INDEX	Company group
Aegon	○	●	●	●	○	○	○	○	53	Aegon N.V.
Allied Dunbar	○	●	●	●	●	●	○	○	41	Zurich Financial Services
Animal Friends	●	●	●	●	●	○	○	○	65	Animal Friends Insurance
Aviva	●	●	●	●	●	○	○	○	65	Aviva
Axa	○	●	●	●	●	○	○	○	35	Axa
Britannic	○	●	●	●	●	●	○	○	53	Britannic Group
Churchill	●	●	●	●	●	○	○	○	29	Royal Bank of Scotland
Clerical Medical	●	●	●	●	●	○	○	○	53	HBOS
Co-operative Insurance Society (CIS)	●	●	●	●	●	●	●	○	76	Co-operative Group
Cornhill	○	●	●	●	●	○	○	○	59	Allianz Group
Direct Line	●	●	●	●	●	○	○	○	29	Royal Bank of Scotland
Eagle Star	○	●	●	●	●	●	○	○	41	Zurich Financial Services
Ecclesiastical	○	●	●	●	●	●	●	○	65	Allchurches Trust Limited
Egg	○	●	●	●	●	●	○	○	41	Prudential
ETA	●	●	●	●	○	○	●		76	Environmental Transport Association
First Direct	○	●	●	●	○	○	○	○	12	HSBC
Halifax	●	●	●	●	○	○	○	○	53	HBOS
Legal & General	○	●	●	●	○	○	○	○	47	Legal and General Group Plc
Liverpool Victoria	●	●	●	●	●	●	○		59	Liverpool Victoria Friendly Society
Lloyds TSB	●	●	●	●	○	○	○	○	29	Lloyds TSB
NatWest	●	●	●	●	○	○	○	○	29	Royal Bank of Scotland
Naturesave	●	●	●	●	○	○	○	○	65	Naturesave Policies Ltd
Northern Rock	○	●	●	●	●	○	○	○	53	Northern Rock
Norwich Union	●	●	●	●	○	○	○	○	65	Aviva
Prudential	○	●	●	●	●	○	○	○	41	Prudential
Royal & Sun Alliance	●	●	●	●	○	○	○	○	65	Royal & Sun Alliance Insurance Group Plc
Royal Bank of Scotland	●	●	●	●	○	○	○	○	29	Royal Bank of Scotland
Royal London	●	●	●	●	●	●	○		59	Royal London Group
Scottish Equitable	○	●	●	○	○	○	○	○	53	Aegon N.V.
Standard Life	○	●	●	●	○	○	○	○	47	Standard Life Group
Zurich	○	●	●	●	●	●	○	○	41	Zurich Financial Services

Column headers (bottom): ENVIRONMENTAL REPORT · ENVIRONMENTAL DEVASTATION · OTHER IRRESPONSIBLE LENDING · THIRD WORLD DEBT · POLITICAL ACTIVITY · ETHICAL INVESTMENT POLICY · LEGAL STATUS · ETHICAL ACCREDITATION · ETHICAL COMPANY INDEX

Key
- ● Top rating
- ○ Middle rating
- ● Bottom rating

Source: The Ethical Company Organisation

Internet banks

The internet allows us to bypass the physical realities of geography: savers no longer need to travel to their local branch to sort out their finances, but can check balances and handle transactions from the comfort of their own home. Online banking has grown rapidly in recent years, but the same old big banks lurk behind most new internet brands, and many still have their fingers in morally-questionable pies across the globe.

BRAVE NEW WORLD

Online banking services include being able to check balances and statements, setting up monthly transactions, making and receiving one-off payments, and paying bills and salaries. Most banks offer free financial planning software to be used in tandem with the internet service.

Internet banks allow savers to see their statements at any time, meaning that it is easy to follow the progress of a cheque, or find out when money paid out on a debit card has left the account. There is no longer any need to wait for the statement to arrive at the end of the month, and many banks allow their customers to print the pages off directly from the screen.

73 per cent of Barclays' customers say they will switch to online services by 2009, and already more than half of Royal Bank of Scotland business customers bank online.

The online financial arena is developing fast. One recent innovation, founded by the creators of online bank Egg and financed by the company that originally backed eBay, was launched in March 2005 and aims to allow millions of people to borrow from and lend money to each other. Zopa (*www.zopa.com*) seeks to do away with "faceless corporations" and put people who wish to lend money in touch with those who would like to borrow. It claims to offer better rates of interest for borrowers and investors than banks or building societies.

SECURITY

There have been numerous newspaper stories about website scams exposing loopholes in the security of online banking. In one such scam, bogus emails claiming to be from your bank ask for your password and other details, enabling the sender to take money from your account.

Despite this, research published in November 2004 showed an increased confidence in online banking: more than one in five adults surveyed by TNS, a market information specialist, said they were either likely to start using or to increase their use of online banking in the future.

All internet-users should know that banks never send emails asking for your account details; if you get one, delete it, block the sender and inform your bank. And, as a further reassurance, the chance of anyone hacking into your account is very slim, since banks use the strongest encryption available to protect customer details. Keep your passwords safe and your money will be safe too.

The independent Financial Services Authority (FSA) has a register of financial organisations that are authorised in the UK, including those that operate over the internet. It keeps an up-to-date list of firms that can safely be dealt with – and those that are not registered and should probably be approached with caution.

INTERNET BANKS

According to research carried out in 2003 by Virtual Surveys, big banks were rated less highly than their online rivals in terms of customer satisfaction. Smile, First Direct and Nationwide scored highest, while Bank of Scotland, Abbey National, Natwest and Lloyds TSB floundered at the bottom of the table.

There has been a recent growth in 'stand-alone' internet banks, such as Smile, Egg, Cahoot, and First Direct. While the brands may be distinct from their high-street counterparts, they usually just represent the online arm of one of the major banks. Be sure to check which one before you sign up for an account.

- Co-op Bank
- Nationwide
- NetmasterGold
- smile

- 365 online
- Alliance & Leicester
- Bank of Scotland
- Charcolonline
- Halifax
- Intelligent Finance
- Internaxx
- Newcastle Net Savings
- Yorkshire Bank

- Abbey
- Barclays
- cahoot
- Citibank
- egg
- HSBC
- Lloyds TSB
- Natwest
- Royal Bank of Scotland
- Woolwich Open Plan

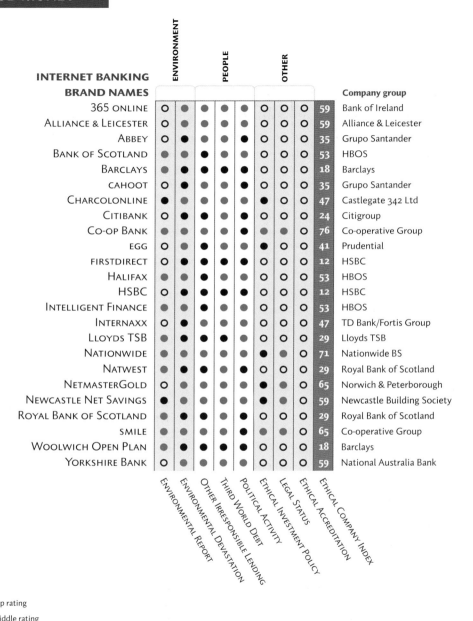

INTERNET BANKING BRAND NAMES

Brand name		ENVIRONMENT		PEOPLE			OTHER			Ethical Company Index	Company group
		Environmental Report	Environmental Devastation	Other Irresponsible Lending	Third World Debt	Political Activity	Ethical Investment Policy	Legal Status	Ethical Accreditation		
365 ONLINE		○	●	●	●	●	○	○	○	59	Bank of Ireland
ALLIANCE & LEICESTER		○	●	●	●	●	○	○	○	59	Alliance & Leicester
ABBEY		○	●	●	●	●	○	○	○	35	Grupo Santander
BANK OF SCOTLAND		●	●	●	●	●	○	○	○	53	HBOS
BARCLAYS		●	●	●	●	●	○	○	○	18	Barclays
CAHOOT		○	●	●	●	●	○	○	○	35	Grupo Santander
CHARCOLONLINE		●	●	●	●	●	●	○	○	47	Castlegate 342 Ltd
CITIBANK		○	●	●	●	●	○	○	○	24	Citigroup
CO-OP BANK		●	●	●	●	●	●	●	○	76	Co-operative Group
EGG		○	●	●	●	●	●	○	○	41	Prudential
FIRSTDIRECT		○	●	●	●	●	○	○	○	12	HSBC
HALIFAX		●	●	●	●	●	○	○	○	53	HBOS
HSBC		○	●	●	●	●	○	○	○	12	HSBC
INTELLIGENT FINANCE		●	●	●	●	●	○	○	○	53	HBOS
INTERNAXX		○	●	●	●	●	○	○	○	47	TD Bank/Fortis Group
LLOYDS TSB		●	●	●	●	●	○	○	○	29	Lloyds TSB
NATIONWIDE		●	●	●	●	●	●	●	○	71	Nationwide BS
NATWEST		●	●	●	●	●	○	○	○	29	Royal Bank of Scotland
NETMASTERGOLD		○	●	●	●	●	●	●	○	65	Norwich & Peterborough
NEWCASTLE NET SAVINGS		●	●	●	●	●	●	●	○	59	Newcastle Building Society
ROYAL BANK OF SCOTLAND		●	●	●	●	●	○	○	○	29	Royal Bank of Scotland
SMILE		●	●	●	●	●	●	●	○	65	Co-operative Group
WOOLWICH OPEN PLAN		●	●	●	●	●	○	○	○	18	Barclays
YORKSHIRE BANK		○	●	●	●	●	○	○	○	59	National Australia Bank

Key

● Top rating
○ Middle rating
● Bottom rating

Source: The Ethical Company Organisation

Mortgages

Ten years ago, most mortgages were taken out with building societies, but since de-mutualisation, about four out of five mortgages are now provided by either a bank, a life insurer or a specialist mortgage lender. All of the companies examined here offer standard 'repayment' mortgages. These include a few of the remaining building societies, some of the major lenders and some companies that offer mortgages with an ethical or 'green' conscience.

WHO GETS THE MONEY?

Mortgages make up most of Britain's £1 trillion debt mountain. In the course of our lives they are likely to be our single biggest outlay; an outlay that may be indirectly funding some of the most ruthless and destructive business activities. As a result, the mortgage company's lending policies are as important as the kind of mortgage on offer.

The corporate social responsibility reports from banks and corporations have evolved into detailed, elaborate documents, and most banks now make some reference to socially responsible investment. It is easy to be sceptical about how much these flashy PR jobs match up to reality, since the major banks so often provoke condemnation from NGOs around the world.

According to Christian Aid (*www. christian-aid.org.uk*), in 2002 HSBC marketed a bond issue for two oil companies, Petronas of Malaysia and Talisman of Canada, both of which were major investors in Sudan. A UN special reporter for Sudan said that revenue from international oil companies such as these fuelled the country's civil war.

More recently, in December 2004, Barclays' involvement in the Trans-Thai-Malaysia gas pipeline, and in the Omkareshwar Dam in India, provoked a human rights protest supported by Friends of the Earth (*www.foe.co.uk*). The bank was accused of failing to uphold the Equator Principles, a code of environmental and social conduct that is designed to prevent organisations from violating human rights through their choice of lending.

GREEN MORTGAGES

Homes are one of the largest sources of carbon dioxide emissions in the UK. While most mortgage lenders offer valuation surveys as part of the mortgage deal, relatively few at this stage are offering specialised environmental surveys. These environmental surveys assess how energy efficient the house is, and give advice on energy saving measures. Currently, the Co-Operative Bank offers this kind of survey free with its green mortgage, as do the Norwich & Peterborough and the Ethical Mortgage Service.

The Ecology Building Society currently lends only on properties that give 'ecological payback'. This translates as houses that it considers to be energy-saving, such as back-to-backs and derelict houses which would otherwise have been abandoned. This strict lending policy means that it won't be suitable for every person seeking a mortgage.

The Norwich & Peterborough offers a carbon-neutral mortgage. For the first five years of each of its Green Mortgages, it will plant eight trees a year. Its leaflet claims that the trees will absorb carbon dioxide to the equivalent of the estimated emissions of the property. It also offers a 'brown' mortgage scheme which aims to encourage the renovation and restoration of buildings for residential use.

The Co-operative Bank's green mortgage will 'pay Climate Care to offset around 20 per cent of an average home's carbon dioxide production for every mortgage we grant'. It claims that over a 20-year mortgage just under a fifth of an acre of forest would be planted.

FINDING ADVICE

The Ethical Investors Group is a collaboration between the Ethical Investment Co-operative (a group of independent financial advisors) and consultants called Thirdwave. It offers advice on mortgages from a panel of lenders that it has ethically screened. This panel includes the Skipton, Scottish and Yorkshire Building Societies.

- Co-op Bank
- Ecology BS
- Ethical Mortgages
- Nationwide BS
- Norwich & Peterborough BS

- Alliance & Leicester
- Halifax

- Abbey
- Barclays
- Cheltenham & Gloucester
- Lloyds TSB
- Royal Bank of Scotland
- Woolwich

MORTGAGES BRAND NAMES	ENVIRONMENT		PEOPLE			OTHER				Company group
	Environmental Report	Environmental Devastation	Other Irresponsible Lending	Third World Debt	Political Activity	Ethical Investment Policy	Legal Status	Ethical Accreditation	Ethical Company Index	
Abbey	○	●	●	●	●	○	○	○	35	Grupo Santander
Alliance & Leicester	○	●	●	●	●	○	○	○	59	Alliance & Leicester
Barclays	●	●	●	●	●	○	○	○	18	Barclays
Cheltenham & Gloucester	●	●	●	●	●	○	○	○	29	Lloyds TSB
Co-op Bank	●	●	●	●	●	●	●	○	76	Co-operative Group
Ecology BS	●	●	●	●	●	●	●	○	71	Ecology BS
Ethical Mortgages	●	●	●	●	●	●	○	○	76	Ethical Investors Group
Halifax	●	●	●	●	●	○	○	○	53	HBOS
Lloyds TSB	●	●	●	●	●	○	○	○	29	Lloyds TSB
Nationwide BS	●	●	●	●	●	●	●	○	71	Nationwide BS
Norwich & Peterborough BS	○	●	●	●	●	●	●	○	65	Norwich & Peterborough BS
Royal Bank of Scotland	●	●	●	●	●	○	○	○	29	Royal Bank of Scotland
Woolwich	●	●	●	●	●	○	○	○	18	Barclays

Key
- ● Top rating
- ○ Middle rating
- ● Bottom rating

Source: The Ethical Company Organisation

GOOD
FOOD & DRINK

Introduction

With lurid headlines about Britain's 'obesity epidemic' filling the newspapers on an almost daily basis, it's no surprise that eating well has become something of a national obsession. It is also the source of more contradictory information than almost any other area of public health. From fad diets to food labels, getting your meals right is a tricky business.

As Jamie Oliver showed with his *Jamie's School Dinners* series for Channel 4, it is vital that good habits are learned from a young age. Part of the extensive response to his programme has been a move towards a ban on 'junk' food (including the now infamous Turkey Twizzler) from schools.

Oliver has also re-ignited the debate over food advertising aimed at children. Criticisms of irresponsible marketing reached a head in 2003 following Cadbury's launch of a vouchers scheme to provide sports equipment for schools, which sparked complaints that it encouraged the counter-productive consumption of large quantities of chocolate.

The proliferation of largely unhealthy, processed food has also been a problem occupying the Food Standards Agency during the development of its new Traffic Light Colours food-labelling scheme (*www.eatwell.gov.uk*). The system, which has so far been adopted by supermarkets Waitrose and Sainsbury's, involves indicating how much salt, fat and sugar is in a product using the familiar red, orange and green colours.

While these are steps in the right direction, there is more to a good diet than what's on the label. This section of *The Good Shopping Guide* contains details of the companies whose foods meet the highest ethical standards. These include products that are fair trade, organic and GM-free, and do not involve the use of factory-farming methods. It also looks at the environmental records of each company, and whether their products are produced and packaged in a sustainable manner. In the final part of the chapter, we reveal which supermarkets are the most progressive and responsible – and you can find out how far your Sunday lunch travelled before it reached your dinner table.

Baby food

Everyone wants what's best for baby, and that usually means the most natural available forms of care and nutrition. There has long been a high level of awareness in Britain about the marketing of baby milk substitutes, but in many countries this is still not the case. When choosing products from the shelves, parents need to be confident that the brands act responsibly, in all areas of production and marketing, both here and abroad.

BREAST MILK SUBSTITUTES

The WHO/UNICEF International Code of Marketing of Breast Milk Substitutes has been developed in response to serious criticisms of the marketing practices of baby milk and food manufacturers over many years. In response to the massive amount of evidence in favour of prolonged breastfeeding, the Code proposes various guidelines to promote this, including solid foods being labelled as suitable only from six months.

In poorer countries in particular, moving from breast milk to substitutes can have severe consequences for a baby's health. The International Baby Food Action Network (IBFAN) released a report in 2004 which condemned aggressive marketing from the major baby food companies across the developing world. The report listed Royal Numico's Nutricia as the second-worst violator of the code, behind Nestlé, but companies including Hipp Organics and HJ Heinz were also listed (see *www.ibfan.org* for more details).

DIFFERENT KINDS OF FOODS

Baby food comes in three main types:

- 'Wet' foods, which are pre-cooked and puréed meals packaged in jars or cans
- 'Dry' foods, in boxes or sachets, which have to be rehydrated to make meals
- Cereals, rusks and rice cakes, eaten plain or with milk

The companies included in the table opposite produce a combination of these three types – check their websites for more information.

ORGANIC BRANDS

Parents are increasingly looking for organic food for their babies. These are guaranteed to be free from the pesticide residues, growth hormones and nitrates that can appear in conventionally-grown foods. They also contain fewer artificial additives, such as E-numbers and flavourings.

There are now exclusively organic companies such as Baby Organix and Hipp, while Heinz and Boots also produce their own organic ranges. *The Organic Baby Book* lists the different organic brands available in the UK.

One strong argument in favour of buying organic food for babies is that they are more vulnerable than adults to toxins such as pesticide residues. This is partly because they eat more food in proportion to their overall body weight than adults, meaning that they will be exposed to a relatively higher level of chemicals.

LABELLING AND PACKAGING

Since 1999 there has been legislation in Britain setting compulsory standards for the nutritional value and labelling of baby foods. The regulations set minimum quantities for the main vitamins, minerals and protein, and maximum quantities for fats, carbohydrate and sodium. All the baby food examined by the Ethical Company Organisation's researchers complied with these regulations.

Most of the packaging for baby foods is in theory recyclable, but very little attention is drawn to this fact.

ALTERNATIVES AND NICHE BRANDS

Baby food can of course be made at home. One simple and healthy process is to liquidise or sieve cooked fruit or vegetables (preferably organic, if available). Some good baby food recipe books are available, including *Cooking for your Baby* (Laraine Toms, Penguin), *Complete New Guide to Preparing Babyfoods* (Sue Castle, Bantam) and *The New Vegetarian Baby* (Baird and Yntema, McBooks).

Yoghurt and fromage frais makers have entered the baby food market with varieties labelled as being suitable for four to six months. There are also niche brands such as Mother Nature Babyfoods (which produces halal foods), Original Fresh Babyfood Co and Osska. Both of the latter companies make fresh meals that are sold in the cold cabinets of health food stores and supermarkets.

- Babynat
- Baby Organix

- Boots
- Hipp Organics

- Cow & Gate
- Farley
- Heinz
- Milupa

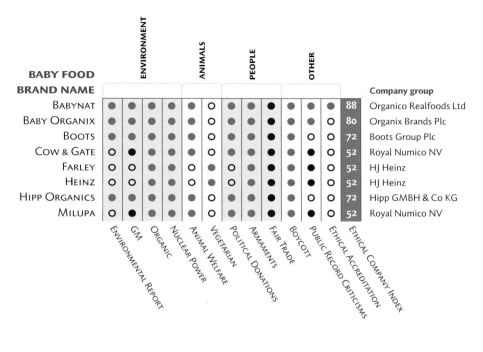

BABY FOOD BRAND NAME	Ethical Company Index	Company group
BABYNAT	88	Organico Realfoods Ltd
BABY ORGANIX	80	Organix Brands Plc
BOOTS	72	Boots Group Plc
COW & GATE	52	Royal Numico NV
FARLEY	52	HJ Heinz
HEINZ	52	HJ Heinz
HIPP ORGANICS	72	Hipp GMBH & Co KG
MILUPA	52	Royal Numico NV

Column categories: ENVIRONMENT (Environmental Report, GM, Organic, Nuclear Power), ANIMALS (Animal Welfare, Vegetarian), PEOPLE (Political Donations, Armaments, Fair Trade, Boycott), OTHER (Public Record Criticisms, Ethical Accreditation)

Key

● Top rating

○ Middle rating

● Bottom rating

Source: The Ethical Company Organisation

Bananas

As with many farmed products from tropical countries, bananas have become a strong seller in the fair trade movement. They are particularly important to the campaign because of the threat from big plantation companies to the livelihoods of people living in the Windward Islands of the Caribbean, where bananas often provide the only reliable employment. Another major issue is the use of pesticides, which can harm both plantation workers and the environment.

BANANA WARS

The US and the EU went through a long dispute about the trading conditions for bananas during the 90s. The European countries tried to keep preferential access for bananas from former colonies, but the World Trade Organisation eventually ruled in favour of the US. This means that the 'dollar banana companies' like Chiquita, Dole and Del Monte have been able to expand their business in Europe. European companies like Fyffes import their fruit mainly, but not exclusively, from the Windward Islands.

Windward bananas are grown much less intensively and more sustainably than those from other countries, especially those in Central America. Most production is done by small producers with better employment conditions and fewer chemicals than elsewhere. Windward bananas also tend to be smaller and sweeter.

However, these improvements can cause other financial problems for the growers. When supermarkets compete to force down prices in the UK, it is not their profits that are being cut, but those of the wholesalers and, ultimately, the growers. In areas such as the Windward Isles, where production prices are higher, farmers are forced to either sell their goods for less than they cost to produce, or be driven out of the market.

Fair trade offers one solution to this cycle, by guaranteeing the growers a minimum price that is set in relation to the production costs in their area. Until the day when consumers refuse to buy products that are sold at unsustainably low prices, their input is crucial – and particularly so for bananas. According to the Fairtrade Foundation they are the UK's most popular fruit, and with 140 million being eaten every week they account, cost-wise, for 28 per cent of all fruit sales. That's a lot of potentially unfair trade.

WAGES AND CONDITIONS

The big multinationals operating in Central and South America own sprawling plantations where workers may toil for 12 hours a day in poor conditions, as well as facing intimidation by owners. Workers have been trying to organise trade unions to bargain for better wages and conditions, but have encountered company harassment, especially in Costa Rica and Honduras.

As before, a good way for customers to influence the way workers are treated in these countries is to opt for fair trade bananas which, after some delay, are now widely available in all major supermarket chains.

PESTICIDES AND CHEMICALS

Since the 1960s, companies have been increasingly growing the varieties of bananas that have the highest yields. However, these are also very susceptible to pests and diseases, so the industry uses an enormous amount of chemicals throughout the growing process, before and after harvesting, as well as to preserve the fruit in transit. While the average usage of pesticides on farms in industrialised countries is 2.7kg per hectare, within the Costa Rican banana industry

the figure is 44kg per hectare, with aerial spraying occurring up to 50 times a year. The workers are exposed to appalling health hazards and the surrounding areas can become seriously contaminated. At the time of going to press, Dole, Del Monte and Chiquita were all facing allegations of exposing workers to harmful levels of these pesticides.

ORGANIC OPTIONS

Planting varieties of bananas that are more resistant to infection is the most obvious way of reducing the justification for such heavy use of pesticides. Growing numbers of bananas are being imported from farms where they are produced without chemical assistance. This market has increased as customers have become more aware of the issues and more observant of the different brands available. Alongside fair trade bananas, organic options are now widely available.

- Fyffes

- Chiquita
- Del Monte

- Bonita
- Dole

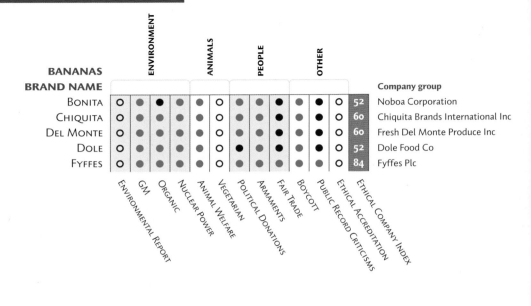

BANANAS

BRAND NAME	Ethical Company Index	Company group
BONITA	52	Noboa Corporation
CHIQUITA	60	Chiquita Brands International Inc
DEL MONTE	60	Fresh Del Monte Produce Inc
DOLE	52	Dole Food Co
FYFFES	84	Fyffes Plc

Key

● Top rating

○ Middle rating

● Bottom rating

Source: The Ethical Company Organisation

CAFÉDIRECT® sponsors Bedtime Drinks
BRINGING QUALITY TO LIFE

Bedtime drinks

Even in this coffee-fuelled country, most people don't want to drink anything containing caffeine last thing at night, which is why there is such a big market for bedtime beverages such as hot chocolate. Many of these products are cocoa-based, so the treatment of the farmers who produce the beans is a major concern. Despite cocoa market prices hitting a record high, many farmers have not found themselves better off.

THE FARMERS

The average cocoa farmer earns just £50 a year from cocoa. New varieties of cocoa have been developed, which can grow in the sun, but the trees decline quicker than traditional varieties, and require high doses of pesticides. One of these pesticides is lindane, which is banned in the EU for health reasons. Also some chocolate companies, especially those buying from suppliers in the Ivory Coast, have been unable to confirm that their cocoa is not picked under conditions of slavery.

To avoid these problems, choose products such as Cocodirect (from Cafédirect, *www.cafedirect.co.uk*), which is certified by the Fairtrade Foundation. This means that the farmers and their communities benefit from a fair price for their goods, and guarantees no forced or child labour. Cafédirect guarantee via their Gold Standard a price higher than the market price, and the Cocodirect drink contains 40 per cent pure cocoa, which means more revenue for farmers.

Also look out for organic brands, certified by the Soil Association. This helps bio-diversity and guarantees no GM ingredients or pesticides.

BOYCOTT CALLS

As the companies table demonstrates, Horlicks, Galaxy and Maltesers are subject to boycott calls. In contrast to the drink's somewhat old-fashioned image, Horlicks's parent company is multinational pharmaceutical giant GlaxoSmithKline. According to campaigners, GSK is being boycotted due to its attempts to block cheaper versions of its anti-AIDS drugs, unnecessary animal testing, and for being one of the ten largest donors to the US Republican party. In addition, the company has admitted to making misleading claims about the vitamin C content of its Ribena soft drink in Australia and New Zealand. Two teenagers discovered the discrepancy during a school experiment.

Mars, which owns Galaxy and Maltesers, is subject to a boycott call for animal testing undertaken by its pet food division (see

www.buav.org). *The Food Magazine* found that it had also partaken in questionable marketing by citing confectionery as a good source of carbohydrate in a promotional health and awareness pack.

Cadbury has also been criticised for irresponsible marketing. It launched a promotion called Get Active, where children were encouraged to buy chocolate bars and save the wrappers to get free sports equipment for their schools. To receive a 'free' basketball, 170 chocolate bar wrappers (representing a total 2kg of fat and over 38,000 calories) would have to be submitted – hardly a beneficial way to get health-promoting sports equipment.

More recently, Cadbury has been involved in a high-profile health scare surrounding an outbreak of salmonella. In July 2007 the company was fined £1m for its involvement in the outbreak, in which 42 people fell ill. It was criticised for implementing a testing policy which, according to reports, allowed for a "tolerance" level of the bacteria – meaning that foods that tested positive could still go on sale to the public. Cadbury has since changed its policy.

Also, Cadbury Schweppes, Mars and GlaxoSmithKline have yet to confirm that their hot drinks contain no GM ingredients. GM issues also crop up with a subsidiary of Ovaltine's owner, Associated British Foods Plc, which has been running trials to assess the commercial viability of oil seed rape for the GM giant Monsanto.

PACKAGING

The packaging used for bedtime drinks products often cannot be recycled, as the combination of tough plastics, cardboards and foils are difficult to separate for re-use. Some companies sell their drinks in glass bottles, which are a much more environmentally-friendly option.

Stick to *The Good Shopping Guide*'s ethically certified brands – they leave a much better taste in your mouth.

- Clipper
- Cocodirect

- Cadbury
- Green & Black's

- Galaxy
- Horlicks
- Maltesers
- Ovaltine

CAFÉDIRECT BRINGING QUALITY TO LIFE sponsors Bedtime Drinks

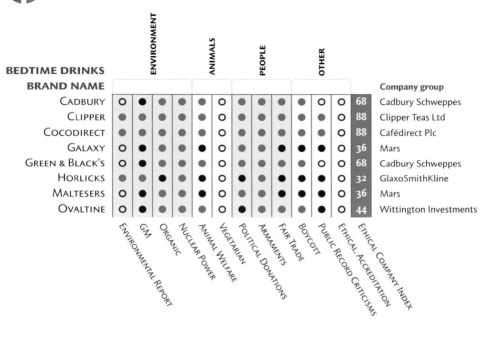

BEDTIME DRINKS BRAND NAME	ENVIRONMENT				ANIMALS		PEOPLE			OTHER			Ethical Company Index	Company group
	Environmental Report	GM	Organic	Nuclear Power	Animal Welfare	Vegetarian	Political Donations	Armaments	Fair Trade	Boycott	Public Record Criticisms	Ethical Accreditation		
CADBURY	○	●	●	●	●	○	●	●	●	●	○	○	68	Cadbury Schweppes
CLIPPER	●	●	●	●	●	○	●	●	●	●	●	○	88	Clipper Teas Ltd
COCODIRECT	●	●	●	●	●	○	●	●	●	●	●	○	88	Cafédirect Plc
GALAXY	○	●	●	●	●	○	●	●	●	●	●	○	36	Mars
GREEN & BLACK'S	○	●	●	●	●	○	●	●	●	●	○	○	68	Cadbury Schweppes
HORLICKS	●	●	●	●	●	○	●	●	●	●	●	○	32	GlaxoSmithKline
MALTESERS	○	●	●	●	●	○	●	●	●	●	●	○	36	Mars
OVALTINE	○	●	●	●	●	○	●	●	●	●	●	○	44	Wittington Investments

Key

● Top rating

○ Middle rating

● Bottom rating

Source: The Ethical Company Organisation

Beer, lager & cider

The big brewers may all be thinking globally these days, but seasoned drinkers usually prefer their local brews when they can find them. Where the big companies often win is by persuading us that a 'local' brew from far away contains something special or unique – hence the success of brews from Mexico, South Africa, India and Thailand. This section covers brands of bitter, lager, stout and cider that are available nationwide.

How many miles?

Our increasingly exotic tastes could be causing horrendous and fairly pointless pollution of the globe. Ingredients for a real ale from a local brewery may have travelled about 600 miles in all, which might seem far enough, but for some imported lagers produced by the multinationals, the ingredients can travel as many as 24,000 miles. There may be some consolation in the fact that many of the so-called 'export' or 'continental' lagers are really brewed under licence in the UK, but there is ever more beer moving across European borders.

What's in the stuff?

Conventional hop farming uses a lot of pesticides – which results in what the pressure group Sustain describes as 'scorched earth' farming methods, where the ground between and beneath the hops is kept barren and dusty. Organic farming methods use mustard mixed with the hops to attract predators and combat aphid attacks.

Traditionally, the barley for malting has come from the highest-quality spring crops, but recently there has been massive development of new winter barley varieties, on which farmers use almost double the number of pesticides. These changes, and the decrease in planting of summer barley, have badly damaged bird populations.

Under current UK legislation, drinks containing over 1.2 per cent alcohol are exempt from the compulsory labelling applicable to other products for consumption. This means that brewers don't tell us when they use chemical additives, as many do to increase the shelf life of the beer or to alter the colour or flavour of the brew. The lack of mandatory labelling causes problems for vegetarians, as most beers do still use animal-derived products.

Organic options

Organic beers have begun to take off, although there are real problems finding organic hops – the main source of supply being far-off New Zealand. Organic production of hops in the UK is not only possible but potentially highly profitable.

Brewing your own beer can give you control over many elements of the brewing process. There are no UK homebrew suppliers currently stocking organic hops. However, these are available by mail order from the US (*www.seven-bridges-cooperative.com*). While this increases beer miles, the weight of the product is only around 3lbs. Online brewing classes are now available on the web (such as *www.breworganic.com*), where you will find lots of the information you need.

NONE FOR THE ROAD

The legal driving alcohol limit in the UK is 80mg%, compared with 50mg% in most of Europe and 20mg% in Sweden.

Although any alcohol will affect all drivers, accident rates for young people double after only two drinks, and increase tenfold after five drinks.

- ESB
- Grolsch
- Scottish & Newcastle

- Beck's
- Blackthorn
- Carling
- Carlsberg
- Foster's
- Heineken
- Holsten
- Merrydown
- Old Speckled Hen
- Stella Artios
- Wadworth's 6X

- Budweiser
- Diageo

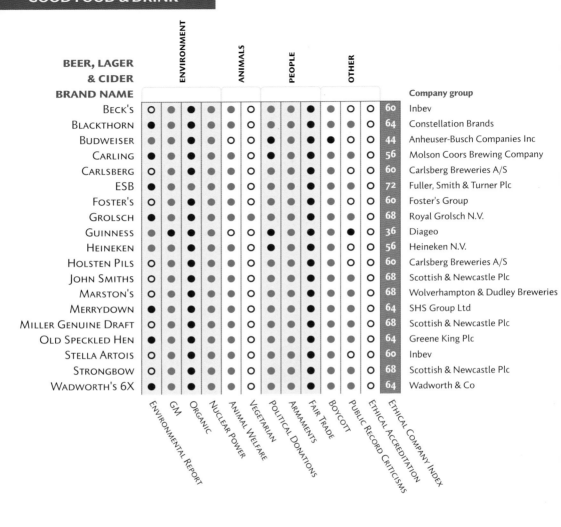

BEER, LAGER & CIDER BRAND NAME	ENVIRONMENT				ANIMALS		PEOPLE			OTHER			ETHICAL COMPANY INDEX	Company group
	Environmental Report	GM	Organic	Nuclear Power	Animal Welfare	Vegetarian	Political Donations	Armaments	Fair Trade	Boycott	Public Record Criticisms	Ethical Accreditation		
BECK'S	O	●	●	●	●	O	●	●	●	●	O	O	60	Inbev
BLACKTHORN	●	●	●	●	●	O	●	●	●	●	●	O	64	Constellation Brands
BUDWEISER	●	●	●	●	O	O	●	●	●	●	O	O	44	Anheuser-Busch Companies Inc
CARLING	●	●	●	●	●	O	●	●	●	●	●	O	56	Molson Coors Brewing Company
CARLSBERG	O	●	●	●	●	O	●	●	●	●	O	O	60	Carlsberg Breweries A/S
ESB	●	●	●	●	●	O	●	●	●	●	●	O	72	Fuller, Smith & Turner Plc
FOSTER'S	O	●	●	●	●	O	●	●	●	●	O	O	60	Foster's Group
GROLSCH	●	●	●	●	●	O	●	●	●	●	O	O	68	Royal Grolsch N.V.
GUINNESS	●	●	●	●	O	O	●	●	●	●	●	O	36	Diageo
HEINEKEN	●	●	●	●	●	O	●	●	●	●	O	O	56	Heineken N.V.
HOLSTEN PILS	O	●	●	●	●	O	●	●	●	●	O	O	60	Carlsberg Breweries A/S
JOHN SMITHS	O	●	●	●	●	O	●	●	●	●	●	O	68	Scottish & Newcastle Plc
MARSTON'S	O	●	●	●	●	O	●	●	●	●	●	O	68	Wolverhampton & Dudley Breweries
MERRYDOWN	●	●	●	●	●	O	●	●	●	●	●	O	64	SHS Group Ltd
MILLER GENUINE DRAFT	O	●	●	●	●	O	●	●	●	●	●	O	68	Scottish & Newcastle Plc
OLD SPECKLED HEN	●	●	●	●	●	O	●	●	●	●	●	O	64	Greene King Plc
STELLA ARTOIS	O	●	●	●	●	O	●	●	●	●	O	O	60	Inbev
STRONGBOW	O	●	●	●	●	O	●	●	●	●	●	O	68	Scottish & Newcastle Plc
WADWORTH'S 6X	●	●	●	●	●	O	●	●	●	●	●	O	64	Wadworth & Co

Key

● Top rating

O Middle rating

● Bottom rating

Source: The Ethical Company Organisation

Biscuits

So-called 'healthy' biscuits are one of the fastest-growing sectors in an already saturated food market. Yet the whole idea of a biscuit is hardly healthy: it is just a sugary, fatty treat to be enjoyed, hopefully, in moderation. It is for this reason that some of the major companies have come under fire for marketing more and more of their products towards children, and for labels that mask their biscuits' true, fat-filled content.

CORPORATE CRUNCH-UP

At the time of writing, the biscuit market was a perfect example of global corporate crunching. A lowly Somerfield 'basics' digestive was made by McVities, which is owned by United Biscuits, which is owned by Finalrealm, which is a consortium of Nabisco, DB Capital, Cinven and PAI. Of those in the consortium, Nabisco is owned by Kraft, which is owned by Philip Morris, the company that makes Marlboro cigarettes but has changed its name to Altria. Cinven is a leverage buy-out operation which owns companies as diverse as Odeon Cinemas, Foesco chemicals and William Hill bookmakers. DB Capital Partners is owned by Deutsche Bank, which has been involved in financing controversial dams amongst other things. So what's new?

INGREDIENTS

Vegetarians and vegans should be aware that many biscuits contain dairy products such as butter or whey powders. Some brands may contain non-specific animal fat. Companies are slowly realising that consumers do often look at the labels. In the mid-1990s, Greenpeace famously persuaded McVities to stop making biscuits with fish oil from industrial fishing.

One biscuit-maker, Northern Foods, says that none of its biscuits are tainted with GM because consumers won't buy GM food. While this is a positive step, it is not supported by the powerful food industry lobby the Food and Drink Federation, which believes that 'biotechnology, including genetic modification, offers enormous potential to improve the quality and quantity of the food supply'.

In the US, Kraft has been using untested and unlabelled genetically modified ingredients for several years, although in Europe the company has so far been respectful of consumer pressure. Now, more than ever, is a time for vigilance against the stealthy introduction of GM technology. Try to buy Walkers, Traidcraft, Doves Farm or Bahlsen, who do not use genetically modified ingredients.

LABELLING

Biscuits are more than likely to be one of the targets of the government's new 'traffic light' food labelling system. As fat-filled confectioneries they will almost certainly come under the 'red' section of the three-colour system, showing that they have fewer health benefits than other foods and should be consumed in moderation.

Nevertheless, it looks as if there will still be plenty of scope for companies to try and market their biscuits as healthy. While regulations prevent a product from being labelled as 'reduced' (such as reduced fat) unless there has been a 25 per cent reduction in that particular nutrient, there is nothing to stop them from using other terms such as 'lite' or 'low fat' to describe a minimal change in ingredients. The term 'lite' could refer to the colour of a product, its weight or, finally, the amount of fat it contains.

Equally, an '85 per cent fat free' biscuit is still 15 per cent fat. Consumers tend to think these are better for you when in fact they could have just as much fat as a slice of cheesecake. While the Food Standards Agency advises that potentially misleading labels such as these should be avoided, many companies capitalise on their customers' trust to market their alternative products. And they're right to think we're confused: surveys have shown that the majority of shoppers have no idea what the labels actually mean.

As a general rule biscuits made from oats, and which don't include chocolate, sugar icing or cream centres, will be marginally more healthy, but the only way to truly know is to take a good look at the ingredients.

- Doves Farm
- Traidcraft
- Walkers

- Bahlsen
- Hill

- Burton's
- Fox's
- Jacob's
- Kitkat
- McVities
- Ritz

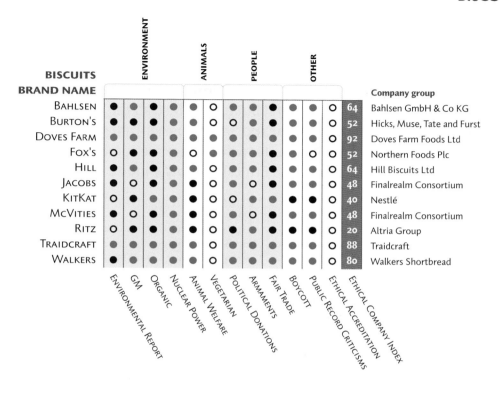

BISCUITS BRAND NAME	ENVIRONMENT – Environmental Report	GM	Organic	Nuclear Power	ANIMALS – Animal Welfare	Vegetarian	PEOPLE – Political Donations	Armaments	Fair Trade	Boycott	Public Record Criticisms	OTHER – Ethical Accreditation	Ethical Company Index	Company group
Bahlsen	●	●	●	●	●	○	●	●	●	●	●	○	64	Bahlsen GmbH & Co KG
Burton's	●	●	●	●	●	○	○	●	●	●	●	○	52	Hicks, Muse, Tate and Furst
Doves Farm	●	●	●	●	●	●	●	●	●	●	●	○	92	Doves Farm Foods Ltd
Fox's	○	●	●	●	○	●	●	●	●	●	○	○	52	Northern Foods Plc
Hill	●	●	●	●	○	●	●	●	●	●	●	○	64	Hill Biscuits Ltd
Jacobs	●	○	●	●	●	○	●	○	●	●	●	○	48	Finalrealm Consortium
KitKat	○	●	●	●	●	○	○	●	●	●	●	○	40	Nestlé
McVities	●	○	●	●	●	○	●	○	●	●	●	○	48	Finalrealm Consortium
Ritz	○	●	●	●	●	○	●	●	●	●	●	○	20	Altria Group
Traidcraft	●	●	●	●	●	○	●	●	●	●	●	○	88	Traidcraft
Walkers	●	●	●	●	●	○	●	●	●	●	●	○	80	Walkers Shortbread

Key

● Top rating

○ Middle rating

● Bottom rating

Source: The Ethical Company Organisation

Bottled water

In the mineral industry, the multinationals are in charge – even when it comes to brands such as Malvern and Buxton. In fact, all the world-wide market leaders (Evian, Volvic, Perrier and San Pellagrino) are under the control of either Danone or Nestle. However there are some local UK brands which do score highly on the Ethical Company Index.

Go local

Try and choose the most local brand you can find - those that are sourced in the UK and therefore have a much smaller carbon footprint.

Every bottle of Perrier sold around the world is bottled at source in Vergèze, France. Readers in, say, Glasgow, could be drinking water that has travelled over 900 miles.

An environmental packaging solution is the re-usable glass bottle. In other European countries, such as Germany, higher proportions of all drinks come in returnable bottles. The mineral water producers are members of a pool system, with their brands being distinguished by label but the bottles shared, allowing short transport distances from consumer to refiller.

In the UK, it seems that the big national breweries, soft drinks producers and supermarkets are reluctant to use refillable glass bottles because of the extra effort (floor space and staff time) it would cause them. They would rather deal with plastics and prefer to encourage recycling, which hands the work over to the consumer. Most councils will collect bottles bearing the numbers one (PET) or two (HDPE), but it is still difficult to find a recycling point for any other type of plastic.

Pure, but how pure?

Although bottled water claims a natural, pure and healthy image, all waters must meet strict quality requirements. The area surrounding a Natural Mineral Water spring requires protection against pollution, and although Natural Mineral Water is legally 'pure', this is not true of all water that is sold in bottles.

When you look at the rows of bottled water in supermarkets (there are up to forty varieties) whose purity is emphasised by waterfalls and mountains, it's easy to forget the complexity of treatment that all water from a source goes through before being bottled.

Those with high blood pressure, or others who need to follow a low sodium (salt) diet should check the mineral content of their water carefully. Natural mineral waters can only claim they're suitable for a low sodium diet if they contain less than 20mg per litre. Current advice from the Food Standards Agency is that some bottled waters shouldn't be used for babies: 'Waters to avoid are those with high levels of nitrate, nitrite, sodium, fluoride and sulphate. There are limits for these in tap, spring and other bottled drinking waters, but not in natural mineral waters.'

CHOOSE THE RIGHT BRAND!

The only bottled waters we recommend are Highland Spring and Campsie Spring as they have a very clean ethical record, are local to the UK, and score very highly on the Ethical Company Index (especially when compared to other leading brands like Evian, Buxton and Volvic). Highland Spring are also the only bottled water brand to join the Ethical Accreditation scheme.

There has been much cynicism about the bottled water industry from some quarters. A report by the Canadian non-governmental Polaris Institute (*www.polarisinstitute.org*) argued that the big companies pay next to nothing for water they take from rural springs or public water systems, and, after turning water into water through elaborate treatment processes, sell a product that is not as well-regulated as tap water, but is vastly more expensive.

For instance, in 2004 Coca Cola launched Dasani, a new brand of bottled water.

Although the water was actually drawn from the mains (Thames Water in fact), Coca Cola talked of a 'highly sophisticated Volvic spacecraft technology. It emerged, however, that this was simply reverse osmosis, used in many domestic water purification units. Then, to complete the PR catastrophe, 500,000 litres of the brand had to be recalled from British supermarkets because of high levels of bromate, a cancer-causing chemical which is not found in Thames Water.

MIX IT UP

The Drinking Water Inspectorate has warned that if opportunities are not taken to improve public perception of tap water, consumers will never appreciate the plentiful low cost water supplied to their taps. So don't be afraid to ask for tap water as it is very healthy too.

- Campsie Spring
- Highland Spring

- Ballygowan
- Spa
- Strathmore

- Aqua Pura
- Buxton
- Evian
- Malvern
- Perrier
- Vittel
- Volvic

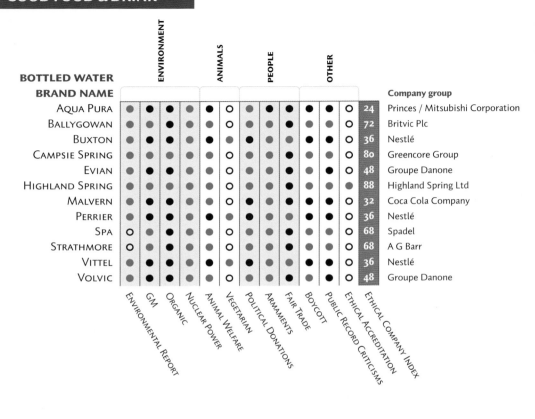

BOTTLED WATER BRAND NAME

Categories: ENVIRONMENT · ANIMALS · PEOPLE · OTHER

Column labels: Environmental Report, GM, Organic, Nuclear Power, Animal Welfare, Vegetarian, Political Donations, Armaments, Fair Trade, Boycott, Public Record Criticisms, Ethical Accreditation, Ethical Company Index

Brand Name	Ethical Company Index	Company group
Aqua Pura	24	Princes / Mitsubishi Corporation
Ballygowan	72	Britvic Plc
Buxton	36	Nestlé
Campsie Spring	80	Greencore Group
Evian	48	Groupe Danone
Highland Spring	88	Highland Spring Ltd
Malvern	32	Coca Cola Company
Perrier	36	Nestlé
Spa	68	Spadel
Strathmore	68	A G Barr
Vittel	36	Nestlé
Volvic	48	Groupe Danone

Key
- ● Top rating
- ○ Middle rating
- ● Bottom rating

Source: The Ethical Company Organisation (2008)

To keep our water pure, we have to get a little dirty.

Highland Spring is sourced from land that is **certified organic** by the Soil Association. To maintain our organic status we must protect our land, keeping it free from pesticides and pollution of any kind. So each day we head up the hillside to make sure everything is just as nature intended.

We have, and always will have, the best interests of the environment at the heart of everything we do, and we will always strive to protect the land, to protect the water, for you.

Reassuringly **pure**.

Bread

From such simple ingredients as flour, water and yeast, an industry of amazing complexity has risen. What was once a simple loaf of bread can now be white, wholemeal, granary, farmhouse, organic or any combination of the above – and probably contains an abundance of additives as well. Home baking is the only sure way to guarantee your bread is free from artificial ingredients, but organic bread from a local bakery comes a close second.

CHEMICALS AND ADDITIVES

Sliced and wrapped loaves are by far the biggest-selling kind of bread in the UK, representing 80 per cent of bread consumption. The main manufacturers are Allied Bakeries and British Bakeries, each controlling about a third of the market. Allied make Kingsmill, and British Bakeries make Hovis. The biggest bakery specialist is Greggs, which controls the Bakers Oven, Olivers, Bartletts and Crawfords outlets, as well as Greggs stores.

Since 1961, plant bakeries have used a fast-track production system known as the Chorleywood Bread Process (CBP). It replaces traditional slow fermentation with a short burst in a high-speed mixer, using a much greater quantity of yeast. More water is absorbed into the dough, which rises up and reaches its desired volume more quickly. Many additives are used in this type of bread, including chemical 'improvers' which oxidise newly-milled flour. As the bleaches used to whiten and sterilise the flour manage to strip it of much of its nutritional value, vitamins and minerals have to be added back in.

The drawback of conventional wholemeal bread, in which the whole of the wheatgrain is retained, is that higher residue levels of fertilisers, pesticides and post-harvest storage treatment chemicals are present in wholemeal than in ordinary white or brown flour. This is a very good reason to choose the organic option when buying bread.

QUESTIONABLE INVESTMENTS

Until recently Doughty Hanson owned RHM, the manufacturer of the Hovis, Mother's Pride, Granary and Nimble brands. Doughty Hanson also invests in SAFT. This multinational company is a major manufacturer of batteries for military applications including intercontinental and ballistic missiles, torpedoes and aircraft, and is a supplier to the US army. Doughty Hanson also owned Dunlop Standard Aerospace, which services military aircraft engines.

Although RHM has since been floated on the stock market, Doughty Hanson still retains a 30 per cent share.

ALTERNATIVES

One alternative to the major brands is bread from a local bakery. However, many bakers are now using technology similar to CBP, which can render the bread rather tasteless, lightweight and insubstantial.

The fashion for eliminating potentially aggravating foods such as wheat and dairy from the diet has brought increased publicity for food intolerance, and led to many supermarkets stocking gluten-free breads. There are some concerns, however, that people are being persuaded to cut foods from their diet unnecessarily, and without proper nutritional advice. Low salt, wholemeal bread is perfectly healthy for most people, but those who do have a diagnosed intolerance can now find the products they require outside the specialist shelves. Even so, the greatest variety of breads is still to be found in health food stores.

Organic bread is now widely available in major UK supermarkets as well as the smaller specialist stores. For those with an interest in purchasing locally baked goods, Goswells produces organic bread on behalf of Doves Farm and Whole Earth Foods in London and the South East, while in the North West there's Sakers and in the Gloucestershire region there's Hobbs House.

Good bread only needs to contain flour, yeast, water and salt and can easily be made at home, either in a breadmaker or by hand. If making bread by hand, look out for recipes that only require one rising, as this will reduce the time it takes to prepare – and don't forget that a standard dough can also be used for pizza bases and other meals.

- Authentic Bread
- Doves Farm
- Village Bakery

- Greggs
- Vogel
- Warburtons
- Whole Earth
- William Jackson

- Allinson
- Burgen
- Granary
- Hovis
- Kingsmill
- Mother's Pride
- Nimble
- Sunblest

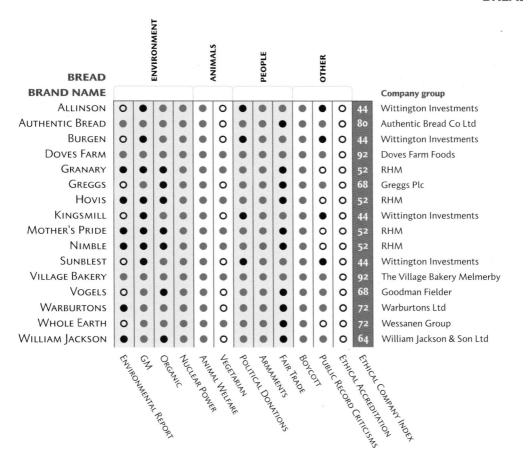

BREAD BRAND NAME	ENVIRONMENT	ANIMALS	PEOPLE	OTHER	Ethical Company Index	Company group
Allinson					44	Wittington Investments
Authentic Bread					80	Authentic Bread Co Ltd
Burgen					44	Wittington Investments
Doves Farm					92	Doves Farm Foods
Granary					52	RHM
Greggs					68	Greggs Plc
Hovis					52	RHM
Kingsmill					44	Wittington Investments
Mother's Pride					52	RHM
Nimble					52	RHM
Sunblest					44	Wittington Investments
Village Bakery					92	The Village Bakery Melmerby
Vogels					68	Goodman Fielder
Warburtons					72	Warburtons Ltd
Whole Earth					72	Wessanen Group
William Jackson					64	William Jackson & Son Ltd

Column categories:
ENVIRONMENT — Environmental Report, GM, Organic, Nuclear Power
ANIMALS — Animal Welfare, Vegetarian
PEOPLE — Political Donations, Armaments, Fair Trade
OTHER — Boycott, Public Record Criticisms, Ethical Accreditation

Key

● Top rating
○ Middle rating
● Bottom rating

Source: The Ethical Company Organisation

Breakfast cereals

There was a time when a bowl full of sugar-drenched cornflakes and cold milk was thought (at least by the breakfast cereal manufacturers) to be the ideal start to the day. The high levels of salt and sweeteners in many of these products have since come under close scrutiny by healthy eating campaigners, and the companies themselves have been criticised for persistently targeting the least nutritious of these brands at children.

A HEALTHY START?

Breakfast cereals have long been a neat way for the food companies to take perfectly healthy food apart and put it back together again for profit. Inevitably, these foods lose much of their nutritional benefit in the process, which is why the companies have to put all those vitamins back in again at the end. They can then claim that these 'added vitamins' make their products healthier and more nutritious than any others.

Some companies make healthy eating claims about their products which are not, according to the Food Commission, substantiated with proper evidence. There was concern when Kellogg's claimed that they were 'serving the nation's health', while their Corn Flakes had been found to contain one of the highest salt levels on the cereals market. In July 2006, *Which?* published a report which found that over three quarters of the 275 cereals it tested rated 'high' for sugar content if measured according to the Food Standards Agency's guidelines. Many products which were marketed as healthy contained alarmingly high levels of salt.

SWEETENING THE KIDDIES

The children's sector makes up about a third of the British market for breakfast cereals, and that is why many products such as Quaker's Sugar Puffs are deliberately packaged to attract children. Such cereals can be high in salt as well as low in fibre. One food author has complained that with sugar accounting for up to half the weight of the ingredients, some products are 'twice as sweet as a jam doughnut'.

It is for this reason that the Food Standards Agency has made efforts to introduce more transparent labelling on foods such as breakfast cereals. The system is becoming more familiar as it is adopted by the major supermarkets, and often involves the companies giving percentage values for each of the main ingredients in the cereal. These will usually include salt, fat and sugar, as well as recommended daily amounts of vitamins and minerals.

Be warned though – the figures may be skewed according to what the company decides is a 'recommended serving' of their product. Suffice to say that 30g of cornflakes may be enough for a child, but the average adult might fill their bowl with twice that amount.

OTHER CONCERNS

Pesticide residues are regularly detected in corn-based cereals even after processing, and research has shown that these residues find their way into 10-30 per cent of conventional breakfast cereals.

Until the tide turned against GM products, there was considerable doubt about the GM content of products made from soya or maize. Now Kellogg's products are reportedly free from proteins from GM crops. Weetabix Ltd stated that no GM ingredient, additive or derivatives are used in any of its processes. Quaker Oats Ltd claimed that it does not use ingredients containing GM material in any Quaker product and that it had tested all lecithin used in its products to ensure freedom from any such material. The company also said it would only consider using ingredients derived from GM crops in the longer term if they had been fully approved by the relevant regulatory and scientific authorities.

A HEALTHIER START

There are now a number of companies offering organic cereals, such as cornflakes and bran flakes, which use reduced quantities of pesticides and are free from GM ingredients. Most of these are easiest to find in specialist health food shops, although some are slowly making their way into the mainstream retailers.

Many nutritionists believe that one of the best ways to start the day is not with cereal but a hearty bowl of porridge. Look for organic oats from one of the companies with a good ethical rating on the table opposite, heat with a little water or organic milk and serve with a sliced (fair trade) banana on top.

- Doves Farm
- Infinity
- Jordans
- Mornflake

- Kallo
- Kashi
- Kellogg's
- Weetabix
- Whole Earth

- Shredded Wheat
- Quaker Oats

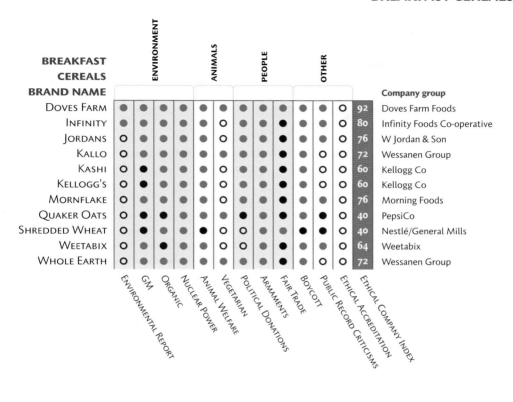

BREAKFAST CEREALS BRAND NAME	ENVIRONMENT				ANIMALS		PEOPLE				OTHER		Ethical Company Index	Company group
	Environmental Report	GM	Organic	Nuclear Power	Animal Welfare	Vegetarian	Political Donations	Armaments	Fair Trade	Boycott	Public Record Criticisms	Ethical Accreditation		
Doves Farm													92	Doves Farm Foods
Infinity													80	Infinity Foods Co-operative
Jordans													76	W Jordan & Son
Kallo													72	Wessanen Group
Kashi													60	Kellogg Co
Kellogg's													60	Kellogg Co
Mornflake													76	Morning Foods
Quaker Oats													40	PepsiCo
Shredded Wheat													40	Nestlé/General Mills
Weetabix													64	Weetabix
Whole Earth													72	Wessanen Group

Key

● Top rating

○ Middle rating

● Bottom rating

Source: The Ethical Company Organisation

Butter & margarine

The world has long been divided into lovers of pure butter, who defy the risks of too much cholesterol, and those who search for a palatable alternative. Although butter is still holding its own in the market, there have recently been huge advances in the development of nice-tasting margarines, dairy spreads and vegan butters. The drawback is that these tend to use a wide variety of different ingredients and additives.

WHAT'S IN THEM?

Butter is a simple product. It consists mainly of the fat found in cows' milk and it is not highly processed, beyond the churning that makes it solid. Some of the 'spreadable' butters, the ones that stay soft in the fridge, may be blended with vegetable oil. Others are processed by breaking down the hard fats.

Margarine is usually more complex. It contains at least 80 per cent oils and fats – which can be of animal, fish or vegetable origin – as well as ingredients such as whey, vegetable colouring, flavouring and emulsifiers. Vitamins are also often added.

Any product with less than 80 per cent oils or fats has to be called a 'spread'. To be labelled as 'reduced fat' a spread may contain up to 60 per cent fat, and to be labelled as 'light' or 'low fat' it may have up to 40 per cent fat. Spreads contain at least as many added ingredients as margarine and some of the lower fat ones have added gelatine and water. The dairy spreads – the ones marketed as being 'butter-like' – contain added cream or buttermilk.

Major supermarkets have now begun stocking vegan-friendly spreads such as Pure, although for a greater choice of products, wholefood shops are still the best option.

THE SEARCH FOR HEALTH

During the 1980s, fears over the health risks of saturated fat convinced many people to switch from butter to margarine. However, in the 1990s it was discovered that trans fatty acids (TFAs) in margarine could raise the level of LDL, the 'bad cholesterol' in the blood, by as much as saturates, while decreasing the level of HDL, the 'good cholesterol'. This is why some products, including some of the dairy spreads, are now marketed as having 'vitrually no TFAs'.

ORGANIC BUTTER

Organic cows receive better treatment than most, because they are never kept permanently indoors, which keeps them healthier, and their calves are suckled for around nine weeks.

GM ISSUES

Some spreads and spreadable butters contain soya oils, which may be labelled simply as vegetable oil or fat. Many of these may be from GM soya beans. That's why it's better to look for products labelled as GM-free or organic.

Lecithin is a common additive derived from soya, and if it is of GM origin it need not be labelled as such on the grounds that there will be no DNA present.

Butter may not be unaffected by the GM issue, as the cows may have been given GM feed. Only organically certified products will avoid GM entirely.

PACKAGING

Butter normally comes wrapped in a single piece of paper, and this is clearly better than the plastic tub packaging used for margarine and spreads. Although the tubs are marked as recyclable, very few of us actually recycle them.

The main reason for this is that polypropylene (identified by a number five on the packaging), the substance used to make margarine tubs, is difficult and expensive to recycle, and there is currently little demand for the resultant materials. Until this changes, few authorities are likely to provide facilities for recycling.

- Pure
- Suma
- Yeo Valley

- Anchor
- Castle Dairies
- Country Life
- GranoVita
- Lurpak
- St Ivel Shirgar
- Utterly Butterly
- Vitalite
- Willow

- Benecol
- Flora
- I Can't Believe It's Not Butter
- Kerrygold

BUTTER & MARGARINE

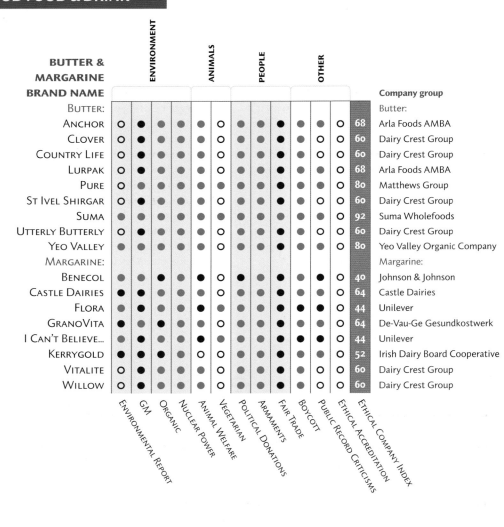

BRAND NAME	Ethical Company Index	Company group
Butter:		**Butter:**
Anchor	68	Arla Foods AMBA
Clover	60	Dairy Crest Group
Country Life	60	Dairy Crest Group
Lurpak	68	Arla Foods AMBA
Pure	80	Matthews Group
St Ivel Shirgar	60	Dairy Crest Group
Suma	92	Suma Wholefoods
Utterly Butterly	60	Dairy Crest Group
Yeo Valley	80	Yeo Valley Organic Company
Margarine:		**Margarine:**
Benecol	40	Johnson & Johnson
Castle Dairies	64	Castle Dairies
Flora	44	Unilever
GranoVita	64	De-Vau-Ge Gesundkostwerk
I Can't Believe...	44	Unilever
Kerrygold	52	Irish Dairy Board Cooperative
Vitalite	60	Dairy Crest Group
Willow	60	Dairy Crest Group

Column categories: ENVIRONMENT (Environmental Report, GM, Organic, Nuclear Power); ANIMALS (Animal Welfare, Vegetarian); PEOPLE (Political Donations, Armaments, Fair Trade, Boycott); OTHER (Public Record Criticisms, Ethical Accreditation); Ethical Company Index

Key

● Top rating
○ Middle rating
● Bottom rating

Source: The Ethical Company Organisation

Cafés

The demand for premium coffee has led to a rapid increase in the number of coffee shops in the UK, with 2,299 branded outlets open in June 2004. Major companies' influence on the world coffee market has contributed to the weak bargaining position of the small-scale producers, many of whom face debt and poverty. However, supporting ethical schemes such as fair trade can reconcile our enjoyment of coffee shops with the needs of the producers.

UK COFFEE SHOP MARKET

The retail coffee market was predicted to be worth £2.2 billion in 2005. Branded cafés account for £700 million of this business, and the three main players (Starbucks, Caffè Nero and Costa Coffee) make up over half of the branded market – and that market is still growing. Predictions that demand for premium coffee would only be a short-lived trend in Britain have been discredited, as the country embraces a European-style café culture. An annual growth rate of at least 5 per cent is expected in this sector for the foreseeable future.

The growth of chain cafés throughout Europe and North America has made a small number of companies very influential in the coffee market as a whole. Most notably, Starbucks now buys 2.2 per cent of the world's coffee. Large companies are able to dictate terms to smaller producers and force down the price of coffee, pushing many small producers below the poverty line. This is a serious problem that all coffee drinkers should be aware of.

FAIR TRADE

The fair trade scheme is the most effective and well-known way to help the 20 million people involved in the production of coffee. Fair trade protects small producers from fluctuating prices and acquisitive middlemen by guaranteeing a minimum price for their coffee and ensuring that farmers are paid regularly. The scheme also charges a premium of 15 US cents per pound of coffee to fund future development. The growing popularity of coffee shops means that cafés can make a significant difference by embracing fair trade. For example, Café Revive's decision to buy only fair trade coffee in 2004 led to a 14 per cent increase in the UK's consumption of ethically sourced coffee.

Developments in the coffee shop sector show what can be achieved by considerate consumerism. In 2004, AMT announced that the reason for their change to fair trade was 'due to your demand'. As more and more consumers seek out fair trade coffee, it its likely that other cafés will also consider ethical purchasing as a means of improving their profits.

Of the larger chains, Starbucks and Costa Coffee both offer a fair trade alternative on request. Whilst this is commendable, large coffee shops could do more. In 2004, Starbucks purchased just 1.6 per cent of its coffee from fair trade sources, despite campaigners calling for the company to buy at least 5 per cent from this market. An effective way of persuading any café to source more of their products ethically is to request fair trade.

Building on the success of fair trade schemes in the coffee shop market, Oxfam launched a new chain of 'Progresso' cafés in 2004. Although initially only trading in London, the charity aims to operate 20 shops nationwide by 2007. As well as embracing fair trade, 25 per cent of Progresso is owned by producer co-operatives, giving them a direct share in the company's profits.

CAFÉ WARS

The growth of branded coffee shops has contributed to the growing monotony of Britain's high streets. Starbucks in particular has been criticised for its aggressive expansion. The resources of the company enable it to sacrifice immediate profits in order to ensure that the brand is visible in prime locations and town centres. Starbucks has also been accused of deliberately locating branches near other established cafés in order to force competitors out of the market. Readers who are concerned about these tactics, and those who value diversity on the high street, can easily vote with their wallet by supporting the smaller coffee shops, which (at the moment) are still more common than their branded rivals. Tea drinkers may want to support their local tea rooms rather than buying from branded coffee shops.

- Café Revive
- Progresso

- AMT
- Caffè Nero
- Coffee Republic
- Costa Coffee
- Puccinos

- Pret a Manger
- Starbucks

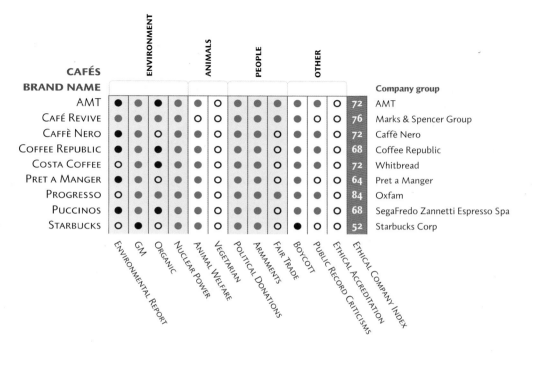

CAFÉS BRAND NAME	ENVIRONMENT				ANIMALS		PEOPLE			OTHER			ETHICAL COMPANY INDEX	Company group
	Environmental Report	GM	Organic	Nuclear Power	Animal Welfare	Vegetarian	Political Donations	Armaments	Fair Trade	Boycott	Public Record Criticisms	Ethical Accreditation		
AMT	●	●	●	●	●	○	●	●	●	●	●	○	72	AMT
CAFÉ REVIVE	●	●	●	●	○	○	●	●	●	●	○	○	76	Marks & Spencer Group
CAFFÈ NERO	●	●	○	●	●	○	●	●	○	●	●	○	72	Caffè Nero
COFFEE REPUBLIC	●	●	●	●	●	○	●	●	○	●	●	○	68	Coffee Republic
COSTA COFFEE	○	●	●	●	●	○	●	●	○	●	●	○	72	Whitbread
PRET A MANGER	●	●	○	●	●	○	●	●	○	●	○	○	64	Pret a Manger
PROGRESSO	○	●	●	●	●	○	●	●	●	●	●	○	84	Oxfam
PUCCINOS	●	●	●	●	●	○	●	●	○	●	●	○	68	SegaFredo Zannetti Espresso Spa
STARBUCKS	○	●	○	●	●	○	●	●	○	●	○	○	52	Starbucks Corp

Key

● Top rating

○ Middle rating

● Bottom rating

Source: The Ethical Company Organisation

Trophy Holistic Premium Dog Food

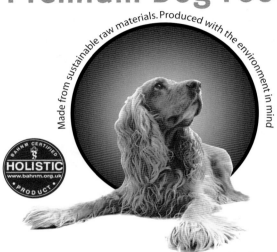

Made from sustainable raw materials. Produced with the environment in mind

A premium, complete, holistic food offering superior nutrition, quality British ingredients and full certification from BAHNM; for lifelong health and vitality.

A natural holistic food with the added benefit that it is made from sustainable raw materials, produced in the U.K. with the environment in mind to complement our green policy.

Benefits:

- Unique holistic formula
- Whole grains for energy and stamina
- Quality animal protein sources
- Natural Omega 3 & 6
- Naturally Hypo-Allergenic & wheat gluten free
- Balanced nutrition
- No fillers, artificial colours, flavourings or preservatives
- Fortified with Glucosamine, Chondroitin, Cranberry & MOS
- Available in two bite sizes

Quality Petfoods, Accessories and Petcare Products

www.trophypetfoods.co.uk

BRITISH MADE

Proudly made in the U.K. Supporting British Agriculture

Call our Nutritional Hotline 01367 240333 for advice, a free sample of Trophy Holistic and an information pamphlet or visit

www.trophypetfoods.co.uk

Cat & dog food

The choice of cat and dog foods in the main supermarkets tends to be rather limited, because most of them source their products from only two manufacturers: Mars and Nestlé. Organic brands are beginning to appear alongside these big names, although they are still easiest to find in specialist shops. Animal testing is an important issue in the manufacture of pet foods, and some owners even consider vegetarianism for their animals.

ORGANIC

Buying organic pet food is a way of avoiding factory-farmed meat, especially where a vegetarian diet is unsuitable. Yarrah is one of the organic brands which is available within supermarkets. New foods should always be introduced slowly, as they may not be readily accepted at first.

To avoid shop-bought feeds altogether, it is possible to give pets home-cooked food. However, it is advisable to consult the vet before embarking on a new diet, as there is a risk of the animal developing imbalances in vitamins and minerals. Dogs need the right phosphorous/calcium ratio to maintain healthy bones, and without taurine (an amino acid that comes almost exclusively from animal sources) cats can go blind. Feeding them too much raw fish can cause neurological problems.

Just like humans, animals are increasingly suffering from weight problems. An estimated 40 per cent of pet cats and dogs in the UK are obese.

ANIMAL TESTING

The British Union for the Abolition of Vivisection (BUAV) has discovered serious cases of animal testing by the pet food industry. The big four pet food companies include Purina Petcare (Nestlé), Hills Pet Nutrition (Colgate Palmolive), Iams (Procter & Gamble), and Pedigree (Mars). Investigation by the BUAV has shown that all of these companies provide funding for, or carry out their own, animal testing.

Procedures in the UK may involve some of the following: isolation of animals for long periods, endoscopy, periods of complete fasting or food restriction, application of skin irritants, frequent changes of diet during trials and plucking hair from near the base of the tail, as well as regular sedation, anaesthetics and enemas. Many animals become too sick as a result of the testing and have to be withdrawn from trials. The fate for others can be worse still; according to the BUAV, an experiment supported by Iams artificially induced kidney failure in cats, resulting in the death of two animals.

Alternative brands to try are Lily's Kitchen, Burns Pet Nutrition, Europa Pet food, OrganiPets and Trophy Pet Foods – none of whom test on animals. These brands have also been accredited by the Ethical Company Organisation, which indicates that they are ethically and environmentally sound.

Buy dried formulations

Some dried food formulations are thought to be healthier than tinned food. Pets need to eat more tinned food than dried to gain the same amount of nutrition.

The environmental evidence is also in favour of dried food. Tinned foods are at least 60 per cent water, making the transported volume and weight much greater. Paper bags are obviously a lower environmental impact choice than tins. Bulk buying is preferable, whether in the form of large sacks or tins.

The new innovation of single-serve portions in plastic pouches and foil trays is utterly wasteful of resources.

Vegetarian pets?

It is highly controversial, but some argue that dogs can be fed a vegan diet, and some companies like Yarrah (Roelevink Beheer BV) make vegan and vegetarian dog food.

Cats, however, do need meat because they require taurine. If they are deprived of it they will soon turn to hunting birds and mice for meat. The Vegan Society imports something called Vegecat from the US, a supplement designed to be added to home-cooked cat food.

- Burns
- Europa
  Pet Foods
- Lily's Kitchen
- OrganiPets
- Trophy Pet
  Foods
- Yarrah

- Butcher's
- Hi-Life
- Pascoe's
- Wagg
- Webbox

- Bakers
  Complete
- Eukanuba
- Felix
- Friskies
- Iams
- Pedigree
- Whiskas

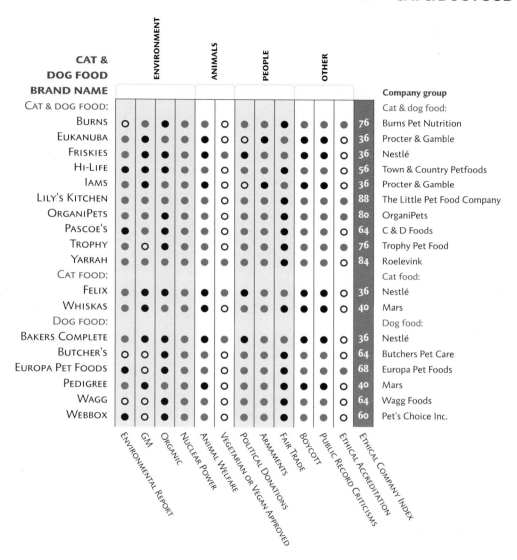

CAT & DOG FOOD BRAND NAME	Ethical Company Index	Company group
Cat & dog food:		Cat & dog food:
Burns	76	Burns Pet Nutrition
Eukanuba	36	Procter & Gamble
Friskies	36	Nestlé
Hi-Life	56	Town & Country Petfoods
Iams	36	Procter & Gamble
Lily's Kitchen	88	The Little Pet Food Company
OrganiPets	80	OrganiPets
Pascoe's	64	C & D Foods
Trophy	76	Trophy Pet Food
Yarrah	84	Roelevink
Cat food:		Cat food:
Felix	36	Nestlé
Whiskas	40	Mars
Dog food:		Dog food:
Bakers Complete	36	Nestlé
Butcher's	64	Butchers Pet Care
Europa Pet Foods	68	Europa Pet Foods
Pedigree	40	Mars
Wagg	64	Wagg Foods
Webbox	60	Pet's Choice Inc.

Rating category columns (left to right): ENVIRONMENT (Environmental Report, GM, Organic, Nuclear Power), ANIMALS (Animal Welfare, Vegetarian or Vegan Approved), PEOPLE (Political Donations, Armaments, Fair Trade, Boycott), OTHER (Public Record Criticisms, Ethical Accreditation).

Key

● Top rating
○ Middle rating
● Bottom rating

Source: The Ethical Company Organisation (2008)

Chocolate

Consumers in the Western world are much more interested than they used to be in where their favourite foods come from and how they are grown. They need to be, because the processes behind the trading of the most important commodities, such as cocoa, can be very ugly indeed. Major concerns include the use of child labour and exposure of workers to dangerous pesticides such as lindane. As ever, one solution is to buy fair trade.

CHILD LABOUR

Thanks to press investigations and television documentaries, the issue of child labour in cocoa farming has been revealed as a serious problem in several countries. One survey carried out by the International Institute of Tropical Agriculture in Ivory Coast, Cameroon, Ghana and Nigeria found that the majority of children working on cocoa farms were under 14, and that approximately one-third of school-age children living in cocoa-producing households had never been to school.

The chocolate industry has developed a Global Industry Protocol (also known as the Harkin-Engel Protocol), and initially promised a method of certifying that cocoa had been grown 'under appropriate labour conditions'. The Protocol also aimed to eliminate the worst forms of child labour on cocoa farms in West Africa. Unfortunately, although some progress has been made, *www.labourrights.org* states that the industry is not doing enough to address labour and associated issues, and consequently the commitments of the Protocol have not been met. Illegal labour may still be prevalent on many farms.

In normal times, Ivory Coast produces nearly half of the world's cocoa, but, according to a report published in the Earth Island Journal, it is hard to ensure that Ivory Coast cocoa is 'slavery free'. The country's cocoa industry has a history of human rights problems. For example, in 2002 most of the foreign workers in the cocoa plantations were driven away by thugs encouraged by the ruling party. Mars and Nestlé have tended to buy large amounts of cocoa from Ivory Coast, whereas Cadbury's has said that it buys 90 per cent of its cocoa from Ghana, which is a signatory to a tough code of conduct against trafficking of child workers.

FAIR TRADE

Buying fair trade chocolate is currently the best way to avoid support for child labour and commodity traders. All of Traidcraft and Day Chocolate Company's chocolate is fair trade marked, as is Green & Black's Maya Gold. Traidcraft's organic chocolate contains fair trade sugar as well as cocoa, and so has the highest proportion of fairly traded ingredients. Another great ethical choice is Chococo from The Purbeck Chocolate Company which has full Ethical Accreditation.

Plamil, a vegan company, doesn't use the fair trade mark on the grounds that it only protects humans from exploitation and not animals, but it says that its cocoa is all sourced from the Dominican Republic and fulfils the social standards set out by the Fairtrade Labelling Organisation.

Perhaps one of the biggest shake-ups in the chocolate industry in recent years has been the controversial Cadbury Schweppes take-over of Green & Black's in May 2005. Cadbury's has, however, promised to run Green & Black's as a standalone business and to take the brand's ethical agenda seriously. Nevertheless, as a result of the take-over Green & Black's no longer fall in *The Good Shopping Guide*'s ethical company category.

TRICKY ISSUES

One major concern about the cocoa industry is how many chemical fertilisers and pesticides the farmers use. The best protection for the cocoa trees is for farmers to do mix planting, which also enables them to provide their own food, as well as using the income from cocoa to pay for health care, education and other costs. The Day Chocolate Company highlights how prone cocoa is to diseases. Therefore, in order not to threaten the livelihoods of the farmers and also the Ghanaian economy, the company has made a choice not to be organic.

The pesticide lindane has been banned from agricultural and horticultural use in the EU, on the grounds that it is a hormone disrupter linked to health problems such as breast cancer. It is still used on cocoa plantations, exposing the workers to potential health risks. Chocolate companies say they have no way of knowing whether their cocoa is sprayed with lindane, as they don't buy direct from the growers. They should be encouraged to do their own tests.

- Chococo
- Divine
- Plamil
- Traidcraft

- Dairy Milk
- Green & Black's
- Lindt
- Ritter Sport
- Thornton's

- Chocolate Orange
- Kitkat
- Mars Bar

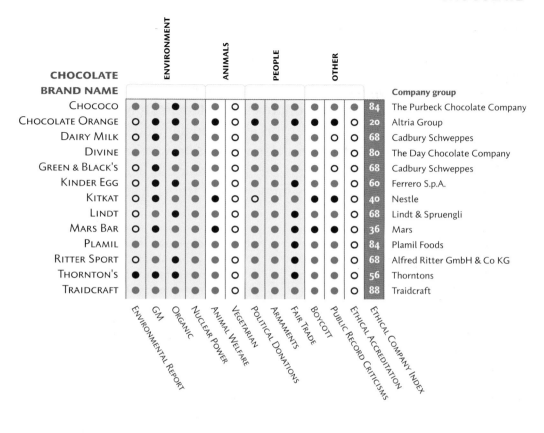

Key

● Top rating

○ Middle rating

● Bottom rating

Source: The Ethical Company Organisation

Cooking oil

With olive oil being touted as an antidote to ageing, it's little wonder it has suddenly become incredibly popular as a salad dressing and a cooking ingredient. The great rush to meet this increased demand has led to expanded production in Mediterranean countries, which is now threatening local ecology and causing large-scale soil erosion. Buying organic oils helps to prevent these problems – and ensures that the product is free from GM ingredients.

TROUBLE IN SPAIN

An important advantage of most olive oil is that it is almost certain to be GM-free, but the food and development organisation Sustain reports that over-intensification of olive oil production in Spain has resulted in erosion and other agronomic and environmental problems, causing irreversible damage in over 40 per cent of Andalucia. The new methods of production have also involved increasing the use of herbicides, pesticides and fungicides. Sustain recommends that consumers choose organic olive oil wherever possible.

PURITY AT A COST

Most of the UK's oilseed rape is grown as a winter crop, which Sustain argues has had a detrimental effect on Britain's environment, causing biodiversity to suffer and bird populations to decline. Winter crops have also at times provided an excuse for mass shooting of wood pigeons.

Although British farmers are not likely to be introducing GM crops just yet, the whole issue remains important for cooking oils. Worryingly for consumers concerned about GM issues, vegetable oil produced from GM plants does not have to be labelled as GM. This is because the processing is thought to eliminate any proteins or DNA that might otherwise be present. Consumers should be aware that maize oil, soya oil and canola (rapeseed) oils may be processed from GM plants, especially if they originate from North America, whose international trade in grains is based on a commodity flow system where no distinction is made between GM and non-GM crops.

In 2002, the Food Standards Agency considered options for food labelling proposed by the European Commission. One of these options was to extend the current labelling to include foods derived from GM material, as well as food containing GM. This would cover vegetable oils. However, the more likely outcome will be that current labelling regulations will remain, with a new additional label of 'GM free' being introduced to denote products which are free from all GM technology. In the meantime, those who want to avoid any GM links should opt for sunflower oil, olive oil or organic oils.

60-SECOND GREEN GUIDE

- Buy glass bottles instead of plastic ones
- There is little risk of active GM materials being present in any oil
- For the lowest risk of GM 'contamination', use olive oil
- Most vegetable oils are equally good for you

OWN-BRAND OILS

Most supermarkets refuse to say which companies produce their own-brand cooking oils. Pressure from consumers may change his policy eventually, but until we can be certain of the identity of the own-brand suppliers, the brand will continue to be rated with the supermarket. Unlike other companies, supermarkets are rated according to their stocking policies. A recent positive development, however, is that supermarkets are beginning to produce their own brand organic olive oils.

BRAND OWNERSHIP

The multinationals Unilever and Mitsubishi own most of the recognised olive oil brands. Neither of these companies boast particularly respectable ethical records. Both have received criticism for their animal rights and welfare policies, as well as for using GM in some of their products. Mitsubishi is involved in nuclear and armament activities and Unilever have had a number of labour complaints levelled against them. Suma and Meridian received the highest rating. There is yet to be a major brand which practices fair trade.

PACKAGING

More expensive oils are likely to come in glass bottles, which are easy to recycle. Products in the lower price range are almost always packaged in plastic bottles, some of which may be made from PVC (which is identifiable by a '3' inside a recycling symbol on the base of the bottle). Plastic recycling in the UK is still very poorly developed, with about 95 per cent of waste being landfilled or incinerated.

- Meridian
- Suma

- Filippo Berio

- Crisp & Dry
- Mazola
- Olivio
- Princes
- Pura

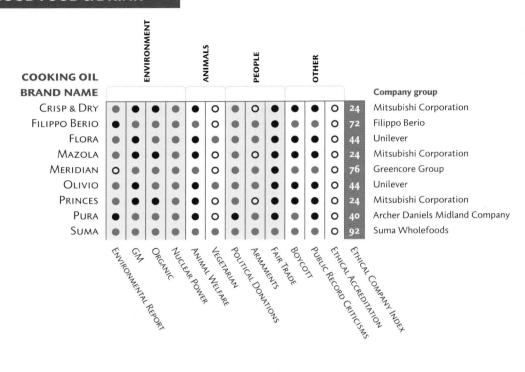

COOKING OIL BRAND NAME / Company group

Brand	Index	Company group
CRISP & DRY	24	Mitsubishi Corporation
FILIPPO BERIO	72	Filippo Berio
FLORA	44	Unilever
MAZOLA	24	Mitsubishi Corporation
MERIDIAN	76	Greencore Group
OLIVIO	44	Unilever
PRINCES	24	Mitsubishi Corporation
PURA	40	Archer Daniels Midland Company
SUMA	92	Suma Wholefoods

Categories: ENVIRONMENT, ANIMALS, PEOPLE, OTHER

Columns: ENVIRONMENTAL REPORT, GM, ORGANIC, NUCLEAR POWER, ANIMAL WELFARE, VEGETARIAN, POLITICAL DONATIONS, ARMAMENTS, FAIR TRADE, BOYCOTT, PUBLIC RECORD CRITICISMS, ETHICAL ACCREDITATION, ETHICAL COMPANY INDEX

Key

● Top rating

○ Middle rating

● Bottom rating

Source: The Ethical Company Organisation

Crisps

The big crisp manufacturers make a lot of noise about the taste of their products, but prefer to only whisper about what they are made of. The label will usually reveal a lengthy list of ingredients, most of which are artificial flavourings and other additives. Alongside the health problems associated with fried and fatty foods, these additives are thought to exacerbate hyperactivity in children. A better option is the (slightly less unhealthy) organic equivalent.

KEEPING KIDS HEALTHY

The Food Commission has sharply criticised snacks promoted by footballers, and accused food marketing firms of undermining children's nutrition. A supermarket survey failed to find any healthy children's food promoted using football imagery. Walkers was the main culprit with its tartrazine-laced Footballs, promotions in association with Gary Lineker and David Seaman, and an FA Premier League sticker offer in its other brands. One mother on the Food Commission's Parents' Jury said: 'It would be better if children were shown that the way to emulate their sporting heroes is to eat and drink healthily.'

Crisps can be healthier than a lot of junk foods, but they should be eaten in moderation. A recent study by Baby Organix found that children are consuming more than twice as much salt in their diet as the government recommends. The UK Asthma & Allergy Research Centre says that 'significant changes in children's hyperactive behaviour could be produced by the removal of colourings and additives from their diet'. It is recommended that brilliant blue (E133), tartrazine (E102), quinoline yellow (E104) and sunset yellow (E110) – colours which appear most commonly in snacks such as Monster Munch – should be eliminated from kids' diets. Monosodium glutamate (E621) is another controversial additive present in many crisps, despite being banned for use in baby foods.

Some crisp manufacturers are also moving into the wholesale use of artificial sweeteners because they cost a fraction of the price of sugar. Many are then ignoring their legal obligation to state directly under the brand name that a product contains sweeteners, consigning it instead to the small print.

NATURAL AND ORGANIC

Tra'fo, Kettle, Cape Cod and Jonathan Crisp products contain only 'natural' ingredients.

Companies have a small circle in the GM column on the table if not all of their products can be guaranteed free from GM-derived ingredients. Although companies in Britain have made considerable progress in sourcing non-GM derivatives, many on the 'red list' are there because of a lack of assurance that dairy ingredients such as whey are from non-GM fed cows.

Certified organic products are always totally GM-free. Many supermarkets are now selling own-brand organic crisps, which are being manufactured for them by companies such as Stour Valley Foods. Jonathan Crisp and Tra'fo crisps are all organic, and Kettle has one organic variety.

Monsanto is currently developing bruise-free potatoes, as well as a 'higher-solids' potato, which will absorb less oil during processing. It remains to be seen whether they will fare better than its Bt potatoes, which companies such as McDonalds,

P&G and Pepsi subsidiary Frito-Lay are now refusing to use, even in the US, due to the high level of public concern about the technology.

PACKAGING

Old-fashioned polypropylene packets, as used by Seabrooks and a lot of the '10p snacks', are in theory easier to recycle than the plasticated foils which most manufacturers now use.

Pringles cartons are the ultimate packaging excess. They contain six different materials, including steel, aluminium, PET and polyethylene, some of them in composite form. As Pringles now make up at least ten per cent of the entire UK 'bagged snacks' market, they are becoming a significant contributor to landfill waste.

- Jonathan Crisp
- Tra'fo

- Cape Cod
- Golden Wonder
- Highlander Snacks
- Kettle Chips
- Mission Foods
- Red Mill
- Seabrook
- Stour Valley

- Brannigans
- KP
- Pringles
- Walkers

CRISPS

BRAND NAME

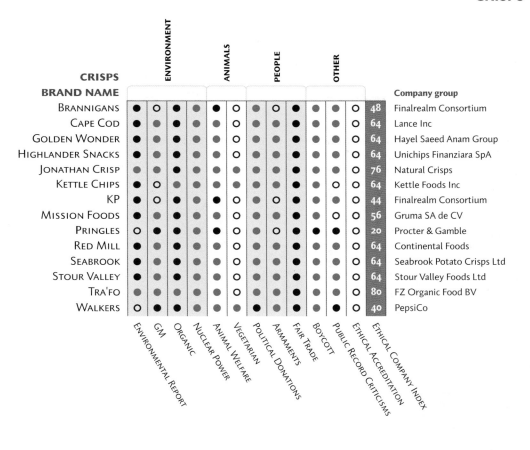

Brand Name	Ethical Company Index	Company group
BRANNIGANS	48	Finalrealm Consortium
CAPE COD	64	Lance Inc
GOLDEN WONDER	64	Hayel Saeed Anam Group
HIGHLANDER SNACKS	64	Unichips Finanziara SpA
JONATHAN CRISP	76	Natural Crisps
KETTLE CHIPS	64	Kettle Foods Inc
KP	44	Finalrealm Consortium
MISSION FOODS	56	Gruma SA de CV
PRINGLES	20	Procter & Gamble
RED MILL	64	Continental Foods
SEABROOK	64	Seabrook Potato Crisps Ltd
STOUR VALLEY	64	Stour Valley Foods Ltd
TRA'FO	80	FZ Organic Food BV
WALKERS	40	PepsiCo

Column headers (left to right):

ENVIRONMENT: Environmental Report, GM, Organic, Nuclear Power
ANIMALS: Animal Welfare, Vegetarian
PEOPLE: Political Donations, Armaments, Fair Trade
OTHER: Boycott, Public Record Criticisms, Ethical Accreditation
Ethical Company Index

Key

● Top rating
○ Middle rating
● Bottom rating

Source: The Ethical Company Organisation

Fish

It was once thought that the sea was an inexhaustible source of fish, but over-exploitation has resulted in depleted stocks and damaged marine ecosystems. Overfishing is one of the world's most pressing environmental issues, and has severe social and economic repercussions. Billions of people depend upon fishing for food, and thousands more for employment. The prevention of overfishing is paramount to the survival of the industry, those who depend on it, and the natural marine environment.

THE ISSUE

A fishery is an area of the sea where the target fish species is caught by net, line or another fishing method. Fisheries that are ecologically balanced and are not depleted of natural resources are becoming increasingly rare. According to the Food and Agriculture Organisation, only one quarter of the world's fish stocks are within safe environmental levels. The remaining stocks are either partly or fully overfished or in a serious stage of depletion. This means that the majority of the world's fisheries are in need of management reviews if they are not to be lost forever.

The consequences of overfishing are already manifest. In 1992, one of the world's richest natural resources, the cod stocks off the Canadian Grand Banks, Newfoundland, disappeared virtually overnight as a result of poor fisheries management. This had a devastating impact on the marine environment and the local community. About 40,000 jobs were lost and the fishery still remains closed today.

There are numerous reasons for the collapse of fisheries and the depletion of fish stocks. Technological advances have enabled the fishing industry to target the resource more precisely and take more from our seas than is sustainable.

Bigger boats, more powerful engines, developments in radar and sophisticated refrigeration systems mean that fishermen can stay out at sea for longer, travel further and locate fish more easily. Catching fish, therefore, is no longer a lottery and as a result more fish are being caught than ever before. Another reason for the collapse of fisheries is the marketplace, which sanctions overfishing by allowing the sale of endangered fish for profit. The problem is that the market is about today and tomorrow and maybe next week, but certainly not about ten years' time.

PEOPLE AND FOOD

In the developed world, seafood is regularly enjoyed by billions of people for taste and health reasons. However, the current unsustainable fishing climate is more of a threat to developing countries, where 3.5 billion people currently depend upon the ocean for their primary source of food (UNEP 2004). If fish stocks continue to deplete, then demand for fish in these coastal areas may outstrip the supply.

LIVELIHOOD AND EMPLOYMENT

As a major renewable resource, fisheries provide a livelihood for hundreds of thousands of people around the world, sustaining coastal towns and villages and representing a valuable source of income for the global community. The role of fishermen is crucial in the lives of many communities that fish for local needs. 90 per cent operate on a small scale, but they account for over half of the global fish catch (UNEP 2004). These are the fishermen who will be increasingly squeezed by the large operators who come in search of new stocks as they exhaust the old. It is the greed of the rich world that has produced the shortages and it will be the wealth of the rich world that buys what fish are left, even though they are essential to the very existence of the poor.

For the sake of their livelihoods, fishermen around the world need to be assured that the fishing industry has a secure future, whether they fish locally or on a much larger scale. Unsustainable fishing affects fishermen in both developed and developing countries alike.

CALL TO ACTION

Raising awareness of overfishing is the first step towards tackling the problem.

Ethical consumers can demand fish from sustainable and well-managed stocks to help safeguard the world's seafood supply. This will put pressure on retailers to stock sustainably harvested seafood products. This in turn will help to provide incentives for the seafood industry to fish in a responsible way.

ONE SOLUTION: THE MARINE STEWARDSHIP COUNCIL (MSC)

In the mid 1990s, conservationists and industrialists alike saw that they had a common interest in changing the marketplace in terms of its operation. This led to the creation of the Marine Stewardship Council (MSC), an international charity dedicated to saving the world's fish stocks. The MSC created an environmental standard to reward well-managed and sustainable fisheries. Fisheries of any size, scale, type or location can voluntarily apply to be assessed against the MSC Standard by independent certification bodies.

The MSC Standard considers the condition of the fish stock, the impact of fishing on the marine ecosystem and the management of the fishery. If they pass, certified fisheries win the right to use the MSC blue eco-label on their products, harnessing consumer preference for sustainable seafood. It is possible to protect fish stocks and marine ecosystems whilst continuing to fish, if the fishing is conducted in a responsible manner.

Examples of responsible fishing include building escape hatches into lobster creel pots, as in the Western Australian Rock Lobster fishery, the first in the world to receive the MSC environmental standard. These hatches enable small lobsters to escape and reproduce while the adults remain within the creel. Another example from the Scottish Loch Torridon and Nephrops fishery, certified to the MSC Standard, is fisherman throwing juvenile fish back into the sea to allow them to reproduce, ensuring that the fish stock remains healthy. Measures to reduce by-catch are also being adopted in order to maintain healthy ecosystems. By-catch, such as fish, marine mammals and seabirds, can be caught accidentally by fishing gear and then thrown back into the ocean dead, disrupting the natural balance of the marine ecosystem. The New Zealand hoki fishery, certified to the MSC Standard, is implementing various measures at the fishery to reduce by-catch.

At the end of 2005 there were 15 fisheries certified to the MSC Standard and many more are at some stage of the fishery assessment process. In total these equate to approximately 4 per cent of the total wild global fish supply.

The MSC provides a solution to the global problem of overfishing and is a market driven programme. Today there are over 300 seafood products carrying the MSC label in 17 countries. New products are appearing every week. The consumer is empowered to make the best environmental choice in seafood, which is needed to complete the circle of influence that uses market forces to ensure the future of sustainable fisheries.

For information on where to buy MSC labelled products, please visit <*www.msc.org*, or see relevant links from *www.gooshing.co.uk*. Through our specific buying habits we can all help place a global industry back on the path to stability and long-term sustainability.

THE FOLLOWING FISHERIES ARE CURRENTLY CERTIFIED BY THE MARINE STEWARDSHIP COUNCIL:

- Alaska Pollock – Bering Sea and Aleutian Islands
- Alaska Pollock – Gulf of Alaska
- Alaska Salmon
- Australian Mackerel Icefish
- BSAI Pacific Cod Freezer Longline
- Burry Inlet Cockles
- Hastings Fleet Dover Sole Fishery
- Hastings Fleet Pelagic Fishery
- Loch Torridon Nephrops
- Mexican Baja California Red Rock Lobster
- New Zealand Hoki
- North Sea Herring
- South African Hake
- South Georgia Toothfish
- South West Mackerel Handline
- Thames Herring
- US North Pacific Halibut
- US North Pacific Sablefish
- West Australian Rock Lobster

Ice cream

It's a safe bet that the traditional recipe for ice cream didn't include 'E110 sunset yellow' and residues of bovine somatotropin, but for some of the big-brand versions this may be the case. Many companies are now making an effort to reduce the number of additives in their desserts, but the only safe way to ensure an E-number free ice cream is to stick to the small producers and buy organic or dairy-free.

INGREDIENTS TO AVOID

Real ice cream should be made like an egg custard, then churned and frozen, but it inevitably becomes more expensive as the purity increases. The cheaper ice creams on the market are combinations of skimmed milk or milk powders, with lots of sugar and sweeteners, and added ingredients such as hardened vegetable fats, emulsifiers, colourings, flavourings, acidity regulators and other artificial processing aids, whipped up with lots of air.

A quick look at the ingredients list should be enough to tell us what level of additives a product contains. Look out for the worst E-numbers, such as annatto (E160b), sunset yellow (E110) and carmoisine (E122), as these have been linked to health problems including asthma, rashes and hyperactivity. Some have also been linked to cancer in test animals. Particular concern has been raised about E110, a coal-tar dye which is a by-product of the petrochemical industry: because of its potential toxicity, manufacturers have been persuaded not to use it in baby food.

The growth hormone bovine somatotropin (commonly called rBST here, or BGH in the US) was designed to be given to cows daily to increase their milk yield. Due to serious health concerns for the cows and for humans, the EU introduced a moratorium on the drug. This is still in effect, meaning the use of rBST is not currently legal in the EU. The Soil Association say that their organic standards prohibit the use of rBST in the production of milk, and naturally none of the non-dairy alternatives contain this hormone. The Organic Consumers Association in the US has an ongoing boycott of Haagen-Dazs in protest against its use of milk from cows injected with rBST.

OTHER OPTIONS

Manufacturers of organic ice cream are generally more aware of the benefits of natural ingredients than the big name brands. All the smaller producers included in the table opposite state their commitment to minimising the use of artificial ingredients in their ice creams.

Some larger retailers are also reducing the number of artificial additives in their ranges and selling more organic goods, which by definition are likely to contain a higher proportion of natural ingredients.

Dairy-free and vegan alternatives to ice cream are also available, most of which use soya in place of animal ingredients such as milk and cream. Soya is a good source of protein and essential amino acids, and has been linked to reductions in 'bad' cholesterol when eaten as part of a balanced diet – although in this case the added sugars in ice cream might outweigh any potential benefit!

Choose organic brands and those certified as GMO free to ensure no genetically modified soya has found its way into the product. Soya is one of the most widely produced GM crops, so it is worth keeping an eye on the label.

TASTE TESTS

The UK Consumers' Association has held taste tests for a range of ice creams and frozen desserts. Green & Black's chocolate ice cream came out as a favourite, and its vanilla range went down well too. Rocombe Farm's chocolate and vanilla flavours also tingled the taste buds, both coming out with an 'above average' rating. The Swedish Glace vanilla flavour came up trumps, although Tofutti's equivalent didn't fare so well, scoring an 'average' rating, as did its chocolate dessert.

Many ice cream cartons are not suitable for remanufacturing, even though they can be recycled. At the moment, facilities to carry out the process are rare. The best option is to find a new use for the tubs at home, rather than throwing them away.

- Cream O'Galloway
- Mother Hemp
- Oat Supreme
- Rocombe Farm
- Swedish Glace
- Yeo Valley

- Green & Black's
- Little Big Food Co
- Tofutti

- Ben & Jerry's
- Carte D'Or
- Haagen Dazs
- Magnum
- Wall's

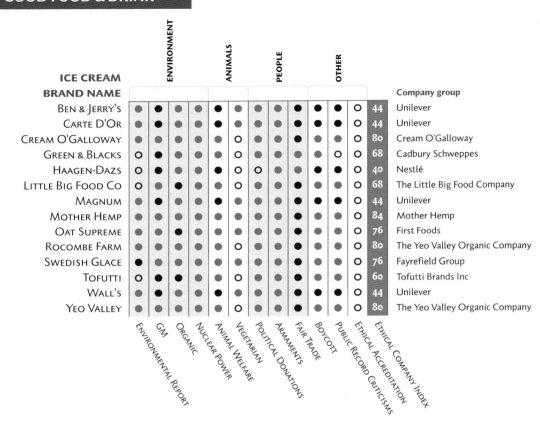

ICE CREAM

BRAND NAME	ENVIRONMENT				ANIMALS		PEOPLE			OTHER			Ethical Company Index	Company group
	Environmental Report	GM	Organic	Nuclear Power	Animal Welfare	Vegetarian	Political Donations	Armaments	Fair Trade	Boycott	Public Record Criticisms	Ethical Accreditation		
BEN & JERRY'S													44	Unilever
CARTE D'OR													44	Unilever
CREAM O'GALLOWAY													80	Cream O'Galloway
GREEN & BLACKS													68	Cadbury Schweppes
HAAGEN-DAZS													40	Nestlé
LITTLE BIG FOOD CO													68	The Little Big Food Company
MAGNUM													44	Unilever
MOTHER HEMP													84	Mother Hemp
OAT SUPREME													76	First Foods
ROCOMBE FARM													80	The Yeo Valley Organic Company
SWEDISH GLACE													76	Fayrefield Group
TOFUTTI													60	Tofutti Brands Inc
WALL'S													44	Unilever
YEO VALLEY													80	The Yeo Valley Organic Company

Key

● Top rating

○ Middle rating

● Bottom rating

Source: The Ethical Company Organisation

Jams & spreads

Although home-made jams, marmalade, lemon curd and other spreads usually have much tastier ingredients than those on the supermarket shelves, few of us have the time, opportunity or indeed inclination to slave over a hot stove making it ourselves. So for the healthiest spreads at breakfast and tea-time, seek out the brands whose jams have the highest percentage of real fruit, rather than concentrates, and don't include artificial sweeteners and preservatives.

FRUIT LEVELS

To be called jam, a preserve only needs to have a minimum of 25 per cent fruit content, while marmalade can have as little as 20 per cent fruit. It is not always obvious that in many commercial jams some of the fruit can be from frozen or concentrated sources. The fruit and sugar is also heavily boiled, which reduces its nutritional value.

'Extra' jam has 45g of fruit per 100g. Compotes are preserves with very high fruit levels, so they do not set in the same way as traditional jam, but they retain much more of the nutritional value of the fruit.

OTHER INGREDIENTS

To be labelled as jam or marmalade, a preserve has to have at least 60g of sugar per 100g of product – even for the extra-fruit varieties. Reduced-sugar jams have 30-55g, but will often have added colour, emulsifier, preservative and stabiliser. Fruit spreads are usually purely derived from fruit, relying on a fruit juice such as apple for sweetness. This means they are best kept in the fridge as they do not keep as long as sugar-rich jam or marmalade.

Vegetarians and vegans need to check the labels of jams and spreads before they buy, as some contain animal-derived ingredients. Lemon curd contains eggs, which are likely to be battery-produced except in the case of organic products. Some jellies and jams may contain gelatine, an animal by-product, to aid with setting.

No genetically engineered fruit is permitted in the UK but the enzymes used to process the fruit, gelatine or added sweeteners could have involved GM. Choosing organic products helps to avoid all these additives. The only brand that is exclusively organic is Bionova. Other companies, such as Meridian, Whole Earth, Hartleys (Wm P Hartley brand) and Baxters make some organic jams. The Herb Stall was the only organic lemon curd producer found at the time of the research.

SWEETENERS AND PRESERVATIVES

Artificial sweeteners may be used in 'diet' products, under a variety of guises such as aspartame, saccharin or xylitol. The first of these, aspartame, can be found in over 6,000 products (including crisps, vitamin pills and soft drinks), and has been the subject of numerous health scares. The most recent, in 2005, centred on an Italian study that linked it to cancer in rats, and sparked a public call by one MP for the sweetener to be banned.

Moreover, some campaigners believe there is reason to doubt the original research that led to aspartame being approved for consumption, because they say there was pressure on the scientists from the sweetener industry. Nevertheless, the European Food Safety Authority has said that no changes will be made to its position on aspartame until a thorough review of the Italian study has been carried out.

Alongside sweeteners, preservatives may be used in higher fruit-content products. Preservatives such as potassium sorbate (E200-213) are suspected of causing allergic reactions, gastric irritation and problems with conception in some people. Manufacturers could avoid using them by noting a shorter shelf life and recommending refrigeration.

PACKAGING

Although most fruit preserves are still packed in glass jars, there has been increasing use of squeezy plastic bottles or pouches by companies such as Hartleys and Robertsons. Some honey manufacturers are starting to pack their products in rigid plastic jars, and this could happen in the jam market too. Before you buy, check for the triangle symbol on the back of packaging to see if the product is suitable for recycling.

- Bionova
- Meridian
- The Herb Stall

- Baxters
- Bonne Maman
- Duerr's
- Stute
- Tiptree
- Whole Earth

- Frank Cooper
- Hartley's
- Robertsons

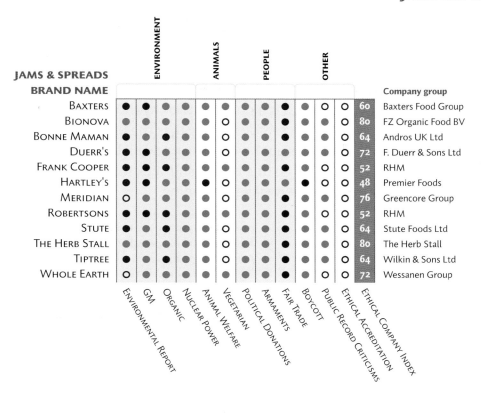

JAMS & SPREADS BRAND NAME	ENVIRONMENT				ANIMALS		PEOPLE				OTHER		Ethical Company Index	Company group
	Environmental Report	GM	Organic	Nuclear Power	Animal Welfare	Vegetarian	Political Donations	Armaments	Fair Trade	Boycott	Public Record Criticisms	Ethical Accreditation		
BAXTERS	●	●	●	●	●	●	●	●	●	●	O	O	60	Baxters Food Group
BIONOVA	●	●	●	●	●	O	●	●	●	●	●	O	80	FZ Organic Food BV
BONNE MAMAN	●	●	●	●	●	O	●	●	●	●	●	O	64	Andros UK Ltd
DUERR'S	●	●	●	●	●	O	●	●	●	●	●	O	72	F. Duerr & Sons Ltd
FRANK COOPER	●	●	●	●	●	●	●	●	●	●	O	O	52	RHM
HARTLEY'S	●	●	●	●	●	O	●	●	●	●	O	O	48	Premier Foods
MERIDIAN	O	●	●	●	●	O	●	●	●	●	●	O	76	Greencore Group
ROBERTSONS	●	●	●	●	●	●	●	●	●	●	O	O	52	RHM
STUTE	●	●	●	●	●	O	●	●	●	●	●	O	64	Stute Foods Ltd
THE HERB STALL	●	●	●	●	●	O	●	●	●	●	●	O	80	The Herb Stall
TIPTREE	●	●	●	●	●	O	●	●	●	●	●	O	64	Wilkin & Sons Ltd
WHOLE EARTH	O	●	●	●	●	●	●	●	●	●	O	O	72	Wessanen Group

Key

● Top rating

O Middle rating

● Bottom rating

Source: The Ethical Company Organisation

Pasta

Tagliatelli, linguine, fusilli or just good old spaghetti. Whichever kind you fancy, there is no doubt that pasta is a popular carbohydrate, whether in a salad or mixed with vegetables, seafood or meat as the basis of a main meal. Although most of the different kinds of pasta available are equally healthy, there is always scope to go one better and seek out the organic or fresh varieties – or perhaps even make it at home.

PURE WHEAT

Traditional quality pasta should be made with 100 per cent durum wheat, in wholewheat or semolina form. However, with growth in the own-brand market pushing prices down, many of the cheaper pastas now contain 'soft wheat' substitutes, which can result in a slightly sticky or slimy texture.

A richer pasta is produced with the addition of egg, making it unsuitable for vegans. Tomato or spinach is added to produce the distinctive red or green pastas, and some pasta-makers are fond of ingredients such as nettles, beetroot and chilli.

FRESH PASTA

In Italy, fresh pasta is available in over a hundred variations of shape and filling, and is sold in specialist shops to be eaten on the day of purchase. In the UK, most of the fresh pasta available is not quite so fresh, as it is usually preserved in a modified environment to extend the shelf life. Pasta from specialist shops is often very good, but many of the ready-prepared fresh pasta meals on the supermarket shelves are rather stodgy with few authentic ingredients.

Fresh pasta most often contains egg, which again is not good news for vegans, and if the pasta is from a non-organic company the eggs will probably be from battery farms. All brands certified as organic by the Soil Association will contain only free-range eggs.

ORGANIC, WHOLEWHEAT AND GM

As the supermarket own-brands are responsible for more than three quarters of all UK pasta sales, the introduction of organic own-brand pasta ranges is a positive step towards sustainable agriculture.

Shoppers need to be wary of wholewheat pasta varieties (unless they are clearly marked as organic) because they are far more likely to contain chemical residues, as the husk or bran of the wheat absorbs more of the pesticides and fertilisers than the semolina used in white varieties.

As there are no GM varieties cleared for sale within the EU, dry pasta in its standard form should be free from GM ingredients, with the possible exception of the red tomato pasta, which could contain GM tomato paste. All the pasta certified as organic by the Soil Association is sure to be GM-free.

PACKAGING

Most pasta is packaged in polypropylene, which although recyclable will usually end up in landfill. Given the expansion of the dried product during cooking and the need for thicker packaging for fresh pasta (in order to maintain the seal around the modified environment), far greater volumes of plastic are needed for the fresh product. This makes it a less environmentally-friendly option than cheaper dried pasta.

ALTERNATIVES

For those with wheat or gluten intolerance, Orgran produces a rice pasta which has been produced in isolation from all other foodstuffs. Another possible alternative may be one of the speciality pastas produced by La Terra e Cielo, which are made from farro wheat or 'spelt' (an ancient forerunner to modern wheat), which contains considerably less gluten, and which the company claims may be suitable for people with a mild wheat intolerance.

For those looking for an organic alternative, Organico (*www.organico.co.uk*), one of the Ethical Company Organisation's accredited brands, produce high quality organic pasta sourced from dedicated suppliers.

An alternative to expensive fresh pasta is to make your own by rolling out flour and water in the right quantities.

- La Terra e Cielo
- Organico
- Traidcraft

- Barilla
- Dellugo
- Fiorucci
- Marshalls
- Orgran
- Pastificio Rana
- Puglisi

- Buitoni
- Seeds of Change

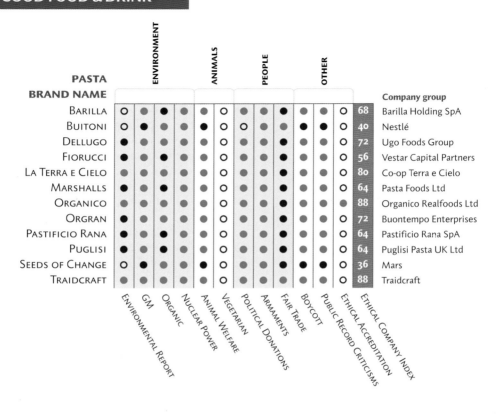

PASTA BRAND NAME	ENVIRONMENT	ANIMALS	PEOPLE	OTHER		Company group
Barilla					68	Barilla Holding SpA
Buitoni					40	Nestlé
Dellugo					72	Ugo Foods Group
Fiorucci					56	Vestar Capital Partners
La Terra e Cielo					80	Co-op Terra e Cielo
Marshalls					64	Pasta Foods Ltd
Organico					88	Organico Realfoods Ltd
Orgran					72	Buontempo Enterprises
Pastificio Rana					64	Pastificio Rana SpA
Puglisi					64	Puglisi Pasta UK Ltd
Seeds of Change					36	Mars
Traidcraft					88	Traidcraft

Column headings: Environmental Report, GM, Organic, Nuclear Power, Animal Welfare, Vegetarian, Political Donations, Armaments, Fair Trade, Boycott, Public Record Criticisms, Ethical Accreditation, Ethical Company Index

Key

● Top rating
○ Middle rating
● Bottom rating

Source: The Ethical Company Organisation

Soft drinks

Sweet, sugary fizzy drinks are loved by children – and more than a few adults too. We all know they're unhealthy, but how many of us are aware of what actually goes into the average soft drink? Additives, preservatives and caffeine can be found in many of the most well known brands, all of which can be potentially harmful if consumed in excess. Pure fruit juices and smoothies are a good alternative.

SWEET AND DAMAGING

The average person consumes four pints of liquid each day. In the UK, around 20 per cent of this is in the form of soft drinks, with the volume slowly rising. High consumption of soft drinks means that other, healthier drinks are being replaced. Apart from the water, there is very little in soft drinks that is even vaguely beneficial.

Whether still or fizzy, off-the-shelf soft drinks can contain the equivalent of up to 15 cubes of sugar – well over half the recommended daily maximum. This can lead to dental cavities and other health problems associated with high intakes of sugar. The acids in many soft drinks (found in both ordinary and no-sugar varieties) can also cause tooth decay and erosion of the hard enamel on the surface of the tooth. Research has found that dental erosion as a result of drinking acidic drinks and other sources affects about 30 per cent of 13-year-olds. Even Ribena's 'tooth-kind' drink failed dental tests carried out in two different studies.

All soft drinks given to children should be diluted to avoid tooth decay, given with meals if possible and in cups rather than bottles, as sipping drinks causes greater damage.

OTHER NASTIES

It's not just the sugar in soft drinks which can cause health problems. Caffeine, found in many fizzy drinks in varying levels, is addictive and can cause hyperactivity, disrupted sleep and withdrawal symptoms in children and adults. In Glasgow, a survey found an unusually high level of orofacial granulomatosis – an oral version of Crohn's disease, which has been linked to a sensitivity to preservatives and flavourings in carbonated soft drinks.

Research in the US has also found links between cola consumption and kidney stones in men. Artificial sweeteners – such as those found in many diet and no-sugar drinks – have also been linked to a number of health problems, although research has yet to prove any conclusive links.

CONFUSED IDENTITIES

Although the Libby's brand is no longer actually produced by Nestlé, it still owns the brand name. Hanover Acceptances' subsidiary, Gerber Foods – the new licensee of the brand – has an agreement with Nestlé for the Libby's name, and consequently Baby Milk Action still lists Libby's in its Nestlé boycott information, because Nestlé still profits from it. This licensing agreement also applies to other ex-Nestlé brands Um Bongo, Libby's C and Jusante. The Nestlé logo is now absent from all packaging, meaning that consumers may have been unwittingly buying Libby's brands believing them to be dissociated from the Nestlé empire.

PACKAGING

Soft drinks are likely to come in aluminium or steel, glass, plastic bottles or cartons.

The volume of packaging used each year is staggering. We use around 6 billion aluminium cans, 225 million plastic containers (mostly plastic bottles) and 6 billion glass containers annually. Less than a third of steel and aluminium cans and only 5 per cent of plastics are recycled in the UK, the remainder being landfilled or incinerated. Glass is the best option, as it can be recycled indefinitely.

SMOOTHIES

A relatively new addition to the soft drinks market are smoothies – juice drinks made from pure crushed fruit. Government guidelines say they can only count towards one portion of your 'five-a-day', regardless of how many pieces of fruit are used, but there can be no doubt that smoothies are still the healthy option. Try Innocent, who scored well in the research and have been accredited by the Ethical Company Organisation.

- Innocent
- Libby's
- Whole Earth Cola

- Britvic
- Irn Bru
- Purdey's
- Robinsons
- Schweppes
- Smoothiepack
- Sunny Delight
- Vimto
- Virgin Cola

- Coca-Cola
- Pepsi
- PJ Smoothie
- Ribena
- Tropicana

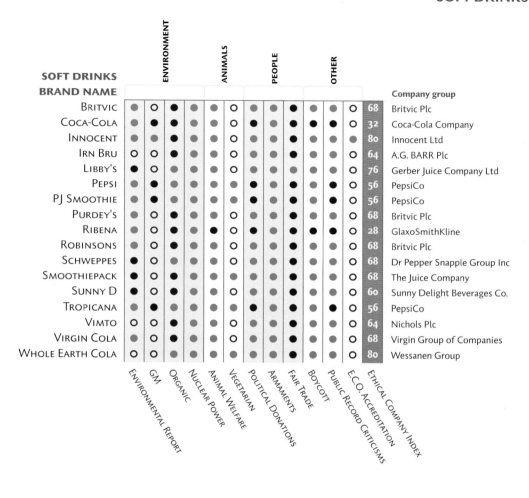

Key

● Top rating
○ Middle rating
● Bottom rating

Source: The Ethical Company Organisation (2008)

Fairtrade food
fights poverty

Buy from Oxfam
Find your nearest
Oxfam shop at:
oxfam.org.uk/shops

Every time you buy from our delicious Fairtrade range, including chocolates, teas, coffees, biscuits, nuts, dried fruit, and spices, you're helping to end poverty! That's because Fairtrade ensures a fairer deal for producers, and all Oxfam's profits are used to overcome poverty and suffering. **Try some today!**

Look for this Mark on Fairtrade products.
www.fairtrade.org.uk

Oxfam GB is a member of Oxfam International. Registered charity No. 202918.
Inhouse Job No. 3464   Photos: Christian Guthier/Oxfam, Fairtrade Foundation

Soup

Soup is often touted as a good all-round meal; healthy, warming and nutritious. Yet there is a big difference between a home-cooked broth and a powdered soup from the supermarket. The latter is likely to be packed with extras, such as added salt and sugar, flavour enhancers and preservatives. It may also come from a company with dubious ethical credentials, and be guilty (like so many processed goods) of environmentally-unfriendly over-packaging.

Healthy diets

Like many types of processed food, ready-made soups have been criticised for containing high levels of sugars, salt and artificial additives such as flavourings and thickeners. Packet soups have been most heavily condemned for offering little of nutritional value, while canned soups often use high levels of sugar and thickeners. Fresh carton soups are usually a healthier option, but many still have a high salt content.

The official guidelines for the 'five-a-day' scheme promoting fruit and vegetables (*www.5aday.nhs.uk*) say that convenience foods such as soups do count as a portion, but advise that consumers check the salt, sugar and fat content before buying. It goes without saying that products which include recognisable vegetables are more likely to count towards your five-a-day than ones that reduce everything to a powder.

Home-made soups, cooked with organic vegetables and with sparing use of salt, make healthy, filling and balanced meals, either on their own or with a helping of crusty wholemeal bread. If made in large quantities, they can be easily refrigerated or frozen for later use.

The famous cabbage soup diet takes the slimming properties of home-made soups to an extreme. By following an all-you-can-eat programme of cabbage soup, plus a few portions of fruit and vegetables a day, the diet promises guaranteed weight loss – not surprising since it restricts the calorie intake to what is essentially a level of controlled starvation. Naturally, reputable dieticians will have nothing to do with it, and even supporters of the plan say it should be followed for no longer than a week.

Companies

Consolidation in the food industry means that supermarket shoppers are faced with an array of companies with problematic ethical records, while the smaller companies and brands are being squeezed out of the mass market.

Although campaigners against the irresponsible marketing of baby foods and breastmilk substitutes usually focus on the activities of Nestlé, Heinz has also been the subject of sustained and serious criticisms on the subject from organisations such as Baby Milk Action. It has been criticised for violations of the International Code of Marketing of Breastmilk Substitutes in countries including Pakistan, Uganda, Peru, Mexico, Ghana and Malaysia. More information on companies involved in this issue is available on the Baby Milk Action website at *www.babymilkaction.org*.

Farleys, a Heinz subsidiary, was also cited back in 1994 as having produced marketing material which played on the insecurities of women, by claiming that breastfeeding harmed the sex lives of many new mothers, and that 'modern women' regarded breasts as 'more than just feeding machines'. Fortunately, the same claims have not been found in recent Farleys marketing materials.

ORGANIC ISSUES

Suma and Just Wholefoods both sell only organic brands of soup, and the New Covent Garden Soup Company has brought out a range of organic choices. Other than these, all the products studied are made from non-organic produce, which generally involves the use of pesticides and potentially environmentally-damaging growing systems.

PACKAGING

Packaging is another issue, as it is for most convenience foods. Ready-made soup comes either in packets, cartons, packets inside cartons or tins. Although most of these can usually be recycled, the inclusion of 'flavour-sealing' materials such as foils and plastics can exclude some products from being remanufactured. None of the products examined in the table had any indication that they were packaged in recycled materials.

- Just Wholefoods
- Suma

- Baxters

- Batchelors
- Campbells
- Carb Options
- Heinz
- Knorr
- New Covent Garden

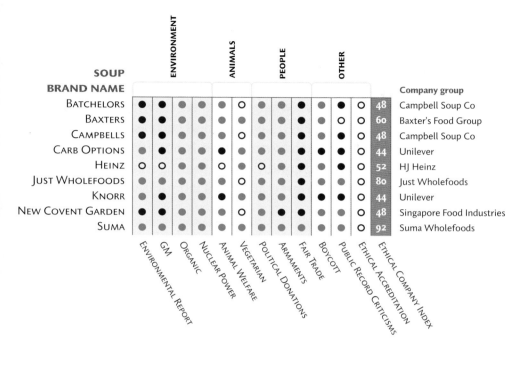

SOUP BRAND NAME	ENVIRONMENT				ANIMALS		PEOPLE			OTHER			Ethical Company Index	Company group
	Environmental Report	GM	Organic	Nuclear Power	Animal Welfare	Vegetarian	Political Donations	Armaments	Fair Trade	Boycott	Public Record Criticisms	Ethical Accreditation		
BATCHELORS	●	●	●	●	●	○	●	●	●	●	●	○	48	Campbell Soup Co
BAXTERS	●	●	●	●	●	●	●	●	●	●	○	○	60	Baxter's Food Group
CAMPBELLS	●	●	●	●	●	○	●	●	●	●	●	○	48	Campbell Soup Co
CARB OPTIONS	○	●	●	●	●	●	●	●	●	●	●	○	44	Unilever
HEINZ	○	○	●	●	○	●	○	●	●	●	●	○	52	HJ Heinz
JUST WHOLEFOODS	●	●	●	●	●	○	●	●	●	●	●	○	80	Just Wholefoods
KNORR	●	●	●	●	●	●	●	●	●	●	●	○	44	Unilever
NEW COVENT GARDEN	●	●	●	●	●	○	●	●	●	●	●	○	48	Singapore Food Industries
SUMA	●	●	●	●	●	●	●	●	●	●	●	○	92	Suma Wholefoods

Key

● Top rating
○ Middle rating
● Bottom rating

Source: The Ethical Company Organisation

Sugar

Sugar, from a nutritional perspective, is pointless. Yet the whole notion of dessert is founded upon its use: where would we be without cakes, chocolate, sweets and pastries? Even savoury food such as processed meats and ready meals can be packed with sugar. But it is not just our own health we should worry about. Working conditions in the sugarcane fields have been the subject of much controversy, and child labour is widespread.

HEALTH FACTORS

Ordinary white sugar supplies little more than cheap calories, as any vitamins and minerals that might be found in the sugar cane are stripped away by the refining process. Eating too much of it puts the body at risk, not only of tooth decay, but of other long-term problems such as diabetes, dyspepsia and heart and liver disease. Sugar has also been associated with a range of health issues, from anxiety to increased symptoms of pre-menstrual tension. Too much sugar can even affect our concentration. It is estimated that almost half of all children are susceptible to increased hyperactivity related to the consumption of sugar – another persuasive argument for the removal of junk food from schools.

Some scientists argue that we are abusing the evolutionary role of our sweet tooth by consuming refined sugar. Until relatively recently, sugar was a delicacy, or wasn't eaten at all. Now, the average American consumes 115lbs of it per year. Our ancestors would have satisfied their cravings for sweetness by eating fruit and sweet vegetables, and in so doing would have obtained necessary nutrients such as vitamin C. In places where sugar cane is eaten raw, people have healthy teeth because of the vitamins and minerals that occur naturally in the juice.

Unrefined or raw brown sugars have been processed to some degree but they retain more nutrients than white sugar. Any superior brown sugar will have been derived from cane. Brown sugar from beet has been coloured with caramel or molasses.

EU SUGAR DUMPING

EU sugar subsidies have helped keep developing countries mired in poverty while rewarding massive refiners like British Sugar (who are behind the Silver Spoon brand) with huge profits. Five million tonnes of surplus sugar are dumped every year on world markets, destroying opportunities for exporters in poorer countries. As a result, in 2004 Ethiopia made losses equivalent to its total national spending on HIV/Aids programmes, and

Malawi's losses actually exceeded its national budget for primary healthcare.

In April 2005, the World Trade Organisation ruled that these subsidies were illegal, and the EU is now planning to reform its policy. This is excellent news, since changes to the EU sugar regime could boost the economies of some of the world's poorest countries: according to Oxfam research, 30,000 jobs could be created in Mozambique and Zambia alone. But Oxfam and the WWF are concerned about the effect of these sudden reforms on developing countries, and say EU proposals are insufficient to alleviate the impact on countries in Africa, the Pacific and the Caribbean, which until now have had (limited) preferential access to European markets. More details on the proposals are available on the Oxfam website at *www.oxfam.org.uk*.

GOOD SUGAR

The sudden growth in the UK of the organic and fair trade market is especially apparent in the sugar business. All the major brands now offer an organic alternative, and Whitworths, Billingtons and Traidcraft each have a fair trade range, although fair trade pioneer Traidcraft is the only company to sell fairly-traded sugar exclusively. The companies that so far have not adopted the fair trade mark for any of their products are British Sugar (a subsidiary of Associated British Foods, which is owned by Wittington Investments, and which bought Billington's in August 2004) and Tate & Lyle, whose factories have been criticised by campaigners for having a history of union busting. We should see more fair trade brands in the future as the power of the ethical pound continues to grow.

- Traidcraft
- Whitworths

- Tate & Lyle

- Billingtons
- Silver Spoon

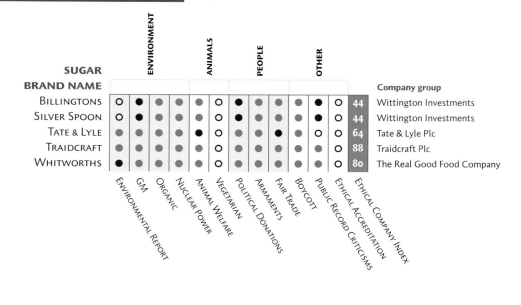

SUGAR

BRAND NAME	Ethical Company Index	Company group
BILLINGTONS	44	Wittington Investments
SILVER SPOON	44	Wittington Investments
TATE & LYLE	64	Tate & Lyle Plc
TRAIDCRAFT	88	Traidcraft Plc
WHITWORTHS	80	The Real Good Food Company

Column categories: ENVIRONMENT (Environmental Report, GM, Organic, Nuclear Power), ANIMALS (Animal Welfare, Vegetarian), PEOPLE (Political Donations, Armaments, Fair Trade, Boycott), OTHER (Public Record Criticisms, Ethical Accreditation, Ethical Company Index)

Key

- Top rating
- Middle rating
- Bottom rating

Source: The Ethical Company Organisation

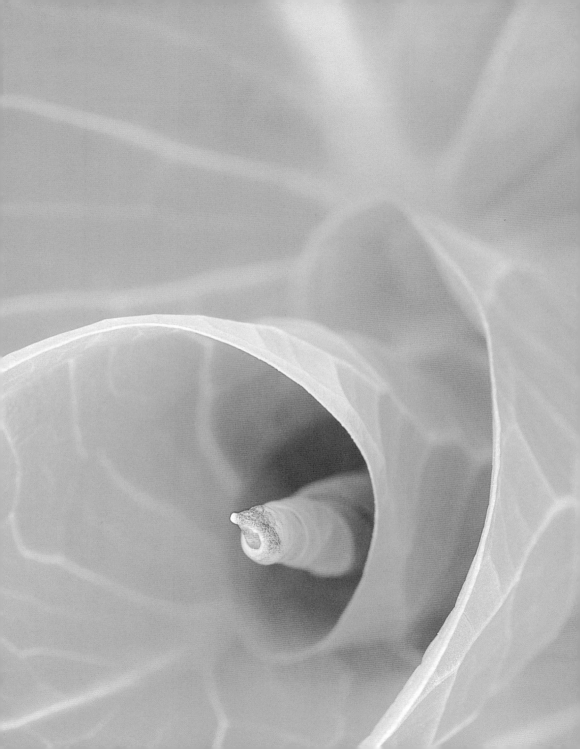

Supermarkets

Love them or loathe them, supermarkets are highly convenient and the majority of the British public uses them regularly. They hold a central place in the retail economy and have a great deal of power – over producers, consumers, and the way food is farmed and transported. While some supermarkets still have a very long way to go, others are making significant efforts to use their power more benignly and conduct their business in an ethical manner.

A HUGE POWER

For every £1 of household expenditure around 49p is spent in supermarkets. And of this, 33p is spent in just the four largest supermarket groups (Asda, Morrisons, Sainsbury's, Tesco). So, for the ethical shopper, the choice of supermarket is probably one of the most crucial decisions to make.

The first supermarkets as we know them today opened in the 19th century, when the Co-operative Movement formed a group of local retailers. Today the UK shopping landscape looks quite different, with 80 per cent of grocery shopping being done in supermarkets. As William Moyes, Director General of the British Retail Consortium, said: 'Let's be honest, life without supermarkets would be hell... What used to take all day now takes a couple of hours.' With better value, more choice and more convenience, no wonder British consumers seem to be in love with supermarkets. But however much we try to ignore it, this convenience comes at a cost.

SUPERMARKET PROGRESS

There are some ethical areas in which supermarkets have made a lot of progress, and are even showing the way for other big businesses. The four product sectors below have increased in availability as a result of support from supermarkets, which have the selling power to move an alternative brand into the mainstream market. In each case, however, consumer demand has had a huge effect in getting the changes made.

1 More fair trade products

All supermarkets now sell some fair trade products – products which give a fairer price to farmers and producers in the developing world. Furthermore, most of them also have their own fair trade brands.

2 More organic products

The Soil Association says that 'our health is directly connected to the health of the food we eat, ultimately to the health of the soil'. Organic farming refers to the growing

SUPERMARKETS WHICH SELL OWN BRAND FAIR TRADE PRODUCTS INCLUDE:

- Asda
- Co-op
- Marks & Spencer
- Morrison's
- Sainsbury's
- Somerfield
- Tesco
- Waitrose

The major supermarkets have reacted to consumers' opposition to genetically modified food and have taken measures to reduce the number of products containing GMOs. All major supermarket chains now store non-GM products, and Marks & Spencer have a non-GM policy on the whole range of their products.

of food crops without the use of synthetic chemical pesticides or fertilisers. Pests are controlled by cultivation techniques and the use of pesticides derived from natural sources. Organic farmers may use seven out of the hundreds of pesticides available. Moreover, animals are reared without the routine use of drugs, antibiotics and wormers, common in intensive livestock farming.

In response to growing consumer concern about the quality of the food they eat, big retailers have made real efforts to provide a wider range of organic products.

Today the Co-op is considered the largest organic 'farmer' in the UK. Sainsbury's has received its third award from the Soil Association for being best organic retailer. Both received Soil Association approval for their own-brand products.

3 Putting a stop to GM

Genetically modified (GM) foods are foods produced using plant or animal ingredients that have been modified using gene technology. The British public are anxious about the use of GM foods because their effects on human health are unknown. Also, releasing genetically altered organisms into the environment could disrupt ecosystems, and genetically modified crops have been proved to be more harmful to many groups of wildlife than their conventional equivalent.

4 More vegetarian products

Some people choose a vegetarian diet for religious, ethical or environmental reasons, or to save money. Others switch to a plant-based diet for health reasons. A vegetarian diet generally contains less total fat, saturated fat and cholesterol and includes more dietary fibre. Vegetarians have lower rates of some cancers, cardiovascular disease, high blood pressure and type-2 diabetes. The vegetable kingdom provides all the vitamins, minerals, proteins, carbohydrates and fats needed for the human diet, although it is important to watch what you eat to be sure of getting the nutrients from vegetables that you miss from animal foods.

Most people become vegetarians out of concern for animal welfare. The green pastures and pastoral barnyard scenes of years past have been replaced by windowless metal warehouses, wire cages and gestation crates in the factory farms of today. On factory farms, animals often spend their entire lives confined to cages or stalls barely larger than their own bodies. And death for these animals doesn't always come quickly or painlessly.

Today, it is possible to find a good range of vegetarian products in our supermarket aisles. Compared to Europe, the UK has quite an advanced approach to labelling their products as suitable for vegetarians.

LOCAL ISSUES

The opening of a big out-of-town supermarket inevitably has an effect on smaller high street shops. By 2005 there were only 9,000 local butchers, compared to 23,000 in 1985, and in 2001 small newsagents were closing at the rate of one per day. This situation has been exacerbated by the growth of branded convenience stores, which, due to their town-centre locations, pitch themselves directly against independent shops.

Crucially, while supermarkets create new jobs, they can also have an impact on existing employment – particularly if small stores lose business as a result of increased competition. Nevertheless, in response to a growing consumer appetite for ethically-traded foods, many communities are pulling together to establish stronger local initiatives, such as farmers' markets and home-delivered vegetable boxes.

The supermarkets themselves are also working harder to improve their reputations, and are in the process of making a number of positive changes to their environmental and sourcing policies. For example, Sainsbury's now sells only line-caught cod and haddock and many of the major stores now source in-season fruit and vegetables from Britain, rather than abroad. The supermarkets have also been instrumental in the drive to phase out energy-hungry incandescent light bulbs.

CONSUMER CONCERNS

Although the supermarkets can be commended for the improvements given above, there are still a number of areas in which more could be done to address consumer concerns. These include:

1) Producers
As large-scale operations, supermarkets rely on industrial farms to produce the huge quantities of food they require. The balance of power in these producer-retailer relationships is usually weighted towards the big stores, which can make it difficult for smaller suppliers to have their voices heard. A public code of conduct, covering issues such as contractual terms, de-listing and product pricing, would reassure shoppers that the people who produce their foods are being treated fairly.

2) Healthy foods
Obesity is a growing problem in the UK, and while supermarkets cannot be blamed for our expanding waistlines, they undoubtedly have a prominent role in influencing our food choices. The introduction of labelling systems such as traffic lights, which indicate the level of fat, sugar and salt in a product, is a major step forward, but clear, straightforward labelling is needed on all products to ensure that consumers really know what they are buying.

3) Loyalty cards
Loyalty cards can be indispensable money-saving devices for regular supermarket shoppers, but they also allow stores to keep an unprecedented amount of data on their patrons. This enables them to build up extensive profiles of their cardholders, a procedure that is currently used to improve the supermarket's quality of service, but which could soon branch into other areas such as security and surveillance. Greater transparency from the supermarkets about the information they hold – and what they plan to do with it – should be a priority.

FOOD MILES

Environmentalists have long been concerned about food miles – the distance food has travelled to get to your plate. Now there is greater awareness of this, and today's shoppers are confronted with the 'food miles dilemma': do you choose a packet of organic beans imported from Africa, helping a local farmer overseas, but which came to England on an aircraft emitting tons of CO_2 into the atmosphere? This transportation also leads to extra packaging, and means the food has been chemically treated to keep it fresh during the journey. What is even more nonsensical is when, thanks to tax-free aviation fuel, we import food we could easily grow ourselves.

The oddities of the global market, and our demand for exotic foods, can lead to ridiculous situations. In 1997, 126 million litres of cow's milk was imported into the UK at the same time as 270 million litres was exported. Animals suffer from our desire to have all products available everywhere; they often have to be carried alive for hundreds of miles before they are slaughtered.

Another economic issue linked with food miles is 'just-in-time' food management. It is an operations approach whereby food is rushed to superstores only when it is needed, to save on expensive storage. This leads to refrigerated trucks doing frequent daily return journeys to farms, only collecting some of the merchandise, with a resultant increase in pollution.

Sustain, an organisation campaigning for ethical farming, warns that as road freight increases and more and more people drive to out-of-town supermarkets, it is even more important to reduce the number of miles travelled by our food. It would like to see the end of air-freighted food altogether.

Tips for your next shopping trip:
1) Buy from the supermarket whose ethical policies you believe in
2) Buy locally-produced, organic and fair-trade goods where possible
3) Buy ethically accredited brands so you know they have been properly checked out - and you are buying more than just ethical claims! (Of the supermarkets, only Sainsbury's has so far gained ethical accreditation from the Ethical Company Organisation)

- Co-op
- Marks & Spencer
- Sainsbury's
- Waitrose

- Budgens
- Morrisons
- Somerfield

- Asda
- Iceland
- Tesco

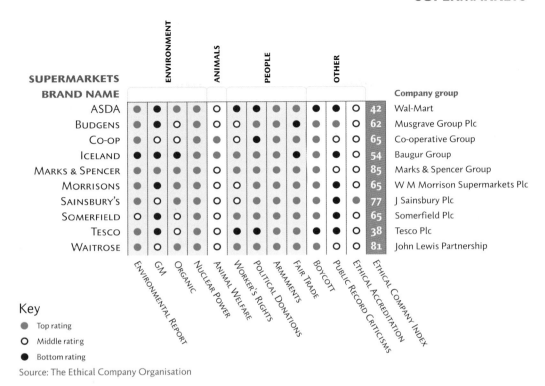

Key
- ● Top rating
- ○ Middle rating
- ● Bottom rating

Source: The Ethical Company Organisation

- Iceland has been given the bottom rating for Organic and Fair Trade as they failed to respond to our requests for further information.
- Morrisons has been given a middle rating for Organic and bottom rating for Fair Trade as they failed to respond to our requests for further information.
- Tesco has been given a middle rating for Organic as they failed to respond to our requests for further information.

THE WELL-TRAVELLED SUNDAY LUNCH

Source: Corporate Watch

Chicken from Thailand	10,691	miles by ship	If you choose products that are in season and purchase them locally at a farmers' market, you could reduce the total journey from 26,234 to just 376 miles!
Runner beans from Zambia	4,912	miles by plane	
Carrots from Spain	1,000	miles by lorry	
Mangetout from Zimbabwe	5,130	miles by plane	
Potatoes from Italy	1,521	miles by lorry	
Sprouts from Britain	125	miles by lorry	
TOTAL	**26,234**	**MILES**	

Quality...
is the heart of Cafédirect

Over the last 3 years we have reinvested an average of 60% of our profits into our growers' businesses and communities.

This funds training and development programmes to continually improve the quality of their produce.

Fatima Lopez was only 18 years old when she took a PRODECOOP Scholarship to study coffee tasting. She is now Head Coffee Taster, ensuring that all the coffee is of the highest quality and tastes delicious.

CAFÉDIRECT®
BRINGING QUALITY TO LIFE

Join our network at
www.cafedirect.co.uk

"Through our long-term relationship with Cafédirect we invested in coffee quality. The co-op is training young people to work in coffee. I am now the head coffee taster. This means I taste the coffees to check the quality and run a training programme for young people. It's creating opportunities for the next generation, like me."

Fatima Lopez
PRODECOOP, Nicaragua

CAFÉDIRECT® sponsors Bedtime Drinks
BRINGING QUALITY TO LIFE

Tea & coffee

Tea and coffee products spearheaded the fair trade campaign for a better deal for Third World farmers and plantation workers. Now, after years of perseverance, the campaign has begun to achieve real success. Two in five people now recognise the Fairtrade mark and know that it signifies a better deal for the producers. Fairly-traded brands are also making a name for themselves by matching the larger coffee brands in terms of taste and quality.

COFFEE CRISIS

Support for fair trade coffee is even more important in the wake of the coffee crisis. In 2000, international coffee prices slumped to an all time low. This price drop benefited transnational companies and 'designer coffee' retailers, as their profits soared while the price of their main raw material crashed. Such corporate gain consigned some of the world's poorest and most vulnerable people to extreme poverty. It is estimated that about 20 million households produce coffee crops, which is often the main – sometimes the only – source of cash income. As a result of the crisis, many farmers have been forced to sell assets such as cattle, and cut down on essential expenses by taking their children out of school or even reducing food consumption.

The underlying cause of the crisis in world coffee prices is production consistently outstripping consumption, resulting in excess stocks driving down prices. The obvious solution is to bring supply back into line with demand and to stabilise prices at more remunerative levels. Northern governments have been unwilling to support supply restrictions, however, as oversupply means good business for politically powerful transnational companies.

In spite of a partial recovery in prices in late 2004, the effects of the crisis are still widely felt and are undermining efforts to achieve the human development targets set for 2015.

SOCIAL CONDITIONS

Wages and conditions for tea plantation workers are often poor, with living facilities falling below acceptable standards. The fair trade campaign hopes to have a long term beneficial effect on their income and overall standards of life.

Cafédirect is tackling these problems by guaranteeing a minimum price for the coffee and tea it buys, and investing on average 60 per cent of its profits (between 2003-6) into the producer partners'

organisations to support a wide range of activities, including market information and management training.

ENVIRONMENT

In most tea plantations, pesticides are mixed in the fields without proper drainage and treatment. Workers say that protective masks, goggles or gloves are rarely provided. In large coffee plantations in Brazil and Colombia, cultivation is so intense that natural nutrients are drained away and have to be replaced by fertilisers.

One ecologically sound production method is shade-grown coffee. Shade trees protect the plants from rain and sun, help maintain soil and water quality, and aid natural pest control, thanks to the birds that are attracted to the forest canopy. Sun-grown coffee, on the other hand, requires chemical fertilisers and pesticides, and leads to greater soil erosion and higher amounts of toxic runoff, endangering both wildlife and people. Equal Exchange's organic coffee is shade grown.

The Ethical Company Organisation can also recommend Ipanema Espresso, who have been accredited by the organisation for their high level of ethical and environmental awareness.

- Cafédirect
- Clipper
- Equal Exchange
- Percol
- Teadirect
- TopQualiTea
- Traidcraft
- Yorkshire Tea

- Lavazza
- Tetley
- Typhoo

- Carte Noir
- Douwe Egberts
- Jacksons of Piccadilly
- Kenco
- Maxwell House
- Nescafé
- PG Tips
- Twinings

CAFÉDIRECT BRINGING QUALITY TO LIFE — sponsors Bedtime Drinks

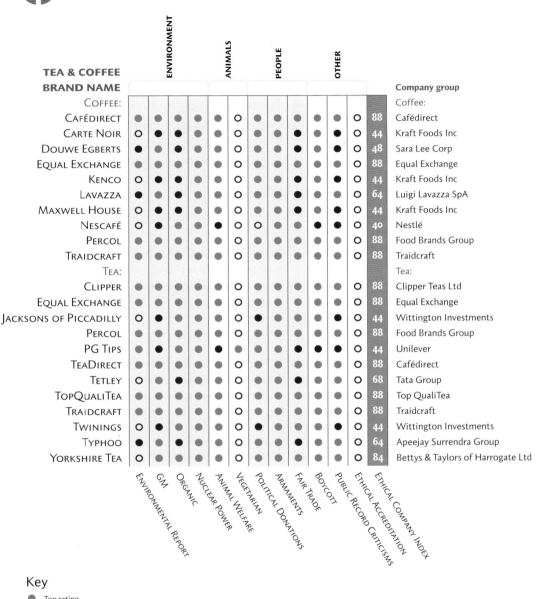

TEA & COFFEE BRAND NAME	ENVIRONMENT				ANIMALS		PEOPLE				OTHER		Ethical Company Index	Company group
	Environmental Report	GM	Organic	Nuclear Power	Animal Welfare	Vegetarian	Political Donations	Armaments	Fair Trade	Boycott	Public Record Criticisms	Ethical Accreditation		
COFFEE:														Coffee:
CAFÉDIRECT													88	Cafédirect
CARTE NOIR													44	Kraft Foods Inc
DOUWE EGBERTS													48	Sara Lee Corp
EQUAL EXCHANGE													88	Equal Exchange
KENCO													44	Kraft Foods Inc
LAVAZZA													64	Luigi Lavazza SpA
MAXWELL HOUSE													44	Kraft Foods Inc
NESCAFÉ													40	Nestlé
PERCOL													88	Food Brands Group
TRAIDCRAFT													88	Traidcraft
TEA:														Tea:
CLIPPER													88	Clipper Teas Ltd
EQUAL EXCHANGE													88	Equal Exchange
JACKSONS OF PICCADILLY													44	Wittington Investments
PERCOL													88	Food Brands Group
PG TIPS													44	Unilever
TEADIRECT													88	Cafédirect
TETLEY													68	Tata Group
TOPQUALITEA													88	Top QualiTea
TRAIDCRAFT													88	Traidcraft
TWININGS													44	Wittington Investments
TYPHOO													64	Apeejay Surrendra Group
YORKSHIRE TEA													84	Bettys & Taylors of Harrogate Ltd

Key

● Top rating
○ Middle rating
● Bottom rating

Source: The Ethical Company Organisation

Vegetarian foods

Once upon a time, a vegetarian looking for a quick shop-bought meal had a choice between bean burgers and bean sausages. Now there are dozens of brands specialising in animal-friendly foods, from meat-free pâtés to non-dairy cheese. Potential buyers of these products should be aware that some of the more prominent brands are owned by much larger manufacturers, who may or may not share their subsidiaries' commitment to the cause.

HIDDEN INGREDIENTS

Even to those who do not follow a vegetarian diet, the number of hidden animal products in everyday foods might come as a surprise. For example, gelatine, which is derived from animal skins and bones, can be found as a gelling agent in sweets, margarine, yoghurt, medicine capsules and jelly. It also appears in some wines and is a key ingredient in photographic film. Animal fats may be used to fry crisps or chips, and in the baking of biscuits and bread, while many E numbers (such as cochineal, E120) are of animal or even insect origin.

While it is illegal for a company to deliberately mislead consumers into believing a product is vegetarian, there is currently no legal definition either in the UK or EU of what the term means when it is used on packaging. The 'suitable for vegetarians' logo is a 'voluntary claim', which means that there is no regulation to protect it. The National Consumer Council (*www. ncc.org.uk*) has found that this provoked significant concerns amongst the general public, and has called for consistent, legal definitions of 'vegetarian' and other terms to be enforced.

THE SEEDLING SYMBOL

Products displaying the Vegetarian Society's seedling symbol are guaranteed to be free from animal ingredients. The Society carries out independent inspections of all its approved brands, to ensure they meet a strict set of criteria. These state that the product must be free from animal flesh or any related ingredients derived from animal slaughter, free from genetically modified organisms and free from cruelty (i.e. not tested on animals). Only free range eggs can be used in Vegetarian Society approved foods, and thorough cleaning of factory equipment must be carried out to ensure there is no contamination of the production line by animal ingredients.

The Vegetarian Society's website (*www.vegsoc.org*) carries a searchable database of all approved brands.

READY MEALS

Some vegetarians' lifestyle choice is in part a conscious decision to distance themselves from the fast-food culture that dominates most mainstream supermarkets. Inevitably, the big sellers have begun to catch on, marketing new varieties of meat-free ready meal to the more health-conscious shopper.

While some are undoubtedly cashing in on a well-meaning but time-poor veggie community, others are producing genuinely innovative vegetarian and vegan products. One such company is Redwood Wholefoods (*www.redwoodfoods.co.uk*), the people behind the Cheatin' meats range, and a member of the Ethical Company Organisation's accreditation scheme. As well as meat-free 'meats', Redwood also sells dairy-free cheeses and is at the forefront of researching new vegetarian lines.

What many of the companies surveyed here show is that vegetarian alternatives are becoming valuable in their own right; they are no longer just substitutes for meat, but rounded, nutritionally complete foods based on strong vegetarian traditions from countries as far apart as Greece and India.

- Cheatin'
- Cauldron Foods
- GranoVita
- Quorn
- Vegi-Deli

- Goodlife
- Granose
- Linda McCartney
- Realeat

- Dalepak
- Tivall
- Wicken Fen

VEGETARIAN FOODS

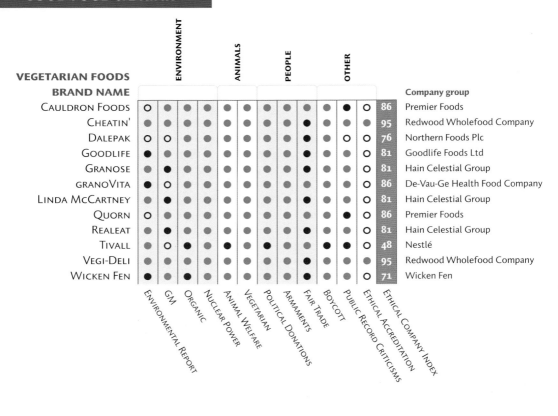

BRAND NAME	ENVIRONMENT				ANIMALS		PEOPLE			OTHER			Ethical Company Index	Company group
CAULDRON FOODS													86	Premier Foods
CHEATIN'													95	Redwood Wholefood Company
DALEPAK													76	Northern Foods Plc
GOODLIFE													81	Goodlife Foods Ltd
GRANOSE													81	Hain Celestial Group
granoVITA													86	De-Vau-Ge Health Food Company
LINDA MCCARTNEY													81	Hain Celestial Group
QUORN													86	Premier Foods
REALEAT													81	Hain Celestial Group
TIVALL													48	Nestlé
VEGI-DELI													95	Redwood Wholefood Company
WICKEN FEN													71	Wicken Fen

Column categories (left to right): ENVIRONMENTAL REPORT, GM, ORGANIC, NUCLEAR POWER, ANIMAL WELFARE, VEGETARIAN, POLITICAL DONATIONS, ARMAMENTS, FAIR TRADE, BOYCOTT, PUBLIC RECORD CRITICISMS, ETHICAL ACCREDITATION, ETHICAL COMPANY INDEX

Key

● Top rating

○ Middle rating

● Bottom rating

Source: The Ethical Company Organisation (2008)

Whisky

The exact origins of whisky are unknown. It is believed that the Ancient Celts were the first to practise distilling. In Scotland, the earliest documented record of distilling was in 1494. Whisky was initially lauded for its medicinal qualities, being prescribed for the preservation of health, the prolongation of life, and for the relief of colic, palsy and even smallpox. Today, it enjoys its position as the world's leading national drink.

WHAT'S IN IT?

The name whisky comes from Irish Gaelic *usque baugh*, or Scottish Gaelic *uisge beatha*, meaning 'water of life'.

For no good reason, the spirit distilled in Scotland and Canada is spelt 'whisky', while in Ireland and America they spell it 'whiskey'. Wherever it's from, whisky is distilled from the fermented mash of cereal grains. In Scotland, the main grain used is barley. In Ireland, other grains may be used with the barley. In Canada and America, the grains are usually rye and maize (the latter is known over there simply as 'corn'). Whisky can only be referred to as 'Scotch' if it has been matured and distilled in Scotland.

Things distinguishing the flavour include the quality of the water, the drying of the grain (in many Scottish distilleries this is done over peat fires) and the oak casks in which the spirit is matured.

MAKING WHISKY

Traditional Scotch whisky requires only three raw materials: barley, yeast and water. From these basic ingredients an elaborate and lengthy production process arises. The first of the five stages is malting, which makes barley into malt. Mashing, the next stage, produces a sugar solution from crushed malt. Yeast is added to the sugar solution, causing it to ferment. The fermented spirit is then distilled to remove any impurities and separate out any solids that are still in the liquid.

The final stage is maturation, which (for Scotch whisky) takes a minimum of three years in oak casks, and up to 12 years for the most refined blends. No alternative means of maturing whisky has yet been found, so the process is thought to be pretty much the same as when it was first invented.

DIFFERENT KINDS

The following are some of the most popular and readily available types of whisky on the market:

- 'Blended' whisky, which is the type most commonly drunk in Britain, can be a combination of up to 50 different malt and grain whiskies.
- 'Malt' whisky is made from malted (or sprouted) grains. A whisky simply labelled as 'malt' may include malt whiskies from several different distilleries.
- To be labelled 'single malt', a whisky has to come from only one distillery.
- 'Grain' whisky is made from a mixture of malted barley and unmalted grains such as wheat or maize.
- Irish whiskey is distilled three times rather than twice, which is usual for Scotch, and is made from malted and unmalted barley as well as other grains such as maize.

ALL IN MODERATION

Research has shown that drinking in moderation can be beneficial to health. The recommended daily amount for women is three units per day with a maximum of 14 units per week. For men it's four units daily with a maximum of 21 units per week. A single unit is equivalent to a small (25 ml) measure of whisky.

However, some drinks manufacturers have been criticised for irresponsible marketing. Diageo, owner of Bell's whisky, has been accused of advertising to underage drinkers with the marketing of its Smirnoff Ice brand. Alcopops are designed not to taste very alcoholic, so appeal to those who are not used to drinking or who are seeking to consume a large amount of alcohol in a short space of time. As such they have been linked to binge-drinking. At £8 million, Diageo's Smirnoff Ice was the brand with the highest amount spent on marketing in 2002-3.

- Famous Grouse
- Teacher's

- Ballantine's
- Balvenie
- Glenfiddich
- Grant's
- Jameson

- Bell's
- Glenmorangie

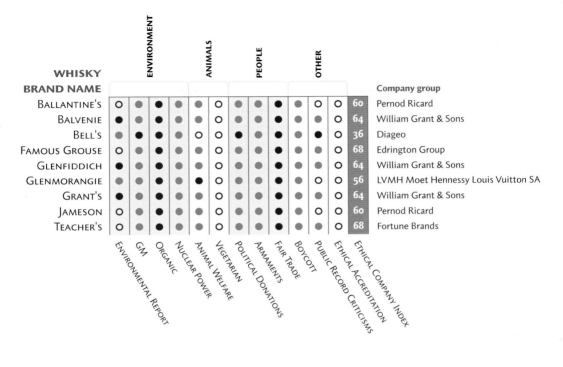

WHISKY BRAND NAME													Ethical Company Index	Company group
BALLANTINE'S													60	Pernod Ricard
BALVENIE													64	William Grant & Sons
BELL'S													36	Diageo
FAMOUS GROUSE													68	Edrington Group
GLENFIDDICH													64	William Grant & Sons
GLENMORANGIE													56	LVMH Moet Hennessy Louis Vuitton SA
GRANT'S													64	William Grant & Sons
JAMESON													60	Pernod Ricard
TEACHER'S													68	Fortune Brands

Column categories: ENVIRONMENT (Environmental Report, GM, Organic, Nuclear Power); ANIMALS (Animal Welfare, Vegetarian); PEOPLE (Political Donations, Armaments, Fair Trade, Boycott); OTHER (Public Record Criticisms, Ethical Accreditation).

Key

● Top rating

○ Middle rating

● Bottom rating

Source: The Ethical Company Organisation

Yoghurt

The main issue in the production of yoghurt is the welfare of the animals producing the milk. Conditions can vary dramatically from farm to farm, and it is often difficult to tell from the labelling whether a product is derived from intensively-reared cattle. The safest option is to choose Soil Association approved brands, or goat and sheep yoghurts, which are also likely to include fewer additives than the mainstream varieties.

THE CASE FOR ORGANIC

Intensive farming of dairy cattle is fraught with animal welfare problems. Cattle can be kept in confined spaces, often being left indoors for long periods of time. The close proximity of the animals means that diseases are rife, so the cattle are regularly treated with antibiotics, even as a precautionary measure. While growth hormones such as rBST are not legal in the UK, other procedures are used to make the cattle produce higher milk yields. This includes using concentrated feeds, which can have an effect on the animals' health, and put unnecessary stress on their bodies.

Organic-standard yoghurt is not only better for the consumer but better for the milk-producing cow. According to the Soil Association, calves on organic farms will have been suckled for around nine weeks, rather than separated from their mothers within a few days, and the disease rates of animals are lower because of better husbandry and a diet of mostly grass and clover. Their health is managed without reliance on antibiotics, using conventional drugs only when a problem is acute. Organic cows are not kept permanently shut up indoors throughout the winter as non-organic herds often are.

Goat and sheep yoghurt also comes from less intensive conditions as it is produced by smaller companies; it is also important for the 10 per cent of the population who are lactose intolerant.

LIVE YOGHURT

Live yoghurts contain two species of bacteria naturally found in the human gut which can, unlike ordinary yoghurt bacteria, pass via the stomach into the intestines, with the claimed benefits of improving digestion and helping to prevent colon cancer. Many yoghurts labelled as 'prebiotics' and 'probiotics' are marketed on the premise that they are good for the immune system. In fact, for people who are already fit, the benefits are probably marginal, but live yoghurt is almost certainly very beneficial for people who are recovering from a stomach bug or who are taking antibiotics.

VEGETARIAN AND VEGAN

Gelatine, a product of animal bones, may be added to thicken reduced-fat yoghurts and so vegetarians should keep a careful eye on the ingredients list.

Most non-dairy yoghurts are made from soya and as such will be highly processed and may contain salt, sugar and other additives, but they contain the same bacterial cultures as conventional yoghurt. As some soya is from GM sources, you may be best advised to look for organic products or those labelled as non-GM.

MARKETING

Nestlé was criticised by the Advertising Standards Authority in July 2006 for marketing its Ski yoghurt with the slogan 'keep it simple – no artificial colour, sweetener or preservative', when the product actually contained synthetic additives. The magazine advert was withdrawn after the ASA ruled that it had misled the public.

Labels such as 'low sugar' or 'lite' on yoghurts can also be misleading, as there is no fixed legislation to define what they mean. In extreme cases, a low sugar variety of one brand may have the same amount of sugar as the regular version of another.

To know exactly what is in your yoghurt, make your own by buying a pot of live yoghurt, adding milk and leaving it in a warm place. It works equally well for soya yoghurts. The system can go on almost indefinitely, but consult a reliable recipe book for useful tips about storage and hygiene.

- Provamel
- Woodlands Park
- Yeo Valley

- Onken
- Rachel's Dairy
- Sojasun
- Total

- Actimel
- Danone
- Muller
- Ski
- Weight Watchers

YOGHURT

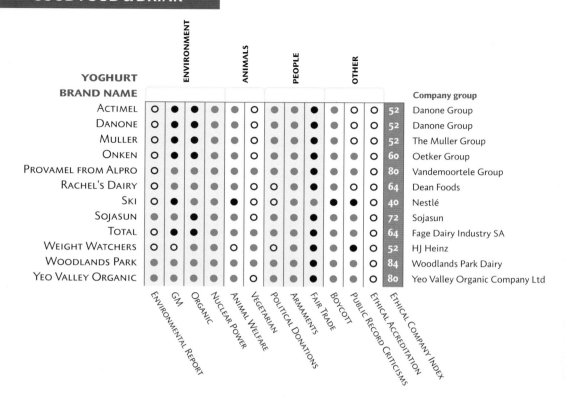

BRAND NAME	ENVIRONMENT				ANIMALS		PEOPLE			OTHER			Ethical Company Index	Company group
	Environmental Report	GM	Organic	Nuclear Power	Animal Welfare	Vegetarian	Political Donations	Armaments	Fair Trade	Boycott	Public Record Criticisms	Ethical Accreditation		
ACTIMEL	○	●	●	●	●	○	●	●	●	●	○	○	52	Danone Group
DANONE	○	●	●	●	●	○	●	●	●	●	○	○	52	Danone Group
MULLER	○	●	●	●	●	○	●	●	●	●	○	○	52	The Muller Group
ONKEN	○	●	●	●	●	○	●	●	●	●	●	○	60	Oetker Group
PROVAMEL FROM ALPRO	○	●	●	●	●	●	●	●	●	●	●	○	80	Vandemoortele Group
RACHEL'S DAIRY	○	●	●	●	●	○	○	●	●	●	○	○	64	Dean Foods
SKI	○	●	●	●	●	○	○	●	●	●	●	○	40	Nestlé
SOJASUN	●	●	●	●	●	○	●	●	●	●	●	○	72	Sojasun
TOTAL	○	●	●	●	●	●	●	●	●	●	●	○	64	Fage Dairy Industry SA
WEIGHT WATCHERS	○	○	●	●	○	●	○	●	●	●	●	○	52	HJ Heinz
WOODLANDS PARK	●	●	●	●	●	●	●	●	●	●	●	○	84	Woodlands Park Dairy
YEO VALLEY ORGANIC	●	●	●	●	●	○	●	●	●	●	●	○	80	Yeo Valley Organic Company Ltd

Key

● Top rating

○ Middle rating

● Bottom rating

Source: The Ethical Company Organisation

gooshing
world shopping revolution

save money . save the planet

from the Ethical Company Organisation, publisher of The Good Shopping Guide

shop at gooshing.co.uk

price search & ethical comparisons on 250,000 products

GOOD

HEALTH & BEAUTY

Cold remedies •

Cosmetics •

Eye care products •

Nappies •

Pain remedies •

Perfumes & aftershaves •

Sanitary protection •

Shampoo •

Skincare •

Soap •

Sun protection •

Toothpaste •

Vitamins •

Introduction

Health and beauty products range from the indispensable to the indefensible, although they are promoted, without exception, as the former. While most of us wouldn't consider going without toothpaste or shampoo, musk-based perfumes and disposable nappies are less easy to justify. The fine line between necessity and luxury has been successfully blurred by decades of marketing, but a small number of companies specialise not only in ethical basics, but in indulgence with a conscience.

These companies generally rely on traditional ingredients, such as natural moisturisers, vegetable fats and non-synthetic fragrances, allaying many consumers' fears about the contents of the cosmetics they use. Particular worries are related to the inclusion of chemicals in many creams and cleansers, including petro-chemical derivatives more readily associated with household than skin-cleaning products. The lack of scientific research in this area means it is difficult to make any proclamations about the safety, or otherwise, of the most popular brands. Unsurprisingly, then, the message is to be cautious.

The animal rights movement has long been associated with the health and beauty industry, and was integral in the campaign to ban animal testing on cosmetics. It remains a vocal critic of those companies that have been slow to change their policies.

Despite the ban on cosmetics testing in the UK, manufacturers are still able to import their ingredients from countries where the rules are less stringent, so the concerns – and the need to check behind the label – remain.

Nevertheless, some breakthroughs have been made. The Co-op recently became the first supermarket to have its own brand products approved by the BUAV, and hopefully other mainstream retailers will follow suit. More products are now available in organic and cruelty-free varieties than ever before, and consumer demand for such brands will enable the companies to increase their supply. Many buyers support these companies partly as a way of avoiding the pharmaceutical giants, whose policies are often difficult to pin down, and who tend to have a much more short-sighted, profit-led outlook.

Cold remedies

Cold remedies can't cure a cold, but instead work by relieving some of the individual symptoms, such as sore throats and headaches. Alongside the hundreds of different cough and cold medicines already on the market, new formulations are constantly being developed to make use of varying combinations of the key ingredients. Despite what the pharmaceuticals giants might claim, the difference between a branded drug and the cheaper generic equivalent is often minimal.

ATISHOO, ATISHOO, WE ALL FALL DOWN

The common cold is caused by a virus infection in the nose, which can be triggered by one of over 2,000 different viruses, most of which are known as rhinoviruses. Adults usually get two to three colds a year, while children are more susceptible and usually average six to ten. Although adults build up an immunity to some of the viruses, there are so many of them and they mutate so quickly that the cold has remained one of the most widespread infectious illnesses around.

The familiar cold symptoms are a blocked nose, sore throat, sneezing and sometimes a headache or a slightly raised temperature. These are caused by the immune system's reaction to the virus. They can't be prevented, but can usually be eased with painkillers or a dedicated cold remedy. Cold remedies are available from the chemist without prescription, and generally include a painkiller, a decongestant and caffeine.

There has been a lot of debate about whether or not cold remedies actually work, but there can be no doubt that many people find they help to relieve the symptoms. Most remedies are now available in non-drowsy formulas so that they can be taken safely during the day, although they should not be combined with other medicines, such as paracetamol, in case of overdose.

PHARMACEUTICAL GIANTS

The companies in the cold remedy business are mostly big players in the pharmaceutical industry. It is an industry often and rightly criticised for inflated prices, animal testing and the marketing of banned or less suitable drugs in the Third World.

The Consumer Association has complained that branded cough and cold remedies are sold at higher prices than the equivalent generic drug, which will be just as effective at treating the symptoms. Some researchers have claimed that the remedies have no strictly medical benefit.

ANIMALS

According to UK law, a number of medical experiments have to be performed before a pharmaceutical product can be licensed. As a result, almost all pharmaceutical companies conduct or fund animal experimentation, making them a major contributor to animal testing. It is not just pharmaceutical products that are tested on animals: companies such as Procter & Gamble are known to test cosmetic ingredients on animals, although this process is not required by law.

The arguments against pharmaceutical testing on animals are well documented, and new technologies such as tissue cultures and computer modelling have increased the number of available alternatives to animal experiments. Despite regulation controlling the manner in which the legally required testing is carried out, animals are often found in appalling conditions.

ALTERNATIVES

A weak immune system will increase susceptibility to colds and other viruses. Eating a balanced diet, including lots of fresh fruit and vegetables, will help to maintain a healthy immune system. Garlic, echinacea and vitamin C are all popular cold-prevention measures. High stress levels have also been shown to weaken the immune system.

The best treatment for cold symptoms is a combination of painkillers and hot drinks with honey and lemon. The drinks are particularly important to prevent the dehydration that might follow a mild fever, and they also have a soothing effect. Steam inhalations with oil vapour such as menthol or eucalyptus can be as effective as branded decongestants at helping to clear the airways. Another popular remedy is to bathe with drops of lavender, tea-tree and eucalyptus essential oils.

- Karvol
- Nurofen Cold & Flu

- Aspar
- Clear Breathe
- Coldenza
- Olbas Oil

- Beecham's
- Benylin 4 Flu
- Cold-Eeze
- Day Nurse
- Lemsip Original
- Sudafed
- Vicks Vapour Rub

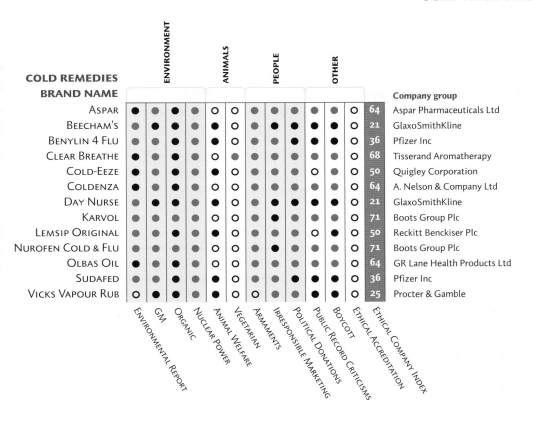

COLD REMEDIES BRAND NAME	ENVIRONMENT				ANIMALS		PEOPLE				OTHER		ETHICAL COMPANY INDEX	Company group
Aspar													64	Aspar Pharmaceuticals Ltd
Beecham's													21	GlaxoSmithKline
Benylin 4 Flu													36	Pfizer Inc
Clear Breathe													68	Tisserand Aromatherapy
Cold-Eeze													50	Quigley Corporation
Coldenza													64	A. Nelson & Company Ltd
Day Nurse													21	GlaxoSmithKline
Karvol													71	Boots Group Plc
Lemsip Original													50	Reckitt Benckiser Plc
Nurofen Cold & Flu													71	Boots Group Plc
Olbas Oil													64	GR Lane Health Products Ltd
Sudafed													36	Pfizer Inc
Vicks Vapour Rub													25	Procter & Gamble

Column labels: Environmental Report, GM, Organic, Nuclear Power, Animal Welfare, Vegetarian, Armaments, Irresponsible Marketing, Political Donations, Public Record Criticisms, Boycott, Ethical Accreditation, Ethical Company Index

Key

● Top rating
○ Middle rating
● Bottom rating

Source: The Ethical Company Organisation

Cosmetics & make-up

The cosmetics industry is big business: in the UK alone we spend £5 billion a year on cosmetics and toiletries. Women, men and even children are under increasing pressure to look good, smell right, and defy the ageing process. With the use of industrially produced synthetic chemicals being linked to worrying side-effects, it seems that a healthy diet, plenty of sleep and lots of water will do more for your complexion than foundation.

ANIMAL TESTING

One of the biggest issues associated with cosmetics is animal testing. Although the testing of cosmetics and their ingredients on animals has been outlawed in the UK since 1998, the sale of products tested elsewhere is not and remains prevalent. Even within the EU, animal tests are only required to assess new ingredients that have no known safety record. Companies that have abandoned animal testing meet the same safety requirements by using existing ingredients which are known to be safe.

The European Union has passed a similar law banning cosmetics testing on animals, and prohibiting the sale and import of new cosmetics that have been animal tested. This was passed despite legal action from the French government (France is home of the cosmetics giant L'Oreal), who claimed that the ban is too severe and will damage European business interests.

The complete animal testing ban will come into force in around 2009. A sale ban for the majority of animal tested products will also come into force in 2009, but the ban on the remaining animal tests will not be implemented until 2013. This last phase will depend on whether sufficient non-animal tests have been developed in time; the BUAV have called this a 'get-out clause' for the cosmetics companies.

A simple solution for the ethical consumer is to support companies that have already stopped all animal testing. the BUAV produce *The Little Book of Cruelty Free*, which is available via their website at *www.buav.org/gocrueltyfree/littlebook.html*.

A SENSITIVE ISSUE

Almost all cosmetics can cause allergic reactions in certain individuals. There is no list of ingredients that can be guaranteed not to cause a reaction, so consumers who are prone to allergies should pay careful attention to what they use on their skin.

Companies can use terms such as 'hypo-allergenic' or 'natural' on cosmetics labels to mean almost anything. Most of the terms have considerable value in promoting cosmetic products to consumers, but dermatologists say they have very little medical meaning.

'Hypoallergenic' implies that products are less likely to cause allergic reactions, but no prescribed scientific studies are required to substantiate this claim. Likewise, the terms 'dermatologist-tested', 'sensitivity tested', 'allergy tested', or 'non-irritating' carry no guarantee that the product won't cause skin reactions.

NANOPARTICLES

Some cosmetics now use nanoparticulate materials to give improved or additional functionality. There are concerns that nanoparticles of zinc, titanium and iron oxides might penetrate the protective layers of the skin and cause reactions with UV light that could result in damage to cell DNA. Widespread use of nanoparticles in products that are washed off will present a diffuse source of nanoparticles to the environment, for example through the sewage system. Whether this presents a risk to the environment will depend on the quantities that are discharged and the toxicity of nanoparticles to organisms, about which almost nothing is known.

At present, products containing nanoparticles do not have to be labelled as such. To be sure of avoiding these and other synthetic chemicals choose organic. Spiezia Organics is one of the few cosmetics companies accredited by the Soil Association. Honesty Cosmetics are certified by the Ethical Company Organisation, and make products suitable for vegetarians and vegans.

- Beauty Without Cruelty (BWC)
- Boots No 7
- Clearasil
- E45
- Honesty Cosmetics
- Spiezia Organics

- Body Shop
- Bourjois
- Chanel
- Clarins
- Clinique
- Lancome
- Maybelline
- Nivea
- Revlon
- Rimmel
- Simple

- Clean & Clear
- Garnier
- Max Factor
- Oil of Olay

COSMETICS & MAKE-UP

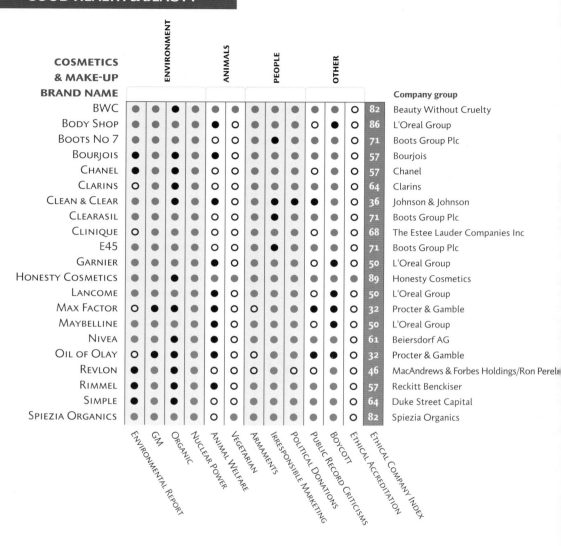

BRAND NAME	Ethical Company Index	Company group
BWC	82	Beauty Without Cruelty
BODY SHOP	86	L'Oreal Group
BOOTS NO 7	71	Boots Group Plc
BOURJOIS	57	Bourjois
CHANEL	57	Chanel
CLARINS	64	Clarins
CLEAN & CLEAR	36	Johnson & Johnson
CLEARASIL	71	Boots Group Plc
CLINIQUE	68	The Estee Lauder Companies Inc
E45	71	Boots Group Plc
GARNIER	50	L'Oreal Group
HONESTY COSMETICS	89	Honesty Cosmetics
LANCOME	50	L'Oreal Group
MAX FACTOR	32	Procter & Gamble
MAYBELLINE	50	L'Oreal Group
NIVEA	61	Beiersdorf AG
OIL OF OLAY	32	Procter & Gamble
REVLON	46	MacAndrews & Forbes Holdings/Ron Perelman
RIMMEL	57	Reckitt Benckiser
SIMPLE	64	Duke Street Capital
SPIEZIA ORGANICS	82	Spiezia Organics

Column headings (left to right):

ENVIRONMENT: Environmental Report, GM, Organic, Nuclear Power
ANIMALS: Animal Welfare, Vegetarian
PEOPLE: Armaments, Irresponsible Marketing, Political Donations, Public Record Criticisms
OTHER: Boycott, Ethical Accreditation
Ethical Company Index

Key
● Top rating
○ Middle rating
● Bottom rating

Source: The Ethical Company Organisation

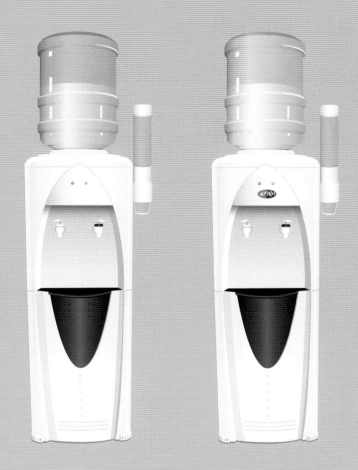

The difference? Hundreds of Bangladeshi lives.

Water is water. One bottled brand is as good for you as the next, isn't it? Wrong. There is one brand that makes for a much healthier world: AquAid. The money it raises goes towards Christian Aid's work in improving the lives of people in the developing world. Just 15 AquAid water coolers used for a year would raise £235: enough to pay for a well in Bangladesh. A well that will provide safe water and could save hundreds of lives for years to come. Please, use whatever influence you have to put AquAid in your office, school, gym, or home. It makes no difference to you which brand you drink. But we know which brand the poor of Bangladesh are rooting for. **To find out more, please call AquAid on 01223 508 109.**

Eye-care products

As spectacles and contact lenses become increasingly sophisticated they tend to use new materials that may have an impact on the environment. One problem associated with contact lens fluids is the time they take to biodegrade, while glasses are often made from complex synthetic substances that require a lot of energy to produce. Many mainstream eye-care products are made by Novartis, a drugs company that has links with GM technology.

SPECTACLES

Chemicals are used to coat both contact and spectacle lenses, and these may degrade into toxic materials when they are disposed of. However, some more ecologically-aware companies have addressed this problem by producing special lens coatings which degrade into harmless substances within seven days.

Many plastic spectacle lenses are made from 'CR39', a synthetic material that is kept in cold storage and cleaned with freon gas before coating. These may have a greater effect on the environment than glass lenses.

Frames with a higher environmental impact include those made from titanium or petroleum-based plastics. Danish label Orgreen uses all kinds of unusual and old-fashioned materials in its spectacles, including wood and even steel. However, many of its lighter designs still require titanium-based frames.

The frames recommended here are those made from cellulose acetate, which are derived from plant cellulose and acetic acid, both of which are sustainable materials.

SOLUTION MYSTERIES

Although contact lens solution may not appear to include animal-derived ingredients, most brands are likely to have been tested on animals. The Vegan Society publishes a list of vegan-friendly contact lens solutions.

The new breed of 'daily' disposable lenses are likely to have a more detrimental effect on the environment than those which can be changed monthly or even yearly. This is because they use up much more packaging and resources than the longer-lasting lenses. However, the advantage of dailies is that they tend not to need cleaning with a solution.

FRANKENSTEIN FARMING?

Drug giant Novartis, which is behind the CIBA Vision brands, has a majority share in (former subsidiary) Syngenta, the world's largest agrochemical company and a pioneer of GM technology. As a huge producer of insecticides, fungicides, herbicides, and genetically-modified seeds, Syngenta epitomises many campaigners' concerns about global farming.

The whole biotech industry, composed largely of Bayer, Syngenta and Monsanto, has been beset by controversy since the late 90s, when there was a public outcry over research into 'Terminator' seeds. These were genetically engineered to become sterile, denying poor farmers their right to save and re-plant seeds from the harvest, and increasing their dependence on biotech and agrochemical companies. According to ActionAid, the big biotech companies are still developing technology that could restrict the use of GM seeds and strengthen their control over the world's farmers.

In March 2005, Syngenta admitted that it had accidentally sold hundreds of tonnes of unapproved GM maize seed to US farmers over four years. Since 16,000 tonnes of US maize was imported into the UK in 2004 alone, it is not unlikely that the unapproved GM crop found its way over the Atlantic.

ALTERNATIVES

Laser treatment and the 'Bates method' of eyesight correction are possible alternatives to spectacles or contact lenses. Laser treatment is extremely expensive, however, while the Bates method – which involves exercises to retrain the eyes to relax and refocus – has not convinced a lot of people that it actually works!

Branded or 'designer' glasses may be produced by a company that is included elsewhere in this book, such as the Good Fashion section, so be sure to check their credentials before you buy.

Another ethical option is to choose your favourite pair of glasses, but make a donation to a charity that provides ophthalmic help to people in poor countries, such as Vision Aid Overseas (who can also recycle your spectacles).

- Sauflon

- Allergan

- Alcon
- Bausch & Lomb
- CIBA Vision
- Johnson & Johnson
- Pilkington Barnes-Hind
- Wesley-Jessen

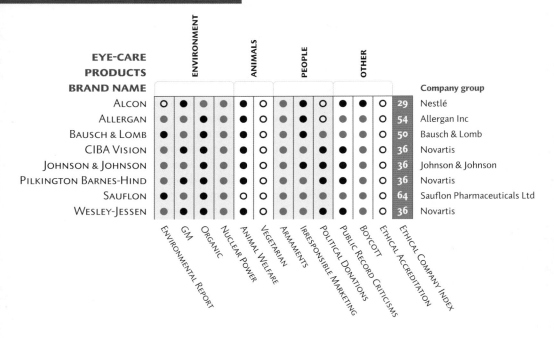

EYE-CARE PRODUCTS BRAND NAME	ENVIRONMENT	ANIMALS	PEOPLE	OTHER	ETHICAL COMPANY INDEX	Company group
ALCON					29	Nestlé
ALLERGAN					54	Allergan Inc
BAUSCH & LOMB					50	Bausch & Lomb
CIBA VISION					36	Novartis
JOHNSON & JOHNSON					36	Johnson & Johnson
PILKINGTON BARNES-HIND					36	Novartis
SAUFLON					64	Sauflon Pharmaceuticals Ltd
WESLEY-JESSEN					36	Novartis

Column categories: ENVIRONMENTAL REPORT, GM, ORGANIC, NUCLEAR POWER, ANIMAL WELFARE, VEGETARIAN, ARMAMENTS, IRRESPONSIBLE MARKETING, POLITICAL DONATIONS, PUBLIC RECORD CRITICISMS, BOYCOTT, ETHICAL ACCREDITATION

Key
- Top rating
- Middle rating
- Bottom rating

Source: The Ethical Company Organisation

Nappies

Three billion disposable nappies are thrown away every year in the UK – that's a lot of waste to end up in landfill or, even worse, in the sea. The estimated cost of disposal for landfilled disposable nappies (which make up 4 per cent of all landfilled domestic waste) is £40 million. A lot of money could be saved if parents went back to reusable terry nappies, an established and environmentally-friendly alternative.

BUM FLUFF

The main disposable nappy brands are Procter & Gamble's Pampers and Kimberly-Clark's Huggies.

The bulkiest component of disposable nappies (or diapers, as they are known in the US) is paper pulp fluff, the rising demand for which is beginning to threaten old-growth forests in Canada, Scandinavia and the Baltic states. Valuable wetlands, moors and meadows risk being destroyed in the quest for new plantations.

Other components of nappies include plastics and chemicals derived from non-renewable sources. There is controversy about the safety of some commonly-used chemicals such as the absorbing agent sodium polyacrylate. Babies with sensitive skin may react to absorbent gels.

HYGIENE

The average baby gets through about 5,000 nappies on his or her way to being potty trained. Disposables are commonly binned or, much worse, flushed away. Putting them in the bin without first cleaning off waste is unhygienic and, though few people know it, actually illegal. Chucking them down the toilet happens far too commonly, and they can cause serious maintenance problems in sewers and sewage farms. Many of them also end up in the sea: a Marine Conservation Society report found an average of between one and two washed up disposable nappies per kilometre of shoreline surveyed.

THE NAPPY DEBATE

Last year the Environment Agency published a report on the comparable environmental impact of disposable and reusable 'terry' nappies, which came to the controversial conclusion that there was little or no difference between the two. It found that the use of fossil fuels involved in cleaning reusable nappies outweighed the impact of production for disposables, and suggested that parents should be free to choose the type of nappy that suits them best.

Nevertheless, the report recommended that nappy manufacturers should:

- Consider using recycled paper in their products
- Use renewable energy for the production process
- Seek out sustainable sources of pulp from managed forests
- Investigate technology for recycling disposable nappies
- Lower the weight of their products

The Women's Environmental Network criticised the report, saying the research was 'seriously flawed'. In particular, it drew attention to the recommendation that nappy companies aim to reduce the weight of their nappies, even though lighter superabsorbent polymers have a higher environmental impact. The Network suggests that the global warming potential of real nappies can be reduced by using an 'A' rated washing machine (see Good Home and Office, page 104), washing at 60°C and air-drying rather than using a tumble dryer. The full Environment Agency report is available at *www.environment-agency.gov.uk*.

REUSABLES

Reusable nappies really do offer a viable alternative to disposables. Only a small percentage of UK parents use them, but there is much higher use of reusables in North America and Australia.

Terries used to be seen as hard work, but washing machines have reduced this and there are plenty of nappy washing services available around the country, some run by local authorities. There are also many new varieties, with specially fitted shapes and pin-free fastening systems, and re-usable overpants for added safety and comfort. The Real Nappy Association advocates the use of thin liners placed inside a terry, allowing solid waste to be peeled away and safely disposed of. These are biodegradable.

Real nappies help to counter nappy rash as they are breathable. But perhaps the best argument for them is the saving in cash terms – total nappy expenditure has been estimated at £250 for re-usables compared with as much as £700 - £1,000 per baby for disposables.

- Bambino Mio
- Modern Baby
- Nature Boy & Girl
- Sam I Am

- Cotton Bottoms
- Huggies
- Svenska Own-Brands

- Moltex Oko
- Pampers

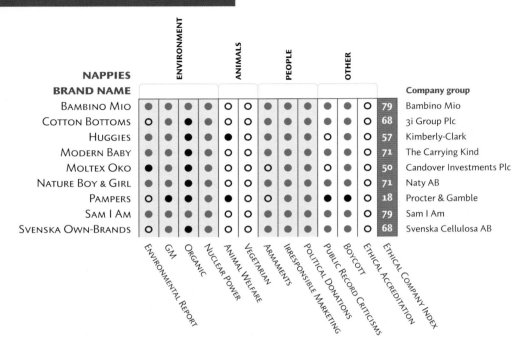

NAPPIES BRAND NAME	ENVIRONMENT				ANIMALS		PEOPLE			OTHER			Index	Company group
	Environmental Report	GM	Organic	Nuclear Power	Animal Welfare	Vegetarian	Armaments	Irresponsible Marketing	Political Donations	Public Record Criticisms	Boycott	Ethical Accreditation	Ethical Company Index	
Bambino Mio	●	●	●	●	○	○	●	●	●	●	●	○	79	Bambino Mio
Cotton Bottoms	○	●	●	●	○	○	●	●	●	●	●	○	68	3i Group Plc
Huggies	●	●	●	●	●	○	●	●	●	○	●	○	57	Kimberly-Clark
Modern Baby	●	●	●	●	○	○	●	●	●	●	●	○	71	The Carrying Kind
Moltex Oko	●	●	●	●	○	○	○	●	●	○	●	○	50	Candover Investments Plc
Nature Boy & Girl	●	●	●	●	○	○	●	●	●	●	●	○	71	Naty AB
Pampers	○	●	●	●	●	○	○	●	●	●	●	○	18	Procter & Gamble
Sam I Am	●	●	●	●	○	○	●	●	●	●	●	○	79	Sam I Am
Svenska Own-Brands	○	●	●	●	○	○	●	●	●	●	●	○	68	Svenska Cellulosa AB

Key

● Top rating
○ Middle rating
● Bottom rating

Source: The Ethical Company Organisation

Pain remedies

It's pretty difficult to avoid the pharmaceutical giants when buying painkillers, but the alternatives are out there. One option is to choose generic analgesics rather than the attractively packaged brand names, which often contain the same active ingredient at a much higher price. Many of the companies are still involved in animal testing, although the number has decreased on previous years; proof that a combination of public pressure and positive legislation can really make a difference.

BRANDS AND GENERICS

The painkiller market is estimated to be worth over £480 million in 2006, up from about £300 million a decade ago. There are three main types of painkilling drug, based upon the active ingredients paracetamol (acetaminophen in the US), aspirin and ibuprofen, all of which are available over the counter. Aspirin and ibuprofen have an anti-inflammatory effect, as well as acting on the pain and fever reduced by paracetamol.

Like nearly every other consumer product, there is an abundance of different pain remedy brands available, with a choice of between 30 and 50 different analgesics in the shops. Formulations may contain either aspirin, paracetamol, ibuprofen or a combination of these, and may also include codeine and other ingredients, such as caffeine.

There are more brands available than there are formulations, many being identical but for the name. Branded painkillers are a good source of income for the pharmaceutical companies, as simply by branding a well-established drug – such as aspirin – they can sell it at an inflated price, sometimes as much as six times the price of a generic, unbranded version.

Only drugs for which the patent has expired are available as generics and may be produced by any company. For example, since January 1998 it has been possible to purchase ibuprofen, whereas before it was only available as a brand such as Nurofen.

Painkillers come in a range of formats, including capsules, tablets, caplets and soluble tablets. Vegetarians might want to avoid capsules as they often contain gelatine.

OTHER ISSUES

Most of the companies included in the research were known to be involved in animal testing. Although companies are obliged in most countries to test pharmaceutical products on animals, some are involved in testing that is not for medical use. Companies producing generics may be less likely to be involved in animal testing as they simply produce drugs that were developed by others.

Concerns have been raised over a class of painkilling drugs called non-steroidal anti-inflammatories after a trial linked them, when taken at prolonged high doses, to an increased risk of heart attack. One drug, Vioxx, has been taken off the market, and the study's authors have called for further research to be carried out.

Recently, over-reliance on painkillers has been revealed as a cause of some persistent headaches. Discovery of the 'medication overuse headache' has led to drugs companies being criticised for marketing their brands as quick fixes, when milder pain might be better left alone.

BURMA (MYANMAR)

In October 2002 Superdrug was bought by a subsidiary of Hutchison Whampoa, a multinational conglomerate based in Hong Kong. Another subsidiary of the company, Hutchison Port Holdings, has since 1997 managed and developed a major Burmese port facility. The company's continued presence in the country serves to support its brutal regime.

ALTERNATIVES

Dealing with stress is usually preferable to having to deal with the symptoms such as pain. Regular exercise and relaxation techniques such as yoga, meditation and massage can be good stress-busters. Aromatherapy can also be useful, and lavender is often recommended.

It has been suggested that migraines may be triggered by certain foods and drink. The most common triggers are thought to be red wine, chocolate, cheese and citrus fruit. Avoiding these may limit the chance of an attack.

- Boots
- Nurofen

- LloydsPharmacy
- Veganin

- Anadin
- Aspro Clear
- Codis
- Disprin
- Feminax
- Hedex
- Panadol
- Solpadeine
- Superdrug

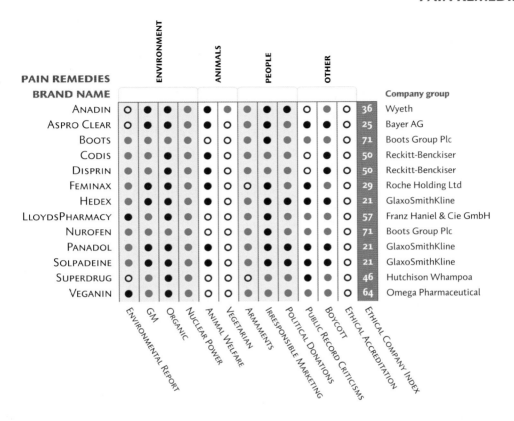

PAIN REMEDIES BRAND NAME	ENVIRONMENT				ANIMALS		PEOPLE			OTHER			ETHICAL COMPANY INDEX	Company group
	Environmental Report	GM	Organic	Nuclear Power	Animal Welfare	Vegetarian	Armaments	Irresponsible Marketing	Political Donations	Public Record Criticisms	Boycott	Ethical Accreditation		
Anadin	○	●	●	●	●	●	●	●	●	○	●	○	36	Wyeth
Aspro Clear	○	●	●	●	●	○	●	●	●	●	●	○	25	Bayer AG
Boots	●	●	●	●	○	○	●	●	●	●	●	○	71	Boots Group Plc
Codis	●	●	●	●	●	○	●	●	●	○	●	○	50	Reckitt-Benckiser
Disprin	●	●	●	●	●	○	●	●	●	○	●	○	50	Reckitt-Benckiser
Feminax	●	●	●	●	●	○	○	●	●	●	●	○	29	Roche Holding Ltd
Hedex	●	●	●	●	●	○	●	●	●	●	●	○	21	GlaxoSmithKline
LloydsPharmacy	●	●	●	●	○	○	●	●	●	●	●	○	57	Franz Haniel & Cie GmbH
Nurofen	●	●	●	●	○	○	●	●	●	●	●	○	71	Boots Group Plc
Panadol	●	●	●	●	●	○	●	●	●	●	●	○	21	GlaxoSmithKline
Solpadeine	●	●	●	●	●	○	●	●	●	●	●	○	21	GlaxoSmithKline
Superdrug	○	●	●	●	○	○	○	●	●	●	●	○	46	Hutchison Whampoa
Veganin	●	●	●	●	○	○	●	●	●	●	●	○	64	Omega Pharmaceutical

Key

● Top rating

○ Middle rating

● Bottom rating

Source: The Ethical Company Organisation

Perfumes and aftershaves

Our sense of smell is linked to our psychological well-being, as anyone who enjoys the scent of freshly mown grass or roasted coffee beans can confirm. Manufacturers of perfumes and aftershaves aim to exploit this link to persuade people to buy their fragrances. Yet there is nothing as natural as mown grass in the average perfume; most contain countless chemicals, none of which legally have to be mentioned on the bottle.

MESSAGE ON A BOTTLE

Manufacturers tap into the aspirational and escapist part of human nature through their advertising campaigns and branding, which suggest an association between a particular fragrance and a glamorous lifestyle. However, the image fostered by the perfume manufacturers is largely illusory. Apart from the dream and a briefly lingering scent, what we are really being sold in our bottle of perfume is nothing more than a container of unnamed chemicals. What is more, many of these chemicals may be harmful.

Manufacturers of perfumes choose from about 8,000 ingredients, and any one bottle may contain as many as 5,000 chemicals. But trying to discover which ingredients are in each perfume is almost impossible. Perfume recipes have so far been protected from compulsory labelling by the highly effective lobbying of multinational companies. These companies have claimed that perfumes contain 'too many ingredients' to list. Without compulsory labelling the fragrance industry relies heavily on self-regulation. However, the potential health and environmental risks associated with some of the ingredients regularly found in fragrances suggests that this situation is inadequate.

HEALTH RISKS

Many ingredients in perfumes, such as benzene derivatives, are associated with health risks. In particular, perfumes can cause headaches, asthma and sinus problems, and a conservative estimate suggests that 2 per cent of the population have a skin allergy to fragrances. There are even suspicions that the phthalates in fragrances could lead to male infertility, and other chemicals in perfumes may be carcinogenic.

The lack of transparency compounds the problems that consumers face when choosing a perfume. Even careful searching cannot help a consumer to avoid known irritants. Until the laws relating to the testing and transparency of perfume ingredients are revised, consumers would be best advised to seek out products with a high proportion of essential oils. Or you could try the cheaper and safer option of using your own pheromones to attract attention.

SMELLING A RAT?

Some perfumes contain ingredients cruelly derived from animals, such as musk (a dried secretion from the preputial follicles of the musk deer), civet (taken from the scent glands of the Ethiopian civet cat), ambergris (taken from sperm whales), and castor (from follicles near the genitals of beavers). Animal substances are often used as fixatives, and therefore are not essential to the fragrance itself. Synthetic substitutes for these ingredients exist and enable companies such as Dolma to guarantee that their perfumes are made with no cruelty towards animals.

Manufacturers have also been accused of harming the environment in their search for fragrance ingredients, Friends of the Earth campaign against companies buying talc mined from the Indian rainforest, which damages the habitat of the tiger.

TARGETING THE KIDS

Child protection authorities have criticised the perfume industry for marketing scents at children. Since 1995, Versace, Agnes B, Nina Ricci, Givenchy and Guerlain have all introduced perfumes for children aged 4 to 15. Some watchdog groups have expressed a fear that the premature sexualisation of children in certain advertisements could legitimise and encourage sexual interest in children.

- Amethyst
  Mist
- Sirius

- Activist
- Aramis
- Cacharel
- Calvin Klein
- Chanel
- Christian Dior
- Estee Lauder
- Gucci
- Opium
- Ralph Lauren
- White Musk
- Youth Dew

- Lynx
- Old Spice
- Revlon

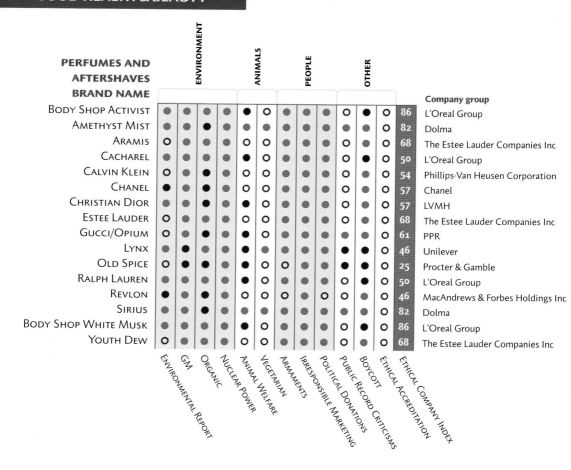

PERFUMES AND AFTERSHAVES

Column headings (left to right): ENVIRONMENT (GM, Organic, Environmental Report, Nuclear Power), ANIMALS (Animal Welfare, Vegetarian), PEOPLE (Armaments, Irresponsible Marketing, Political Donations), OTHER (Public Record Criticisms, Boycott, Ethical Accreditation), Ethical Company Index

Brand Name	Ethical Company Index	Company group
Body Shop Activist	86	L'Oreal Group
Amethyst Mist	82	Dolma
Aramis	68	The Estee Lauder Companies Inc
Cacharel	50	L'Oreal Group
Calvin Klein	54	Phillips-Van Heusen Corporation
Chanel	57	Chanel
Christian Dior	57	LVMH
Estee Lauder	68	The Estee Lauder Companies Inc
Gucci/Opium	61	PPR
Lynx	46	Unilever
Old Spice	25	Procter & Gamble
Ralph Lauren	50	L'Oreal Group
Revlon	46	MacAndrews & Forbes Holdings Inc
Sirius	82	Dolma
Body Shop White Musk	86	L'Oreal Group
Youth Dew	68	The Estee Lauder Companies Inc

Key
- ● Top rating
- ○ Middle rating
- ● Bottom rating

Source: The Ethical Company Organisation

Sanitary protection

It has been estimated that the average woman will throw away 250 to 300lb worth of sanitary protection, and use up to 15,000 tampons during her lifetime. This, and other expenses on sanitary protection, will cost her over £150 a year. Part of this expense is likely to be down to the 'every-day panty liner', a relatively new product that has been successfully marketed on the somewhat controversial claim that it is intrinsic to 'daily freshness'.

BIG BRANDS

The sanitary protection market is dominated by one company, Procter & Gamble, who produce the well known brands Tampax, Always and Allday. This large and extensive company has been criticised for less-than ethical practices in relation to the environment and animal welfare. Fortunately, alternatives are available, and they are well worth seeking out because they reduce health and environmental concerns to a near-zero.

HEALTH

Manufacturers estimate that 10 per cent of women have permanently deserted the tampon due to fears of the blood infection Toxic Shock Syndrome (TSS). This is a rare but painful, and potentially fatal, disease. 99 per cent of TSS cases are found in women wearing rayon-blend tampons, the most common kind. Natracare does 100 per cent cotton tampons, which may therefore be safer.

The superabsorbent polyacrylate gel AGM was banned from tampons in 1995 because of links to TSS, but it is still used in some towels. The main safety issue arises from the temptation to change gel-filled towels less frequently, causing a build-up of bacteria. Additionally, a Canadian study on babies' nappies found that when dry, AGM powder can travel up the urethra to the kidneys and cause scarring.

The Women's Environmental Network (WEN) has campaigned on the issue of GM cotton in tampons and towels. Aside from the environmental objections to modification of the cotton crop, the organisation is concerned about potential alterations in absorbency levels increasing the risk of TSS, and about the potential transfer of antibiotic resistance marker genes.

Using disposable sanitary products risks putting toxins next to your skin or vaginal tissue. Some residues, such as pesticides and dioxins from the bleaching process, have been linked to birth defects, reproductive disorders, depressed immunity and cancer.

THE ENVIRONMENT

Casual flushing of sanitary protection waste means that much of it ends up in rivers and sewage outfills, acting as a breeding ground for diseases and potentially being mistaken by sea mammals for prey. Otherwise, it festers in landfill sites, where it takes six months for a tampon to degrade. Plastic packaging and applicators may persist indefinitely in the environment. Reusable sanitary protection, such as the Keeper, washable sanitary towels, and sponges are the best environmental option as there are no disposal issues to consider.

The percentage of waste paper pulp in tampons and towels has increased during the last ten years, but it has recently taken a dive again due to a move away from recycled products to a focus on premium ones. Manufacturers play to the fact that around half of women declare themselves prepared to pay more if they sense a higher quality and comfort level – hence the extra wings, gels and gauzy layers that keep appearing.

ALTERNATIVES

For those who are concerned about sanitary waste ending up in landfill, there are now a number of eco-friendly mail-order companies that produce washable sanitary towels. These are usually made from soft terry cotton in a range of sizes, and have adjustable fastenings. Most products can be machine washed and tumble-dried.

In addition to washable sanitary towels and sponges, which are similar in principle to ordinary tampons and towels, it might be worth considering the menstrual cup. Made by companies such as Mooncup (an Ethical Company Organisation accredited company), it has received positive feedback from customers and women's groups. The cup is re-useable, which makes it a financially and environmentally viable option, and it does not contain rayon, or any other harmful chemicals and substances. This means that it has not been linked to Toxic Shock Syndrome. The Mooncup can be obtained from *www.mooncup.co.uk*.

- Keeper
- Luna sponges
- Many Moons pads
- Mooncup
- Natracare

- Bodyform
- Helen Harper
- Kotex
- Libresse
- Lil-lets
- Soft-tampons

- Alldays
- Always
- Carefree
- Tampax

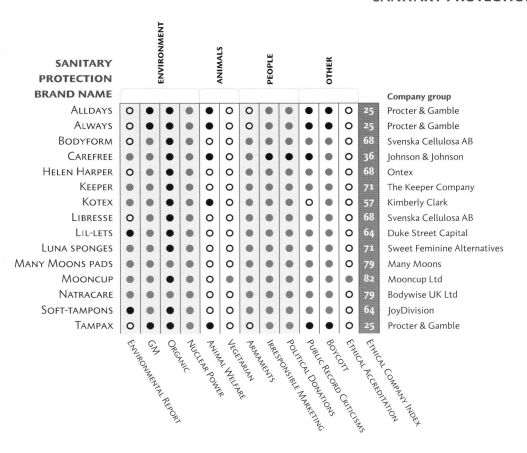

SANITARY PROTECTION BRAND NAME	ENVIRONMENT				ANIMALS		PEOPLE				OTHER		Ethical Company Index	Company group
	Environmental Report	GM	Organic	Nuclear Power	Animal Welfare	Vegetarian	Armaments	Irresponsible Marketing	Political Donations	Public Record Criticisms	Boycott	Ethical Accreditation		
ALLDAYS	○	●	●	●	●	○	○	●	●	●	●	○	25	Procter & Gamble
ALWAYS	○	●	●	●	●	○	○	●	●	●	●	○	25	Procter & Gamble
BODYFORM	○	●	●	●	○	○	●	●	●	●	●	○	68	Svenska Cellulosa AB
CAREFREE	●	●	●	●	●	○	●	●	●	●	●	○	36	Johnson & Johnson
HELEN HARPER	○	●	●	●	○	○	●	●	●	●	●	○	68	Ontex
KEEPER	●	●	●	●	○	○	●	●	●	●	●	○	71	The Keeper Company
KOTEX	●	●	●	●	●	○	●	●	○	●	●	○	57	Kimberly Clark
LIBRESSE	○	●	●	●	○	○	●	●	●	●	●	○	68	Svenska Cellulosa AB
LIL-LETS	●	●	●	●	○	○	●	●	●	●	●	○	64	Duke Street Capital
LUNA SPONGES	●	●	●	●	○	○	●	●	●	●	●	○	71	Sweet Feminine Alternatives
MANY MOONS PADS	●	●	●	●	○	○	●	●	●	●	●	○	79	Many Moons
MOONCUP	●	●	●	●	○	●	●	●	●	●	●	●	82	Mooncup Ltd
NATRACARE	●	●	●	●	○	○	●	●	●	●	●	○	79	Bodywise UK Ltd
SOFT-TAMPONS	●	●	●	●	○	○	●	●	●	●	●	○	64	JoyDivision
TAMPAX	○	●	●	●	●	○	○	●	●	●	●	○	25	Procter & Gamble

Key

● Top rating

○ Middle rating

● Bottom rating

Source: The Ethical Company Organisation

Shampoo and conditioner

Elaborate hair care is intrinsic to the modern beauty routine, even though some claim that all it really needs is soap and water. Shampoo and conditioner manufacturers often succeed in seducing even the conscious consumer with their apparently 'natural' or 'organic' products, but we should not always believe what we read on the label. Choose companies whose ethical claims have been verified by the BUAV and the Soil Association – and by the Ethical Company Organisation.

THE NATURAL LOOK

Over the past few years, booming interest in organic produce has caused the mainstream cosmetics companies to flirt heavily, and successfully, with the natural image in launching their new product lines. This corporate romance with nature can be criticised as a cheap attempt to appear ecologically sound, as the few token 'natural' ingredients invariably mask the usual chemical cocktail. Alternative groups have called for Elida Fabergé to withdraw or rename its Organics line until all ingredients are certified organic. Of course, alternative producers have long been proclaiming the benefits of natural ingredients, with product lines true to their principles.

SUDS LAW

The long list of ingredients on the back of a shampoo bottle can be hard to decipher without specialist chemical knowledge. A commonly-used shampoo ingredient, due to its propensity to foam, is sodium laurel sulphate, or its milder form sodium laureth sulphate. Claims about the former's damaging health effects point to it being an allergen, with symptoms including skin and eye irritation. Industry replies to such concerns emphasise that these chemicals are used in measured amounts that have been legally decreed as safe for use.

Dandruff is a problem that many people are tackling with medicated shampoos. Anti-dandruff shampoos can contain potentially toxic chemicals and can even aggravate the problem. Eating foods that contain the right fats – such as raw nuts and cold-pressed vegetable oils – is one way to address the imbalance.

ANIMAL TESTING

Some companies skirt around the issue of animal testing, and at the same time keep themselves open to new ingredients, by adhering to the 'five-year rolling rule'. This means that five years must have elapsed since the ingredient was tested on animals. Naturewatch and the BUAV support use of the 'fixed cut-off date', whereby companies refuse to use ingredients tested on animals after a certain date.

ALTERNATIVES

In the days before shampoo, people resorted to more imaginative methods of achieving glossy locks. Soap was used as an all-round cleanser for hair and body, but as water has become more alkaline (hard) its effectiveness has declined, leaving hair rough and tangled. In areas with a soft water supply, using a plain soap with conditioner is an option. Otherwise adding something acidic to soap, such as vinegar or lemon juice, can neutralise the hard water. If you follow up with conditioner, your hair should be left healthy. It is possible to dispense with shampoo completely. However, many people find the transitional period unpleasant, as the scalp's naturally-produced oils (washed out by shampooing) kick back into action.

For a slightly easier option, try shampoos and conditioners from the companies that have been accredited by the Ethical Company Organisation. Green People, Hemp Garden, Honesty and Natura Organics are all members of the accreditation scheme, which indicates that they are ethically and environmentally compassionate. See the Good Network section at the back of the book for more information on these companies and how to buy their products.

- Botanics
- Faith in Nature
- Green People
- Hemp Garden
- Honesty
- Natural Organic Soap
- Nature Organics
- Neem Care
- Weleda

- Body Shop
- Henara
- L'Oreal
- Original Source
- VO5

- Aussie
- Head and Shoulders
- Organics
- Pantene Pro-V
- Superdrug

SHAMPOO AND CONDITIONER

Rating categories (left to right): **ENVIRONMENT** (Environmental Report, GM, Organic, Nuclear Power) · **ANIMALS** (Animal Welfare, Vegetarian) · **PEOPLE** (Armaments, Irresponsible Marketing, Political Donations, Public Record Criticisms) · **OTHER** (Boycott, Ethical Accreditation) · Ethical Company Index

Brand Name	Ethical Company Index	Company group
Aussie	32	Procter & Gamble
Body Shop	86	L'Oreal Group
Botanics	71	Boots Group Plc
Faith in Nature	86	Faith Products
Green People	89	Green People Company
Head and Shoulders	32	Procter & Gamble
Hemp Garden	86	Hemp Garden Ltd
Henara	61	Henkel
Honesty	89	Honesty Cosmetics
L'Oreal	50	L'Oreal Group
Natura Organics	86	Villa Natura
Neem Care	79	Bioforce
Organics	46	Unilever
Original Source	68	PZ Cussons
Pantene Pro-V	32	Procter & Gamble
Shampoo & Conditioner Bars	86	Natural Organic Soap
Superdrug	46	Hutchison Whampoa
V05	57	Alberto Culver
Weleda	79	Weleda Group

Key

● Top rating
○ Middle rating
● Bottom rating

Source: The Ethical Company Organisation

GREENPEOPLE
organic lifestyle

natural, organic and ethical beauty
for radiant skin and healthy hair

"The closest you can get to organic food for your skin"
Pamper yourself and your family with skin, hair, body &
sun care products from Green People containing active
ingredients, nourishing organic oils and plant extracts.

WINNER
Natural Health
Beauty Awards
2008

we don't use...

lanolin, parabens, sodium lauryl /laureth sulphate, proplyene

glycol, synthetic fragrances, petrochemicals, phthalates

for a FREE catalogue and sachet please visit
www.greenpeople.co.uk or call 01403 740350

Skincare

Even though the big cosmetics firms love to use the word 'natural' on their products, most skincare creams use man-made chemicals, some of which are potentially toxic. Consumer groups have expressed concern about 'bio-accumulation', where chemicals build up in our systems because we do not have the capacity to get rid of them. The only way to ensure the safety of what we buy is to look at the small print behind the slogan.

HOW NATURAL?

Lack of proper industry regulation means that a product can be called 'natural' even if it contains as little as 1 per cent natural ingredients. Most skincare creams contain dozens of synthetic and chemical ingredients, many of which are a potential cause for concern.

Specific ingredients that are probably best avoided include: propylene glycol, formaldehyde, ammonia derivatives (diethanolamine, triethanolamine and monoethanolamine), alpha hydroxy acid and benzoic acid. Of these, propylene glycol (also found in industrial form in antifreeze and brake fluid) has been associated with kidney damage, alpha hydroxy acid has been linked with damage to skin cells, and formaldehyde is a known irritant.

Skin irritation is a common complaint with cosmetics. Irritation and allergies tend to be more common in people with eczema, asthma and hay fever, and usually involve the appearance of inflammation, itchiness or redness. As all cosmetics have the potential to cause a reaction if enough people use them, warnings tend to be given only for high-risk products such as hair dyes. Synthetic chemicals such as propylene glycol are known to cause problems for sensitive individuals. Fragrance-free skincare creams, and those which are made from certified natural ingredients, are less likely to irritate the skin.

BIO-ACCUMULATION

According to Friends of the Earth, our bodies are on average contaminated with 300 man-made chemicals. Many of these chemicals 'bio-accumulate', meaning that they aren't broken down by the body. Some can also interfere with the hormone system and may cause cancer. The long-term effects of these chemicals are so far unknown and, more worryingly, even if they were found to be harmful, our bodies would be unable to eliminate them. Friends of the Earth believes that these chemicals should be identified, then phased out and replaced with safer alternatives as soon as possible.

ANIMAL TESTING

The labelling of cosmetics products may imply that they have not been tested on animals, when in fact the opposite is the case. Even if a finished product has not been animal tested, the ingredients used to make it may have been. When a company says 'we don't test our products or ingredients on animals', it could mean that someone else is doing the testing for them. Equally, the statement 'against animal testing' doesn't necessarily mean the company puts this into practice. Manufacturers will often use these vague statements as a way of concealing their (and their suppliers') involvement in practises that the consumer may not agree with.

The only way to guarantee a cruelty-free cosmetic is to look for the BUAV's rabbit and stars symbol, which confirms that the product meets the Humane Cosmetics Standard.

PACKAGING

A particular problem with moisturisers is the amount of packaging they create. Most brands use plastic packaging, which is most likely to end up in landfill, with only a small amount being recycled or incinerated. Culpeper is one of the rare brands that uses glass to package its skincare products. The Body Shop used to refill old bottles, although these days not every shop offers this facility (and we have concerns over their parent company since the takeover!).

- Aromatherapy Direct
- Bulldog
- Essential Care
- Fushi
- Green People
- Hemp Garden
- Honesty
- Lush
- Natura Organics
- Weleda

- Aveda
- Boots
- Clarins
- Culpeper
- E45
- Nivea
- Origins

- Body Shop
- L'Oreal
- Neutrogena
- Oil of Olay
- Ponds

SKINCARE BRAND NAME	ENVIRONMENT				ANIMALS		PEOPLE				OTHER		Ethical Company Index	Company group
	Environmental Report	GM	Organic	Nuclear Power	Animal Welfare	Vegetarian	Armaments	Irresponsible Marketing	Political Donations	Public Record Criticisms	Boycott	Ethical Accreditation		
Aromatherapy Direct	●	●	●	●	○	○	●	●	●	●	●	●	88	Aromatherapy Direct
Aveda	○	●	●	●	●	○	●	●	●	●	●	○	63	The Estee Lauder Companies Inc
Body Shop	●	●	●	●	●	○	●	●	●	●	●	○	50	L'Oreal Group
Boots	●	●	●	●	○	○	●	●	●	○	●	○	71	Alliance Boots Plc
Bulldog	●	●	●	●	○	○	●	●	●	●	●	●	79	The Little Wing Trading Company Ltd
Clarins	○	●	●	●	○	○	●	●	●	●	●	○	71	Clarins Group
Culpeper	●	●	●	●	○	○	●	●	●	●	●	○	75	Culpeper Ltd
E45	●	●	●	●	○	○	●	●	●	○	●	○	71	Alliance Boots Plc
Essential Care	●	●	●	●	○	○	●	●	●	●	●	●	88	Essential Care (Organics) Ltd
Fushi	●	●	●	●	○	○	●	●	●	●	●	●	88	Fushi
Green People	●	●	●	●	○	●	●	●	●	●	●	●	92	Green People Company
Hemp Garden	●	●	●	●	○	●	●	●	●	●	●	●	83	Hemp Garden Ltd
Honesty	●	●	●	●	●	●	●	●	●	●	●	●	100	Honesty Cosmetics
L'Oreal	●	●	●	●	●	○	●	●	●	●	●	○	50	L'Oreal Group
Lush	●	●	●	●	○	●	●	●	●	●	●	○	79	Lush Ltd
Natura Organics	●	●	●	●	○	○	●	●	●	●	●	●	88	Villa Natura
Neutrogena	●	●	●	●	●	○	●	●	●	●	●	○	50	Johnson & Johnson
Nivea	○	●	●	●	○	○	●	●	●	○	●	○	67	Beiersdorf AG
Oil of Olay	●	●	●	●	●	○	○	●	○	●	●	○	42	Procter & Gamble
Origins	○	●	●	●	●	○	●	●	●	●	●	○	63	The Estee Lauder Companies Inc
Ponds	●	●	●	●	●	●	●	●	●	●	●	○	54	Unilever
Weleda	●	●	●	●	○	○	●	●	●	●	●	○	83	Weleda Group

Key

● Top rating
○ Middle rating
● Bottom rating

Source: The Ethical Company Organisation (2008)

natural ◎ collection ™

Our award-winning range includes organic cotton and fair trade clothing and accessories, items for your home and garden, energy-saving gadgets, organic cosmetics, eco cleaning products like Ecover and much more.

Each item is carefully researched and selected to promote ecological and sustainable manufacturing practices. Our philosophy is that small positive choices by the many can have a tremendous impact on our collective ethical evolution.

Eternal Organic Wool Cache Coeur Top

Florame Organic Men's Grooming Collection

naturalcollection.com
0845 36 77 001

Soap

Most people probably wouldn't want to wash themselves with a petrochemical-fragranced bar of animal fats, but these ingredients may be contained in even the simplest bar of soap – and they might not be easy to identify on the label. Fortunately, some smaller manufacturers make their soaps to vegetarian or vegan standard, using natural essential oils for scent, dried flowers for colour and herbs for exfoliation. Hand-made and cruelty-free, these are an ideal alternative.

INGREDIENTS

Soap is made from animal or vegetable fats, oils or grease, and forms when the fats interact with an alkali. Preservatives, salts, colours, perfumes, moisturisers and emulsifiers may then be added, with the more adventurous brands including fruits, spices and essential oils. Traditionally, soaps were produced from animal fats such as fish oils or tallow, listed in the ingredients as 'sodium tallowate'. The Vegan Society describes tallow as 'hard animal fat, especially that obtained from the parts about the kidneys of ruminating animals'. Although there are vegetable alternatives, many of the major soap brands still contain animal fats and consequently are not suitable for vegetarians or vegans.

Vegetable soaps may also contain added ingredients such as honey, lanolin and milk, preventing them from being suitable for vegans. Lush, Caurnie, Suma, Faith and Body Shop soaps are all suitable for vegetarians. Caurnie and Faith soaps are all vegan, while all except Suma's honey soaps are suitable for vegans. The Body Shop produces a list of its 'vegan non-friendly' products and Lush clearly labels those soaps which are suitable for vegans.

The Good Shopping Guide can recommend Caurnie, Ecosoapia, Hemp Garden and Natural Organic Soap, all of whom received particularly good marks in the survey and have been accredited by the Ethical Company Organisation.

MAKING SOAP CLEANLY

Most of the bigger brand soaps are made from a common soap bar, manufactured by large commercial producers who sell it on in the form of dried soap nodules to individual soap makers for reprocessing.

Soaps made by the 'alternative' producers, such as Caurnie, Faith and Suma, are hand-made, which provides employment and promotes traditional soap-making techniques. According to information from Suma, the cold saponification process used by Suma and Caurnie is more energy-efficient, as 'all the ingredients remain in the mix, with only such heat input as is required to raise the temperature of the mix to body heat'.

A commercial processor may use a boiling process which could consume up to 65kw hours of electricity and 15 tonnes of water in producing one tonne of soap. The alternative soap makers claim that commercial products extract the glycerine, selling it as a by-product, instead of leaving it in the soap. Since glycerine is a natural moisturiser, this explains why many soaps can dry the skin.

SYNTHETICS AND PACKAGING

Most of the major soaps contain synthetic (petrochemical-based) ingredients, but many of the smaller producers use natural ingredients, such as essential oils, rather than artificial fragrances to scent their soaps. The synthetic ingredients used by the larger companies are often irritants for sensitive skin.

The packaging used by the major brands is often excessive, with Imperial Leather (the UK's best-selling soap) using three wrappers, including a box. In comparison, Suma's soap is sold completely loose and just wrapped in a brown envelope, and other sellers such as Caurnie have made a commitment to using only minimal packaging.

Bits of soap that are too small to be used for washing can be kept in a soap jar, and dissolved in hot water to make a soft jelly for washing-up.

- Caurnie Soaps
- Ecosoapia
- Faith in Nature
- Hemp Garden
- Lush
- Natural
  Organic Soap
- Suma

- Body Shop
- Imperial Leather
- Nivea
- Pearl
- Simple

- Camay
- Dove
- Fairy
- Palmolive
- Pears

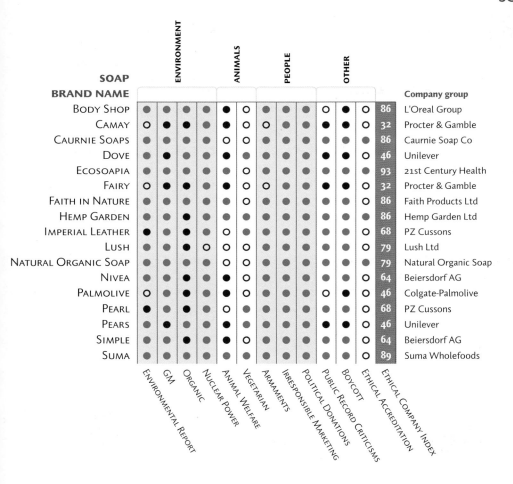

SOAP BRAND NAME	ENVIRONMENT				ANIMALS		PEOPLE				OTHER		Ethical Company Index	Company group
	Environmental Report	GM	Organic	Nuclear Power	Animal Welfare	Vegetarian	Armaments	Irresponsible Marketing	Political Donations	Public Record Criticisms	Boycott	Ethical Accreditation		
Body Shop	●	●	●	●	●	O	●	●	●	O	●	O	86	L'Oreal Group
Camay	O	●	●	●	●	O	O	●	●	●	●	O	32	Procter & Gamble
Caurnie Soaps	●	●	●	●	O	O	●	●	●	●	●	●	86	Caurnie Soap Co
Dove	●	●	●	●	●	●	●	●	●	●	●	O	46	Unilever
Ecosoapia	●	●	●	●	●	O	●	●	●	●	●	●	93	21st Century Health
Fairy	O	●	●	●	●	O	O	●	●	●	●	O	32	Procter & Gamble
Faith in Nature	●	●	●	●	●	O	●	●	●	●	●	O	86	Faith Products Ltd
Hemp Garden	●	●	●	●	●	●	●	●	●	●	●	●	86	Hemp Garden Ltd
Imperial Leather	●	●	●	●	O	●	●	●	●	●	●	O	68	PZ Cussons
Lush	●	●	●	O	O	O	●	●	●	●	●	O	79	Lush Ltd
Natural Organic Soap	●	●	●	●	O	O	●	●	●	●	●	●	79	Natural Organic Soap
Nivea	●	●	●	●	●	O	●	●	●	●	●	O	64	Beiersdorf AG
Palmolive	O	●	●	●	●	O	●	●	O	●	●	O	46	Colgate-Palmolive
Pearl	●	●	●	●	O	●	●	●	●	●	●	O	68	PZ Cussons
Pears	●	●	●	●	●	●	●	●	●	●	●	O	46	Unilever
Simple	●	●	●	●	●	O	●	●	●	●	●	O	64	Beiersdorf AG
Suma	●	●	●	●	●	●	●	●	●	●	●	O	89	Suma Wholefoods

Key

● Top rating
O Middle rating
● Bottom rating

Source: The Ethical Company Organisation

Sun protection

There are over 69,000 new cases of skin cancer diagnosed each year in the UK, but most people are now aware of the necessity of using sun lotion. With a wide range of brands available, and with experts reminding us that the most expensive and well-known products are not necessarily any better than the smaller names, there is no reason not to consider some of the lesser known and more ethical companies when protecting your skin.

SCREENS AND BLOCKS

The British Department of Health and the US Food and Drug Administration claim that, although sunscreen prevents sunburn, there is no proof that it actually prevents cancer. They also warn that the main danger of sunscreen is that people increase their risk of skin cancer by increasing the length of time they spend in the sun. They warn against the use of expensive and very high sun protection factor (SPF) lotions as 'the benefits are minimal'. A study by the Consumers' Association in 2001 found that cheap sunscreens can provide as much sun protection as those at the more pricey end of the market.

Sunscreen only works when it's slapped on thick at least half an hour before going outside, as it doesn't start working immediately. The Department of Health recommends using a sunscreen with a minimum rating of SPF 15. Unfortunately, many alternative cosmetics companies only produce low factor sunscreens. For example, Weleda uses a filter based on the vegetable extract camphor to produce SPF 8 in its highest-rated product. Honesty Cosmetics, a brand approved by *The Good Shopping Guide*, has an SPF 15 product.

Studies suggest that sunscreens with SPF 15 to 20 are generally acceptable, but that those above this level increase their ratings by increasing concentrations of key chemical components, which can cause irritation. Meanwhile, the EU is abolishing the term 'sunblock' because it is potentially misleading to customers.

WHAT CHEMICALS?

Sunscreens may contain one or more of a number of different active compounds to block out the sun's rays, such as OMC (octyl methoxycinnamate), benzophenone, benzophenone 3 (oxybenzone), titanium dioxide, zinc oxide and talc, all of which should be listed on the packaging. Despite the potential risks of some of these ingredients (studies carried out on mice have raised concerns about the safety of OMC), it isn't possible to find a sunscreen with a high SPF that doesn't use at least one of them.

ANIMAL TESTING

Sunscreens are currently classed as cosmetics, which means that animal testing is not required by law. Every year 35,000 animals in the EU are subjected to unnecessary experiments to test cosmetic products. The UK introduced a total ban on the testing of cosmetic products and ingredients on animals in November 1998, but because there is no world-wide ban, many cosmetics sold in the UK will simply have had their tests carried out elsewhere. Until a clear deadline is set, there is little regulatory incentive for widespread industry change. Vegetarians and vegans will be pleased to know that sunscreens by Honesty contain no animal derived ingredients, but they will have to watch out for beeswax, chitin, collagen, elastin, lanolin and stearin, which may be found in other companies' products. Another accredited brand, Green People, sell organic sun care creams.

PACKAGING

The majority of sun lotions come in plastic bottles (usually polyethylene, PE, or high-density polyethylene, HDPE) and can only be recycled where such facilities exist. However, Weleda's sun cream is packaged in an aluminium tube to enable it to be easily recycled.

- Green People
- Honesty
- Soltan
- Weleda

- Banana Boat
- Body Shop
- Calypso
- Clarins
- Delph
- Estee Lauder
- L'Oreal
- Malibu
- Nivea Sun
- Simple

- Coppertone
- Piz Buin

SUN PROTECTION BRAND NAME	Ethical Company Index	Company group
AMBRE SOLEIL	50	L'Oreal Group
BANANA BOAT	57	Playtex products
BODY SHOP	86	L'Oreal Group
CALYPSO	64	Linco Care Ltd
CLARINS	68	Clarins SA
COPPERTONE	25	Schering-Plough
DELPH	64	Fenton Pharmaceuticals
ESTEE LAUDER	68	The Estee Lauder Companies Inc
GREEN PEOPLE	89	Green People Company
HONESTY	89	Honesty Cosmetics
MALIBU	64	Malibu Health
NIVEA SUN	64	Beiersdorf AG
PIZ BUIN	36	Johnson & Johnson
SIMPLE	64	Beiersdorf AG
SOLTAN	71	Boots Group Plc
WELEDA	79	Weleda AG

Rating categories (columns, left to right):

- **ENVIRONMENT:** Environmental Report, GM, Organic, Nuclear Power
- **ANIMALS:** Animal Welfare, Vegetarian
- **PEOPLE:** Armaments, Irresponsible Marketing, Political Donations
- **OTHER:** Public Record Criticisms, Boycott, Ethical Accreditation

REMEMBER

- Skin cancer can be caused by excessive exposure to the sun
- Wear a hat, sunglasses and tightly woven clothes
- Pale clothes let more sun through than darker ones
- During holidays in the hottest weather, have a long lunch and a siesta

Key

● Top rating
O Middle rating
● Bottom rating

Source: The Ethical Company Organisation

Toothpaste

Having clean teeth is much more important for dental health reasons than for the sake of cosmetics. Toothpastes marketed on the basis of their visual effect, such as whitening and smokers' products, should be approached with caution, as they can often contain abrasives. Alongside health worries about excessive fluoride ingestion, other ingredients to look out for are sodium lauryl sulphate and triclosan, both of which have been a source of recent controversy.

LABELLING

The British Dental Health Foundation and the British Dental Association both run labelling schemes which allow oral health and hygiene products to carry the BDHF or BDA logo. Companies have to pay for the initial checks on the products and then pay an annual fee to the relevant body in order to carry the logo. The Consumers' Association has concerns about the scheme, because toothpastes without an accreditation logo are not necessarily any worse.

FLUORIDE

Since fluoride toothpaste came onto the market in the 1970s, tooth decay rates have fallen by 75 per cent. However, there are associated health concerns. Over-exposure to fluoride can lead to fluorosis, with flu-like symptoms and possible links to future thyroid problems, so manufacturers warn against ingestion of toothpaste, particularly for children. However, the amount of fluoride in toothpaste has not been proven to pose a serious health risk, and the benefits of healthy teeth are usually thought to outweigh any potential problems. Readers concerned about their fluoride intake, particularly the 10 per cent of the British population who live in areas where the water is fluoridated, can choose fluoride-free toothpastes such as Green People, Kingfisher, Tom's of Maine or the appropriate Weleda brand.

OTHER INGREDIENTS

Many toothpastes contain sodium lauryl sulphate (SLS), a synthetic foaming agent. Some experts have raised concerns about this ingredient, saying that it is a suspected gastro-intestinal or liver toxicant. Others point to the fact that it has been associated with recurrent mouth ulcers. It is also an industrial-strength detergent, so many people may want to think twice before putting it in their mouths. However, a small application for a short period followed by a thorough rinsing should be harmless for most people. For those with a recurring mouth ulcer problem, Green People and Weleda toothpastes are SLS-free.

Triclosan (which may also be listed under CH 3635, Irgasan Ch 3635 or Ster-Zac) is an antibacterial agent which has caused controversy because it may increase the growth of superbugs, although it has not been shown to be dangerous for human health.

All toothpastes list the active ingredients, so levels of triclosan and fluoride salts present in the paste should always be found on the packet. Toothpaste brands which contain triclosan include Colgate, Crest, Mentadent P, Sensodyne F and Macleans. Other brands marketing themselves as 'antibacterial' may also contain triclosan.

PACKAGING

Most toothpastes now come in plastic tubes, and several in pump dispensers. Some still come in the traditional aluminium tube. Tom's of Maine says that its aluminium tube, lined with food-grade plastic, can be recycled along with aluminium cans. Kingfisher Natural Toothpaste is packed in boxes manufactured from recycled cardboard and its tubes are made from biodegradable cellulose.

ALTERNATIVES

Dabur is an ayurvedic brand and made according to ancient Hindu principles.

If you wish to join the 6 per cent of the population who don't use toothpaste at all, experiment with sea salt, soot, chalk or bicarbonate of soda.

- Green People
- Kingfisher
- Thursday Plantation
- Tom's of Maine
- Weleda

- Dabur
- Nelson
- Sarakan

- Aquafresh
- Arm & Hammer
- Colgate
- Crest
- Euthymol
- Mentadent P
- Oral B
- Pearl Drops

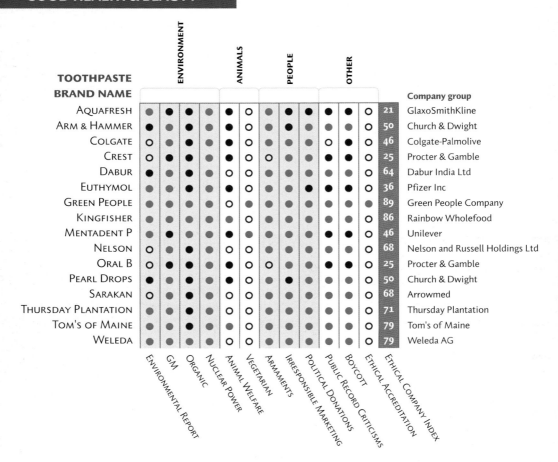

TOOTHPASTE BRAND NAME	ENVIRONMENT				ANIMALS		PEOPLE			OTHER			Ethical Company Index	Company group
	Environmental Report	GM	Organic	Nuclear Power	Animal Welfare	Vegetarian	Armaments	Irresponsible Marketing	Political Donations	Public Record Criticisms	Boycott	Ethical Accreditation		
Aquafresh						O						O	21	GlaxoSmithKline
Arm & Hammer						O						O	50	Church & Dwight
Colgate	O					O				O		O	46	Colgate-Palmolive
Crest	O					O	O					O	25	Procter & Gamble
Dabur					O	O						O	64	Dabur India Ltd
Euthymol						O						O	36	Pfizer Inc
Green People					O								89	Green People Company
Kingfisher						O						O	86	Rainbow Wholefood
Mentadent P												O	46	Unilever
Nelson	O				O	O						O	68	Nelson and Russell Holdings Ltd
Oral B	O					O	O					O	25	Procter & Gamble
Pearl Drops						O						O	50	Church & Dwight
Sarakan	O					O						O	68	Arrowmed
Thursday Plantation					O	O						O	71	Thursday Plantation
Tom's of Maine						O						O	79	Tom's of Maine
Weleda					O	O						O	79	Weleda AG

Key
● Top rating
O Middle rating
● Bottom rating

Source: The Ethical Company Organisation

Vitamins

Given that much of the marketing surrounding them seems to play on our desire for wellbeing, some consumers are understandably cautious about vitamins. However, there are a number of exceptions to the rule that healthy eating is the best way to get all the vitamins and minerals we need, and dietary supplements can be of benefit to many people. Those who choose vitamins need to know exactly what is in the products they take.

A VITAMIN A DAY KEEPS THE DOCTOR AWAY?

Some people argue that the traditional apple will do a better job. Fruit and vegetables have much more varied benefits than one-dimensional vitamin supplements. For example, a vitamin C supplement is usually made of asorbic acid, whereas food with vitamin C also contains other micro-nutrients, such as tyrosinase, which play an important role in the prevention of disease. Vitamin C in food also contains bioflavonoids which help the body to absorb the vitamin itself. Similarly, some vitamin B supplements are manufactured from coal tar, which does not work as effectively as natural sources of the vitamin, such as wheat germ. Therefore, a balanced diet remains the best way to enhance your health, and vitamin supplements shouldn't be used to make up for bad eating habits.

But what if you don't get the recommended five portions of fruit and veg a day? Most doctors agree that taking a low dose multi-vitamin and mineral supplement won't do any harm, and will probably have some benefits. After all, vitamins are essential for a healthy and active lifestyle. Problems only arise if you exceed the recommended dosage.

Vitamin supplements are, however, most beneficial if you have special health needs or a particular gap in your diet. Pregnant women, for example, can benefit from taking folic acid supplements, and it is particularly important for adolescents to get the proper intake of calcium, making a supplement worthwhile if they don't receive the recommended amount through their diet. Advertisements and health editorials commonly target vegetarians and vegans as those who are most in need of supplements. However, both the Vegan and Vegetarian societies argue that a healthy, mixed diet should provide all the nutrients we need.

INGREDIENTS

When the Food Commission conducted a survey into additives it was shocked by the numbers contained in supplements, as well as by the lack of clear labelling of ingredients. Its survey found a colouring in Redoxon which is banned in virtually all foods. Artificial sweeteners, aspartame and sorbitol, as well as talcum powder, silicon dioxide and anti-caking agents were found in some other supplements. More worryingly, an earlier government survey discovered higher-than-permitted levels of lead and arsenic in a number of supplements. Although the government did not at the time conclude that the products posed a significant risk, manufacturers were required to change their formulations.

Information on how supplements should be labelled, and safe dosage levels, are available at *www.food.gov.uk*.

PACKAGING

Many vitamin pills are vastly overpackaged. Some products, such as Seven Seas, are packaged in an outer box as well as the vitamin bottle, while Perfectil vitamins go even further by packaging each individual pill in its own bubble pack.

The majority of vitamin bottles are also made from plastic, although a few brands use glass. Viridian is the only company offering recycling of its bottles. Consumers can return their empty Viridian glass bottle to the place of purchase, and receive a 25p refund when it is taken for recycling. The company also makes a charity donation for every sale.

- Boots
- Viridian

- FSC
- GNC
- Holland & Barrett
- Perfectil
- Quest
- Red Kooga

- Centrum
- Redoxon
- Sanatogen
- Seven Seas
- Solgar

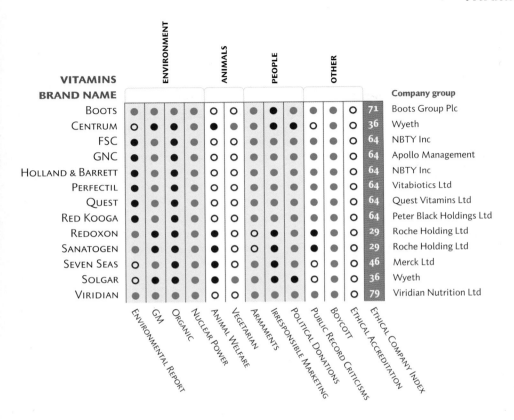

VITAMINS BRAND NAME / Categories: ENVIRONMENT, ANIMALS, PEOPLE, OTHER

Column headings: Environmental Report, GM, Organic, Nuclear Power, Animal Welfare, Vegetarian, Armaments, Irresponsible Marketing, Political Donations, Public Record Criticisms, Boycott, Ethical Accreditation, Ethical Company Index

Brand Name	Ethical Company Index	Company group
Boots	71	Boots Group Plc
Centrum	36	Wyeth
FSC	64	NBTY Inc
GNC	64	Apollo Management
Holland & Barrett	64	NBTY Inc
Perfectil	64	Vitabiotics Ltd
Quest	64	Quest Vitamins Ltd
Red Kooga	64	Peter Black Holdings Ltd
Redoxon	29	Roche Holding Ltd
Sanatogen	29	Roche Holding Ltd
Seven Seas	46	Merck Ltd
Solgar	36	Wyeth
Viridian	79	Viridian Nutrition Ltd

Key
- ● Top rating
- ○ Middle rating
- ● Bottom rating

Source: The Ethical Company Organisation

GOOD
FASHION

High street fashion •

Jeans •

Shoes and trainers •

Alternative clothing directory •

Introduction

Thanks to the efforts of progressive companies across the UK, ethical clothing and fashion are no longer mutually exclusive. While it was once only possible to dress in cruelty-free clothing if you resigned yourself to ill-fitting kaftans and scratchy hemp trousers, now the fashion industry is cluttered with designers offering organic, recycled, fair trade and traditional garments at a comparable cost to the high street.

This development is not just a victory for looking good. More importantly, it is a step towards the eradication of unethical labour policies and exploitation in factories around the world. The term 'sweatshop' has become a by-word for the dubious activities of huge multinationals, but its real meaning should not be forgotten. The word was coined over 200 years ago to describe factory conditions that 'sweated' products out of labourers by forcing them to work long hours. To keep costs down, wages were set low and safety precautions were minimal. Collectives and trade unions were banned, and workers had no guarantee that their jobs were secure.

Sweatshop practices belong in the 19th century, but they still exist in many countries today. The chances are you are wearing something right now that is the product of these conditions. The companies who set themselves apart from these practices are sending a message to the big manufacturers that such exploitation is unacceptable, and that a growing number of consumers not only agree with them, but are willing to act upon their principles.

The choices for the ethical consumer are manifold. High street stores such as Marks & Spencer are beginning to stock fairly traded clothes, which are also available via the internet at People Tree (*www.peopletree.co.uk*) and Plain Lazy (*www.plainlazy.com*), amongst many others. Companies including Seasalt and Howies use organic cotton, and the Worn Again range offers garments made out of everything from car seats to parachutes. A comprehensive list of stockists is available in the Alternative Clothing Directory, while bargain hunters need look no further than the nearest charity shop for second-hand and recycled clothing.

High street fashion

Clothes, like any other consumable goods, have a history. In the case of the fashion industry, that history usually involves people in poorer, less developed countries being sourced for cheap labour. This doesn't necessarily mean exploitation; indeed, many high-street fashion chains are conscientious about human rights issues and have policies to maintain fair standards. Some, however, continue to source from countries such as Burma or allow poor conditions to exist in their workshops.

No sweat

The issue of sweatshops has attracted a good deal of attention in the West, as companies within the fashion industry have been charged with abusing basic human rights abroad in order to keep prices competitive at home. In the worst reported cases, workers have to work seven days a week with no holidays, do not receive decent wages, and are prevented from forming unions. There is now considerable pressure on companies to have a code of conduct, and to make a concerted effort to meet this code. It is essential that companies allow their workers to form unions and to have some kind of external or internal monitoring process.

A code of conduct, however, does not immediately infer ethical credibility, because they are not always rigorously enforced. While Gap has a decent code of conduct it also has a large number of suppliers, who are subject to very few independent inspections. H&M also has a good code of conduct, yet it has recently been criticised for its failure to prevent union busting in its factories. Some companies, including Gap, have signed up to the Ethical Trading Initiative. This is a step in the right direction, but it certainly doesn't guarantee truly ethical practices.

One solution to the problem of finding ethical clothes is to buy from smaller companies that specialise in ethical matters. These are listed in our Alternative Clothing Directory (page 330).

Burma (Myanmar)

Many companies still source from Burma, which is often regarded as one of the most unethical practices around. Burma is ruled by a military dictatorship that is widely considered to be amongst the worst regimes in the world, and has been condemned as such by the United Nations. The regime consistently abuses basic human rights and refuses any kind of democratic political system. Millions of men, women and children are used in forced labour and are often threatened with murder, torture and rape. Only 5 per cent of the national budget is spent on social and health care, while nearly half is spent on defence. Foreign capital merely strengthens the dictatorship and the exploitation of the Burmese people. The situation is unlikely to change; the leader of the democracy party, Aung San Suu Kyi, has been detained by the dictatorship for almost ten years.

A comprehensive list of these companies that still source from Burma can be found at *www.burmacampaign.org.uk*.

COTTON

It is estimated that nearly one third of a pound of chemical fertilisers and pesticides is needed to produce enough cotton for a single T-shirt, and these chemicals are some of the most toxic around. Buy organic if you can: Seasalt are an Ethical Company Organisation accredited company who sell fashionable and long-lasting organic clothing.

For good quality organic cotton on the high street, try New Look, who are also members of the accreditation scheme.

- H&M Hennes
- Marks & Spencer
- Monsoon & Accessorize
- New Look
- Next
- People Tree
- Seasalt

- Dorothy Perkins
- Evans
- Gap
- Karen Millen
- Mango
- Miss Sixty
- Oasis
- Principles
- Topshop
- Warehouse
- Zara

- French Connection
- George
- River Island
- Tesco

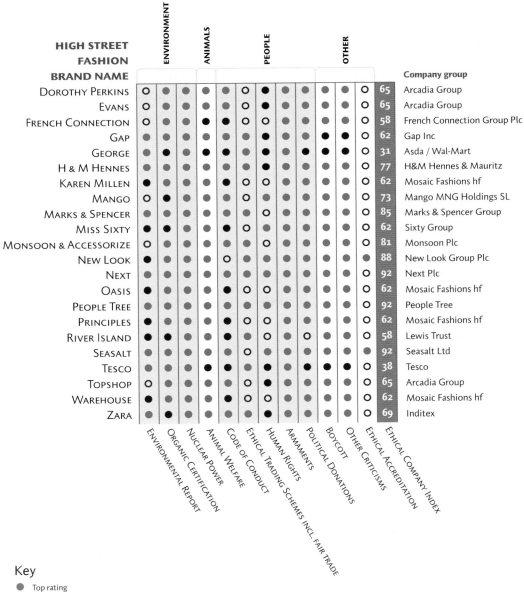

HIGH STREET FASHION BRAND NAME — column categories: ENVIRONMENT, ANIMALS, PEOPLE, OTHER

Sub-columns: Environmental Report · Organic Certification · Nuclear Power · Animal Welfare · Code of Conduct · Ethical Trading Schemes incl. Fair Trade · Human Rights · Armaments · Political Donations · Boycott · Other Criticisms · Ethical Accreditation · Ethical Company Index

Brand Name	Ethical Company Index	Company group
DOROTHY PERKINS	65	Arcadia Group
EVANS	65	Arcadia Group
FRENCH CONNECTION	58	French Connection Group Plc
GAP	62	Gap Inc
GEORGE	31	Asda / Wal-Mart
H & M HENNES	77	H&M Hennes & Mauritz
KAREN MILLEN	62	Mosaic Fashions hf
MANGO	73	Mango MNG Holdings SL
MARKS & SPENCER	85	Marks & Spencer Group
MISS SIXTY	62	Sixty Group
MONSOON & ACCESSORIZE	81	Monsoon Plc
NEW LOOK	88	New Look Group Plc
NEXT	92	Next Plc
OASIS	62	Mosaic Fashions hf
PEOPLE TREE	92	People Tree
PRINCIPLES	62	Mosaic Fashions hf
RIVER ISLAND	58	Lewis Trust
SEASALT	92	Seasalt Ltd
TESCO	38	Tesco
TOPSHOP	65	Arcadia Group
WAREHOUSE	62	Mosaic Fashions hf
ZARA	69	Inditex

Key

● Top rating
○ Middle rating
● Bottom rating

Source: The Ethical Company Organisation (2008)

Jeans

Whether £3 at the supermarket or £300 at an exclusive boutique, our jeans are invariably manufactured as cheaply as possible abroad. Companies subcontract their manufacturing to factories in Central America, Asia, Eastern Europe or Northern Africa, where the costs are low and the working conditions are poor. These factories may subcontract further, which makes monitoring these conditions difficult. The removal of quotas in 2005 may force overseas manufacturers to cut costs even more ruthlessly.

SWEATSHOP LABOUR

The term 'sweatshop' has been used for years to describe conditions throughout the global garment industry, where workers (usually young women) work very long hours for wages that are often insufficient to live on. Reports of intimidation, forced overtime, strip-searching and child labour are also rife.

In the US in January 1999, campaign groups and trade unions filed a federal lawsuit against 18 companies operating in the Pacific island of Saipan, which is part of the US Commonwealth of the Northern Mariana Islands. The lawsuit, which was filed on behalf of 35,000 Saipan garment workers, alleged that the companies had formed a 'racketeering conspiracy' to use indentured labour to produce clothing on the island, that contractors, manufacturers and retailers 'had engaged in and benefited from forced labour', and that 'workers were forced into conditions constituting peonage and involuntary servitude, in violation of human rights laws'.

Since then, companies including Gap, Calvin Klein and Donna Karan have settled claims and have agreed to the independent monitoring of Saipan contractors in future. Levi Strauss was the only company that refused to settle the claim.

Jeans found on sale in the UK are increasingly likely to have been manufactured in Central and Eastern Europe or in North Africa. Labour Behind the Label (*www. labourbehindthelabel.org*) reported that Gap factory workers in Russia had been paid just 11 cents per hour and were kept in 'slave-like' conditions.

In Bulgaria, a factory which manufactured clothing for Levi Strauss stores in the UK was reported to be strip-searching female workers at the end of their shifts on a regular basis, ostensibly to check they had not stolen anything. One worker, interviewed by *The Sunday Times*, reported that she had been sacked after refusing to be strip-searched. In addition the factory allegedly failed to pay sufficient wages for workers to feed and house a family properly.

CODES OF CONDUCT

Documents are sometimes produced by clothing companies which set down minimum standards for working conditions. The companies on the table have been approved if, among the usual stipulations about wages and working hours, they formally recognise the right to collective bargaining (the right to form a union) and they have some kind of monitoring system in place to ensure the code is not ignored. Companies who are approved under the Ethical Trading Schemes heading have signed up to the Ethical Trading Initiative (ETI) or the Fair Labor Association (FLA), and have therefore opened their factory doors to independent scrutiny (even if this scrutiny extends to very few factories).

There are some signs that the clothing industry is beginning to emerge from its moral torpor. Companies with the worst human rights records, such as Gap and Nike, have recently been praised for their attempts to improve working conditions in their supply chain. Gap's 2005 CSR report is admirably honest about the labour abuses that go on in the company's overseas factories, and Levi Strauss has been applauded for working with trade unions and supporting sacked workers at a factory in Mexico.

FAIR TRADE

The Fairtrade Foundation launched certified cotton in the UK in late 2005. Demand for fair trade cotton products has been high, so it is only a matter of time before fair trade jeans become available. Check the Alternative Clothing Directory for details of organic alternatives.

- Calvin Klein
- Easy
- Falmer

- Amazing
- Diesel
- DKNY
- Lee Cooper

- Lee
- Levi
- Wrangler

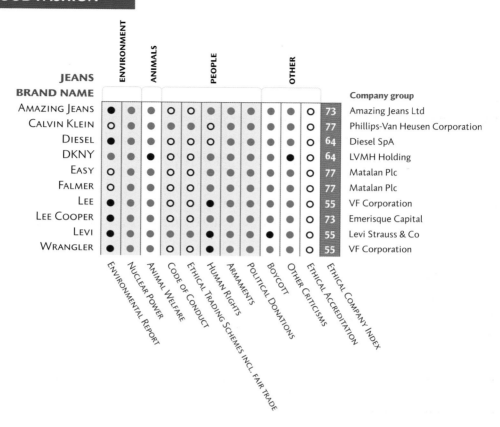

JEANS BRAND NAME	ENVIRONMENT		ANIMALS	PEOPLE					OTHER		Ethical Accreditation	Ethical Company Index	Company group
	Environmental Report	Nuclear Power	Animal Welfare	Code of Conduct	Ethical Trading Schemes incl. Fair Trade	Human Rights	Armaments	Political Donations	Boycott	Other Criticisms			
Amazing Jeans	●	●	●	O	O	●	●	●	●	●	O	73	Amazing Jeans Ltd
Calvin Klein	O	●	●	●	●	O	●	●	●	●	O	77	Phillips-Van Heusen Corporation
Diesel	●	●	●	O	O	O	●	●	●	●	O	64	Diesel SpA
DKNY	●	●	●	O	O	●	●	●	●	●	O	64	LVMH Holding
Easy	O	●	●	O	O	●	●	●	●	●	O	77	Matalan Plc
Falmer	O	●	●	O	O	●	●	●	●	●	O	77	Matalan Plc
Lee	●	●	●	O	O	●	●	●	●	●	O	55	VF Corporation
Lee Cooper	●	●	●	O	O	●	●	●	●	●	O	73	Emerisque Capital
Levi	●	●	●	●	●	●	●	●	●	●	O	55	Levi Strauss & Co
Wrangler	●	●	●	O	O	●	●	●	●	●	O	55	VF Corporation

Key

● Top rating

O Middle rating

● Bottom rating

Source: The Ethical Company Organisation

Shoes and trainers

Over the last twenty years, sweatshops have become synonymous with the big-name shoe brands; Nike, Adidas, Reebok and Puma. By the end of the nineties, these companies had been accused of a whole range of corporate crimes, from involvement in child labour to lacing workers' drinks with amphetamines to keep them going through the night. However, following intensive campaigning things are changing, and 'corporate social responsibility' is now the phrase on everyone's lips.

MATERIAL MATTERS

Polyvinyl chloride (PVC) may be the most damaging plastic to human health and the environment. According to Greenpeace, it is being phased out by Adidas, Asics, Nike and Puma. New Balance has eliminated some PVC but set no start-date for phase-out; Fila, Reebok and Saucony made no commitments. In particular, concerns have been raised over the release of toxic chemicals such as dioxins from PVC products.

Nike has signed up to a Climate Savers pact and aims to reduce greenhouse gas emissions across its operations, replacing sulphur hexafluoride (a greenhouse gas nearly 35,000 times more potent than an equivalent weight of carbon dioxide) in its 'air' trainers.

Sports shoes comprise dozens of mostly synthetic materials. Leather uppers are tanned via a 20-step process using strong chemicals. In countries with little environmental protection, tannery wastes can be discharged untreated into the water systems, making tap water undrinkable.

WORKING CONDITIONS

It was recently calculated that a Thai worker would have to work for 26.5 million days or 72,000 years to receive what Tiger Woods gets during his five-year contract with Nike. Or, in other words, that Nike spends the equivalent of 14,000 workers' daily wages to pay Tiger Woods for one day.

Campaigners hope to ensure that the workers receive fair labour practices and good working conditions. They are trying to persuade companies to agree to:

- No use of forced labour or child labour
- Freedom of association and collective bargaining
- Payment of a living wage
- A 48-hour week maximum
- Safe working conditions
- No race or gender discrimination

On the whole, the campaigns have been successful. Nike, Adidas, Reebok and Puma have all been forced to re-evaluate working conditions in their factories over the last decade. The above stipulations are included in all the codes of conduct for the big brands, and Reebok, Adidas and Nike have agreed to participate in Fair Labor's external monitoring programme.

The problems arise in enforcing the code. Rather than owning factories outright, companies subcontract from factories who have their own management. It is up to the company to ensure that the factories comply with their code of conduct.

To their credit, several companies do this by carrying out unannounced monitoring and audits. Timberland, on hearing of problems in one of their factories, immediately sent in auditors to find out more. Puma have received praise for setting up a scheme called SAFE but many companies are more lax in implementing and monitoring their codes of conduct.

Indeed, while Nike receives all the flak, smaller companies are slipping through the net unnoticed. Very little is known about their standards; they source from around the world but have no code of conduct and presumably no monitoring processes. What *is* known known is that three companies, Shellys, LK Bennett and Dolcis, are on the Burma Campaign UK's 'named and shamed list'.

The problems do not end with the company's conscience: in China, authentic trade union activity is illegal, regardless of what the code of conduct stipulates. Clearly, there is a lot left to be done.

- Birkenstock
- Cheatah

- Clarks
- Converse
- Dolcis
- Faith
- Mizuno
- New Balance
- Nike
- Nine West
- Office
- Puma
- Russell & Bromley
- Timberland

- Adidas
- Fila
- Hush Puppies
- LK Bennett
- Reebok
- Shellys
- Umbro

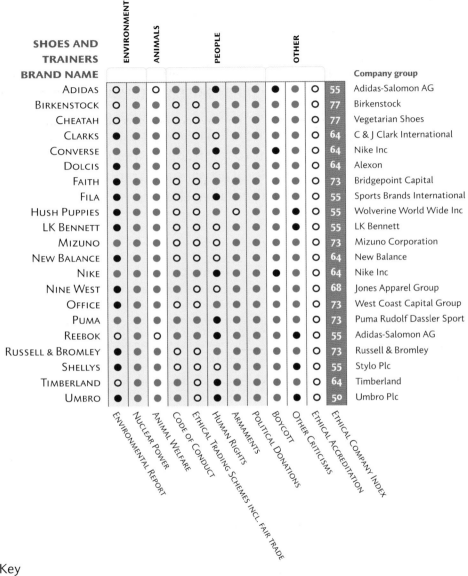

SHOES AND TRAINERS BRAND NAME	ENVIRONMENT — Environmental Report	Nuclear Power	ANIMALS — Animal Welfare	PEOPLE — Code of Conduct	Ethical Trading Schemes incl. Fair Trade	Human Rights	Armaments	Political Donations	OTHER — Boycott	Other Criticisms	Ethical Accreditation	Ethical Company Index	Company group
ADIDAS	○	●	○	●	●	●	●	●	●	●	○	55	Adidas-Salomon AG
BIRKENSTOCK	○	●	●	○	○	●	●	●	●	●	○	77	Birkenstock
CHEATAH	○	●	●	○	○	●	●	●	●	●	○	77	Vegetarian Shoes
CLARKS	●	●	●	○	○	○	●	●	●	●	○	64	C & J Clark International
CONVERSE	●	●	●	●	●	●	●	●	●	●	○	64	Nike Inc
DOLCIS	●	●	●	○	○	○	●	●	●	●	○	64	Alexon
FAITH	●	●	●	○	○	●	●	●	●	●	○	73	Bridgepoint Capital
FILA	●	●	●	○	○	●	●	●	●	●	○	55	Sports Brands International
HUSH PUPPIES	●	●	●	○	○	●	○	●	●	●	○	55	Wolverine World Wide Inc
LK BENNETT	●	●	●	○	○	○	●	●	●	●	○	55	LK Bennett
MIZUNO	●	●	●	○	○	○	●	●	●	●	○	73	Mizuno Corporation
NEW BALANCE	●	●	●	○	○	○	●	●	●	●	○	64	New Balance
NIKE	●	●	●	●	●	●	●	●	●	●	○	64	Nike Inc
NINE WEST	●	●	●	●	○	○	●	●	●	●	○	68	Jones Apparel Group
OFFICE	●	●	●	○	○	●	●	●	●	●	○	73	West Coast Capital Group
PUMA	●	●	●	●	●	●	●	●	●	●	○	73	Puma Rudolf Dassler Sport
REEBOK	○	●	○	●	●	●	●	●	●	●	○	55	Adidas-Salomon AG
RUSSELL & BROMLEY	●	●	●	○	○	●	●	●	●	●	○	73	Russell & Bromley
SHELLYS	●	●	●	○	○	○	●	●	●	●	○	55	Stylo Plc
TIMBERLAND	○	●	●	●	○	●	●	●	●	●	○	64	Timberland
UMBRO	●	●	●	●	○	●	●	●	●	●	○	50	Umbro Plc

Key

● Top rating
○ Middle rating
● Bottom rating

Source: The Ethical Company Organisation

Alternative clothing directory

Ethical clothing is gradually becoming more easy to find, but at the moment the majority of alternative shops still operate over the internet or via mail order. Some brands are also stocked by independent high street stores, whose addresses are included below. The companies in this directory have shown a commitment to fair trading, organic production methods, recycling and supporting local artisans and traditional techniques. They are the future of alternative clothing.

Major Suppliers

Bishopston Trading Company

The Bishopston Trading Company is involved in a workers' co-operative which has grown out of the linking of the southern Indian village of KV Kuppam with Bishopston in Bristol. Supplying through five shops and via mail order, the company sells organic clothes for both children and adults. These include work and leisure clothes and accessories including bags and jewellery.
www.bishopstontrading.co.uk

33 Silver Street, Bradford-on-Avon, Wiltshire BA15 1JX
Tel: 0122 586 7485

8a High Street, Glastonbury BA6 9DU
Tel: 0145 883 5386

33 High Street, Stroud, Glocestershire GL5 1AJ
Tel: 0145 376 6355

193 Gloucester Road, Bishopston, Bristol BS7 8BG
Tel: 0177 924 5598

79 High Street, Totnes, Devon TQ9 5PB
Tel: 0180 386 8488

Chandni Chowk

Supplier of clothes made with hand-spun natural fibres and coloured using vegetable dyes.
www.chandnichowk.co.uk

102 Boutport Street, Barnstaple EX31 1SY
Tel: 0122 548 3541

6 New Bond Street Place, Bath BA1 1BH
Tel: 0127 137 4714

66 Park Street, Bristol BS1 5JN

1 Harlequins, Paul Street, Exeter EX4 3TT

14a The Bridge, Riverside Place, Taunton TA1 1UG
Tel: 0182 332 7377

Siesta

Fairly traded clothes from Latin America.
www.siestacrafts.co.uk

1 Palace Street, Canterbury CT1 2DY
Tel: 0122 746 4614

TRAIDCRAFT PLC

A range of menswear and womenswear, available via mail order and online.

www.traidcraft.co.uk

Kingsway North, Gateshead, Tyne & Wear NE11 0NE
Tel: 0191 491 0591

MAIL ORDER OR ONLINE ORDERING

ANIMAL TAILS

Beautiful certified ethical and organic children's T-shirts featuring original artwork of endangered species.

www.animaltails.co.uk

e-mail: info@animaltails.co.uk

GARTHENOR ORGANIC PURE WOOL

Hand knitted garments from certified organic British sheep – spun locally and not dyed or bleached. Range includes adult, children's and baby clothing.

www.organicpurewool.co.uk

Llanio Road, Tregaron, Wales SY25 6UR
Tel: 0157 049 3347

GOSSYPIUM

Simple modern organic cotton clothing, including underwear and pyjamas. Men's, women's and children's ranges available.

www.gossypium.co.uk

Gossypium House, 210 High Street, Lewes BN7 2NH
Tel: 0800 085 6549

GREENFIBRES

Mail-order supplier of organic clothing (including jeans and sportswear). Also sells bedding and other accessories.

www.greenfibres.com

99 High Street Totnes, Devon TQ9 5PF
Tel: 0180 386 8001

HEMP UNION

Sells a range of hemp clothing, trousers, jeans and tops.

www.hemp-union.karoo.net

24 Anlaby Road, Hull, East Yorkshire HU1 2PA
Tel: 0148 222 5328

HOWIES

Fashionable jeans, hoodies and t-shirts made from organic and recycled cotton.

www.howies.co.uk

Tel: 0123 961 5598

HUG

Organic, fairly-traded modern fashions from Peru. Men's, women's and children's ranges.

www.hug.co.uk

Tel: 0485 130 1525

MARLO CLOTHING

Contemporary organic cotton and hemp clothing, using natural dyes.

www.marlo.co.uk

Tel: 0173 675 5928

NATURAL COLLECTION
Hemp clothing, organic exercise gear, organic t-shirts, organic wool socks, hemp socks, vests, underwear.
www.naturalcollection.com

Dept 7306, Sunderland SR9 9XZ
Tel: 0870 331 3333

ONE WORLD IS ENOUGH
Handmade non-organic clothing for women, men and children, from fair trade suppliers.
www.one-world-is-enough.net

82 Commercial End, Cambridge CB5 0NE
Tel: 0845 257 3026

PEOPLE TREE LTD
UK arm of the Japan-based Fairtrade company, selling organic, fair trade clothes. Aimed at the fashion-conscious.
www.ptree.co.uk

Studio 7, 8-13 New Inn Street, London, EC2A 3PY
Tel: 0207 739 0660

PLAIN LAZY
Funky ethical clothing for men and women.
www.plainlazy.com

Tel: 0127 348 3336

SEASALT
Soil Association certified organic clothing.
www.seasaltcornwall.co.uk

SE CLOTHING
Hemp clothing handmade to order in the UK.

The Grange, All Saints, St Elmham, Halesworth IP19 0NX
Tel: 0198 678 2476

SPIRIT OF NATURE
Organic cotton clothes, including men's workshirts and fleeces.
www.spiritofnature.co.uk

Unit 7, Hannah Way, Gordleton Industrial Park, Lymington SO41 8JD
Tel: 0870 725 9885

SCHMIDT NATURAL CLOTHING
Organic cotton clothing for children and adults. Mail order service available.
www.naturalclothing.co.uk

Tel: 0845 345 0498

SMART TART
Individual designer bags and clothing made from recycled materials, hemp and vegetarian 'leather'.
www.smarttart.co.uk

Blackbird Barn, Bank Square, St Just, Cornwall TR19 7HJ
Tel: 0173 678 7091

WORN AGAIN
Clothing and shoes made from recycled materials, including parachutes and prison blankets.
www.antiapathy.org

OTHER SHOPS

PATAGONIA
Outdor clothing made from organic cotton and hemp, including fleeces made from recycled plastic.
www.patagonia.com

She Active, 21-22 New Row, Covent Garden, London WC2N 4LA (main Patagoinia supplier)
Tel: 0207 836 6222 (phone for details of other shops)

TUMI

Fairly traded clothes from Latin America.

www.tumi.co.uk

8/9 New Bond Street Place, Bath BA1 1BH

Tel: 0122 544 6025

TUCANO

Organic cotton and hemp clothing, including beach wear.

Pound House, Pound Road, West Wittering,
West Sussex PO20 8AJ

Tel: 0124 351 3757

SECOND-HAND CLOTHES

Second-hand or 'recycled' clothes are one of the best environmental options. As well as being a low-cost alternative to high street retailers, the money paid for clothing can also go to a good cause. Second-hand clothing can be found in charity shops, car boot sales and from friends and relatives.

FAIR TRADE SHOPS SELLING TRAIDCRAFT CLOTHES

A WORLD OF DIFFERENCE

13 Narrowgate, Alnwick NE66 IJH

Tel: 0166 560 6005

FAIRER WORLD

84 Gillygate, York YO31 7EQ

Tel: 0190 465 5116

GATEWAY WORLD SHOP

Market Place, Durham DH1 3NJ

Tel: 0191 384 7173

JUST FAIR TRADE

www.justfairtrade.com

10 Bishop Street, Town Hall Square, Leicester LE1 6AF

Tel: 0166 255 9123

JUST TRADING

7 Fountain Street, Nailsworth, Stroud GL6 0BL

Tel: 0145 383 3002

LIVERPOOL WORLD SHOP

71 Bold Street, Liverpool L1 4EZ

Tel: 0151 708 7328

ONE WORLD SHOP

www.oneworldshop.co.uk

71 John's Church, Princes Street, Edinburgh EH2 4BJ

Tel: 0131 229 4541

THE GREEN SHOP

30 Bridge Street, Berwick Upon Tweed TD15 1AQ

Tel: 0128 930 5566

TRADERS FAIR WORLD SHOP

12 Museum Street, Colchester CO1 1TN

Tel: 0120 676 3380

TRAID LINKS

20 Market Place, Wirksworth DE4 4ET

Tel: 0162 982 4393

WORLD OF DIFFERENCE

20 High Street, Rugby CV21 3BG

Tel: 0178 857 9191

GOOD
NETWORK

ACCREDITED COMPANIES •

NGOs •

GOOSHING •

THE ETHICAL MARKETPLACE •

Introduction

The closing chapter of *The Good Shopping Guide* is dedicated to the Good Network; a disparate group of like-minded people who are all working towards making our world a better place. Whether through campaigning, social events or setting an example with their business practices, they have become part of a global 'ethical' movement. And, having nearly reached the end of this book, you can consider yourself one of them!

Throughout *The Good Shopping Guide*, companies have been recommended as members of the Ethical Company Organisation's Accreditation Scheme. The opening pages of this section give more information and contact details for each of them, so that you can find out what progressive changes they have made and how their products compare to the mainstream manufacturers.

The next section is devoted to non-governmental organisations. High-profile groups such as Greenpeace and Friends of the Earth are household names, synonymous with their commitment to, and passion for, the environment and the people who live in it. But behind these big names are dozens of other charities who need our support. Some are campaign groups with express social or political aims; others are working in aid of a particular cause or population group. All are united by their belief that people

power really works. Find out how to support them on page 348.

No campaign would be complete without live events, and the green movement is no exception. The days out included here are not just about hemp smocks and cider (although there will be plenty of both), but are an opportunity to meet people of all ages with similar interests and to find out more about the eco-lifestyle. Many of the events included are local gatherings, while some are established music festivals which share the community ethos that defines the ethical shopping movement.

The final place to look before putting the ethical shopping principles into practice is the Marketplace, which only features companies that meet *The Good Shopping Guide*'s high ethical standards. Finally, we introduce Gooshing, the website that takes the Good Network onto the world wide web.

Accredited companies

The following companies belong to the Ethical Accreditation Scheme, and can display the Ethical Company logo as a symbol of their certification. *The Good Shopping Guide* can recommend them as companies that have been fully surveyed and meet the highest ethical standards. For more information about joining the scheme, call 0207 229 2115 or email *companyaccreditation@ethical-company-organisation.org* for an application pack.

ANIMAL TAILS

Animal Tails believe that there's no greater beauty than our World and the diverse species that populate it. However, the escalating rate of extinction, through loss of habitat caused by human activity, is making many species of beauty pass into nothingness. At Animal Tails they love people, animals and the environment and they doing their bit to support a balanced symbiosis. All their T-shirts and screen-prints are 100% organic, and they are ethically manufactured.
www.animaltails.co.uk

ANNIRAC

The Annirac is a unique drying rack designed for owners of Kitchen Ranges (like AGA's). With an Annirac Drying Rack you can conveniently air and dry clothes, crockery, glassware and much more and help reduce wasted energy rising from your Kitchen Range – avoiding the need to use an alternative heat source for drying/airing (eg. tumble dryings). Annirac offers a variety of models to suit most makes of Kitchen Ranges. Orders can be placed by phone, online or post.
www.annirac.com
Tel: 01371 870 312

ARENA FLOWERS

A leading online florist, Arena Flowers delivers fresh bouquets and arrangements at affordable prices. Their flowers come direct from Holland's flower auctions, meaning that there are no middlemen, and no extra costs are passed on to the consumer. Working with their partner florists overseas, Arena Flowers also offers an international delivery service, so you can send flowers to your loved ones even if they're on the other side of the world. They sell everything from roses to orchids, and are the first UK company to offer bouquets certified by the Fair Flowers Fair Plants organisation. This guarantees that the flowers have been produced using sustainable, environmentally friendly techniques.
www.arenaflowers.com
Tel: 0800 035 0581

AROMATHERAPY DIRECT

Aromatherapy Direct pride themselves in offering the highest quality products and excellent customer service. The company is committed to being environmentally friendly and conscious. Their essential oils and other skin care products contain natural and organic ingredients and they only use recyclable packaging. They source their ingredients very carefully and from sustainable sources. Since their products are hand blended and made to order, quality and freshness are assured.
www.aromatherapydirect.ltd.uk
Tel: 01872 573543

ATMOS HEATING SYSTEMS

Atmos design and install heating and hot water systems for homes and businesses. Their condensing gas boilers and water heating systems have won awards for energy efficiency, and the company is committed to promoting environmentally friendly products. Atmos systems can save up to 50 per cent on fuel consumption, which not only helps reduce your use of fossil fuels, but saves you money as well. An energy-efficient Atmos product is built to last, and will easily pay for itself in the long term. The company also sells a range of Solar hot water systems, and its boilers are specially designed to help customers reduce their water wastage.
www.atmos.uk.com
Tel: 0132 787 1990

BROTHER

Brother is a world-wide electronics and manufacturing company, which sells its products in over 100 countries. They feel it is their duty to do whatever they can to protect and preserve the environment, and have several policies in place to ensure they work towards this goal. Brother aim to reduce their use of water, energy and materials, and run regular audits to assess their progress across all areas of environmental management. The company launched the world's first TCO99 Compliant Printer, which meets 50 stringent ecological, health and safety and ergonomic requirements. Their product range includes printers, all-in-one machines, faxes, labelling systems, laminators and sewing machines.
www.brother.co.uk
Tel: 0845 606 0626

BULLDOG

Bulldog are male grooming products made with natural ingredients to improve performance. They use none of the potentially harmful man-made chemicals often associated with the cosmetics industry - like parabens, sodium laureth sulfate, artificial colours or synthetic fragrances. Bulldog has signed up to the Campaign for Safe Cosmetics – a pledge to remove toxic chemicals and replace them with safer alternatives. The Bulldog packaging has been developed to 'look cool' on the shelf and the range includes shave gel, shave balm, shampoo, shower gel, face wash and moisturiser and can be found at large Sainsbury's stores nationwide.
www.meetthebulldog.co.uk
Tel: 020 8969 6006

BURNS PET NUTRITION

Burns Real Food has been developed over the last ten years using John Burns' experience as a veterinary surgeon. Burns is a simple pet food which is intended to allow the animal's body to function as it should. Owners have reported that when their dogs went onto Burns the skin and coat condition improved, including reductions in hair loss and itching, and the coat became glossy and silky. Unpleasant odours disappeared and older dogs became livelier, less stiff and generally more interested in life. Burns Pet Nutrition has never conducted experiments on animals, and is accredited by the British Union for the Abolition of Vivisection.

www.burns-pet-nutrition.co.uk
Tel: 0800 018 1890

CAURNIE SOAP COMPANY

Working from their organic herb garden in Scotland, Caurnie have been providing quality hand-made vegan soaps since they were founded there in 1922 – the oldest soap-maker in the region. They specialise in traditional soaps, which use the cold process technique and contain natural vegetables and herbs. Their products are cruelty-free and vegetarian, and are suitable for delicate skins and allergy sufferers who would rather avoid synthetic chemicals. Caurnie believe in low-energy, low-impact production, and this is reflected in their dedication to the minimal packaging of their products. Soaps, shampoos and a range of hand-made household cleaning products are available through the website.

www.caurnie.com
Tel: 0141 776 1218

CHARITY BANK

Charity Bank is the UK's first not for profit bank. It is a unique enterprise, combining the compassion of a charity and the strength of a bank. By offering affordable solutions to charity borrowers, Charity Bank helps organisations across the country tackle poverty, exclusion, abuse and prejudice, and breathe life back into under-invested communities. While donations will always be an important part of funding, Charity Bank believes that they are most effective when combined with long-term investment. Saving with Charity Bank offers you a social return on your cash, and ensures that your money is being used for the common good, rather than commercial gain.

www.charitybank.org
Tel: 0173 277 4040

CHELSEA BS

Chelsea Building Society is first building society to qualify for Ethical Accreditation. Chelsea is proud to be a mutual building society with the business built on strong values and with a long standing culture of giving customers fair treatment. Chelsea is not only commited to its members but also to its staff, the communities in which it works and the environment. Chelsea Building Society's ethical score (ECI) is high as it has aligned many of its Corporate Responsibility strategies to those within its Corporate Plan so that best practices within the CR field become part of its business processes and plans in future.

www.thechelsea.co.uk
Tel: 01242 271271

CHOCOCO

Chococo – The Purbeck Chocolate Company. Handmade fresh chocolates are proudly created by husband & wife team in Purbeck, Dorset. They craft all their fresh chocolates by hand every day so that customers get to discover the joy of eating truly fresh pure chocolates. They believe that pure foods tastes better so they don't put preservatives into their chocolates. They are proud of being ethical chocolate makers, just as they care about the taste of their finished product, they also care about the bigger picture - about where the ingredients come from and the people who produce them.

www.chococo.co.uk
Tel: 01929 421777

THE CLEAN SPACE

The Clean Space partnership is a cleaning company with a difference. As a Fairtrade Services provider, it delivers a higher standard of care for its employees, investing in training and support to create a reliable, motivated team that values its work. All employees are invited to invest in the business, giving them an opportunity to share in the pride and responsibility of ownership. Clean Space specialises in office cleaning, and offers services including contract cleaning, waste removal, carpet shampooing, recycling and even getting the crumbs out of your computer keyboard. Contact their offices in London or Manchester to see if they can make your office into a clean space.

www.thecleanspace.com
Tel: 0870 423 3559

CO2 BALANCE

Co2 Balance Ltd is a carbon management company who are actively seeking to reduce the greenhouse gas emissions of both businesses and individuals. They seek carbon offset projects that have positive Co-benefits. For example all of their woodland plantations are open to the public for the benefit of the community and their energy efficiency and renewable energy projects in Africa improve the recipients' standards of living by improving health & safety and reducing user fuel costs.

www.co2balance.com
Tel: 0845 094 2620

DESIGNS BY TARAN

Designs by Taran is the life-long dream of Taran Vernon, a talented and imaginative floral designer based in Farnham, Surrey. They are deeply passionate about floral design, and pride themselves on delivering high quality produce from environmentally sustainable sources wherever possible. The mission to protect the environment has been an issue on Taran's mind for a long time and currently they recycle green waste, plastics wrapping, paper and re-use cardboard boxes. In order to reduce their carbon footprint Designs by Taran have gone to extensive lengths to source stock both from local suppliers, and those who have proven track records in ethical policy, and where possible their International Flower deliveries are flown in on passenger planes rather than on specifically chartered aircraft. They are members of Fair Flowers Fair Plants (FFP).

www.designsbytaran.co.uk
Tel: 0845 468 2572

ECOSOAPIA

21st Century Health have launched Ecosoapia, an organic hand and body wash. This luxurious liquid soap is available in peppermint, lavender, almond, eucalyptus, tea tree, rose and unscented, and is approved by the Soil Association. It has been awarded the Chemical Consumer Award and Consumer Award from Allergy UK, which is important for allergy sufferers. Ecosoapia is free from SLS, artificial colour, fragrances, synthetic preservatives and parabens and is suitable for vegetarians and vegans. As well as being kind to your skin it is kind to the environment. Ecosoapia costs £6.50, with 10 per cent of all profits going to Iracambi to help conserve the rainforests.

www.ecosoapia.com
Tel: 0800 026 0220

ESSENTIAL CARE

Essential Care is a range of truly organic body care, hand-made with pure plan oils and biodynamic herbs. None of the products are tested on animals, nor use artificial fragrances, colourings or other common synthetics and they are the first company to have created a Soil Association certified shampoo. Based in Suffolk, Essential Care is a small family team who have been researching formulations for their products since the 1980s and set up as a mail order company in 2003. The Essential Care range includes moisturisers, cleansers, shampoos, massage oils, essential oils and more. Products can be purchased online, by post or telephone.

www.essential-care.co.uk
Tel: 01638 716593

ETA

The Environmental Transport Association was founded in 1990 to raise awareness of the impact of excessive car use, and to help individuals and organisations make positive changes in their travel habits. They are the world's first climate-neutral motoring organisation, and have firmly established environmental and ethical business policies to ensure that their day-to-day activities respect the environment. For breakdown cover and home, motor, cycle or travel insurance, the ETA is a truly ethical alternative to other motoring organisations. The ETA also compiles an annual Car Buyer's Guide, which ranks cars according to their green credentials and reveals the best and worst motors on the market.

www.eta.co.uk
Tel: 0845 389 1010

EUROPA PET FOODS

Europa pet foods are designed to help your dog stay fit and healthy. Produced in the UK to a highly digestible optimum nutrition formula, the foods are hypo-allergenic and free from wheat or wheat gluten, soya and dairy products. They include a balanced range of vitamins and minerals, as well as Omega 3 & 6 fatty acids, all of which provide health benefits for your dog – as well as helping to reduce feed cost and veterinary bills for you! A full ingredients list is available on the Europa website. The Europa range has been accredited by the BUAV 'Not Tested on Animals' scheme.

www.europa-pet-food.co.uk
Tel: 0845 658 0987

Everything Environmental

Everything Environmental specialise exclusively in the manufacture, sourcing and supply of eco-friendly business gifts. Providing a solution to the upsurge in corporate environmental responsibility, Everything Environmental was established to supply business gift distributors with a one stop source of personalised recycled and eco-friendly products. All items in their core range are made from recycled, organic, sustainable or ethically sourced materials and can all be printed in the client's design.
www.everything-environmental.co.uk
Tel: 0870 739 1458

Fair*

Fair* is an ethical creative communications practice. They provide consultancy services to anyone from small independent traders to large corporate organisations. Fair* believe that the smallest choices can make the biggest differences and by working with them you can make a progressive statement about your brand. They strive to have as minimal an impact on the environment as possible.
www.fairbrand.org

Fushi

Fushi's range of herbal remedies, cosmetics and aromatherapy oils have been developed according to the philosophy that inner health promotes outer well-being. This innovative brand has built its holistic ideology into its outlets, where it offers expert impartial information about issues of health and well-being. Nearly all of the essential oils and extracts used in its products are organic and approved by the Soil Association, and it is committed to providing health and beauty solutions using only 100 per cent natural products. A supporter of fair trade and ethical operations, Fushi has been listed as one of the 50 'businesses to watch out for'.
www.fushi.co.uk
Tel: 0845 338 5251

Good Energy

Good Energy is an independent UK company which supplies only 100 per cent renewable energy products to homes and businesses. The electricity they supply comes from wind, small scale hydro and solar power generators across Britain, and they run a Home Generation scheme to support smaller sites and those who want to produce their own energy. Good Energy is recommended by Friends of the Earth and has come top in their league table of green energy suppliers. The company is growing fast and hopes to encourage as many people as possible to get involved in the world-wide movement to keep the world habitable.
www.good-energy.co.uk
Tel: 0845 456 1640

GREEN ENERGY

Green Energy is a renewable energy supplier created to offer people who are concerned about our shared environment the chance to do something practical, positive and imaginative. Green Energy aim to grow a business that is ethical, responsible and constructive, but also commercially sound, prudently managed and secure in the long term. Green Energy supplies electricity to domestic customers and small business customers in England and Wales. They plan to re-invest up to 50 per cent of their profits into renewable electricity generation projects, encouraging the development of new green solutions and allowing them to have a greater impact in the reduction of greenhouse gas emissions.
www.greenenergy.uk.com
Tel: 0800 783 8851

GREEN GARDEN GROUP

Green Garden Group are an eco friendly and ethical gardening service based in Penzance, Cornwall. The company works mainly in private residential gardens and are able to undertake the majority of gardening requirements, large or small, as well as undertaking commercial and maintenance contracts. Their aim is to operate a business that is underpinned by sound environmental practices and to provide a model of sustainable activity. Their objective is to promote green living, to be an example for others to modify their own attitudes and lifestyles towards increasing environmental responsibility.
www.greengardengroup.co.uk
Tel: 0845 329 8034

GREEN PEOPLE

Green People offer hand-made health and beauty products, with ranges including cosmetics, sun lotions and travel toiletries. They are committed to developing products that are 100 per cent natural, certified organic and highly effective. None of their formulations or products are, or ever have been, tested on animals, and most of their range is approved by the Vegan Society. All Green People products are suitable for vegetarians and full ingredient disclosure is always given on the labelling. Green People support charities with related environmental concerns, and each year 10 per cent of their net profits are donated to charitable causes linked to 'green' or environmental issues.
www.greenpeople.co.uk
Tel: 0140 374 0350

THE GREEN SHOPPING GUIDE

The Green Shopping Guide is a free to use online green business directory. It brings together a range of businesses, organisations and charities from around the UK that provide green and ethical products and services. With the busy lifestyles that we lead, sourcing ethical products and services can be time-consuming, but The Green Shopping Guide website aims to make it easier and quicker, by linking you directly to what you want and to where you can buy it. So whether you're looking for organic pesticides, ethical foot-ware, sustainable architects, bio-degradable nappies or green weddings, The Green Shopping Guide is the place to find them – and much, much more.
www.thegreenshoppingguide.co.uk

GREEN STATIONERY COMPANY

The Green Stationery Company is the only dedicated green stationery dealer in the UK, and is a premier supplier of recycled paper and green office products. They select items that are environmentally benign or have environmental advantages over standard office goods. Green Stationery aim to maintain business practices consistent with their goal of sustaining the fragile environment for future generations, within a culture that respects life and honours its interdependence. Unlike many office product dealers, they do not charge a premium for green items, but believe that choosing the right product is a step towards reducing the throwaway culture that is endemic in many offices.

www.greenstat.co.uk

Tel: 0122 548 0556

HEMP GARDEN

Hemp Garden manufacture a range of fine, safe and effective body-care products, seeking to make these as beautiful, beneficial and pleasurable as they can be. All of their products use hemp as a base ingredient, and they have sought to enhance the properties of this phenomenal plant with botanical extracts and essential oils. Hemp Garden use only the finest natural ingredients and avoid the synthetic substances contained in many body-care products. They subscribe to the principle that businesses should not only be economically viable, but environmentally responsible and socially equitable. The Hemp Garden range includes shampoo and conditioner, soap, hand cream and body lotion.

www.hempgarden.co.uk

Tel: 0142 443 4370

HIGHLAND SPRING

Highland Spring water is drawn from 2000 acres of protected land beneath the Ochil Hills in Pertshire, Scotland. This land has been kept free from farming, agricultural spraying, pesticides and habitation for more than 20 years. As a result of this protection of its catchment area, Highland Spring was the first British bottled water brand to have its land certified organic by the Soil Association. The Highland Spring philosophy is to protect their environment and protect the fruit that it bears, so they have gone to great lengths to ensure that their land is as natural as it can be - as part of this focus they were the first bottled water producer to join EMAS – the voluntary eco-management and audit scheme.

www.highlandspring.com

Tel: 01764 660 500

HOLZ TOYS

Holz Toys was started after owners Rebecca and Christoph Bettin returned from Germany where they had lived for several years. Whilst they were there they began to learn of the special regard and tradition for wooden toys. They believed that wooden toys meant so much more and as parents of four children they decided to make these toys available in England. They have been a retail supplier for 7 years and their offices and warehouses are based in Lostwithiel, Cornwall. Holz Toys strive to bring their customers finely crafted playthings that are both environmentally sound and safe and designed to inspire and awaken the imagination. Concern for the environment being one of their main priorities, they wish to limit the use of plastic particularly for children's playthings. They source ethically produced and manufactured wooden toys from sustainable alder and beech forestry in Europe and from pesticide free rubber wood, recycled from plantations in Thailand. They offset their carbon footprint by planting trees locally and by purchasing plots of rainforest.

www.holz-toys.co.uk

Tel: 0845 130 8697

Honesty Cosmetics

Honesty Cosmetics manufacture a wide selection of skin and hair products, all of which are suitable for vegetarians and vegans. In addition to their own range, they offer a variety of complementary products sourced from a number of other companies who also adhere to compassionate policies. From everyday necessities to more luxurious products, Honesty Cosmetics items have been chosen to ensure their quality. Honesty offer a fast and efficient mail order service, and help and advice on ordering is available between Monday and Friday from 9.30am to 5pm. Their products include bath and shower gel, shampoo and conditioner, moisturising lotion, soap and essential oils.

www.honestycosmetics.co.uk

Tel: 0162 981 4888

Innocent Drinks

Innocent produce 100 per cent natural drinks, made from 100 per cent pure fruit and fresh juices – no concentrates, colourings, preservatives, water or sugar. Their range includes smoothies (fruit in a bottle), thickies (live probiotic yoghurt, real fruit and honey), juices, super smoothies and juicy water. Since 2003 all their drinks have been supplied in bottles made with 25 per cent recycled plastic, which is the maximum that current technology will allow. To offset its environmental impact, Innocent funds social programmes including planting trees and donating money to an NGO that buys mango trees and cows for farmers in poor rural areas of southern India.

www.innocentdrinks.co.uk

Tel: 0208 600 3993

IT Ambulance

IT Ambulance provide IT Support, Computer Support, Network Support, Disaster Recovery and Computer Maintenance. They comply with WEEE directives and recycle customers' old equipment and packaging. They aim to be carbon neutral by 2010 and support local charities.

www.itambulance.co.uk

Tel: 0800 0214 999

Kanzi Home

If you are looking for high quality, contemporary home-wares which are produced ethically, Kanzi Home is the online shop to visit. At Kanzi Home, they believe that any truly beautiful creation cannot exist if tainted with exploitation or unfair trading practices. Therefore many of their products are from suppliers with official Fair Trade certification, and where that is not possible, they strive to ensure that their suppliers are still following Fair Trade guidelines for employment, wages and working conditions. Their website includes hundreds of beautiful products for your home or a unique gift for someone else's.

www.kanzihome.co.uk

Tel: 0845 055 7710

LILY'S KITCHEN

Lily's Kitchen makes a range of truly delicious, nutritious food for pets. They are the first and only company in the UK to be certified as both Organic and Holistic. Their 100% natural recipes come in recyclable packaging and include wholesome, locally sourced ingredients, from butternut squash to apples, from rosehip to marigold petals. They support several charities who make a difference to pets' lives.
www.lilyskitchen.co.uk
Tel: 0845 680 5459

THE LUBERATION LABORATORY

The Luberation Laboratory design, formulate, manufacture and market the world's first certified organic range of intimacy products – the Yes range of water and oil based organic lubricants and mosturisers. Their mission is to change the world from the inside, they have a set of value that describe their commitment to their care for people (and animals), plants, their products and the planet. Their products are both organic and vegetarian.
www.yesyesyes.org
Tel: 0845 094 1141

MOONCUP

Mooncup is an innovative alternative to tampons, offering all the comfort and convenience without the cost, waste or health risks. Manufactured by a small ethical business in the UK, the soft silicone cup is worn internally, collects rather than absorbs menstrual fluid, and can be re-used for every period. There is no mess, no leaks or dryness. You only need one mooncup, which will last for years, so it's eco-friendly, saves money and is ideal for travelling, exercise and overnight use. As more and more women use mooncup, their enthusiastic word-of-mouth keeps the mooncup movement growing: a genuine revolution for women.
www.mooncup.co.uk
Tel: 0127 367 3845

NASH PARTNERSHIP

Nash Partnership are independent estate agents and letting agents, with offices in Berkhamsted, Hemmel Hempstead and Tring. In July 2007 they became England's first CarbonNeutral® estate agency. As a company, they have a good understanding of their environmental impact and have put together an action plan to improve energy efficiency and look at more innovative ways of reducing energy use where possible. Their long-term aim is to encourage other local businesses to think about the environmental impact they have and to do something positive about it. Nash Partnership prides themselves on their hard-earned reputation for service and is committed to getting the very best results for their clients – every time.
www.nashpartnership.co.uk
Tel: 01442 863000

NATURAL BY NATURE OILS

This family-run business was one of the first to promote aromatherapy in the UK, and has established itself as one of the leaders in its field. It was involved in the production of *A Safety Guide on the Use of Essential Oils*, which was based on world-wide research and is widely regarded as one of the most comprehensive books of its kind. Natural by Nature Oils actively supported the BUAV's campaign to end animal testing for cosmetics and toiletries, and donates 5 per cent of the purchase price of its certified organic oils (which won the Best New Organic Essential Oil Range award in 2003) to the organisation.
www.naturalbynature.co.uk
Tel: 0158 284 0848

THE NATURAL CURTAIN COMPANY

The Natural Curtain Company is the first online made-to-measure, hand-made curtain and roman blind company to use natural fabric. They offer a range of modern simple classic fabric designs which are plain, striped or patterned including hand-woven crewel from Kashmir. They have designs to suit formal, informal, kitchen and children's curtains or roman blinds – each of which you can choose to have lined. For curtains, there are a range of heading option from tab top, eyelet and pencil pleat to pinch pleats and inverted pleats. You can design your own curtains or blinds using easy step-by-step tools which guide you through the ordering process.
www.naturalcurtains.com
Tel: 0845 5000 400

NATURA ORGANICS

Natura products are made by a family-based business in Provence using renewable raw materials such as natural oils, plant extracts and essential oils. They are certified organic by the European equivalent of the Soil Association, and are made without the use of chemical products or preservatives. There is no testing on animals at any stage of the production process, even on the raw ingredients, and Natura products are suitable for vegetarians and vegans. The company supports ethical production measures, such as the rights of workers and detachment from political activity. Products in the Natura range include shower gel, bath foam, body lotion, shampoo and hand cream.
www.naturaorganics.com
Tel: 0127 368 5800

NATURAL ORGANIC SOAP

Natural Organic Soap produce mild, glycerin-rich soaps using the traditional cold process method. Their products are registered with the Vegan Society, and were certified organic by the Soil Association in 2005. This means that all the ingredients used in Natural Organic soaps are 100 per cent organic, allowing you to avoid the pesticides, insecticides and synthetic fertilisers used on conventionally-grown plants. They are also GM-free, and do not contain ingredients such as sodium laureth sulphate. Natural Organic soaps include luxurious hempseed and avocado oils, enriched with moisturising cocoa or shea butter, and fragranced with organic essential oils. Flowers, roots and spices bring colour and gentle exfoliating properties.
www.organicsoap.net
Tel: 0208 488 2469

New Look

New Look is one of the UK's leading fashion retailers. With the motto "accessible fashion", they make cool, trendy clothing for everyone, no matter what your age, shape or size. In the last year, they have launched exclusive designer ranges with Giles Deacon and Lily Allen. The company is a member of the Ethical Trading Initiative, and believes in setting the highest possible standards for its suppliers – including seeking and promoting sustainable improvement in working conditions. New Look also has a rapidly expanding organic range, which includes jersey tops and dresses, as well as items in the 915 Generation, Maternity, Tall and Inspire ranges.

www.newlook.co.uk
Tel: 0500 454 094

Organico

Organico are importers of high quality organic foods. Their origins are in the healthfood and wholefood market, which has enabled them to develop a good understanding of what constitutes a healthy, balanced and nutritious diet. Organico work hard to find like-minded suppliers and bring us the type of foods that we enjoy eating every day. Their policy is to sell only 'tasty foods made with natural ingredients, prepared in a manner that respects and does not destroy the earth's limited resources'. Organico pledge to work openly and ethically to find high quality organic foods at fair prices, from dedicated organic farmers and suppliers.

www.organico.co.uk
Tel: 0118 923 8760

OrganiPets

OrganiPets are a pet food company with one passion in life – to make great food for the cat or dog you love. All of their products are organic, hypo-allergenic and use no artificial colours, flavours or preservatives and no wheat, soya or beef. OrganiPets support British farmers by sourcing their ingredients as locally as possible, which helps to minimise transport pollution and reduce the environmental impact of their products. They also sponsor West Oxford Animal Rescue, providing them with the food they need for their animals. OrganiPets are currently working with small suppliers to increase the organic content of their foods from 88 to 100 per cent.

www.organipets.co.uk
Tel: 0845 388 0935

OSMO

OSMO provide high quality wood products made with carefully selected timber for both indoor and outdoor use. Their range includes wood flooring, wall panelling, fencing, garden furniture and decking. They have developed a special micro-porous wood finish which matches the demands of wood as a natural material, and use solvents on their products only when absolutely necessary. OSMO have also developed environmentally-friendly cleaning and maintenance products to ensure that their goods retain their health and durability long after purchase. More and more OSMO-processed wood is being FSC certified, and the company believes that sustainability is key to our continuing use of this valuable natural resource.

www.osmouk.com
Tel: 0129 648 1220

PLAIN LAZY

Plain Lazy is a fresh and funky clothing label specialising in dynamic and imaginative design for both men and women. It produces a broad selection of clothing, as well as stationery, bags, accessories and gifts, all with its unique street-urban twist. The label's ethos of freedom of expression and individuality is encapsulated in its vivid sense of style. Plain Lazy is a keen supporter of ethical and fair trade practices, and refuses to compromise its principles even as the company expands. The Plain Lazy range is supplied to independent retailers across the UK, and is also available through mail order via their website.

www.plainlazy.com
Tel: 0127 348 3336

PO-ZU

Po-Zu are a London based design team who have over ten years' experience working on shoe brands ranging from the high street to haute couture. They believe in embracing and responding to the constant changes and mutations in culture and fashion, and are continuously seeking to merge styles, create hybrids and push footwear design forward. Many footwear companies are beginning to engage with green production, reducing their use of harmful dyes and chemicals, and seeking alternatives to synthetic materials. Po-Zu hope to bring eco-chic to the forefront of shoe design, and are looking to undertake projects from initial ideas right through to the final product.

www.po-zu.com
Tel: 0797 641 0378

REDWOOD WHOLEFOODS

Redwood Wholefoods produce a wide selection of meat free foods. These include a variety of Cheatin' meats (such as Rashers, their much acclaimed alternative to bacon), which are particularly popular with people who enjoy the flavour and texture of meat, but who no longer want to eat it. They have also developed Making Waves, an innovative range of fish-free items, and a number of super-melting dairy-free alternatives to cheese. Their Vegi-Deli products have been specially developed to appeal to vegetarians who are looking for new and exciting foods to eat but do not necessarily want to replace the flavour of meat in their diet.

www.redwoodfoods.co.uk
Tel: 0153 640 0557

SAINSBURY'S

Sainsbury's was listed in EIRIS's top ten greenest companies of 2007, and readers of *The Observer* awarded it "Supermarket Initiative" of the year for its compostable packaging. The supermarket has been commended for a decision to increase its range of Marine Stewardship Council (MSC) certified fish, and is a prominent supporter of fair trade and organic produce. It will be the first UK retailer to convert a fifth of its online delivery fleet to green electric vehicles, and has already met its 2010 target to reduce landfill waste by 10 per cent – all of which shows that even big retailers can do their bit for the environment.

www.sainsburys.co.uk
Tel: 0800 636 262

SATELLITE

Satellite are talented and passionate marketing professionals, who aim to deliver intelligent, effective solutions on brief and on time, every time. With experience of working for the big name agencies, the team are able to produce a good idea for anything – from a matchbox to a poster, a cottage industry to a big multinational. Satellite have worked with some of the most well-known brands around, and their high profile clients include Camden and the Green Party. Whether you are looking for advertising, direct marketing, new media or PR, they can capitalise on the uniqueness of your business to make you stand out from the crowd.

www.satellitemc.com

Tel: 0207 239 4913

SEASALT

Seasalt was the first fashion brand to have its clothing certified to Soil Association standard. 70 per cent of its products (including men's and women's clothing and footwear) are made from organic cotton, grown without the use of chemical pesticides. Other product lines include wellies, waterproof jackets and pullovers. Seasalt believes in the principle that it is worth paying a slightly higher price for a well-designed, functional and long-lasting garment, rather than buying in to the culture of disposable fashion. The company aims to work in the most environmentally-friendly way available, and looks for ways to make its activities as responsible as possible.

www.seasaltcornwall.co.uk

Tel: 0173 635 2032

SHARED INTEREST

Shared Interest was established in 1990 and has grown rapidly to become a prominent ethical lender in the UK. Based in Newcastle-upon-Tyne, it is a co-operative lending society which provides credit facilities to organisations involved in fair trade. The society has around 8,500 members in the UK, and assets of over £20 million – around £14 million of which is available to lend in fair trade. Shared Interest believes in operating under a strong democratic structure, and has an elected council to monitor the work of its Board of Directors. If you are interested in investing in Shared Interest's work, visit their website for more information.

http://cust.shared-interest.com

Tel: 0191 233 9100

TERRAMAR ORGANICS

Terramar Organics is an online and mail order clothing company specialising in the sale of organic and fair trade clothing. Its products are made with fully certified sustainable textiles, which have been assessed at all stages of the production process. The company was founded to sell basic but quality clothing such as shirts and T-shirts which will last well and don't cost the earth. Terramar promotes sustainable living by minimising its exploitation of natural resources, and supports the local community by making use of its resources and talent. It does not source its clothing from factories involved in sweatshop practices or exploitation of labour.

www.terramar.co.uk

Tel: 0799 961 3982

THE TIDE HAS TURNED

The Tide Has Turned is a bespoke travel company for ethical people that won't cost the earth. They organise travel arrangements uniquely suited to your requirements and budget while staying true to their ethical beliefs – and yours. By taking into consideration the impact travel can have on society, cultures and the environment, they can help change how you travel and as a result of the work they do for you, they intend to stimulate social change and to leave the world a better place. Following personal consultation and in-depth research they propose travel arrangements singularly designed to satisfy your requirements – they don't retain commissions to pay for their service, ensuring their bespoke service remains completely unbiased.
www.thetidehasturned.co.uk
Tel: 01308 861488

TROPICAL WHOLEFOODS (FM FOODS)

When the people behind Tropical Wholefoods lived in Uganda, the local farmers were always asking them how they could sell their fruits in Europe. So they began to experiment with sun-drying the fruits in solar dryers. All that was needed was sun, fruit and energy – of which they had plenty! They took their first sun-dried fruits back to England and sold them at markets. Harvested when fully ripe and immediately sun-dried, they had really full flavours, were 100 per cent pure fruit, and were free from all preservatives. Today, Tropical Wholefoods continue to provide a whole range of dried fruit, dried vegetables and snack bars.
www.tropicalwholefoods.com
Tel: 0207 737 0444

TROPHY PET FOODS

Trophy Pet Foods are independent producers of premium pet foods for dogs, cats and small mammals. Their range is designed to provide all the nourishment your pet requires in a carefully balanced meal. Trophy specially selects the best ingredients available ensuring that they are nutritious, wholesome and palatable. They then deliver these products to you. Trophy offer free samples so that your pet can try the food before you buy and they offer a 100% satisfaction guarantee, so if you have not seen a difference in your pet after 28 days or are not satisfied, they refund or replace the product for you. Trophy Pet Foods are also approved under the BUAV 'No Animal Testing' Standard.
www.trophypetfoods.co.uk
Tel: 01367 240333

ZED PR

Zed PR is a small, friendly and flexible PR agency, offering big agency brains without some of the big agency bad habits. It specialises in public relations programmes for ambitious companies, making sure the right people know and hear about its clients – whether that's through the media, brand 'evangelists', direct engagement with audiences or other services. Members of the Zed PR team have worked across many industries, from computer programming tools to environmentally friendly nappies. They have helped launch concepts and companies from online banking to the first digital cameras for consumers, and have the know-how to spread their infectious enthusiasm for your big idea.
www.zedpr.co.uk
Tel: 0118 969 8966

NGOs

The non-governmental organisations listed below (and a great many others not included here) help give a voice to individuals who are concerned about some of the most important issues affecting humans, animals and the environment. NGOs have emerged as a key component of 21st century debate. Free from political and corporate chains, they have the power to present a genuinely independent view of the problems that face us all as human beings.

AMNESTY INTERNATIONAL

Amnesty International is one of the leading human rights organisations in the world, untainted by political, economic or religious bias. Amnesty aims to enshrine universal entitlement to 'physical and mental integrity, freedom of conscience and expression, and freedom from discrimination'.
www.amnesty.org.uk
Tel: 0207 033 1500

BARNARDOS

Barnardos aims to help young people who are in grave need of assistance, and its 357 centres around Britain provide guidance for children and teenagers from difficult backgrounds. Barnardos offers fostering and adoption services, and works to find solutions to problems including sexual abuse and homelessness.
www.barnardos.org.uk
Tel: 0208 550 8822

THE BLUE CROSS

The Blue Cross offers guidance, advice and support for pet and horse owners, and, through several animal adoption centres, re-homes thousands of animals each year. Its network of hospitals offers free veterinary care for animals whose owners cannot afford private vets' fees.
www.bluecross.org.uk
Tel: 0199 382 2651

BRITISH RED CROSS

The British Red Cross is part of the largest independent humanitarian network in the world, offering impartial assistance to those in need. The Red Cross helps the victims of armed conflict, and works against disease and human suffering in the UK and around the world.
www.redcross.org.uk
Tel: 0870 170 7000

BROCKWOOD PARK SCHOOL

Brockwood Park School is a residential school for students aged 14-19 from around the world. Students gain a good academic education and one that nurtures in them human qualities and encourages enquiry about all aspects of life.
www.brockwood.org.uk
Tel: 0196 277 1744

BUAV

The British Union for the Abolition of Vivisection (BUAV) is the world's leading anti-vivisection organisation, campaigning peacefully – through political lobbying, legal challenges and undercover investigations – to end all animal testing both nationally and internationally. The BUAV runs 'No Animal Testing' standards for household and beauty products, which consumers can check by looking for the rabbit and stars logo on product packaging.
www.buav.org
Tel: 0207 700 4888

CAFOD

The Catholic Agency for Overseas Development (CAFOD) aims to alleviate poverty and create a more just world. CAFOD has bases in over 60 countries, attempting to help the poor in each country without racial or religious bias. CAFOD's other aims include campaigning for a fairer world and putting faith into action.
www.cafod.org.uk
Tel: 0207 733 7900

CANCER RESEARCH UK

Aiming to find a cure for cancer though world-class research, Cancer Research UK is the pre-eminent cancer charity in Britain. With an annual scientific spend of around £191 million (raised almost entirely though voluntary contributions), Cancer Research UK is backed by a dedicated team of 3,000 scientists.
www.cancerresearchuk.org
Tel: 0207 242 0200

CHRISTIAN AID

Christian Aid works in some of the world's poorest communities in over 50 countries. It works where the need is greatest, regardless of religion, supporting local organisations which are best placed to understand their communities.
www.christianaid.org.uk
Tel: 0207 620 4444 (UK)
www.christian-aid.ie
Tel: 01 611 0801 (Ireland)

COMPASSION IN WORLD FARMING

Compassion in World Farming (CIWF) is the leading international organisation actively campaigning to improve the lives of all farmed animals by abolishing factory farming and long distance animal transport. Based in the UK, CIWF has offices and representatives across the world.
www.ciwf.org
Tel: 0173 026 4208

COMIC RELIEF

Having attracted over 2,000 celebrities to its cause over the years, Comic Relief aims to redress serious issues through comedy and laughter. As well as raising money, the annual televised Comic Relief show aims to inform and educate the public and promote social change.
www.comicrelief.org.uk
Tel: 0207 820 5555

ENVIRONMENTAL INVESTIGATION AGENCY

BBC Wildlife Magazine has described the Environmental Investigation Agency (EIA) as 'one of Britain's most effective conservation groups'. Last year it celebrated 20 years of protecting wildlife, people and the planet. EIA is an independent, international campaigning organisation committed to investigating and exposing environmental crime.
www.eia-international.org
Tel: 0207 354 7960

THE FAIRTRADE FOUNDATION

The Fairtrade Foundation awards the Fairtrade Mark, the only consumer guarantee that products are independently certified to meet international fair trade standards. The mark can be seen on over 250 products in most major retail outlets. The Foundation raises public awareness about fair trade and organises the nationwide Fairtrade Fortnight in March each year. It is also the UK member of the international Fairtrade Labelling Organisation (FLO), which unites 18 national Fairtrade initiatives across Europe, North America and Mexico.
www.fairtrade.org.uk
Tel: 0207 405 5942

FRIENDS OF THE EARTH

Friends of the Earth is the largest international network of environmental groups in the world, represented in 68 countries. It is one of the leading environmental pressure groups in the UK and has a unique network of local campaigning groups, working in more than 200 communities in England, Wales and Northern Ireland.
www.foe.co.uk
Tel: 0207 490 1555

FOREST STEWARDSHIP COUNCIL

The FSC is an international, non-governmental organisation dedicated to promoting responsible management of the world's forests. It was founded in 1993 in response to public concern about deforestation and demand for a trustworthy wood-labelling scheme. There are national working groups in 28 countries including the UK.
www.fsc.org
Tel: 0168 641 3916

GREENPEACE

Active in 40 countries worldwide, Greenpeace is a non-profit organisation with several environmental aims, including curbing climate change and preserving our oceans and ancient forests. To maintain its independence, Greenpeace only accepts donations from individual supporters and foundation grants.
www.greenpeace.org.uk
Tel: 0207 865 8100

GLOBAL ACTION PLAN

Global Action Plan is an independent charity committed to encouraging the public to be more environmentally sustainable. Working with businesses, schools and local communities it believes that every little helps to make a real difference. You can find out how green you are at the websites *www.greenscore.org.uk* and *www.carboncalculator.com.*
www.globalactionplan.org.uk
Tel: 0207 405 5633

GUIDE DOGS FOR THE BLIND

The Guide Dogs for the Blind association supplies guide dogs and other mobility services to blind and partially sighted people in the UK, and educates people on the need to care for their eyes.
www.guidedogs.org.uk
Tel: 0118 983 5555

HELP THE AGED

Help the Aged aims to enrich the lives of older people by reinforcing their social status. Of the money the charity spends, 28 per cent goes to combating poverty amongst the elderly, 30 per cent goes to reducing isolation, 13 per cent to defeating ageism and 29 per cent to promoting quality in care.
www.helptheaged.org.uk
Tel: 0207 278 1114

INTERNATIONAL TREE FOUNDATION

The International Tree Foundation (ITF) is 80 years old and works towards a world richer in trees, by planting, preserving and educating people on the value of trees worldwide. In the UK, ITF members work in their local communities. On a global scale, ITF tree planting grants help the world's poorest environments and societies.
www.internationaltreefoundation.org
Tel: 0870 774 4269

LEAGUE AGAINST CRUEL SPORTS

Founded in 1924, the League Against Cruel Sports maintains a unique approach to the protection of wildlife – combining campaigning with conservation. The League has always been at the forefront of the campaign to ban hunting with dogs, and to achieve their goals they liaise closely with politicians in pressing for government action.
www.league.uk.com
Tel: 0845 330 8486

MACMILLAN CANCER RELIEF

Offering practical and emotional support for those who have been diagnosed with cancer, Macmillan Cancer Relief recruits dedicated nurses and doctors to provide expert cancer care. It also offers treatment centres, details of financial help and other specialist information.
www.macmillan.org.uk
Tel: 0808 808 2020

MARIE CURIE CANCER CARE

Marie Curie Cancer Care offers high quality nursing free of charge, and allows terminally ill people to spend their last days in the comfort and privacy of their own home. The organisation's team of scientists is also involved in research into the disease.
www.mariecurie.org.uk
Tel: 0207 599 7777

THE MARINE STEWARDSHIP COUNCIL

The Marine Stewardship Council (MSC) is an international non-profit organisation working to prevent the collapse of fish stocks. It has developed an environmental standard for well-managed and sustainable fisheries. Fisheries that meet this standard are awarded with a blue eco-label, enabling consumers to identify sustainable seafood products and make the best environmental choices.
www.msc.org
Tel: 0207 350 4000

National Trust
The National Trust was founded in 1895 to act as a guardian for the nation in the acquisition and protection of threatened coastline, countryside and buildings. The National Trust now cares for over 612,000 acres of beautiful countryside in England, Wales and Northern Ireland, plus almost 600 miles of coastline and more than 200 buildings and gardens of outstanding interest and importance.
www.nationaltrust.org.uk
Tel: 0870 458 4000

Nicaragua Solidarity Campaign
The Nicaragua Solidarity Campaign (NSC) sells fair trade Nicaraguan coffee, Mexican and Guatemalan crafts, books and t-shirts. They also organise fair trade tours to Nicaragua and campaign around issues of trade justice. Email *nsc@nicaraguasc.org.uk* to join, and receive a free world music CD.
www.nicaraguasc.org.uk
Tel: 0207 272 6919

NSPCC
The National Society for the Prevention of Cruelty to Children (NSPCC) is the leading UK charity in the field of child protection, and is currently the only children's charity with statutory powers. This enables it to act decisively against cruelty to children.
www.nspcc.org.uk
Tel: 0207 825 2500

One World Action
One World Action aims to defeat poverty and promote democracy in the less developed world. One World Action works with partner organisations on the ground to promote respect for human freedoms in Africa, Asia and America. The organisation also liaises with senior policymakers in both Britain and the EU.
www.oneworldaction.org
Tel: 0207 833 4075

Oxfam
Oxfam is a development, relief and campaigning organisation. It works to combat poverty and suffering by addressing important issues such as fair trade, conflict, education, debt, aid and employment conditions in developing countries.
www.oxfam.org
Tel: 0870 333 2700

Pesticide Action Network
Pesticide Action Network UK (PAN UK) promotes healthy food, agriculture and an environment which will provide food and meet public health needs without dependence on toxic chemicals, and without harm to food producers and agricultural workers.
www.pan-uk.org
Tel: 0207 065 0905

PDSA
Every working day, PDSA caters for 4,500 sick and injured pets of less fortunate people. With 46 PetAid hospitals and hundreds of associated private practices, PDSA has established itself as Britain's leading veterinary charity.
www.pdsa.org.uk
Tel: 0195 229 0999

Prince's Trust
The Prince's Trust is a UK charity that supports young people who face more obstacles than most, helping them overcome barriers and get their lives on track. The Trust provides practical support such as training, mentoring and financial assistance. Since 1983 they have helped more than 60,00 young people start in business, and have supported many young entrepreneurs. The Prince's Trust website has a directory of nearly 1,500 Trust-supported businesses in 100 categories across the UK.
www.princes-trust.org.uk
Tel: 0800 842 842

The Rainforest Foundation
The Rainforest Foundation provides valuable support for the efforts of native inhabitants of the world's rainforests to protect their environment. The Foundation assists such peoples in securing their rights and natural resources, and obtaining essential services from the relevant state.
www.rainforestfoundationuk.org
Tel: 0207 251 6345

The Ramblers' Association
The Ramblers' Association is the biggest organisation in Britain to support walkers, and has a membership of 139,000. The organisation protects the UK's unique network of public paths and provides information allowing people to plan their walks.
www.ramblers.org.uk
Tel: 0207 339 8500

ROYAL NATIONAL INSTITUTE FOR THE BLIND

The Royal National Institute for the Blind (RNIB) offers practical support and advice for the two million British people with sight problems. RNIB can provide information about Braille, Talking Books and computer training.
www.rnib.org.uk
Tel: 0845 766 9999

ROYAL NATIONAL INSTITUTE FOR DEAF PEOPLE

Through the use of campaigning, education and training courses, the Royal National Institute for Deaf People (RNID) helps to represent the 8.7 million people with hearing disabilities in the UK. It is the largest charity in this field in Britain.
www.rnid.org.uk
Tel: 0207 296 800

ROYAL NATIONAL LIFEBOAT INSTITUTION

The Royal National Lifeboat Institution (RNLI) saves lives at sea through the provision of a 24-hour search and rescue service around the British and Irish coast. It is staffed by volunteer crews and relies on financial contributions from the public. RNLI crews rescue an average of 19 people every day.
www.rnli.org.uk
Tel: 0845 122 6999

ROYAL SOCIETY FOR THE PROTECTION OF BIRDS

The Royal Society for the Protection of Birds (RSPB) aims to create a healthy environment for birds and wildlife, and offers volunteers the chance to watch and observe some of the rarest species of bird in Britain.
www.rspb.org.uk
Tel: 0176 768 0551

ROYAL SOCIETY FOR THE PREVENTION OF CRUELTY TO ANIMALS

By promoting responsible pet ownership, the Royal Society for the Prevention of Cruelty to Animals (RSPCA) attempts to promote kindness towards animals. It also acts to prevent unnecessary animal suffering, and finds new, responsible owners for unwanted pets.
www.rspca.org.uk
Tel: 0189 523 1435

SAVE THE CHILDREN

Save the Children works in the UK and across the world. Emergency relief runs alongside long-term development and prevention work to help children, their families and their communities to be self-sufficient. The organisation learns from the reality of children's lives and campaigns for solutions to the problems they face.
www.savethechildren.org.uk
Tel: 0207 012 6400

SCOPE

Scope is a natural disability organisation which focuses on cerebral palsy, and aims to achieve equality and respect for disabled people. It works towards the idea that disabled people should have the same human and civil rights as everyone else.
www.scope.org.uk
Tel: 0207 619 7100

SPINAL RESEARCH

Spinal Research is a pioneering charity which is making progress in its aim to find ways to repair spinal cord injury and reverse the paralysis that it causes.
www.spinal-research.org
Tel: 0148 389 8786

SPORT RELIEF

Affiliated to Comic Relief, Sport Relief funds projects which use sport to alleviate violence in communities, and provide hundreds of young people with the sense of confidence and motivation that comes from participating in team sports. Sport Relief also sends celebrities abroad to spread the organisation's message in disadvantaged areas.
www.sportrelief.com
Tel: 0207 820 5555

SURFERS AGAINST SEWAGE

Surfers Against Sewage campaign for clean, safe recreational waters, free from sewage effluent, toxic chemicals and nuclear waste. Using a solution-based argument of viable and sustainable alternatives, the group highlights what it sees as inherent flaws in current practises, attitudes and legislation. It challenges industry, legislators and politicians to end their 'pump and dump' policies.
www.sas.org.uk
Tel: 0845 458 3001

SURVIVAL INTERNATIONAL

Survival International is a worldwide organisation supporting tribal peoples. It stands for their right to decide their own future and helps them protect their lives, lands and human rights. Survival International has supporters in 82 countries and is the only organisation to make use of public opinion and public action to secure long-term improvement for tribal peoples.
www.survival-international.org
Tel: 0207 687 8700

Tear Fund

Tear Fund is active throughout the world, with numerous regional strategies. These include providing support for communities in managing healthcare, focusing on children at serious risk in disadvantaged areas, and augmenting food and housing security in poorer regions.
www.tearfund.org
Tel: 0845 355 8355

Tourism Concern

Tourism Concern works with communities in countries which are popular tourist destinations, with the aim of curbing the amount of poverty tourism causes. Through the use of advocacy and publicity, Tourism Concern attempts to find a way of increasing the benefits of tourism to destination countries.
www.tourismconcern.org.uk
Tel: 0207 133 3330

Trees for Cities

Trees for Cities is an independent charity that plants trees and re-landscapes public spaces in urban areas of greatest need. Its aim is to stimulate a greening renaissance in cities around the world. You can get involved by sponsoring trees or volunteering at Trees for Cities events.
www.treesforcities.org
Tel: 0207 587 1320

UNICEF

UNICEF, the United Nations Children's Fund, is a global champion for children's rights which makes a lasting difference by working in partnership with others, from governments and teachers to mothers and youth groups. UNICEF is a driving force for people throughout the world working to ensure a better future for children.
www.unicef.org.uk
Tel: 0870 606 3377

Women's Environmental Network

The Women's Environmental Network (WEN) campaigns on issues that link women and the environment, and is particularly concerned with issues concerning women's health and reproduction. WEN's approach emphasises the belief that women have the right to information to enable them to make fair choices.
www.wen.org.uk
Tel: 0207 481 9004

World Development Movement

The World Development Movement tackles the underlying causes of poverty. It lobbies decision-makers to change the policies that keep people poor. WDM researches and promotes positive alternatives. It works alongside people in the developing world who are standing up to injustice.
www.wdm.org.uk
Tel: 0207 737 6215

World Vision

World Vision is a Christian charity and one of the world's leading relief and development agencies, currently helping over 100 million people in nearly 100 countries in their struggle against poverty, hunger and injustice, irrespective of their religious beliefs.
www.worldvision.org.uk
Tel: 0190 884 1000

World Society for the Protection of Animals

The World Society for the Protection of Animals (WSPA) interacts with over 460 member organisations to improve global standards of animal welfare. WSPA envisages a world in which the welfare of animals is understood and respected by everyone, and enshrined in effective legislation.
www.wspa.org.uk
Tel: 0207 587 5000

World Wildlife Fund

The World Wildlife Fund (WWF) is working around the world to protect endangered wildlife, preserve wild lands and address global threats and challenges. Working with dedicated members and conservation partners, WWF protects endangered wildlife and habitats on a global scale.
www.wwf-uk.org
Tel: 0148 342 6444

You can make easy tax-free donations to many of these NGOs at *www.gooshing.co.uk* – see page 370 for more information.

About GOOSHING

The Ethical Company Organisation operates GOOSHING, an online companion to *The Good Shopping Guide* which is designed to make ethical shopping on the internet easier and cheaper. Consumers around the world can log on to *www.gooshing.co.uk* to compare companies' ethical ratings and make informed choices about what they buy. Saving you money. Saving the planet. GOOSHING has now experienced over 3 million unique users!

The secret of GOOSHING's growing popularity among supporters of animal welfare, human rights and green living is that it is a genuine one-stop shop. It features thousands of different products, providing instant comparisons and a price-search mechanism that guarantees to deliver you the lowest price on your product of choice from over 350 retailers.

GOOSHING uses the rating system of the Ethical Company Organisation's Research Department, focusing on the core criteria that are relevant to products which are commonly bought online. This targeted methodology means that ethical ratings on *www.gooshing.co.uk* will occasionally differ slightly from those found in *The Good Shopping Guide*.

Over 250,000 products are rated, including everything from CD and DVD players, home appliances and computer equipment to electronics and gadgets for the office. Whatever you want to buy, GOOSHING will direct you to the most ethical brand choices – and then the very cheapest place to buy that product. You can buy securely using a credit or switch card, and the goods will be delivered direct to your door.

GOOSHING aims to save you money and put even more consumer pressure on the world's worst offending companies – and to be more respectful towards the people, the animals and the environment of the world we live in. Now that's gooshingly good shopping!

We highly recommend you use *www.gooshing.co.uk* for all your online shopping needs.

save money . save the planet

from the Ethical Company Organisation, publisher of The Good Shopping Guide

gooshing

world shopping revolution

shop at gooshing.co.uk

price search & ethical comparisons on 250,000 products